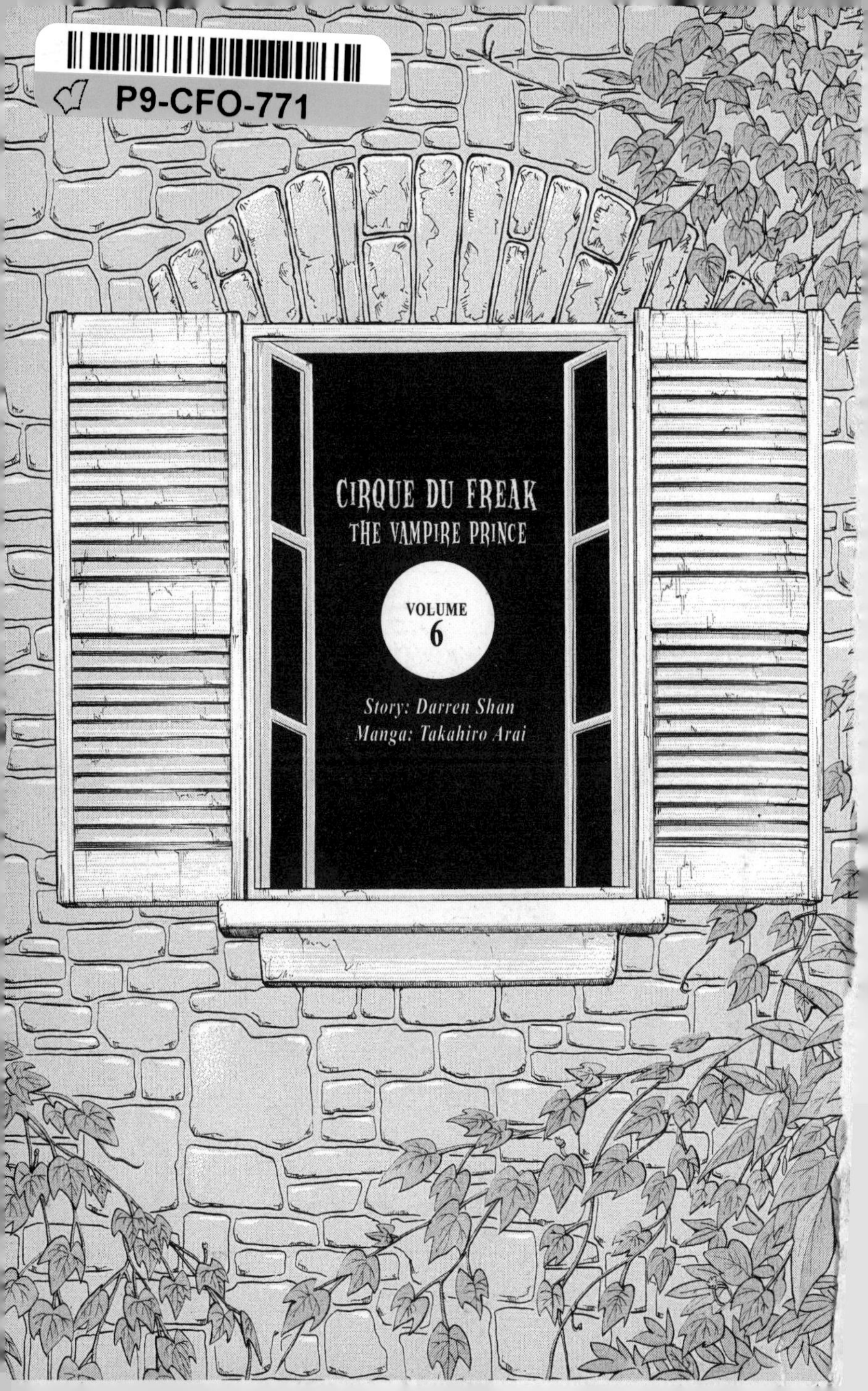

CIRQUE DU FREAK
THE VAMPIRE PRINCE

VOLUME
6

Story: Darren Shan
Manga: Takahiro Arai

A SUMMARY OF TRIALS OF DEATH:

FACING ALMOST CERTAIN DEATH FOR FAIL-
ING THE TRIALS OF INITIATION, DARREN
CONSPIRES WITH KURDA AND GAVNER
TO ESCAPE FROM VAMPIRE MOUNTAIN.
BUT ALONG THE ESCAPE ROUTE, KURDA'S
TRUE ALLIANCE WITH THE VAMPANEZE
BECOMES APPARENT, AND GAVNER IS
KILLED. HIS BEST RESISTANCE PROVEN
FUTILE, CORNERED BY THE VAMPANEZE,
DARREN'S ONLY ESCAPE IS THROUGH THE
MOUNTAIN'S GIANT AQUEDUCT. SPURN-
ING KURDA'S HAND OF RESCUE, DARREN
THROWS HIMSELF INTO THE SWIRLING
MAELSTROM THAT CARRIES HIM AWAY
FROM VAMPIRE MOUNTAIN...

CIRQUE DU FREAK 6
CONTENTS

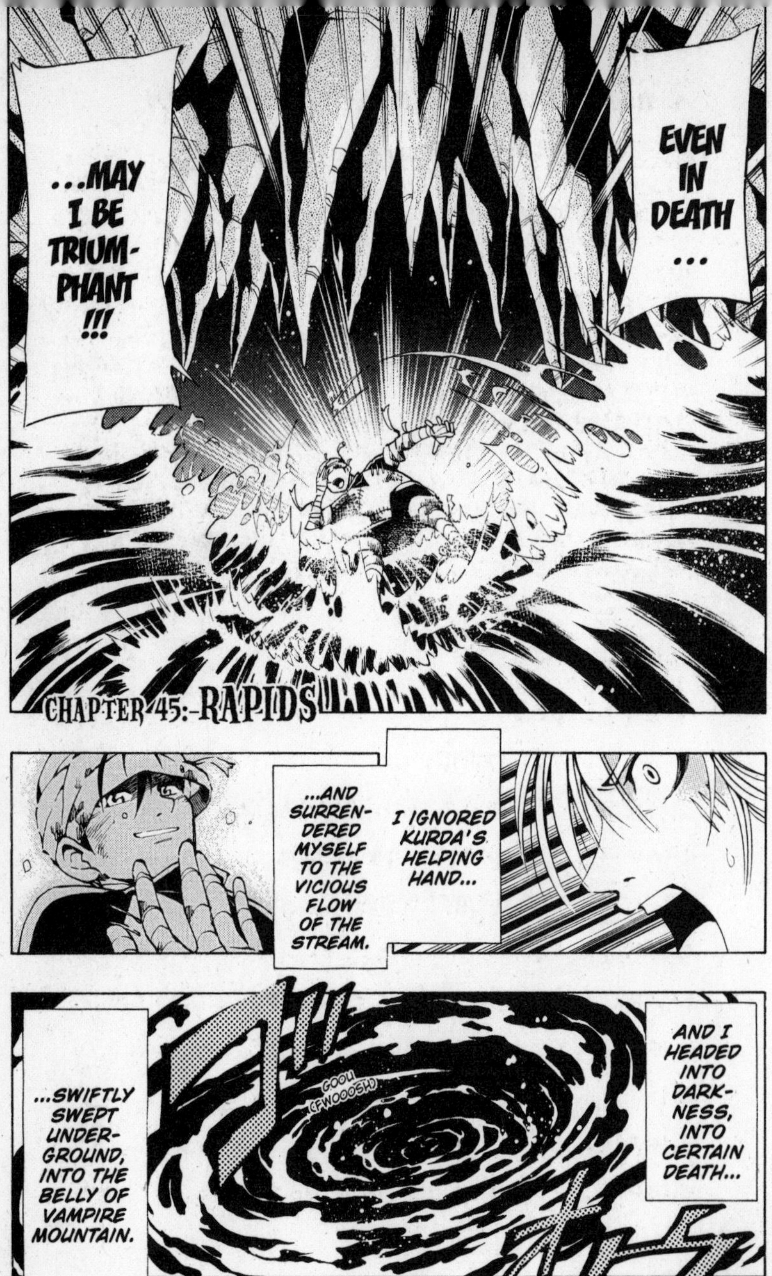
EVEN IN DEATH...
...MAY I BE TRIUMPHANT!!!
CHAPTER 45: RAPIDS
I IGNORED KURDA'S HELPING HAND...
...AND SURRENDERED MYSELF TO THE VICIOUS FLOW OF THE STREAM.
AND I HEADED INTO DARKNESS, INTO CERTAIN DEATH...
GOOU (FWOOOSH)
...SWIFTLY SWEPT UNDERGROUND, INTO THE BELLY OF VAMPIRE MOUNTAIN.

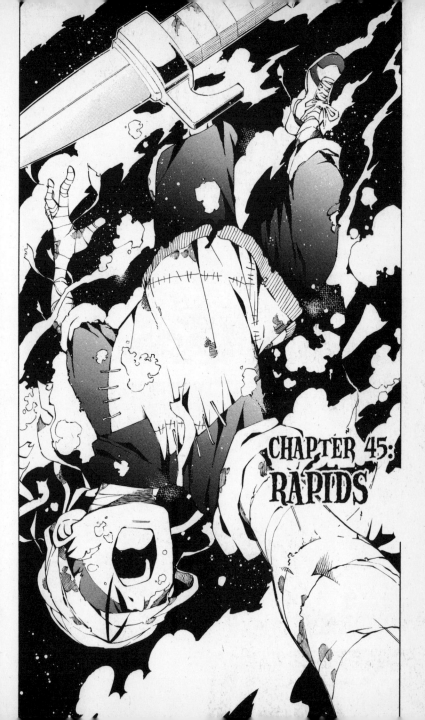

CHAPTER 45:
RAPIDS

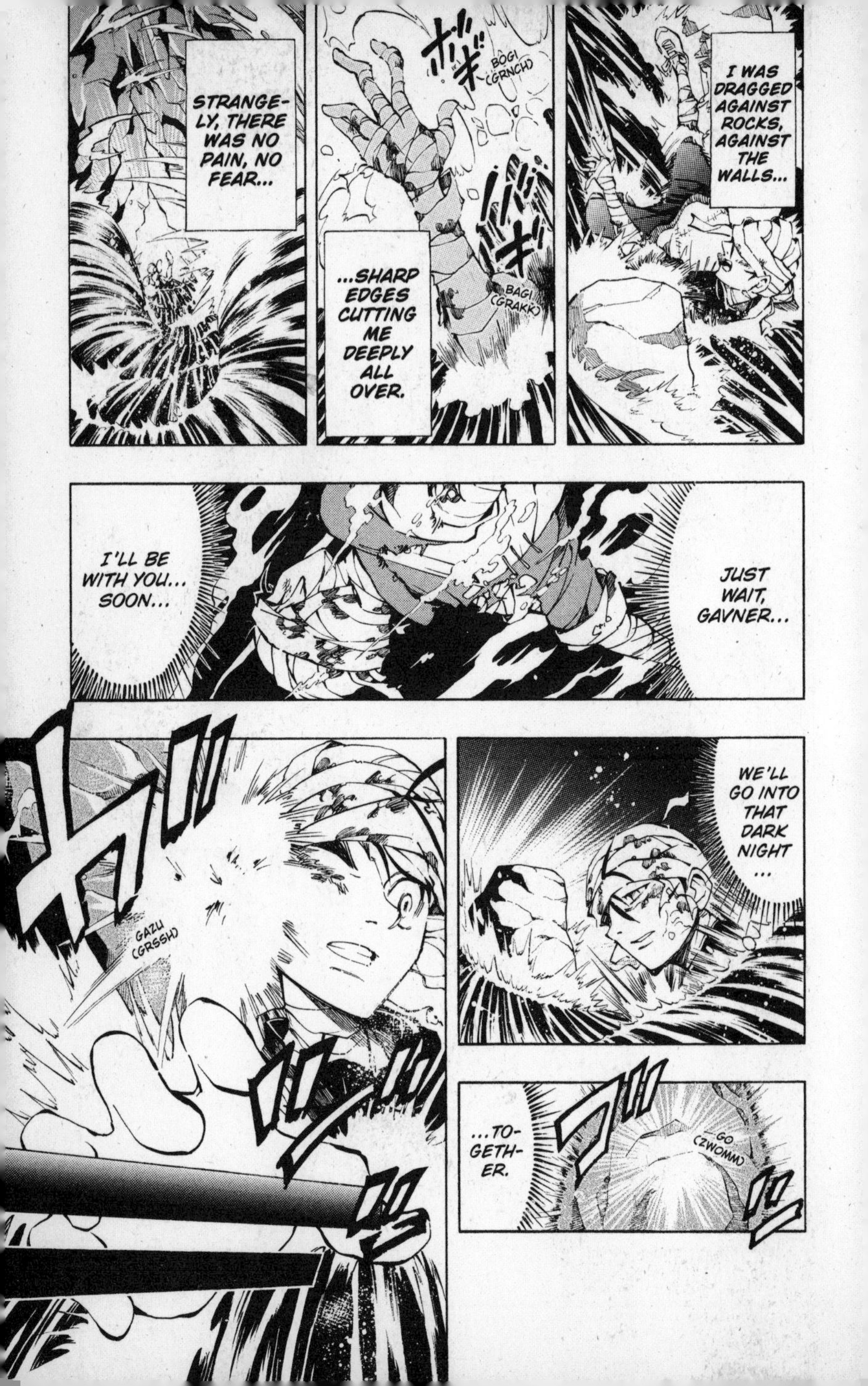
I WAS DRAGGED AGAINST ROCKS, AGAINST THE WALLS...
BOGI (GRNCH)
BAGI (GRAKK)
...SHARP EDGES CUTTING ME DEEPLY ALL OVER.
STRANGE-LY, THERE WAS NO PAIN, NO FEAR...
JUST WAIT, GAVNER...
I'LL BE WITH YOU... SOON...
WE'LL GO INTO THAT DARK NIGHT ...
...TO-GETH-ER.
GO (ZWOMM)
GAZU (GRSSH)

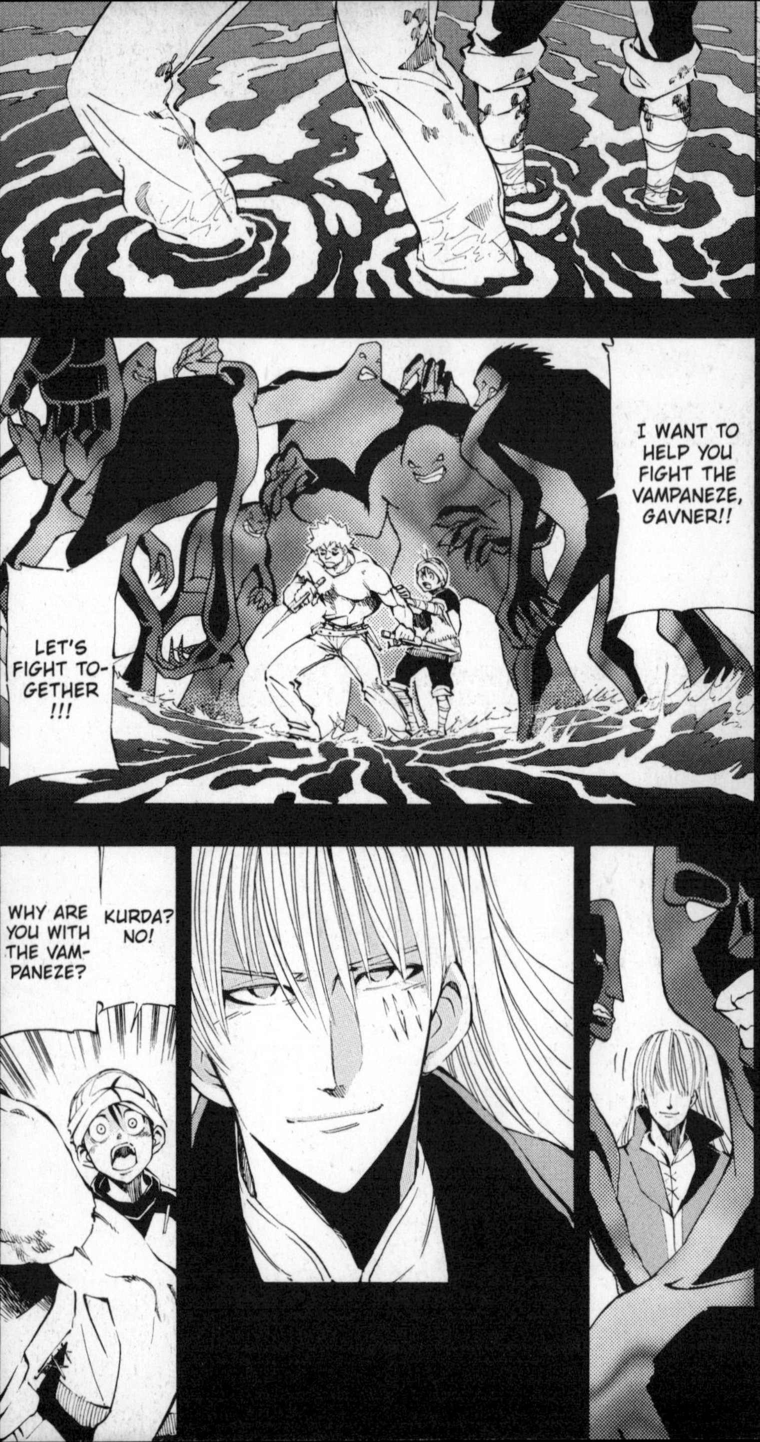
I WANT TO HELP YOU FIGHT THE VAMPANEZE, GAVNER!!
LET'S FIGHT TO-GETHER!!!
KURDA? NO!
WHY ARE YOU WITH THE VAM-PANEZE?

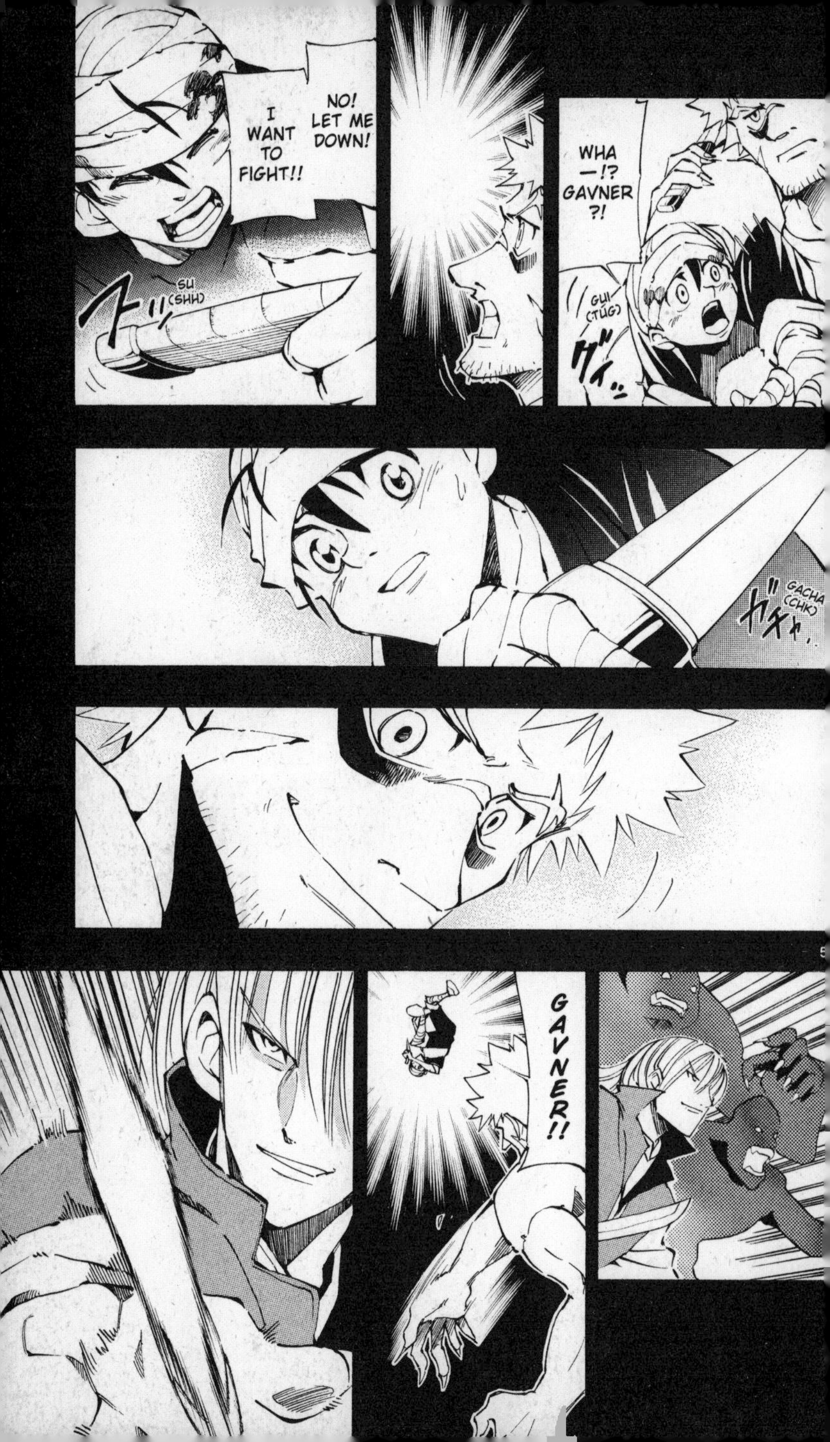
WHA —!? GAVNER ?!
GUI (TUG)
NO! LET ME DOWN!
I WANT TO FIGHT!!
SU (SHH)
GACHA (CHK)
GAVNER!!

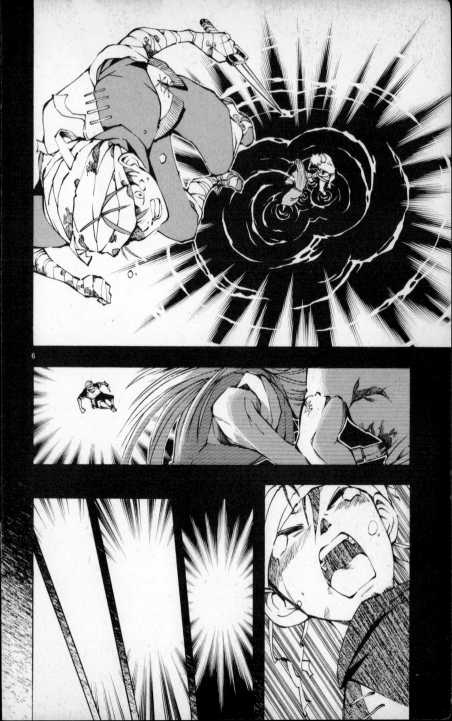

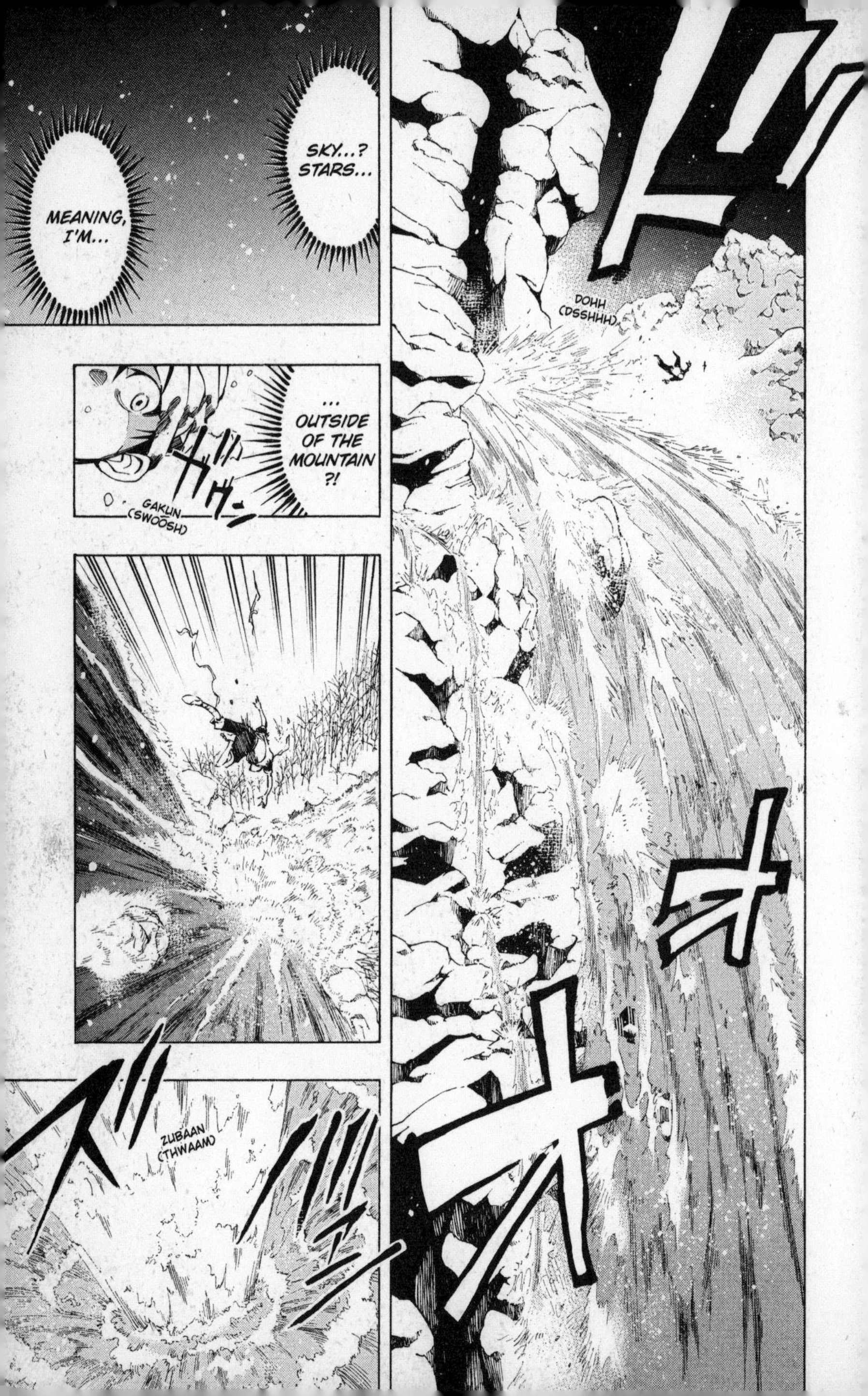
DOHH (DSSHHH)
SKY...? STARS...
MEANING, I'M...
... OUTSIDE OF THE MOUNTAIN ?!
GAKUN (SWOOSH)
ZUBAAN (THWAAM)

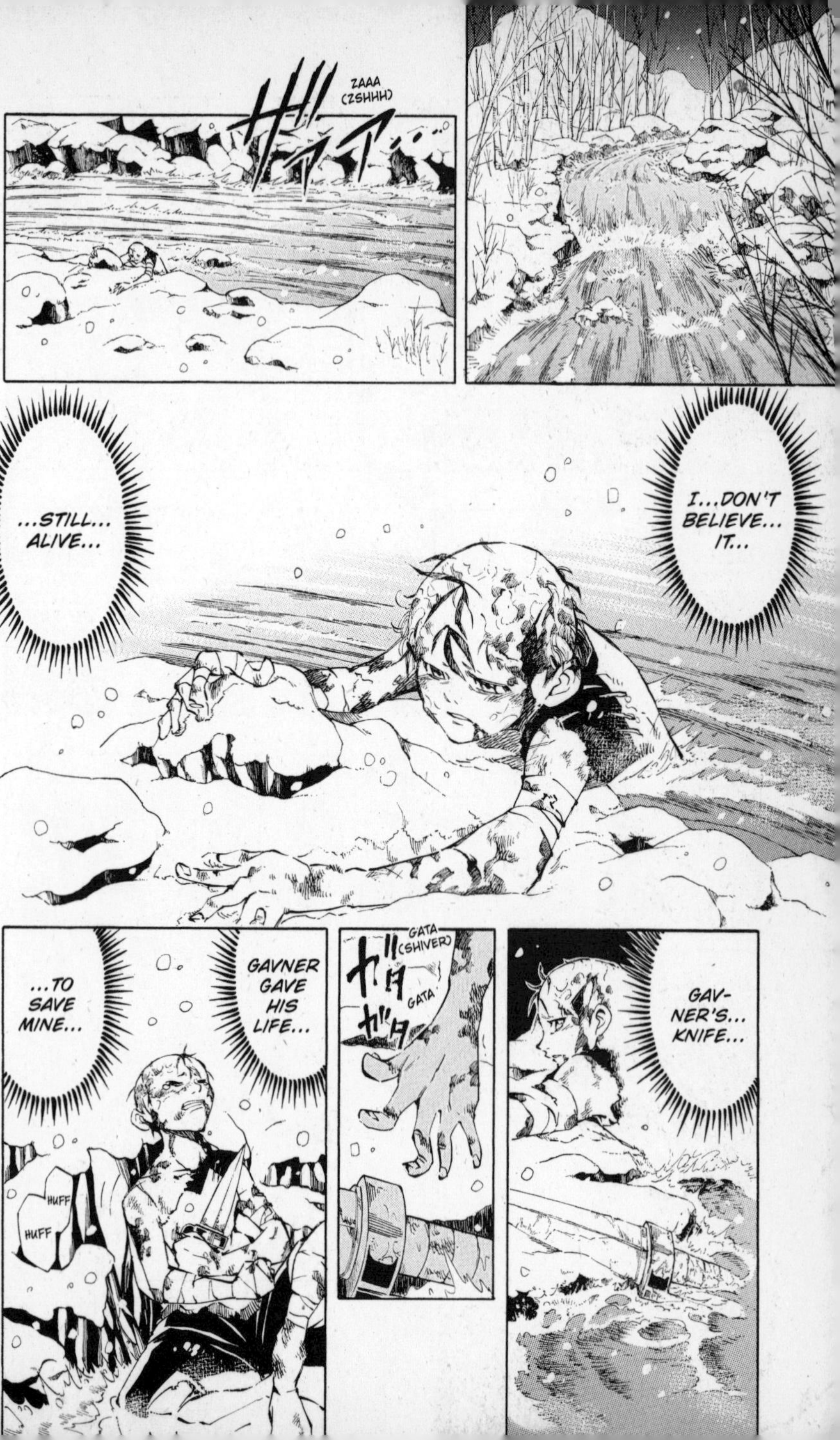
ZAAA (ZSHHH)
I...DON'T BELIEVE... IT...
...STILL... ALIVE...
GAV-NER'S... KNIFE...
GATA (SHIVER)
GATA
GAVNER GAVE HIS LIFE...
...TO SAVE MINE...
HUFF
HUFF

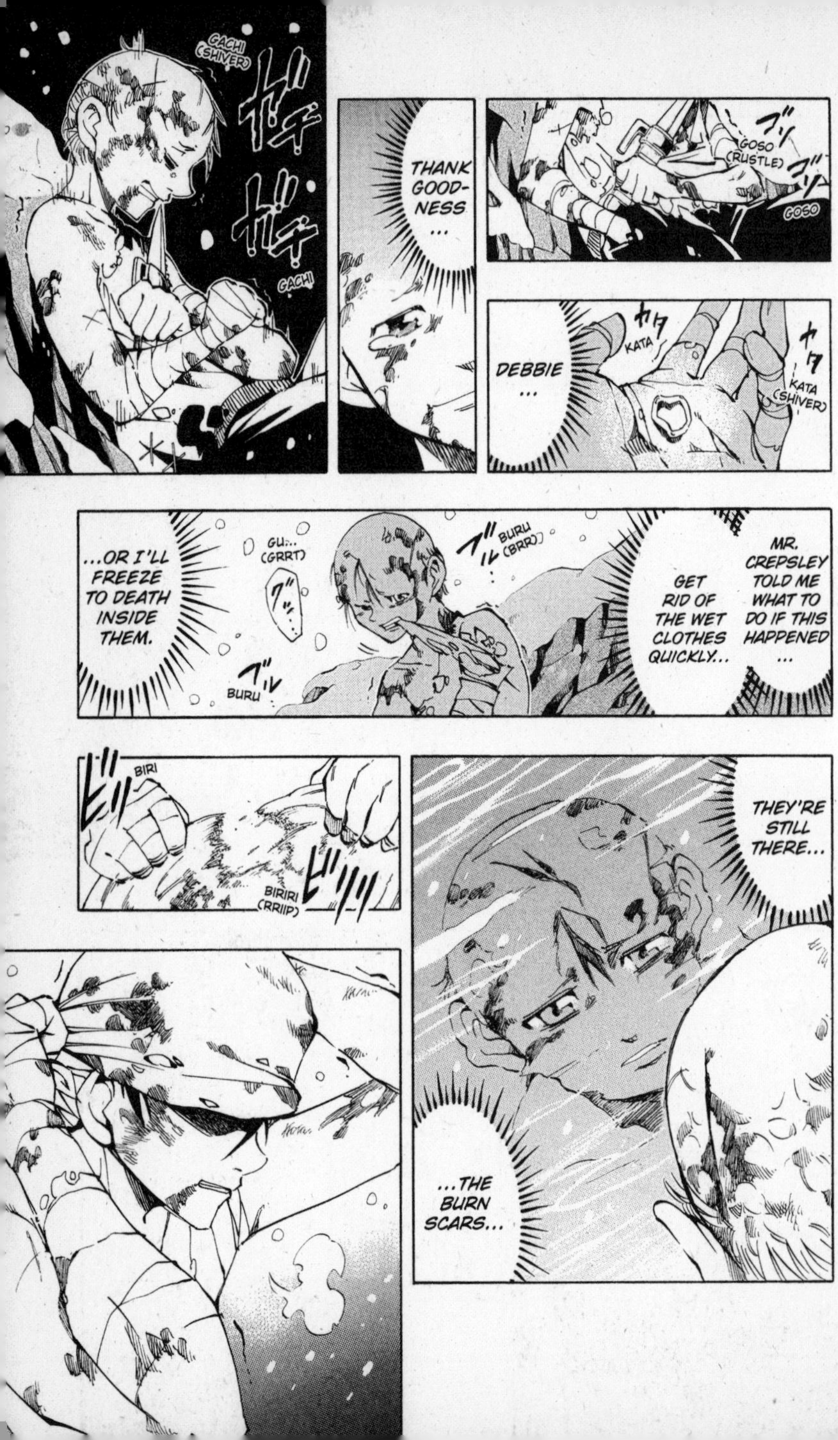
GOSO (RUSTLE)
GOSO
KATA
KATA (SHIVER)
DEBBIE ...
THANK GOODNESS ...
GACHI (SHIVER)
GACHI
MR. CREPSLEY TOLD ME WHAT TO DO IF THIS HAPPENED ...
GET RID OF THE WET CLOTHES QUICKLY...
BURU (BRR)
GU... (GRRT)
...OR I'LL FREEZE TO DEATH INSIDE THEM.
BURU
THEY'RE STILL THERE...
...THE BURN SCARS...
BIRI
BIRIRI (RRIIP)

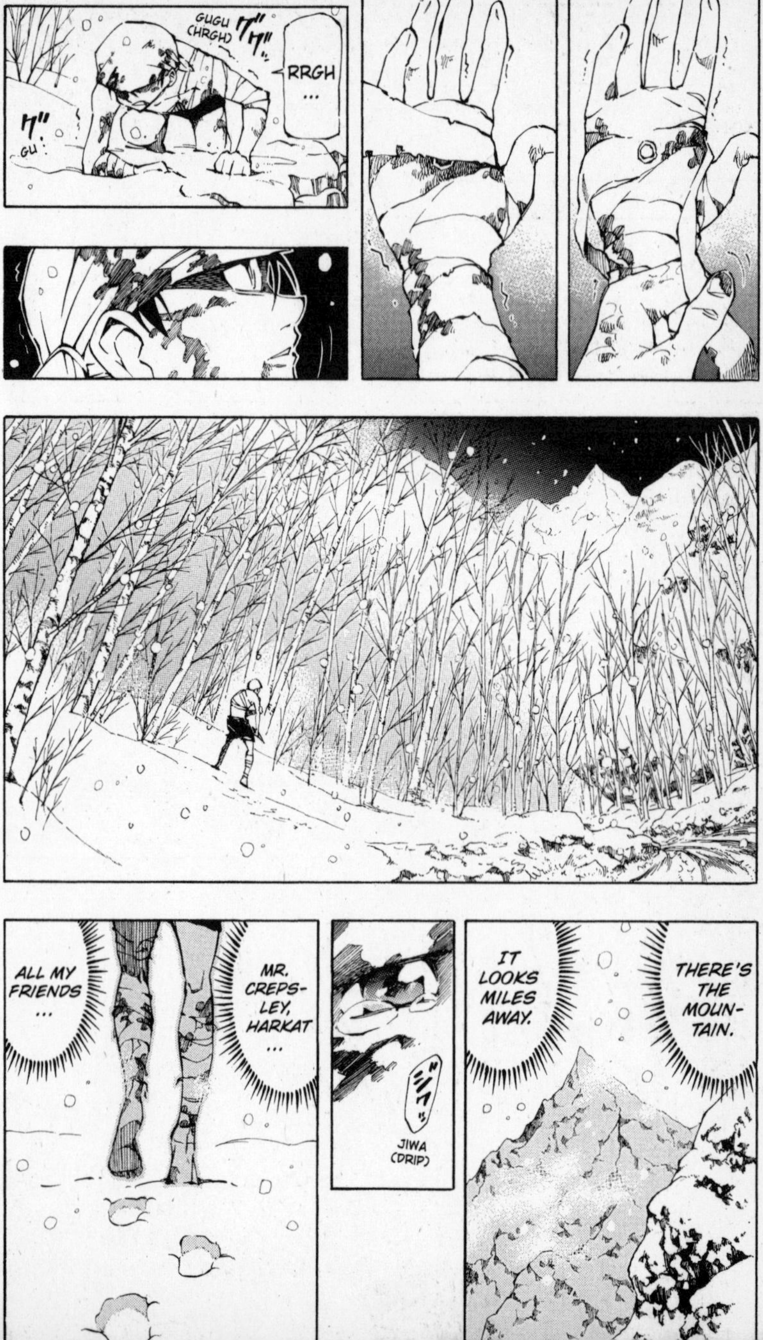
GUGU (HRGH)
RRGH ...
GU
THERE'S THE MOUN-TAIN.
IT LOOKS MILES AWAY.
JIWA (DRIP)
MR. CREPS-LEY, HARKAT ...
ALL MY FRIENDS ...

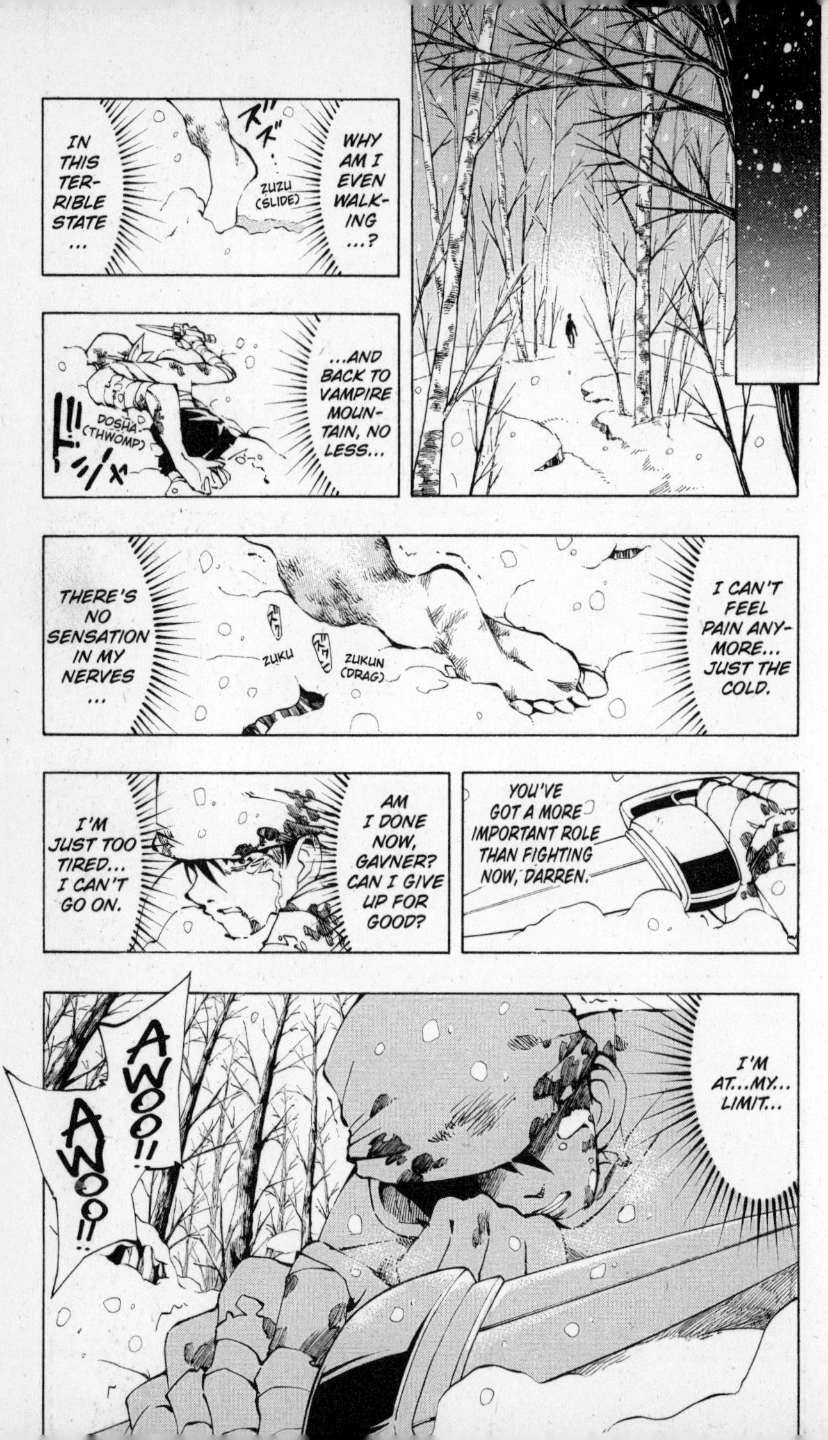
WHY AM I EVEN WALKING...?
ZUZU (SLIDE)
IN THIS TERRIBLE STATE...
...AND BACK TO VAMPIRE MOUNTAIN, NO LESS...
DOSHA (THWOMP)
I CAN'T FEEL PAIN ANYMORE... JUST THE COLD.
ZUKUN (DRAG)
ZUKU
THERE'S NO SENSATION IN MY NERVES...
YOU'VE GOT A MORE IMPORTANT ROLE THAN FIGHTING NOW, DARREN.
AM I DONE NOW, GAVNER? CAN I GIVE UP FOR GOOD?
I'M JUST TOO TIRED... I CAN'T GO ON.
I'M AT...MY... LIMIT...
AWOO!!
AWOO!!

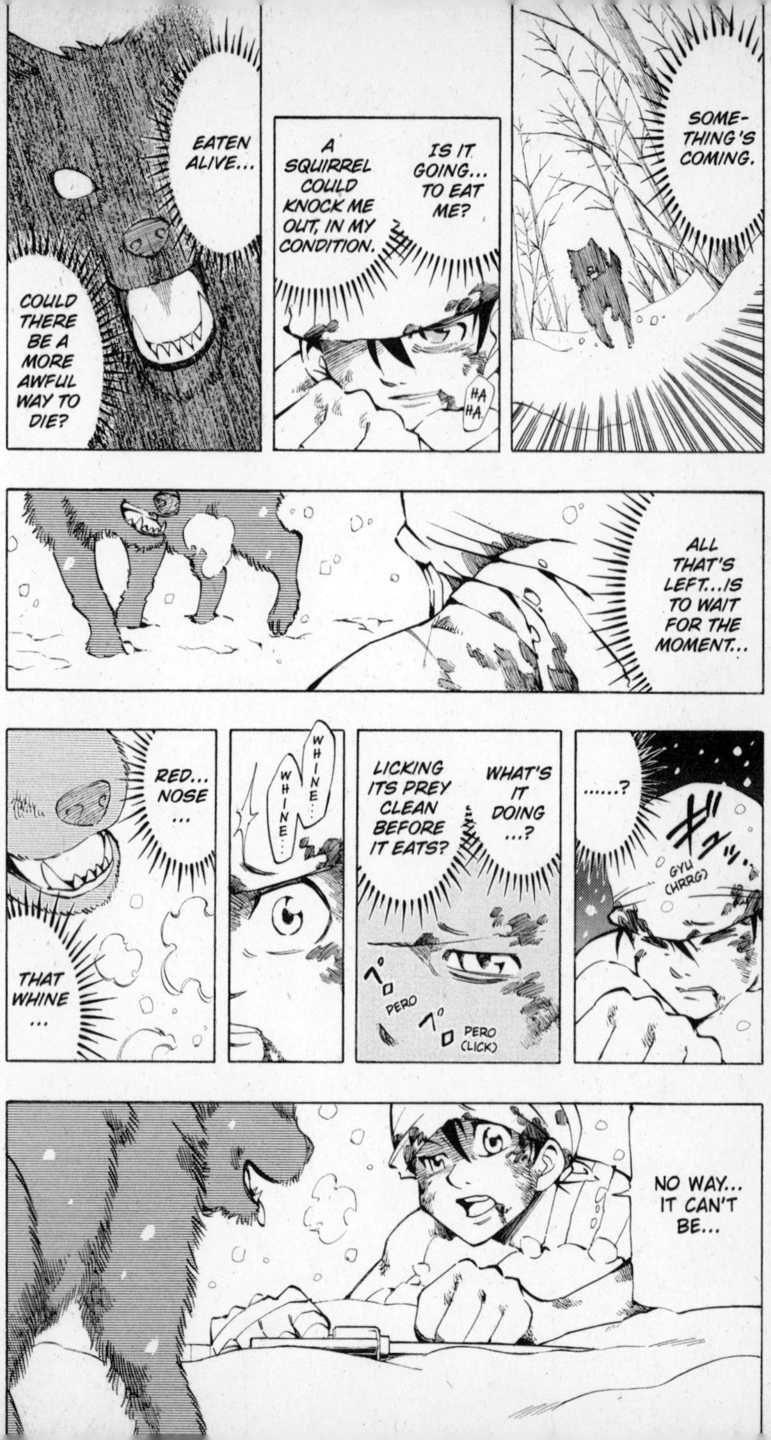
SOME-THING'S COMING.
IS IT GOING... TO EAT ME?
A SQUIRREL COULD KNOCK ME OUT, IN MY CONDITION.
HA HA.
EATEN ALIVE...
COULD THERE BE A MORE AWFUL WAY TO DIE?
ALL THAT'S LEFT...IS TO WAIT FOR THE MOMENT...
......?
GYU (HRRG)
WHAT'S IT DOING ...?
LICKING ITS PREY CLEAN BEFORE IT EATS?
PERO
PERO (LICK)
WHINE...
WHINE...
RED... NOSE ...
THAT WHINE ...
NO WAY... IT CAN'T BE...

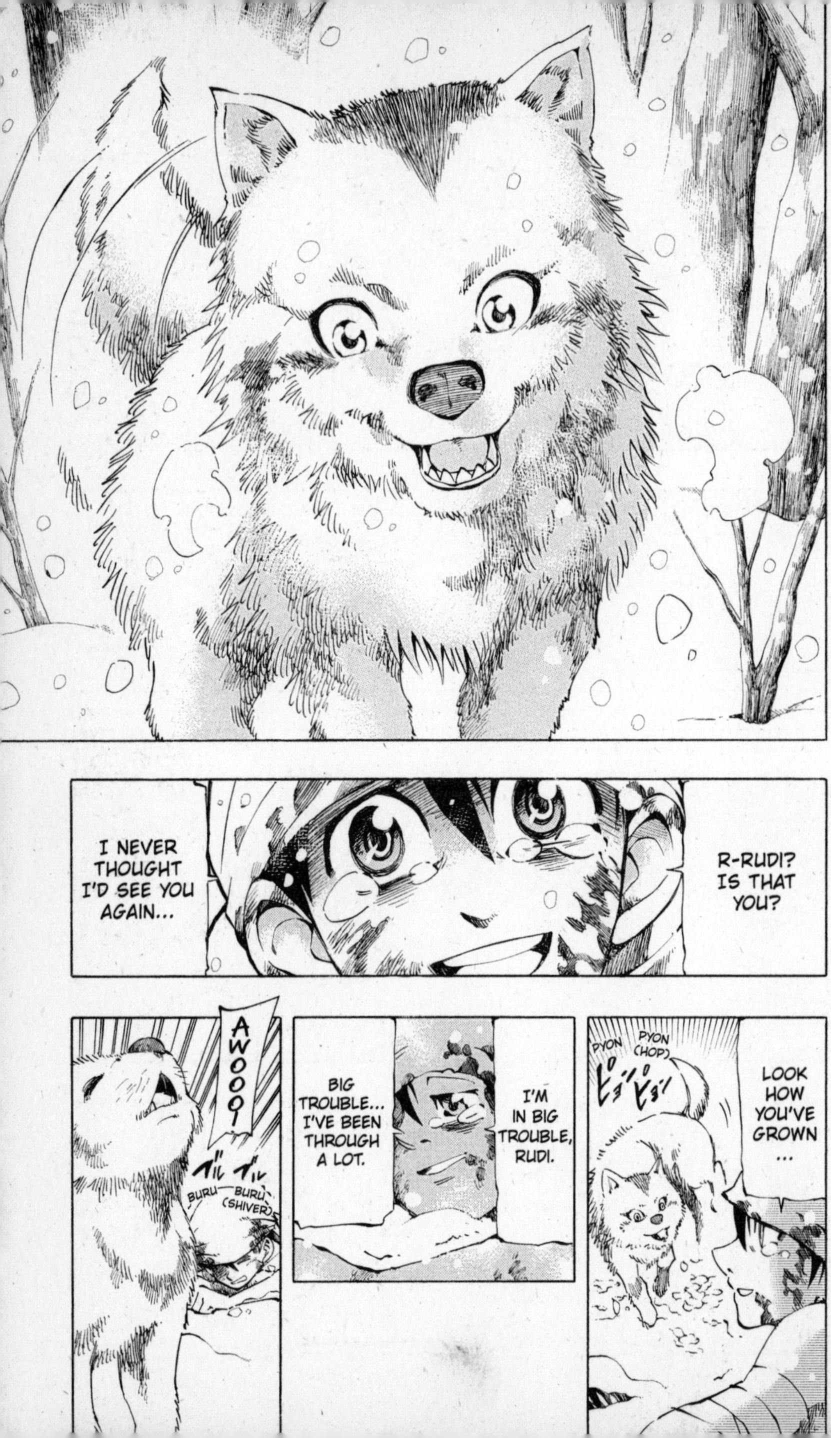
R-RUDI? IS THAT YOU?
I NEVER THOUGHT I'D SEE YOU AGAIN...
LOOK HOW YOU'VE GROWN...
PYON PYON (HOP)
I'M IN BIG TROUBLE, RUDI.
BIG TROUBLE... I'VE BEEN THROUGH A LOT.
AWOOO
BURU BURU (SHIVER)

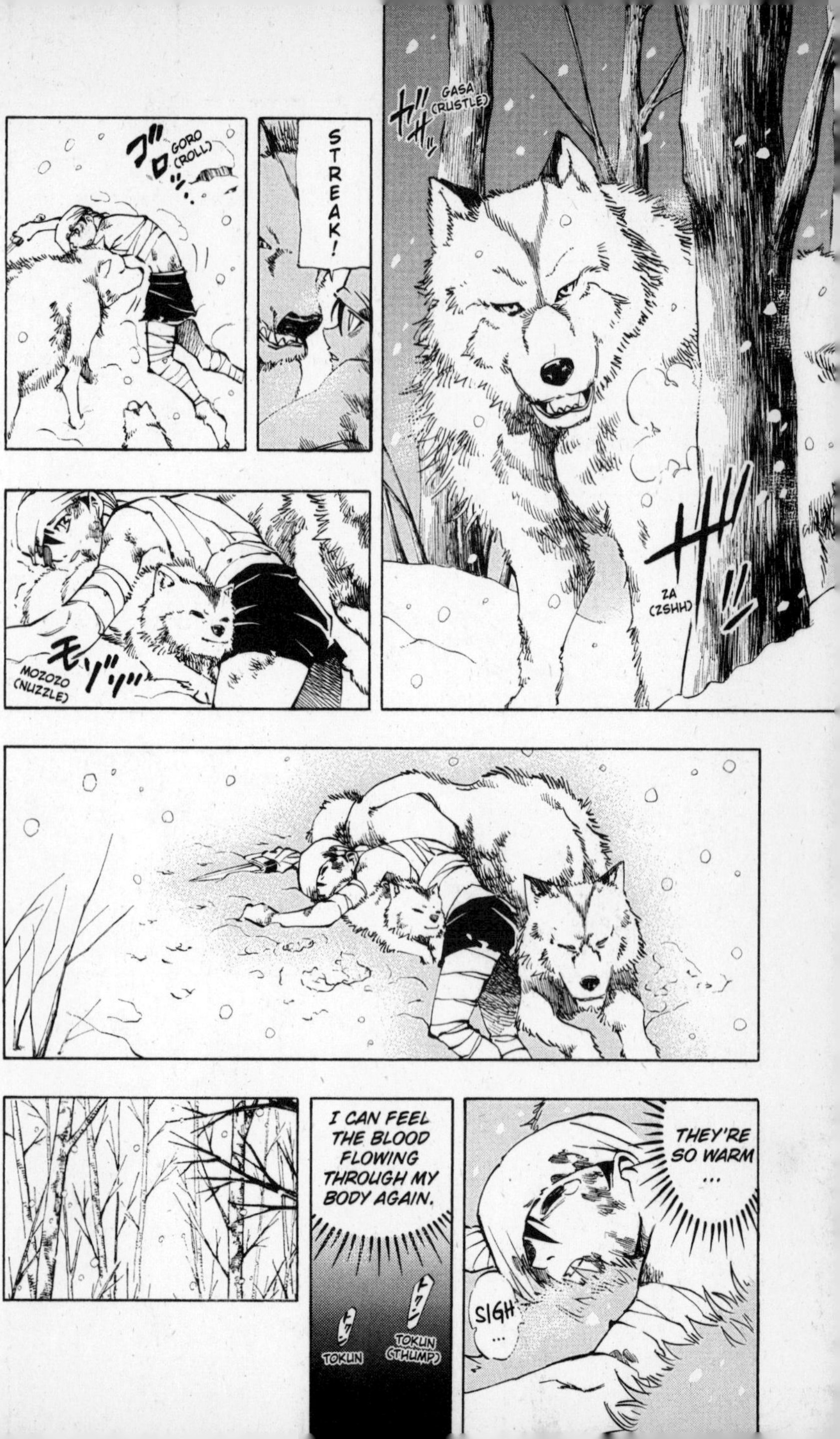
GASA (RUSTLE)
ZA (ZSHH)
STREAK!
GORO (ROLL)
MOZOZO (NUZZLE)
THEY'RE SO WARM ...
SIGH ...
I CAN FEEL THE BLOOD FLOWING THROUGH MY BODY AGAIN.
TOKUN (THUMP)
TOKUN

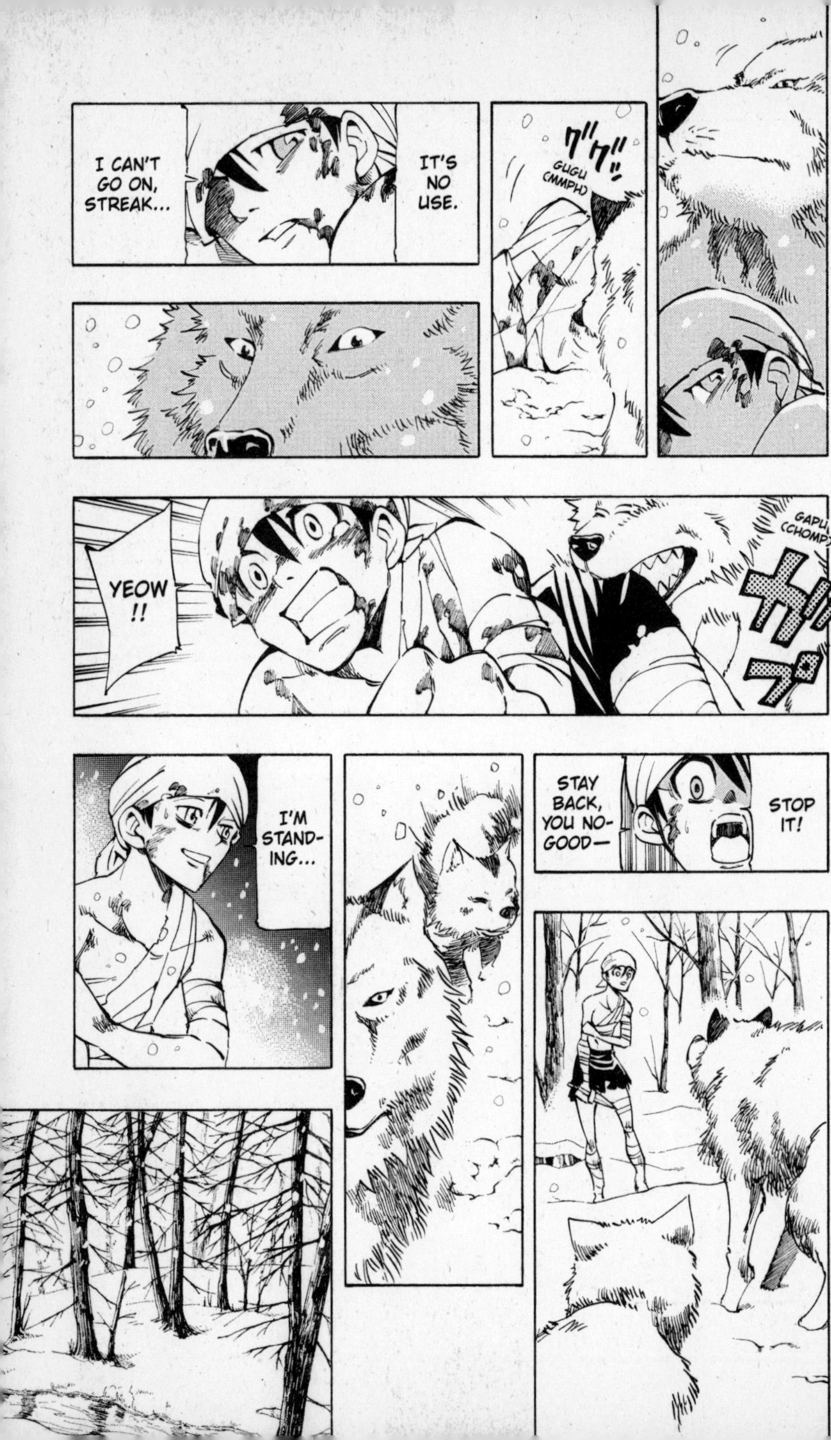
ググ
GUGU (MMPH)
IT'S NO USE.
I CAN'T GO ON, STREAK...
GAPU (CHOMP)
ガブ
YEOW !!
STOP IT!
STAY BACK, YOU NO-GOOD—
I'M STANDING...

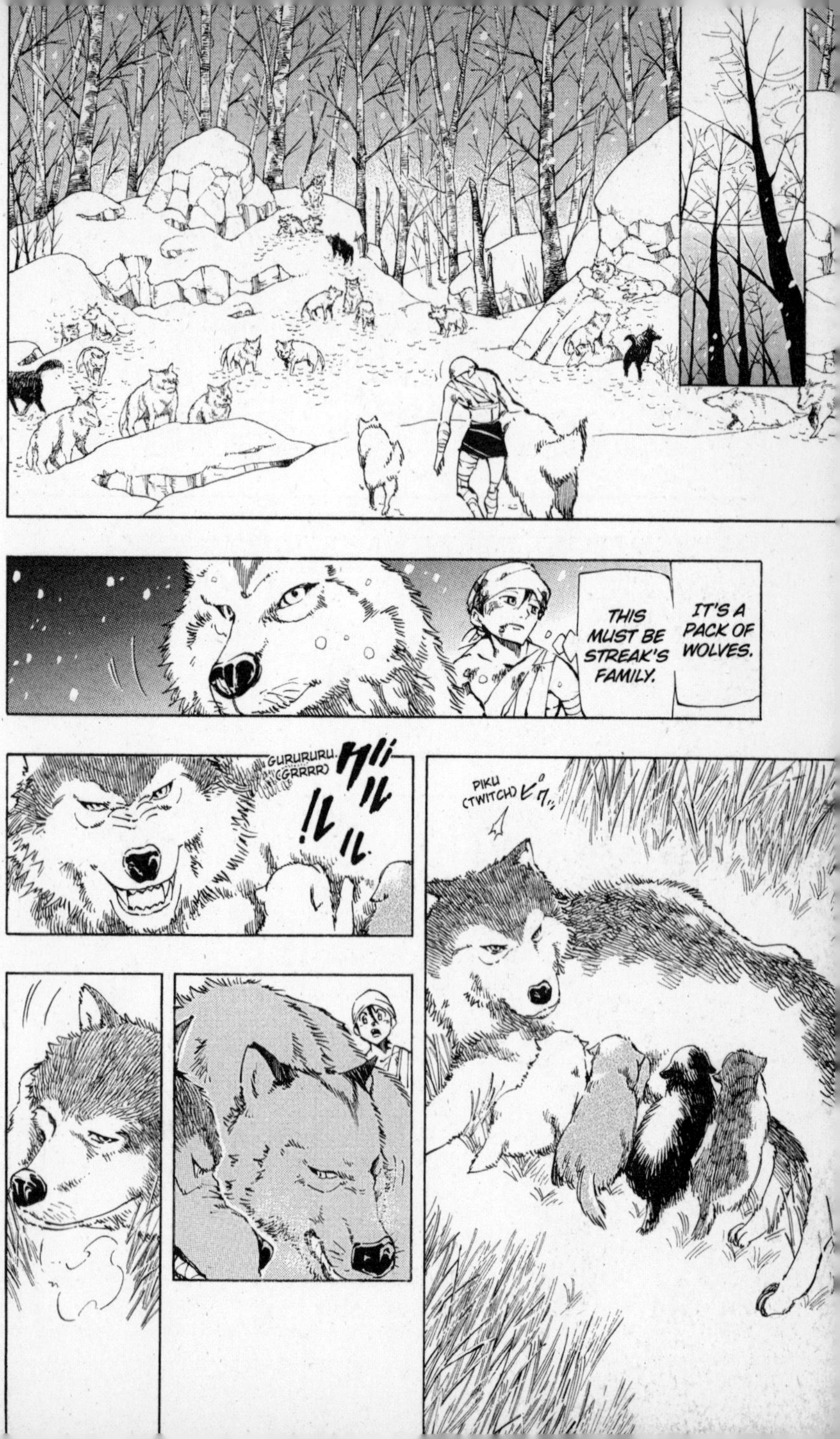

IT'S A PACK OF WOLVES.
THIS MUST BE STREAK'S FAMILY.
PIKU (TWITCH) ピク
GURURURU (GRRRR) グルルル

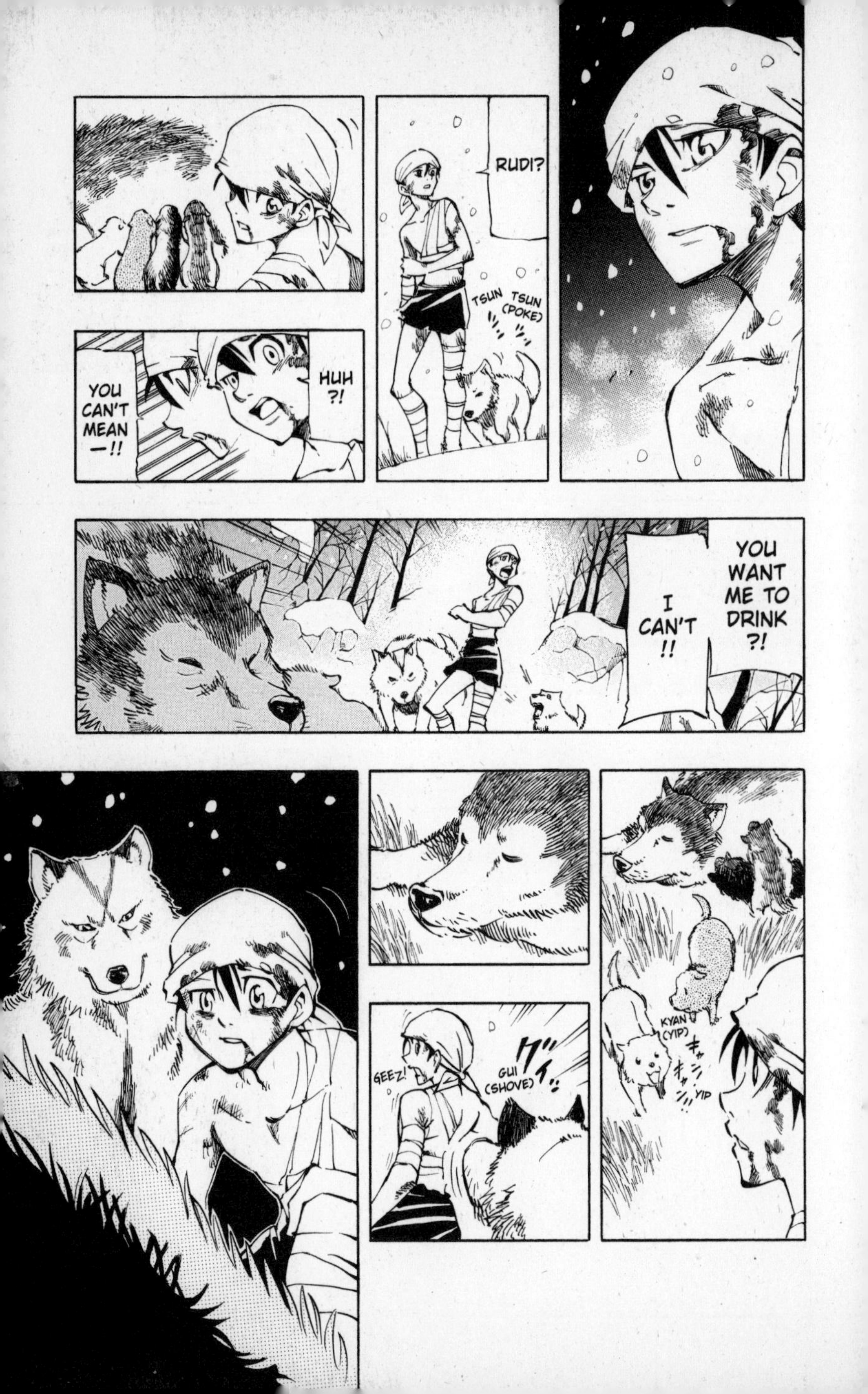
RUDI?
TSUN TSUN (POKE)
HUH ?!
YOU CAN'T MEAN —!!
YOU WANT ME TO DRINK ?!
I CAN'T !!
KYAN (YIP)
YIP
GUI (SHOVE)
GEEZ!

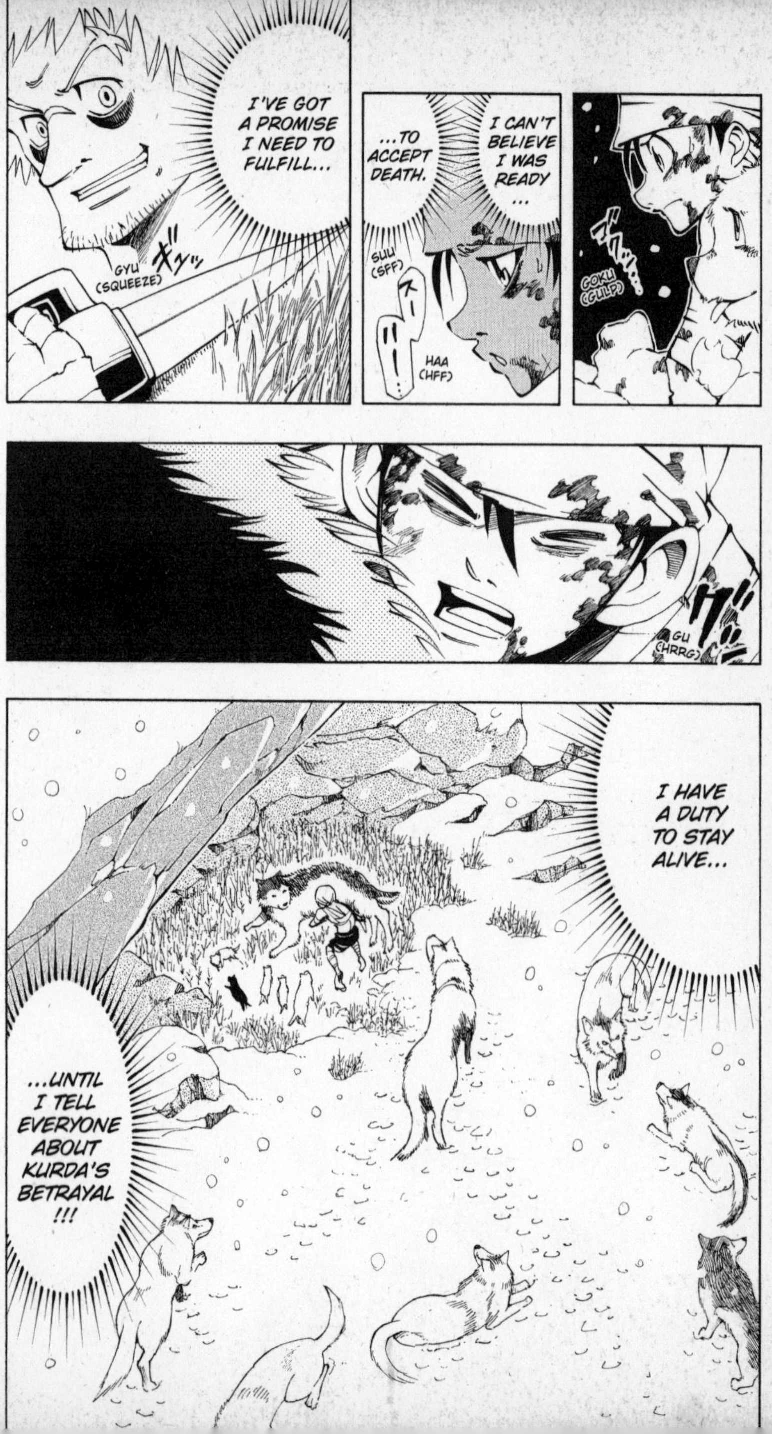

GOKU (GULP)
I CAN'T BELIEVE I WAS READY ...
...TO ACCEPT DEATH.
SUU (SFF)
HAA (HFF)
I'VE GOT A PROMISE I NEED TO FULFILL...
GYU (SQUEEZE)
GU (HRRG)
I HAVE A DUTY TO STAY ALIVE...
...UNTIL I TELL EVERYONE ABOUT KURDA'S BETRAYAL !!!

CHAPTER 46:
THE TRAITOR'S PLOT

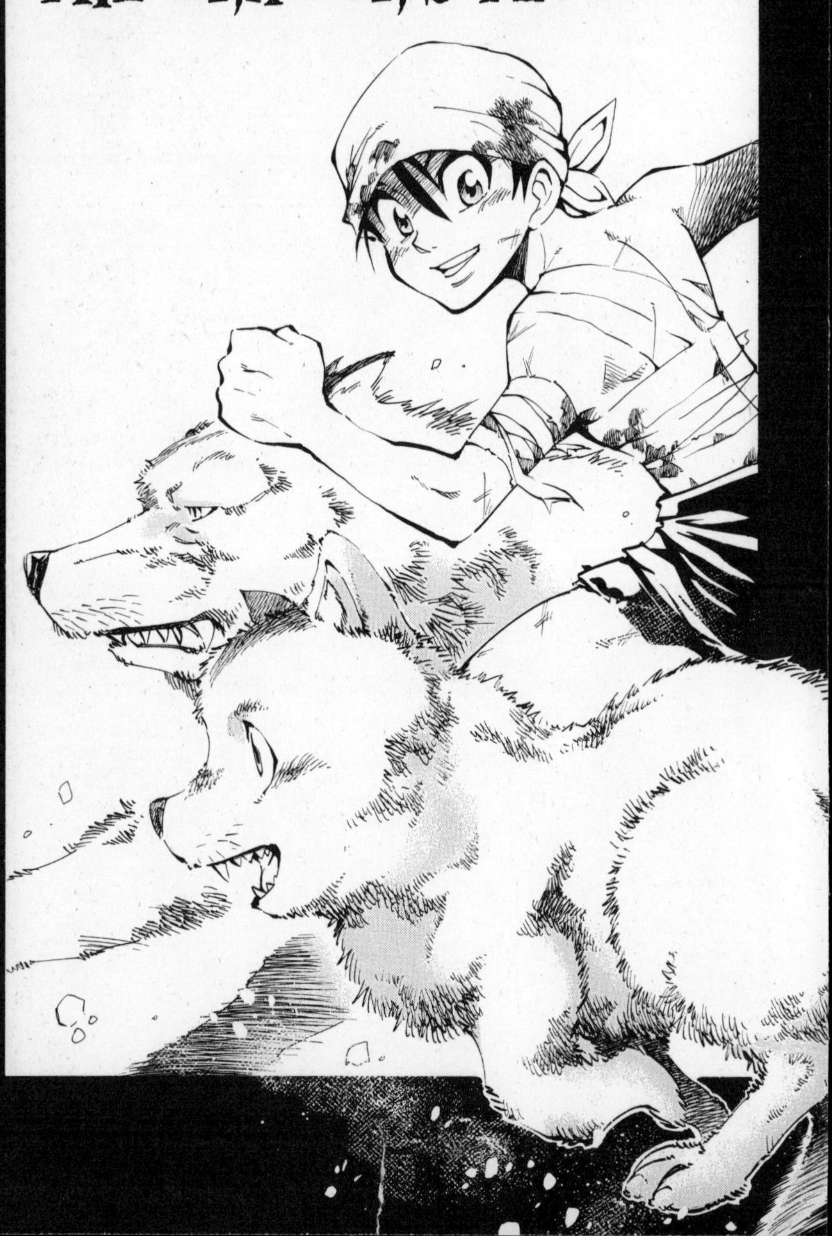

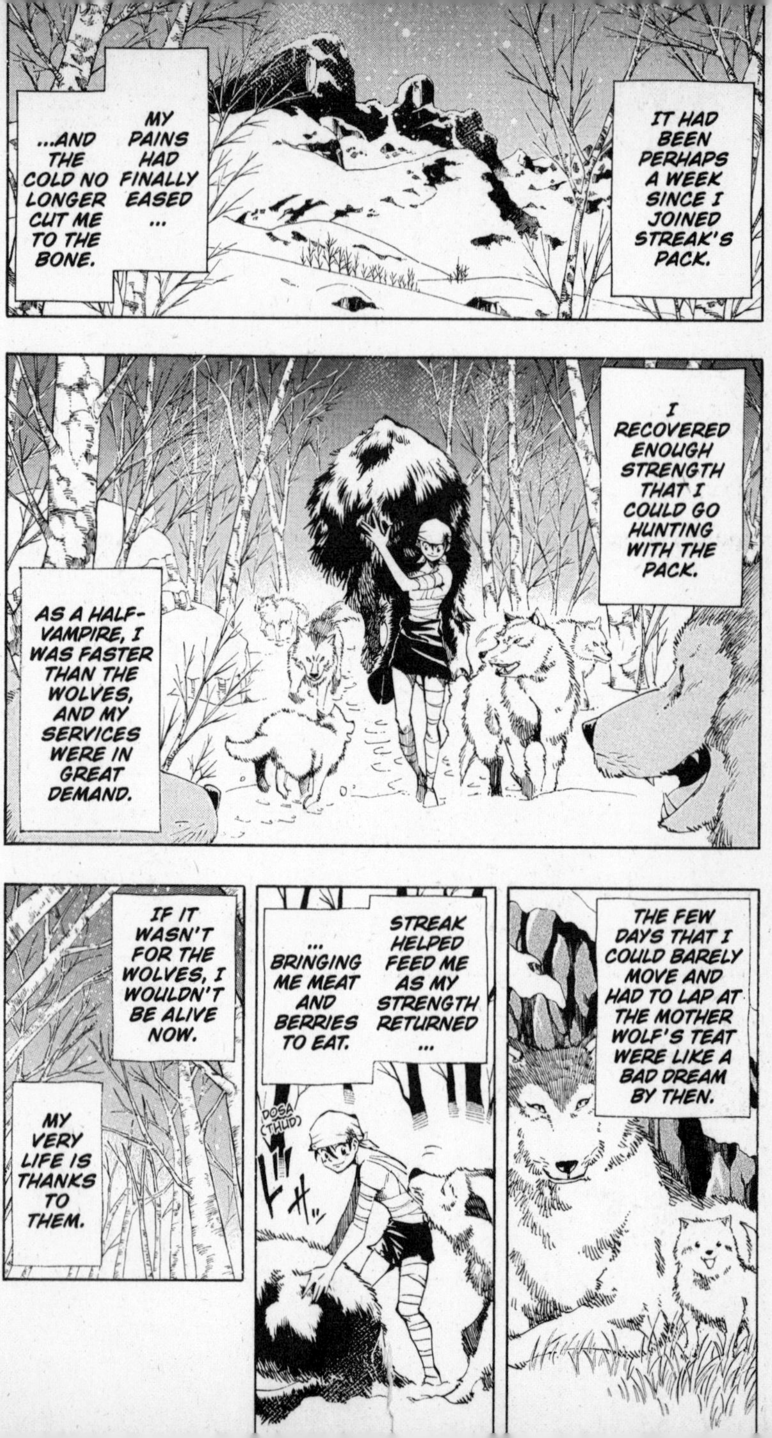
IT HAD BEEN PERHAPS A WEEK SINCE I JOINED STREAK'S PACK.
MY PAINS HAD FINALLY EASED ...
...AND THE COLD NO LONGER CUT ME TO THE BONE.
I RECOVERED ENOUGH STRENGTH THAT I COULD GO HUNTING WITH THE PACK.
AS A HALF-VAMPIRE, I WAS FASTER THAN THE WOLVES, AND MY SERVICES WERE IN GREAT DEMAND.
THE FEW DAYS THAT I COULD BARELY MOVE AND HAD TO LAP AT THE MOTHER WOLF'S TEAT WERE LIKE A BAD DREAM BY THEN.
STREAK HELPED FEED ME AS MY STRENGTH RETURNED ...
... BRINGING ME MEAT AND BERRIES TO EAT.
DOSA (THUD)
ドサッ
IF IT WASN'T FOR THE WOLVES, I WOULDN'T BE ALIVE NOW.
MY VERY LIFE IS THANKS TO THEM.

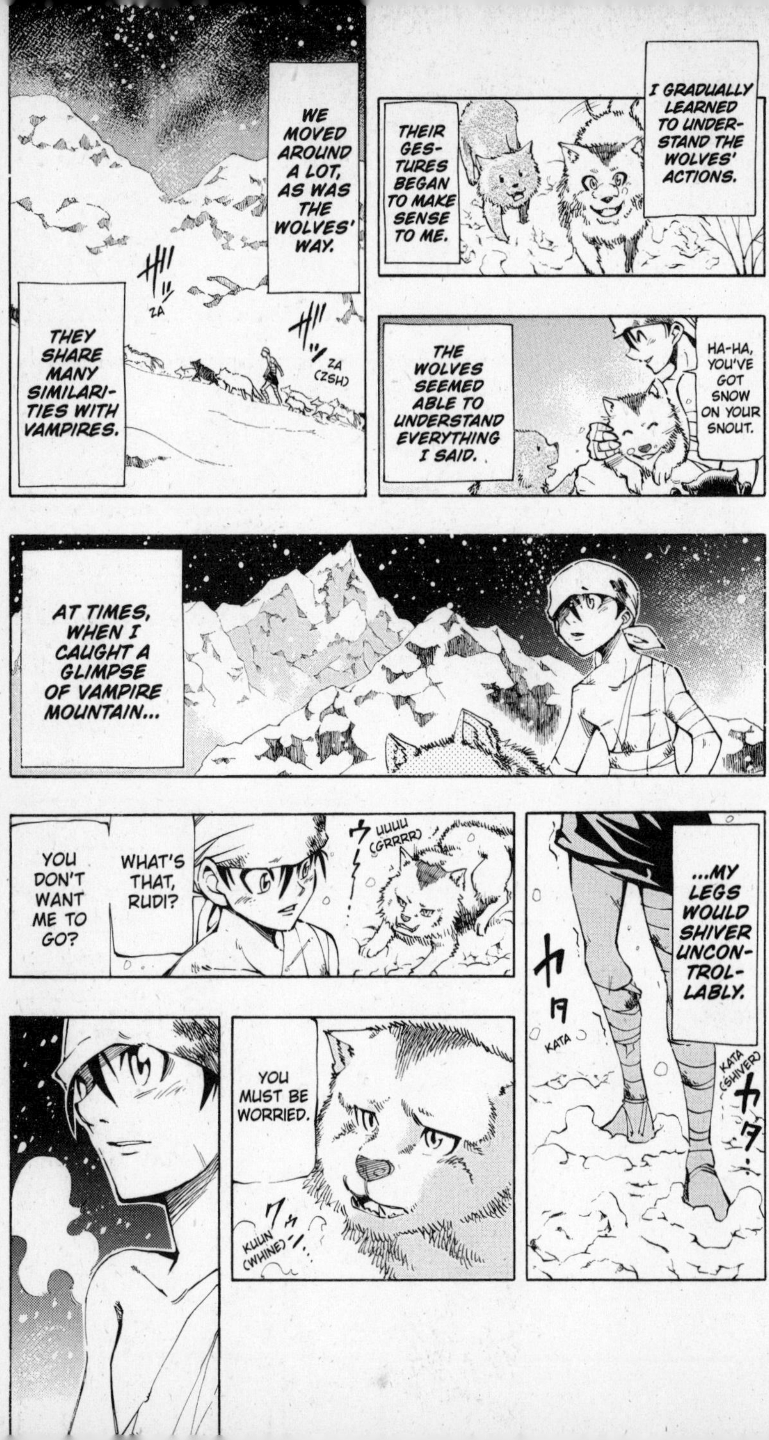

I GRADUALLY LEARNED TO UNDERSTAND THE WOLVES' ACTIONS.
THEIR GESTURES BEGAN TO MAKE SENSE TO ME.
HA-HA, YOU'VE GOT SNOW ON YOUR SNOUT.
THE WOLVES SEEMED ABLE TO UNDERSTAND EVERYTHING I SAID.
WE MOVED AROUND A LOT, AS WAS THE WOLVES' WAY.
ZA
ZA (ZSH)
THEY SHARE MANY SIMILARITIES WITH VAMPIRES.
AT TIMES, WHEN I CAUGHT A GLIMPSE OF VAMPIRE MOUNTAIN...
...MY LEGS WOULD SHIVER UNCONTROLLABLY.
KATA
KATA (SHIVER)
UUUU (GRRRR)
WHAT'S THAT, RUDI?
YOU DON'T WANT ME TO GO?
YOU MUST BE WORRIED.
KUUN (WHINE)

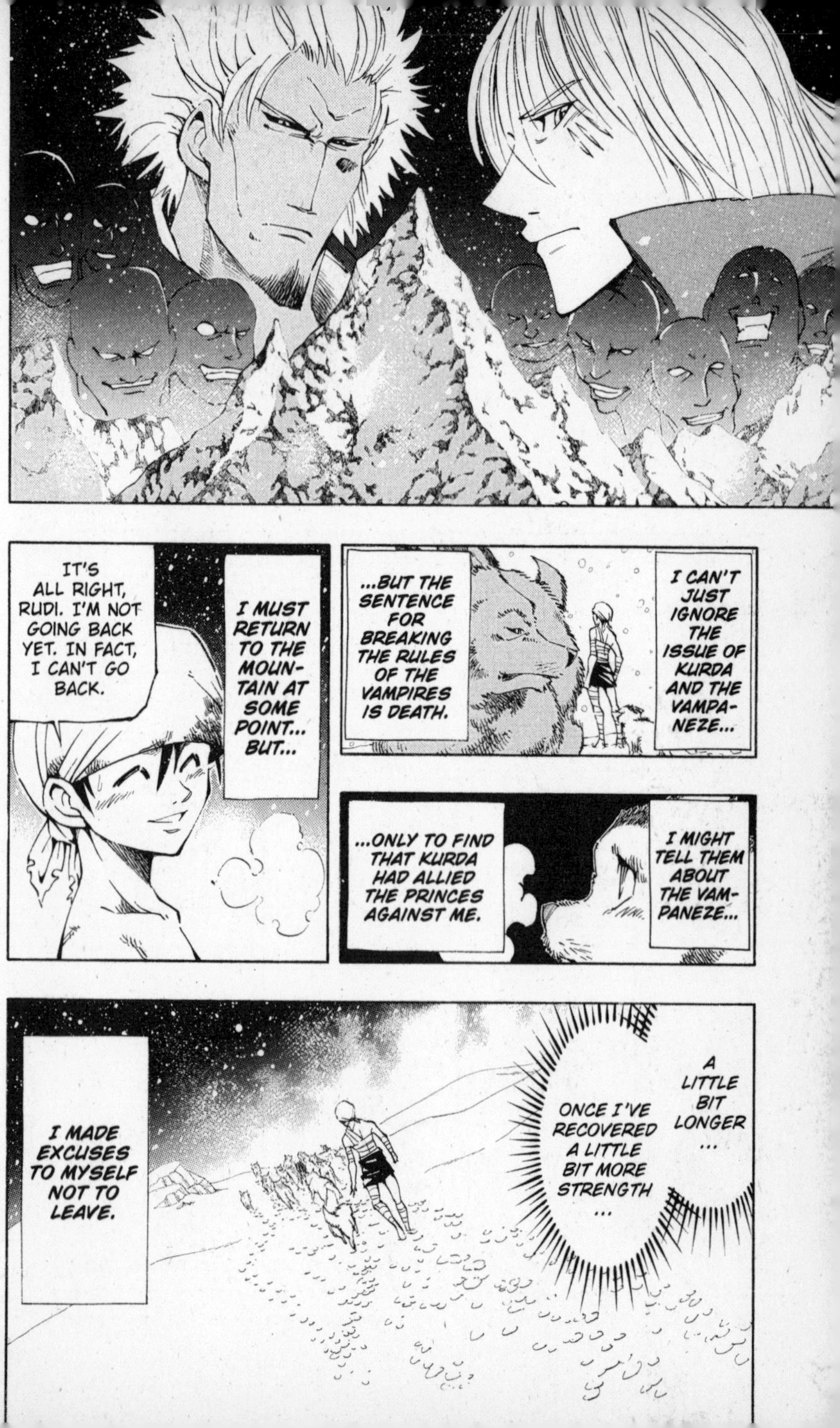

I CAN'T JUST IGNORE THE ISSUE OF KURDA AND THE VAMPANEZE...
...BUT THE SENTENCE FOR BREAKING THE RULES OF THE VAMPIRES IS DEATH.
I MIGHT TELL THEM ABOUT THE VAMPANEZE...
...ONLY TO FIND THAT KURDA HAD ALLIED THE PRINCES AGAINST ME.
I MUST RETURN TO THE MOUNTAIN AT SOME POINT... BUT...
IT'S ALL RIGHT, RUDI. I'M NOT GOING BACK YET. IN FACT, I CAN'T GO BACK.
A LITTLE BIT LONGER ...
ONCE I'VE RECOVERED A LITTLE BIT MORE STRENGTH ...
I MADE EXCUSES TO MYSELF NOT TO LEAVE.

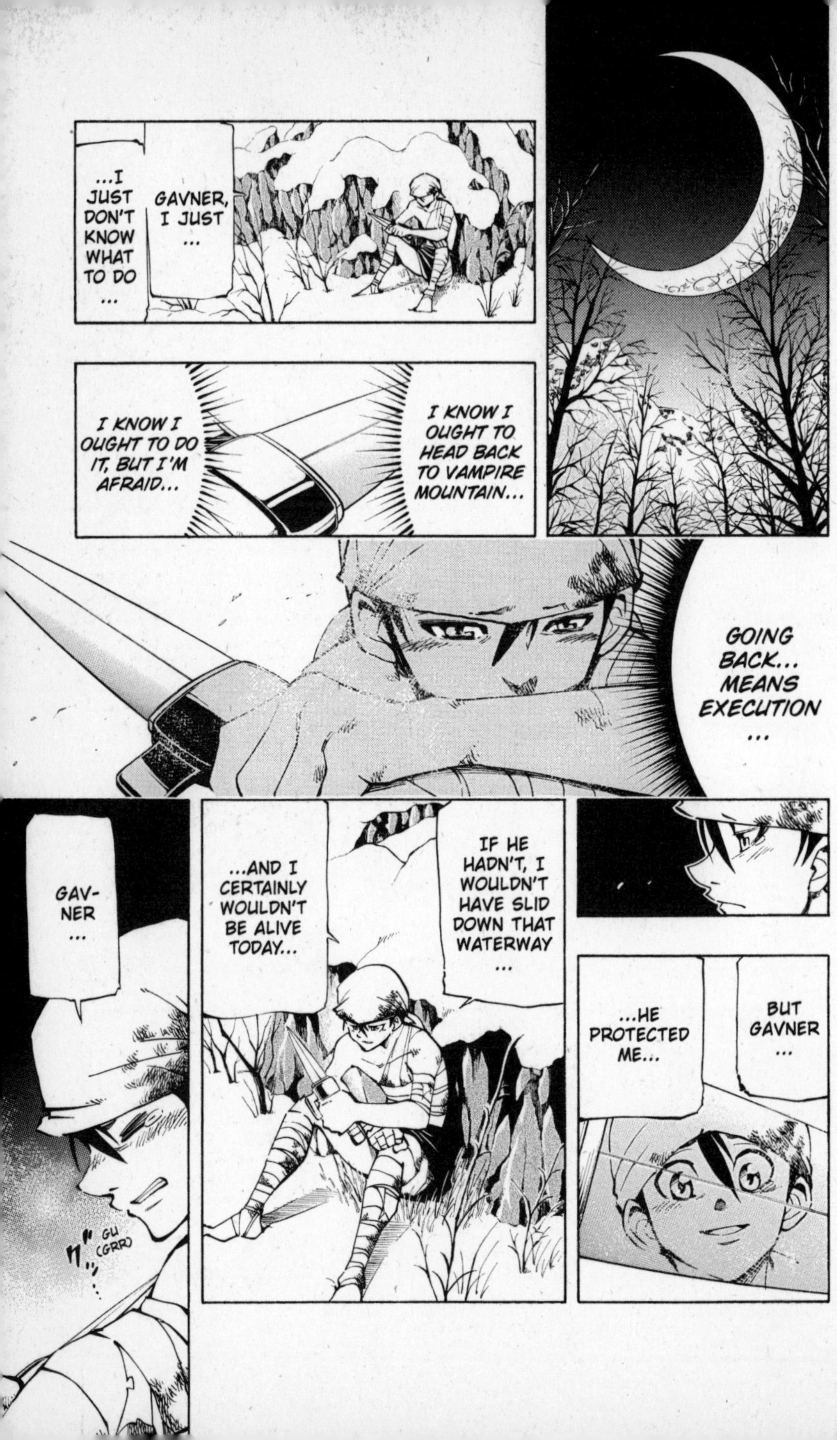
GAVNER, I JUST ...
...I JUST DON'T KNOW WHAT TO DO ...
I KNOW I OUGHT TO HEAD BACK TO VAMPIRE MOUNTAIN...
I KNOW I OUGHT TO DO IT, BUT I'M AFRAID...
GOING BACK... MEANS EXECUTION ...
BUT GAVNER ...
...HE PROTECTED ME...
IF HE HADN'T, I WOULDN'T HAVE SLID DOWN THAT WATERWAY ...
...AND I CERTAINLY WOULDN'T BE ALIVE TODAY...
GAV-NER ...
GU (GRR)

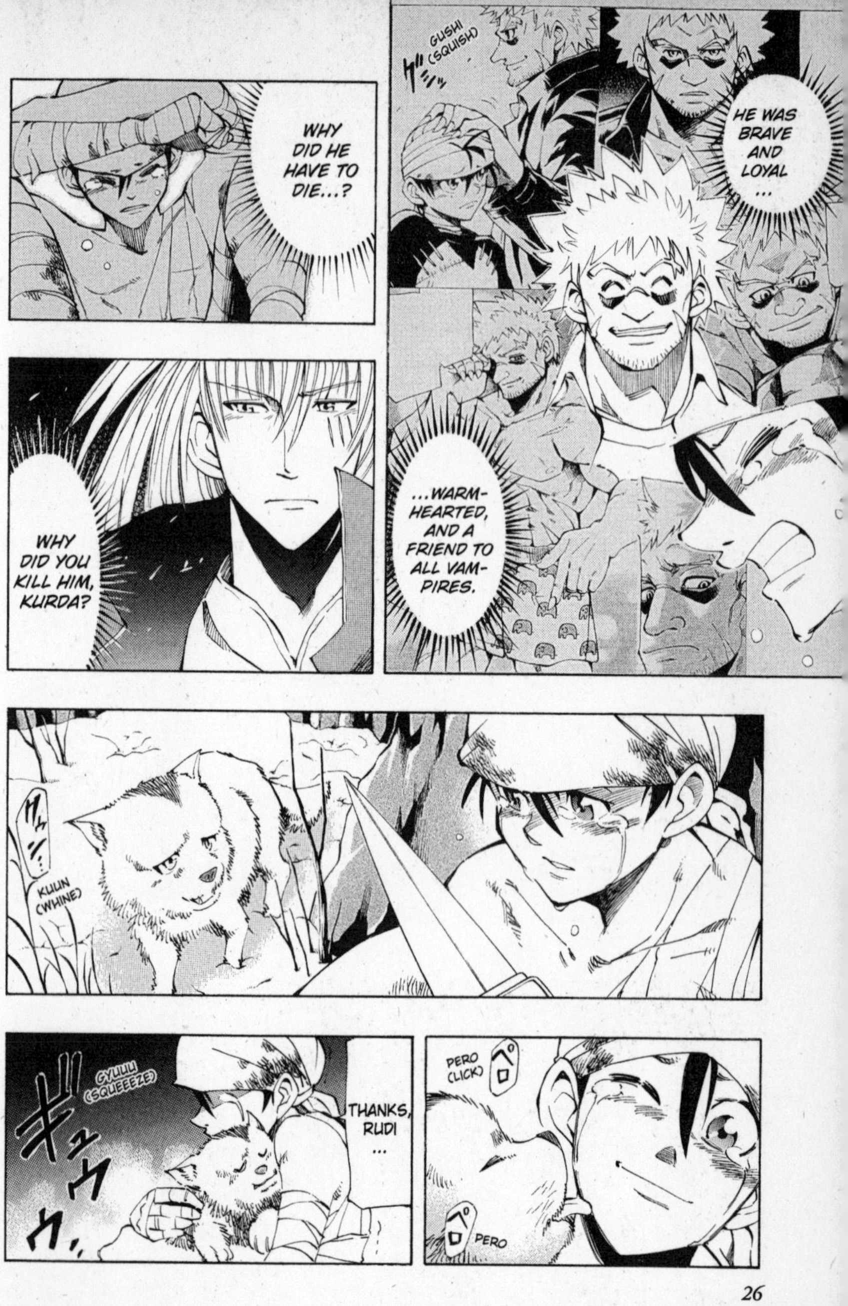
GUSHI (SQUISH)
HE WAS BRAVE AND LOYAL ...
...WARM-HEARTED, AND A FRIEND TO ALL VAMPIRES.
WHY DID HE HAVE TO DIE...?
WHY DID YOU KILL HIM, KURDA?
KUUN (WHINE)
PERO (LICK)
PERO
GYUUU (SQUEEEZE)
THANKS, RUDI ...

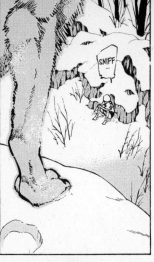

SNIFF
....

FUI
(HRF)

UOU!!
(WOOF!!)

ONE NIGHT,
PERHAPS
BECAUSE
HE SENSED
I WAS
FEELING
DOWN...

...STREAK
TOOK ME
OUT FOR
A HUNT,
JUST THE
TWO OF
US.

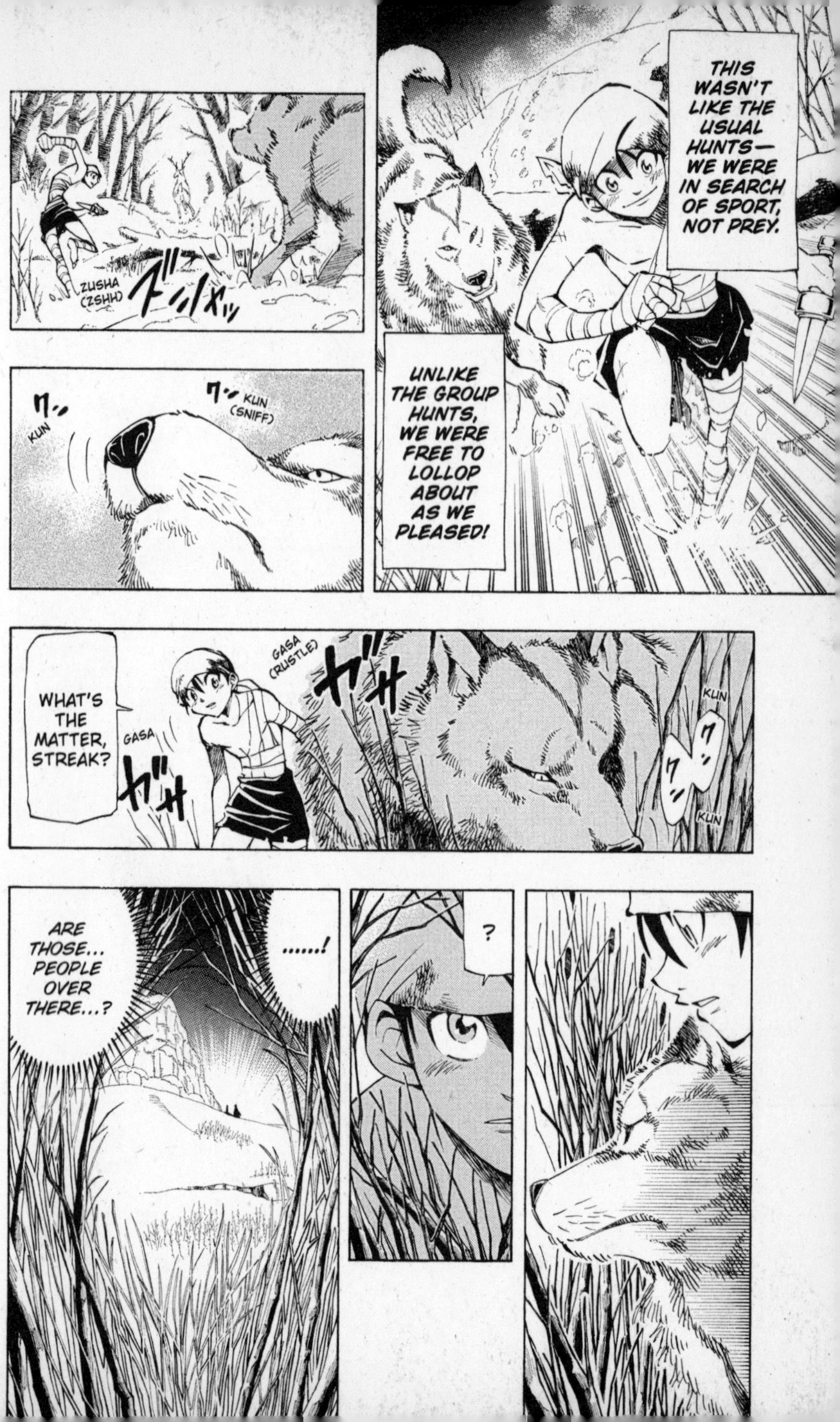
THIS WASN'T LIKE THE USUAL HUNTS—WE WERE IN SEARCH OF SPORT, NOT PREY.
UNLIKE THE GROUP HUNTS, WE WERE FREE TO LOLLOP ABOUT AS WE PLEASED!
ZUSHA (ZSHH)
KUN (SNIFF)
KUN
KUN
KUN
GASA (RUSTLE)
WHAT'S THE MATTER, STREAK?
GASA
?
......!
ARE THOSE... PEOPLE OVER THERE...?

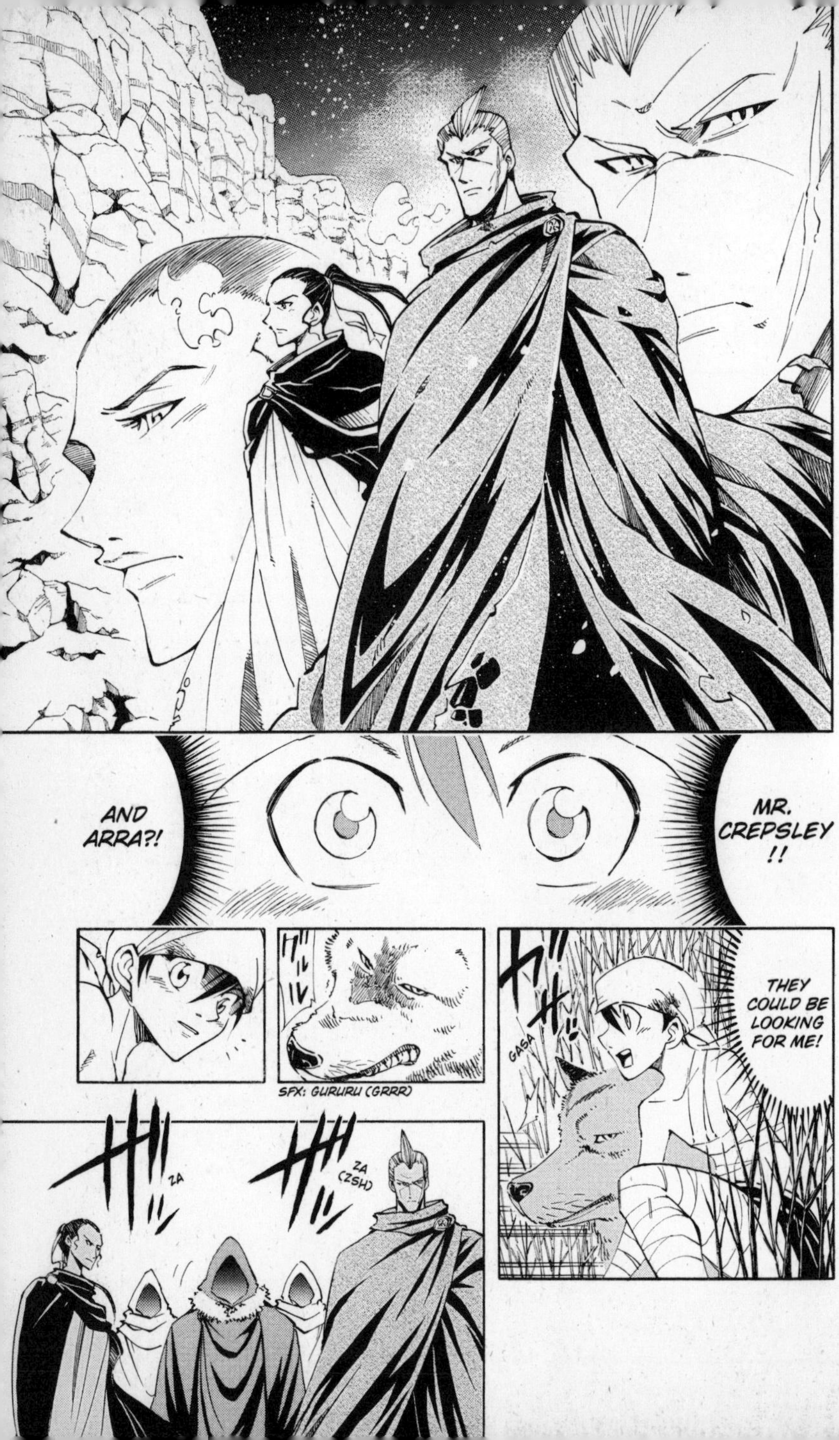
MR. CREPSLEY !!
AND ARRA?!
THEY COULD BE LOOKING FOR ME!
GASA
SFX: GURURU (GRRR)
ZA (ZSH)
ZA

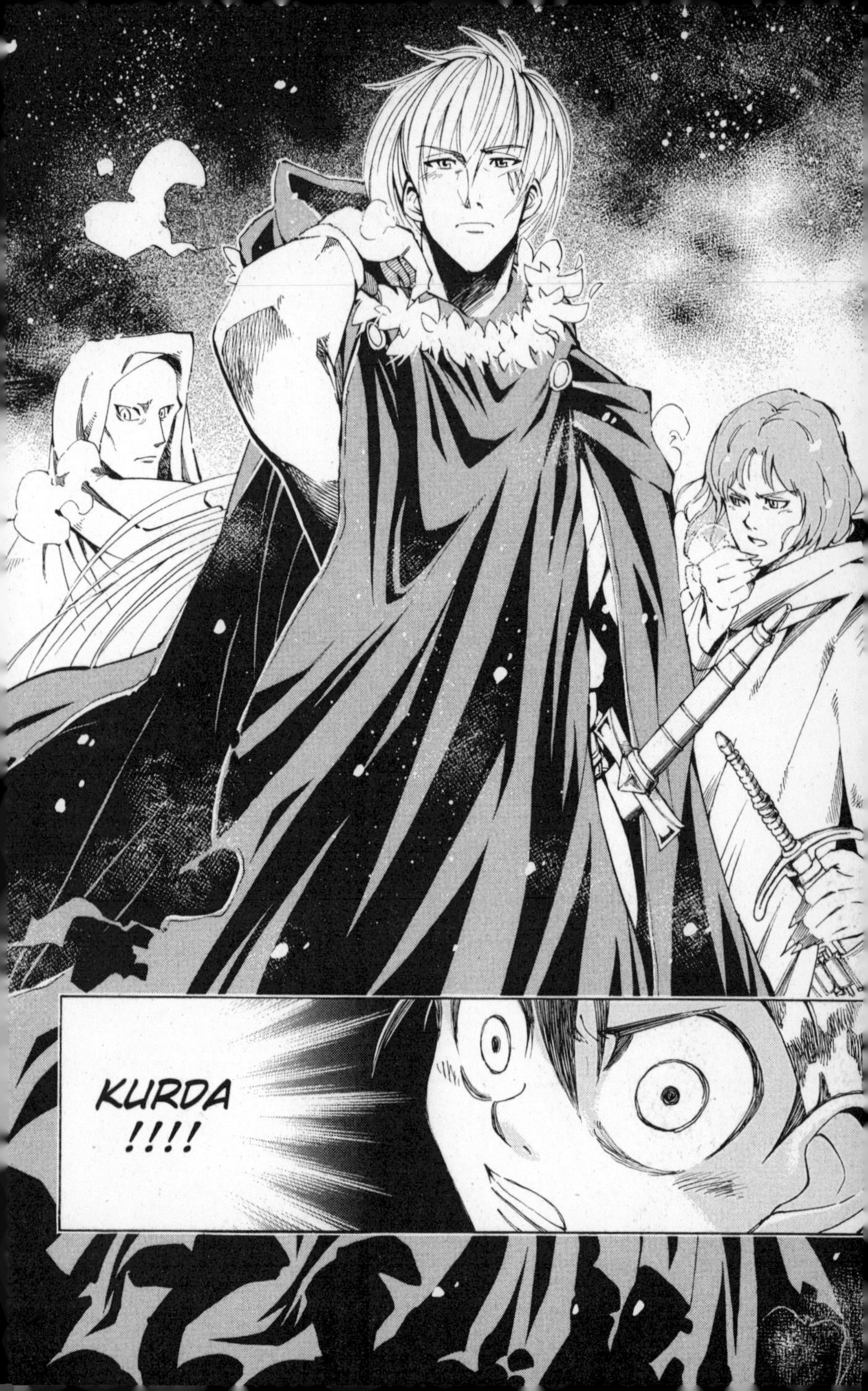
KURDA
!!!!

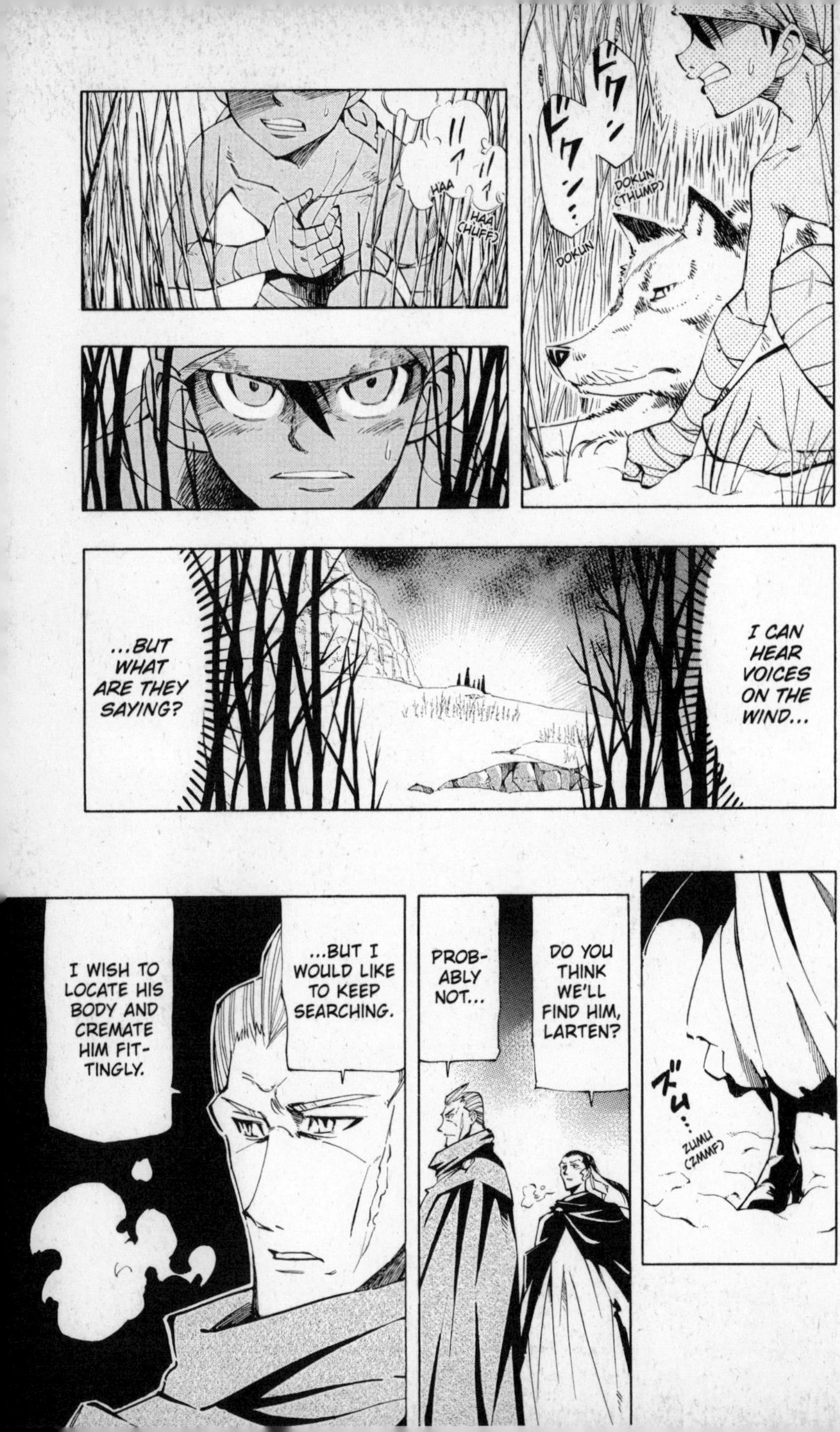

ドクン
ドクン
DOKUN (THUMP)
DOKUN
ハァ
ハァ
HAA
HAA (HUFF)
I CAN HEAR VOICES ON THE WIND...
...BUT WHAT ARE THEY SAYING?
ズム..
ZUMU (ZMMF)
DO YOU THINK WE'LL FIND HIM, LARTEN?
PROB- ABLY NOT...
...BUT I WOULD LIKE TO KEEP SEARCHING.
I WISH TO LOCATE HIS BODY AND CREMATE HIM FIT- TINGLY.

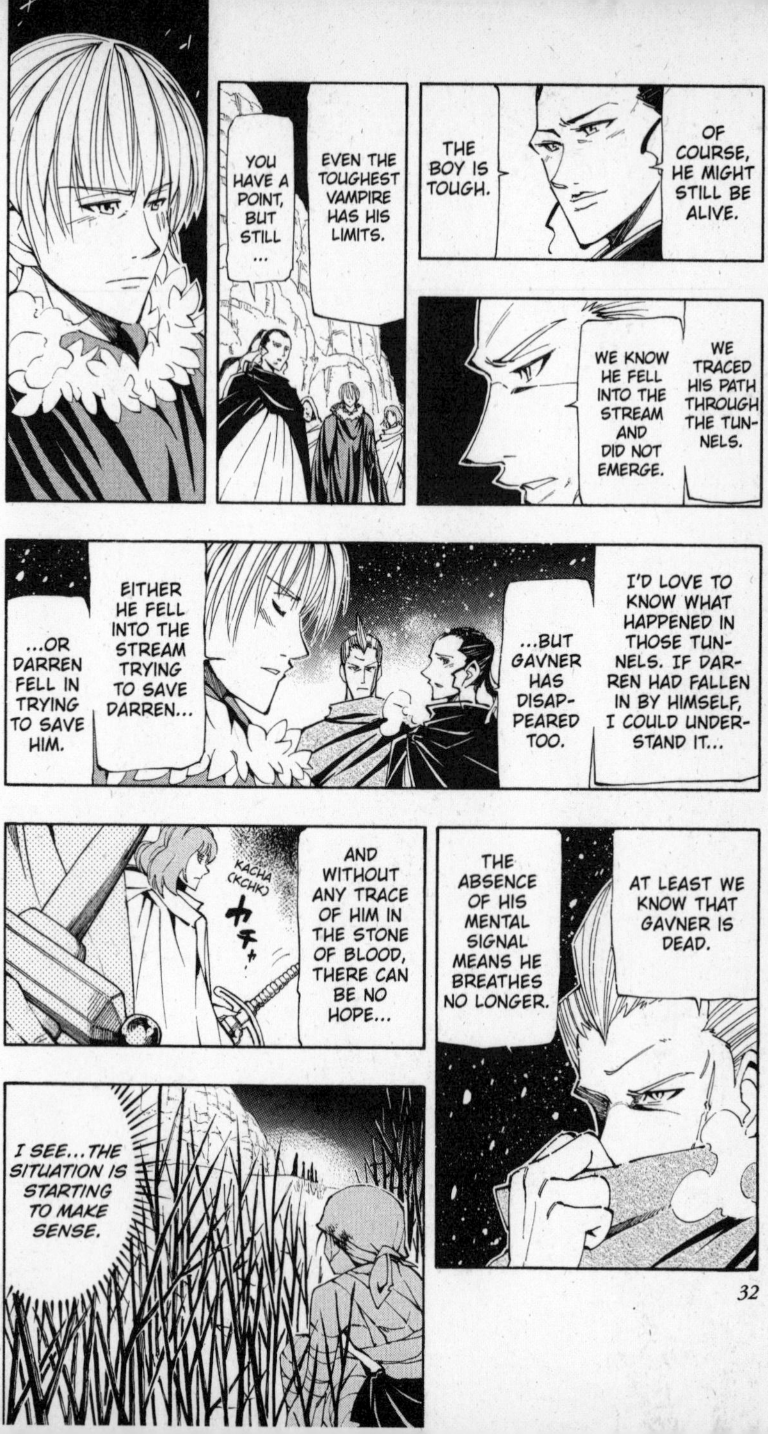
OF COURSE, HE MIGHT STILL BE ALIVE.
THE BOY IS TOUGH.
WE TRACED HIS PATH THROUGH THE TUN-NELS.
WE KNOW HE FELL INTO THE STREAM AND DID NOT EMERGE.
EVEN THE TOUGHEST VAMPIRE HAS HIS LIMITS.
YOU HAVE A POINT, BUT STILL ...
I'D LOVE TO KNOW WHAT HAPPENED IN THOSE TUN-NELS. IF DAR-REN HAD FALLEN IN BY HIMSELF, I COULD UNDER-STAND IT...
...BUT GAVNER HAS DISAP-PEARED TOO.
EITHER HE FELL INTO THE STREAM TRYING TO SAVE DARREN...
...OR DARREN FELL IN TRYING TO SAVE HIM.
AT LEAST WE KNOW THAT GAVNER IS DEAD.
THE ABSENCE OF HIS MENTAL SIGNAL MEANS HE BREATHES NO LONGER.
AND WITHOUT ANY TRACE OF HIM IN THE STONE OF BLOOD, THERE CAN BE NO HOPE...
KACHA (KCHK)
カチャ
I SEE...THE SITUATION IS STARTING TO MAKE SENSE.

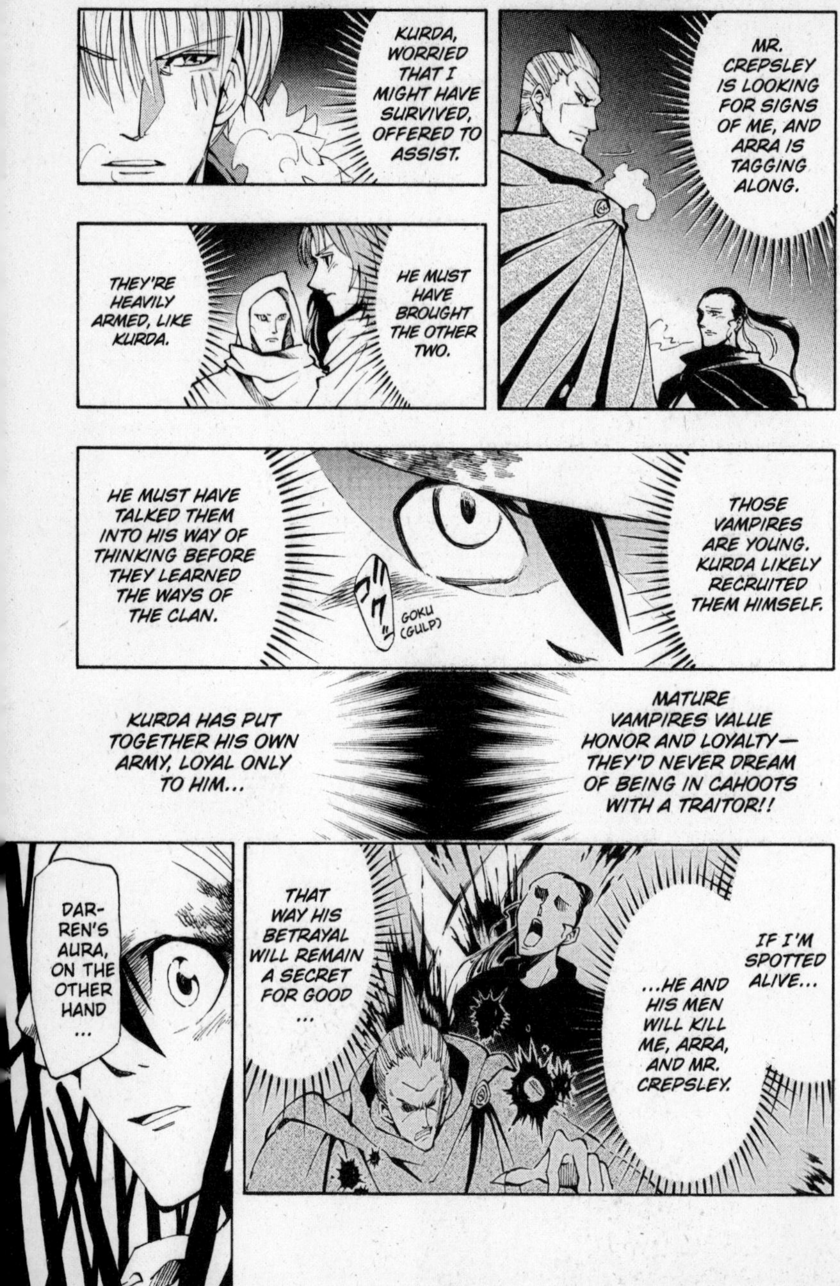
MR. CREPSLEY IS LOOKING FOR SIGNS OF ME, AND ARRA IS TAGGING ALONG.
KURDA, WORRIED THAT I MIGHT HAVE SURVIVED, OFFERED TO ASSIST.
HE MUST HAVE BROUGHT THE OTHER TWO.
THEY'RE HEAVILY ARMED, LIKE KURDA.
THOSE VAMPIRES ARE YOUNG. KURDA LIKELY RECRUITED THEM HIMSELF.
GOKU (GULP)
HE MUST HAVE TALKED THEM INTO HIS WAY OF THINKING BEFORE THEY LEARNED THE WAYS OF THE CLAN.
MATURE VAMPIRES VALUE HONOR AND LOYALTY— THEY'D NEVER DREAM OF BEING IN CAHOOTS WITH A TRAITOR!!
KURDA HAS PUT TOGETHER HIS OWN ARMY, LOYAL ONLY TO HIM...
IF I'M SPOTTED ALIVE...
...HE AND HIS MEN WILL KILL ME, ARRA, AND MR. CREPSLEY.
THAT WAY HIS BETRAYAL WILL REMAIN A SECRET FOR GOOD ...
DAR-REN'S AURA, ON THE OTHER HAND ...

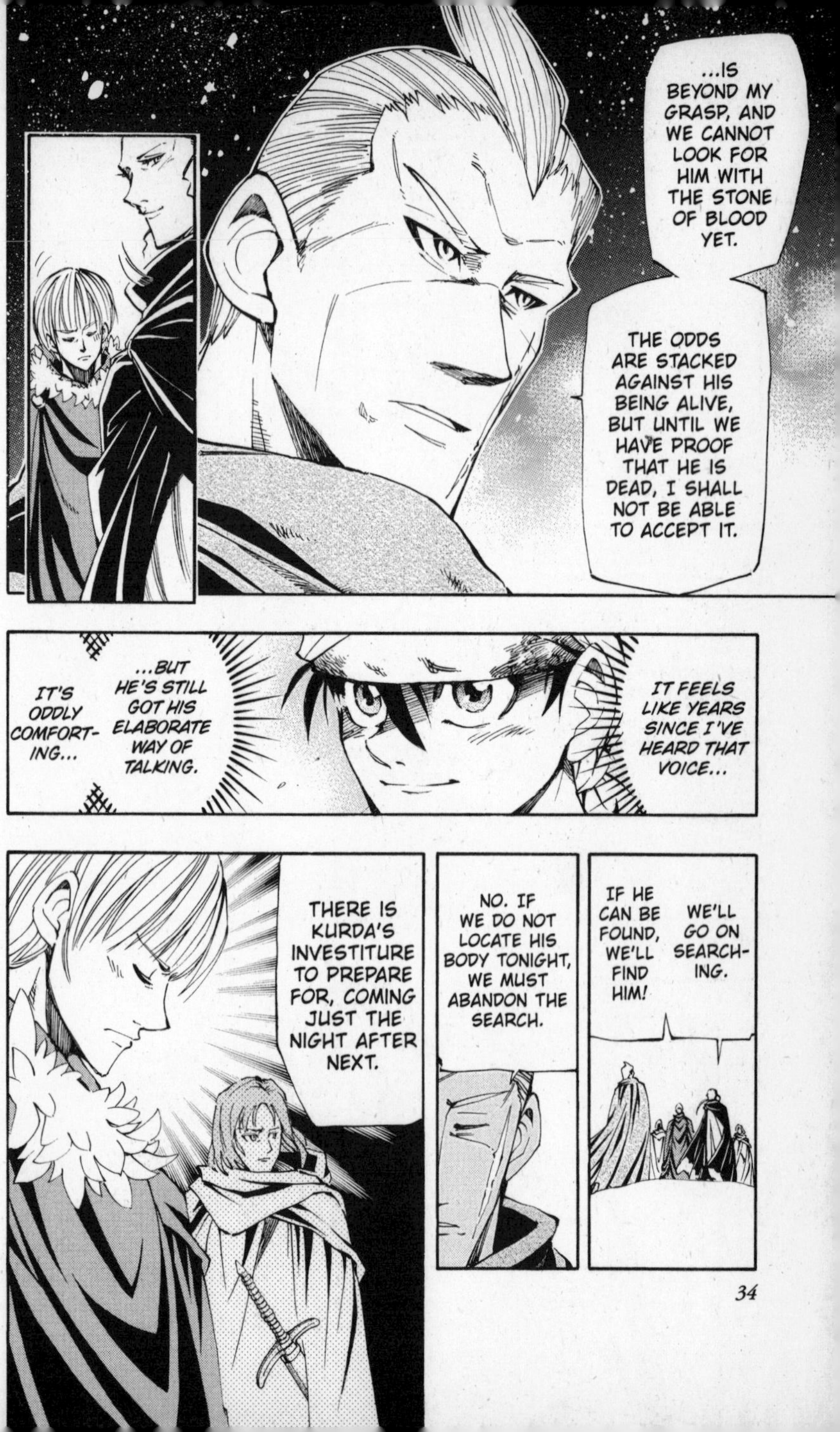
...IS BEYOND MY GRASP, AND WE CANNOT LOOK FOR HIM WITH THE STONE OF BLOOD YET.
THE ODDS ARE STACKED AGAINST HIS BEING ALIVE, BUT UNTIL WE HAVE PROOF THAT HE IS DEAD, I SHALL NOT BE ABLE TO ACCEPT IT.
IT FEELS LIKE YEARS SINCE I'VE HEARD THAT VOICE...
...BUT HE'S STILL GOT HIS ELABORATE WAY OF TALKING.
IT'S ODDLY COMFORTING...
WE'LL GO ON SEARCHING.
IF HE CAN BE FOUND, WE'LL FIND HIM!
NO. IF WE DO NOT LOCATE HIS BODY TONIGHT, WE MUST ABANDON THE SEARCH.
THERE IS KURDA'S INVESTITURE TO PREPARE FOR, COMING JUST THE NIGHT AFTER NEXT.

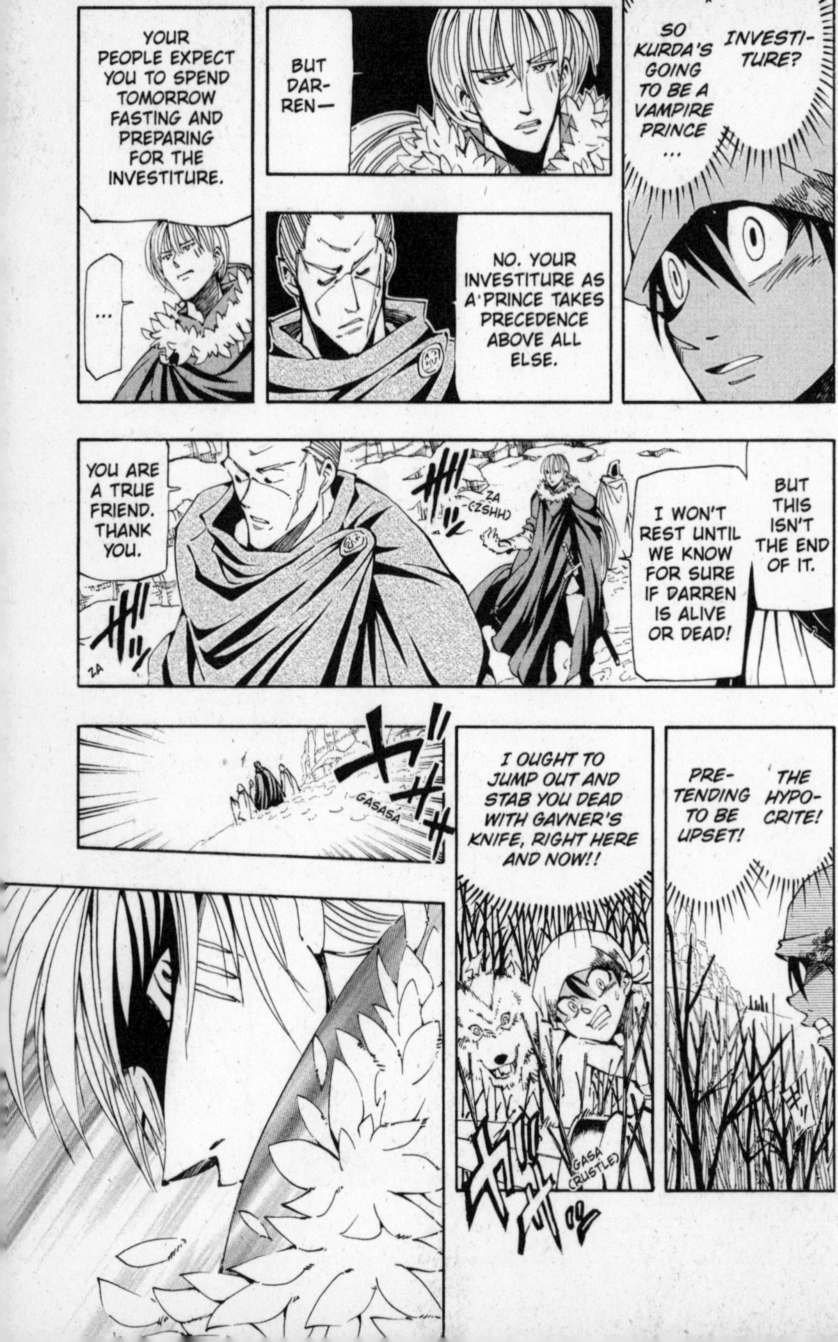
INVESTI-TURE?
SO KURDA'S GOING TO BE A VAMPIRE PRINCE ...
BUT DAR-REN—
YOUR PEOPLE EXPECT YOU TO SPEND TOMORROW FASTING AND PREPARING FOR THE INVESTITURE.
NO. YOUR INVESTITURE AS A PRINCE TAKES PRECEDENCE ABOVE ALL ELSE.
...
BUT THIS ISN'T THE END OF IT.
I WON'T REST UNTIL WE KNOW FOR SURE IF DARREN IS ALIVE OR DEAD!
ZA (ZSHH)
YOU ARE A TRUE FRIEND. THANK YOU.
ZA
THE HYPO-CRITE!
PRE-TENDING TO BE UPSET!
I OUGHT TO JUMP OUT AND STAB YOU DEAD WITH GAVNER'S KNIFE, RIGHT HERE AND NOW!!
GASA (RUSTLE)
GASASA

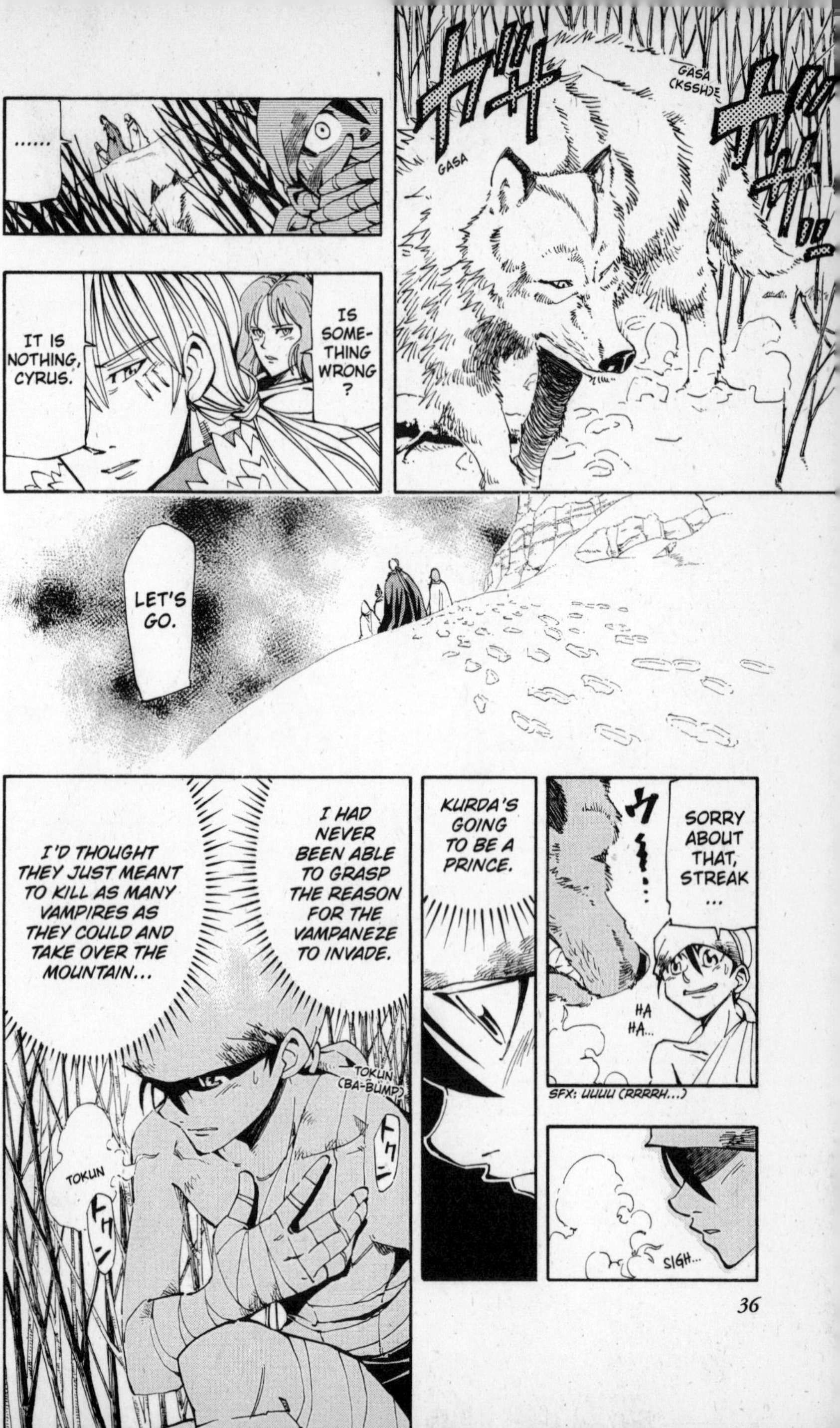
GASA (KSSH)
GASA
......
IS SOMETHING WRONG?
IT IS NOTHING, CYRUS.
LET'S GO.
SORRY ABOUT THAT, STREAK...
HA HA...
SFX: UUUU (RRRRH...)
SIGH...
KURDA'S GOING TO BE A PRINCE.
I HAD NEVER BEEN ABLE TO GRASP THE REASON FOR THE VAMPANEZE TO INVADE.
I'D THOUGHT THEY JUST MEANT TO KILL AS MANY VAMPIRES AS THEY COULD AND TAKE OVER THE MOUNTAIN...
TOKUN (BA-BUMP)
TOKUN

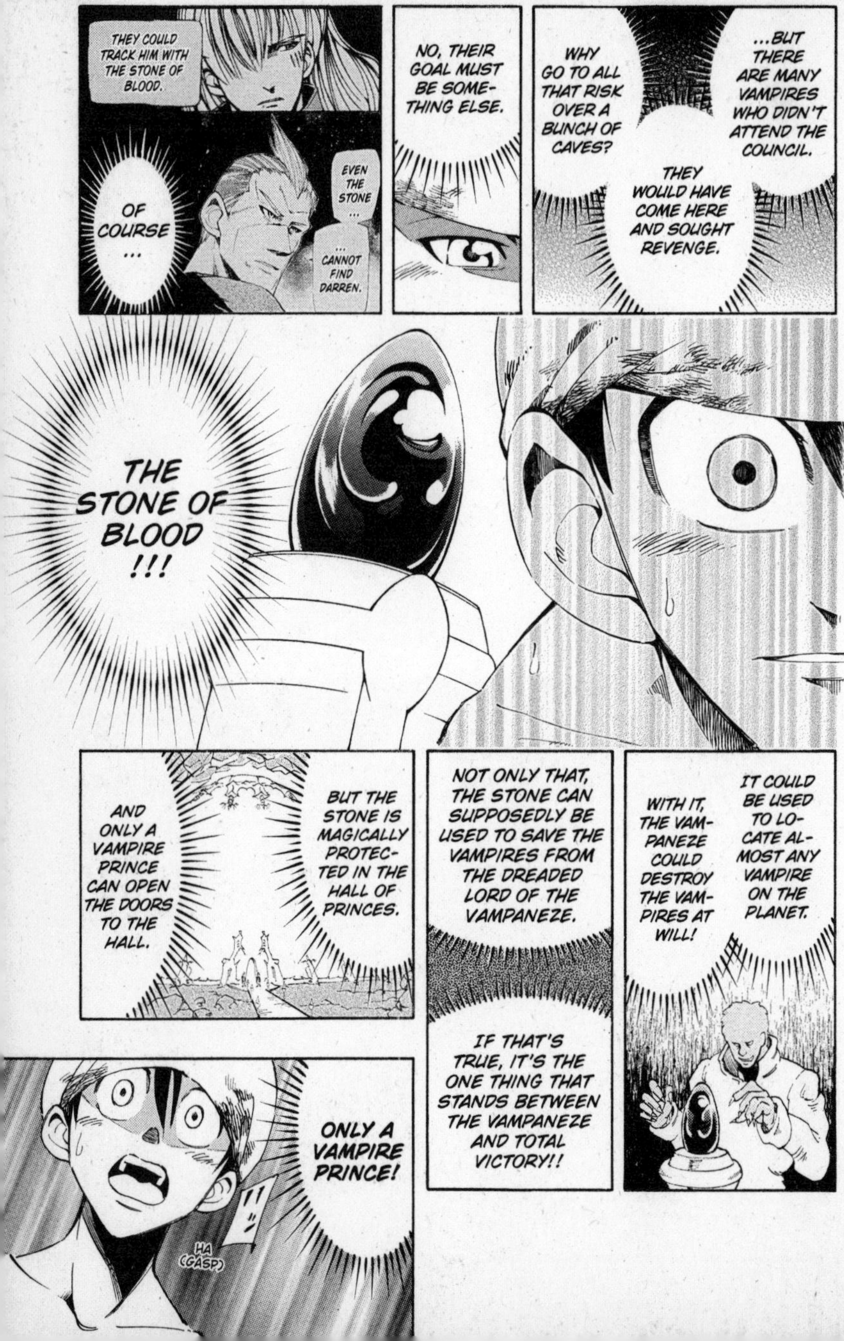
...BUT THERE ARE MANY VAMPIRES WHO DIDN'T ATTEND THE COUNCIL.
THEY WOULD HAVE COME HERE AND SOUGHT REVENGE.
WHY GO TO ALL THAT RISK OVER A BUNCH OF CAVES?
NO, THEIR GOAL MUST BE SOME-THING ELSE.
THEY COULD TRACK HIM WITH THE STONE OF BLOOD.
EVEN THE STONE...
...CANNOT FIND DARREN.
OF COURSE...
THE STONE OF BLOOD!!!
IT COULD BE USED TO LO-CATE AL-MOST ANY VAMPIRE ON THE PLANET.
WITH IT, THE VAM-PANEZE COULD DESTROY THE VAM-PIRES AT WILL!
NOT ONLY THAT, THE STONE CAN SUPPOSEDLY BE USED TO SAVE THE VAMPIRES FROM THE DREADED LORD OF THE VAMPANEZE.
IF THAT'S TRUE, IT'S THE ONE THING THAT STANDS BETWEEN THE VAMPANEZE AND TOTAL VICTORY!!
BUT THE STONE IS MAGICALLY PROTEC-TED IN THE HALL OF PRINCES.
AND ONLY A VAMPIRE PRINCE CAN OPEN THE DOORS TO THE HALL.
ONLY A VAMPIRE PRINCE!
HA (GASP)

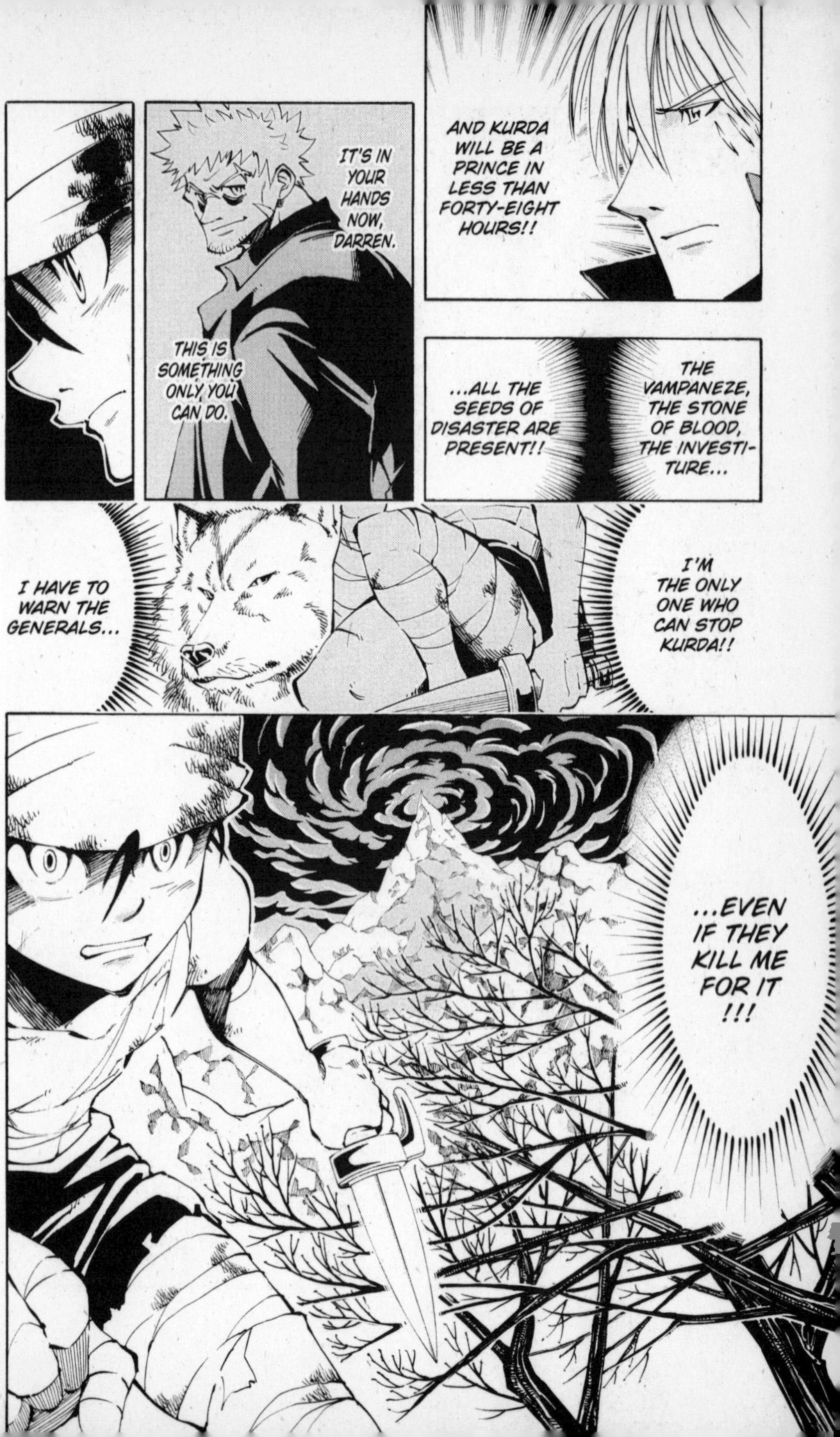
AND KURDA WILL BE A PRINCE IN LESS THAN FORTY-EIGHT HOURS!!
THE VAMPANEZE, THE STONE OF BLOOD, THE INVESTITURE...
...ALL THE SEEDS OF DISASTER ARE PRESENT!!
IT'S IN YOUR HANDS NOW, DARREN.
THIS IS SOMETHING ONLY YOU CAN DO.
I'M THE ONLY ONE WHO CAN STOP KURDA!!
I HAVE TO WARN THE GENERALS...
...EVEN IF THEY KILL ME FOR IT!!!

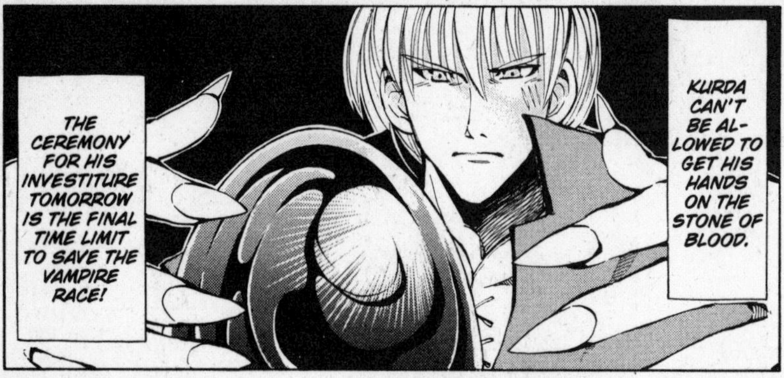
KURDA CAN'T BE AL-LOWED TO GET HIS HANDS ON THE STONE OF BLOOD.
THE CEREMONY FOR HIS INVESTITURE TOMORROW IS THE FINAL TIME LIMIT TO SAVE THE VAMPIRE RACE!

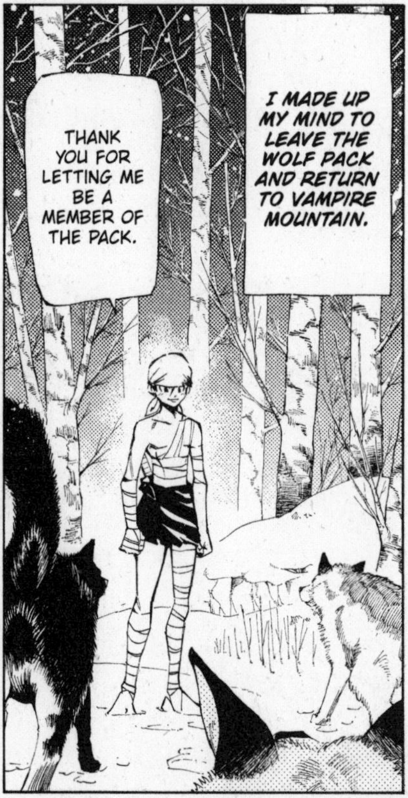
I MADE UP MY MIND TO LEAVE THE WOLF PACK AND RETURN TO VAMPIRE MOUNTAIN.
THANK YOU FOR LETTING ME BE A MEMBER OF THE PACK.

CHAPTER 47: MAGDA THE GUIDE

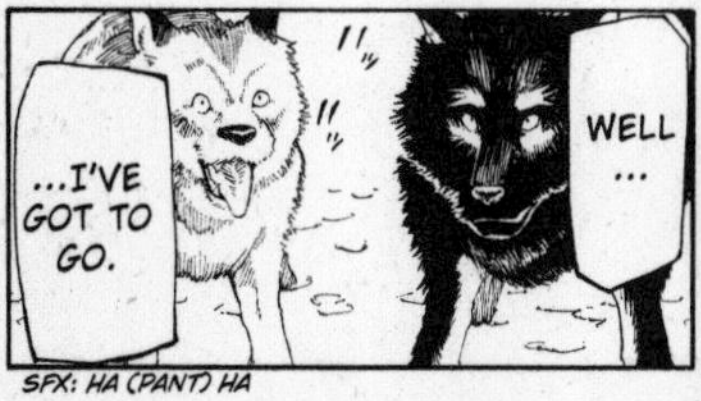
WELL ...
...I'VE GOT TO GO.

SFX: HA (PANT) HA

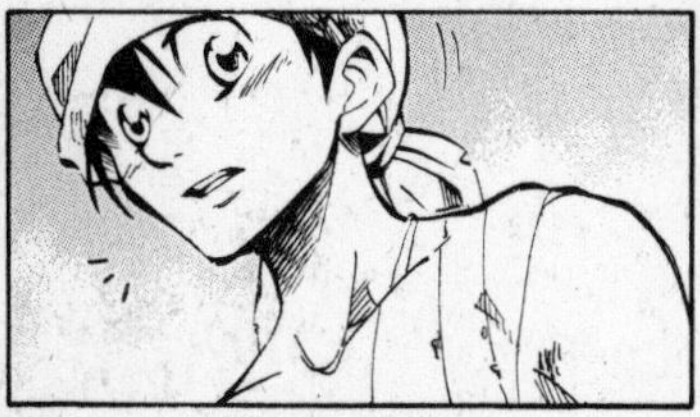

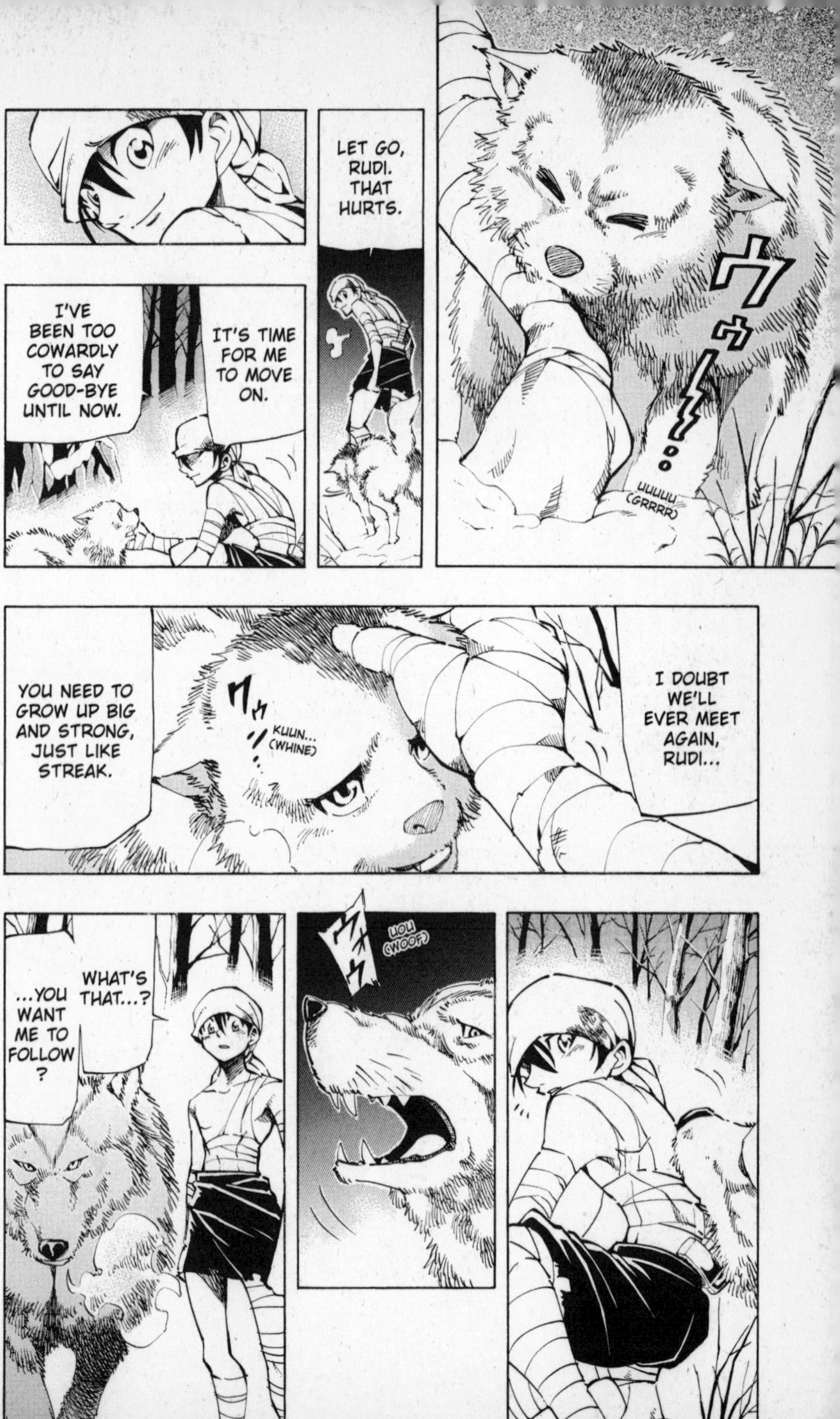

ウゥ…!!
UUUUU (GRRRR)
LET GO, RUDI. THAT HURTS.
I'VE BEEN TOO COWARDLY TO SAY GOOD-BYE UNTIL NOW.
IT'S TIME FOR ME TO MOVE ON.
I DOUBT WE'LL EVER MEET AGAIN, RUDI...
KUUN... (WHINE)
YOU NEED TO GROW UP BIG AND STRONG, JUST LIKE STREAK.
UOU (WOOF)
WHAT'S THAT...?
...YOU WANT ME TO FOLLOW?

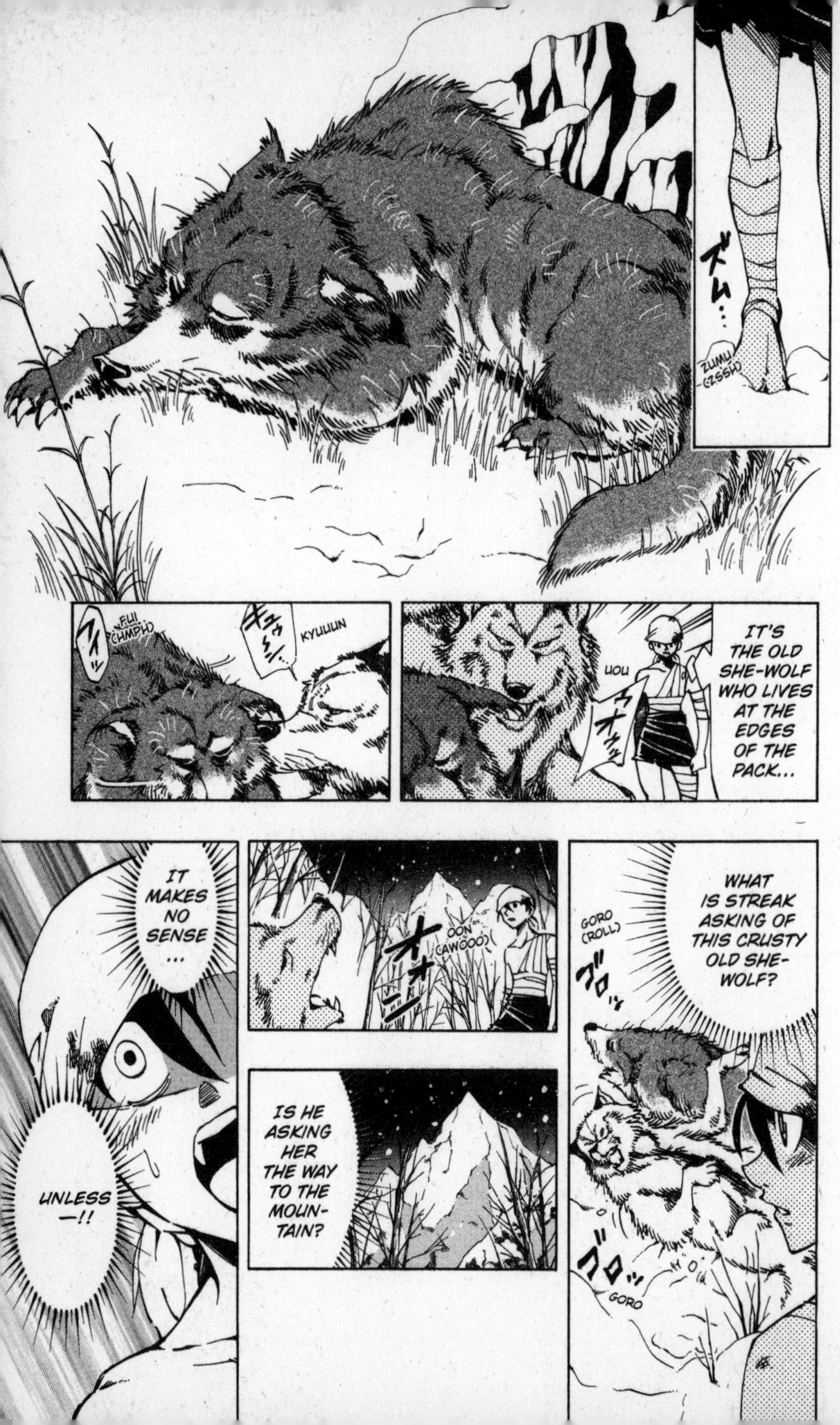

ZUMU (ZSSH)
IT'S THE OLD SHE-WOLF WHO LIVES AT THE EDGES OF THE PACK...
UOU
KYUUUN
FUI (HMPH)
WHAT IS STREAK ASKING OF THIS CRUSTY OLD SHE-WOLF?
GORO (ROLL)
GORO
OON (AWOOO)
IS HE ASKING HER THE WAY TO THE MOUNTAIN?
IT MAKES NO SENSE ...
UNLESS—!!

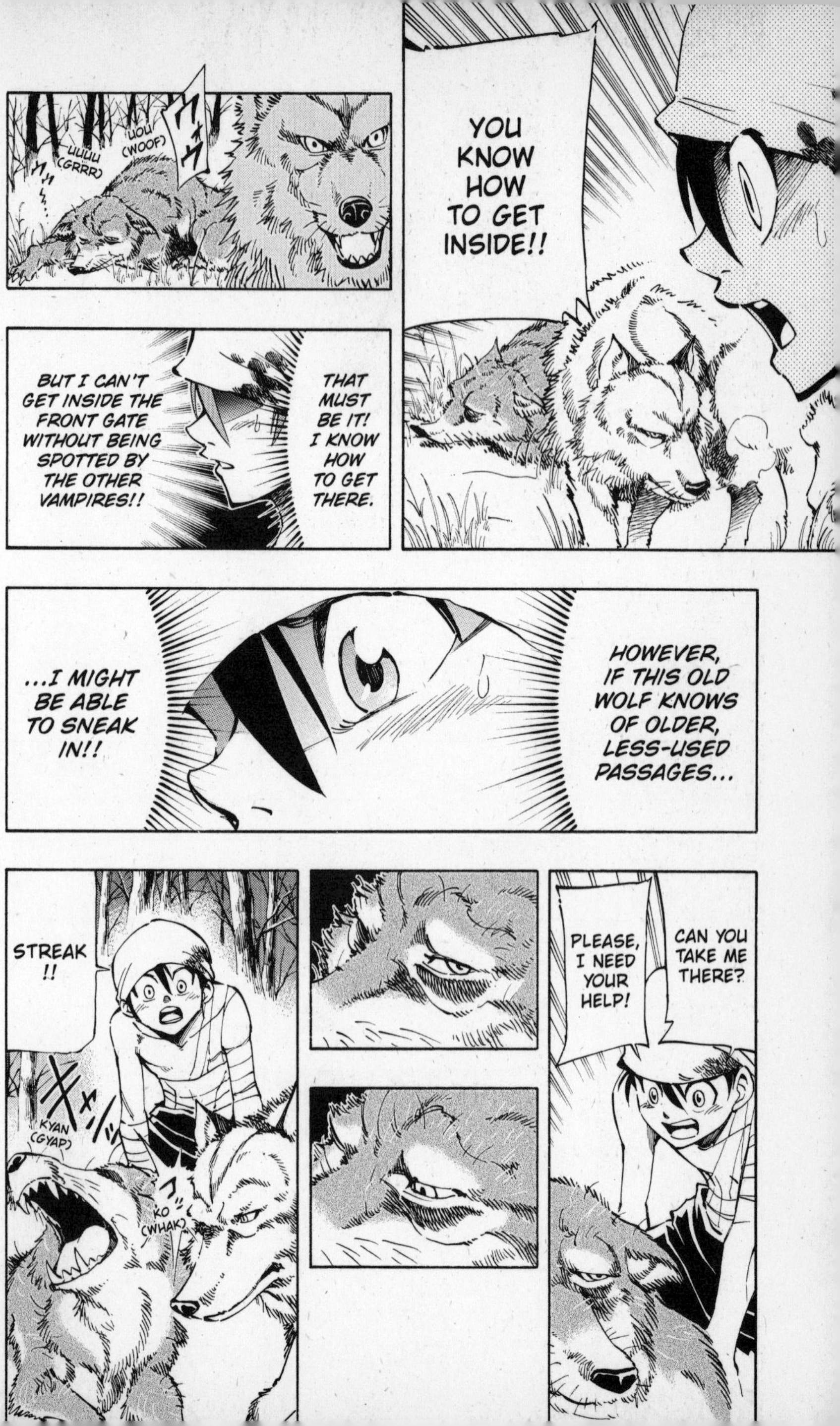
YOU KNOW HOW TO GET INSIDE!!
UOU (WOOF)
UUUU (GRRR)
THAT MUST BE IT! I KNOW HOW TO GET THERE.
BUT I CAN'T GET INSIDE THE FRONT GATE WITHOUT BEING SPOTTED BY THE OTHER VAMPIRES!!
HOWEVER, IF THIS OLD WOLF KNOWS OF OLDER, LESS-USED PASSAGES...
...I MIGHT BE ABLE TO SNEAK IN!!
CAN YOU TAKE ME THERE?
PLEASE, I NEED YOUR HELP!
STREAK !!
KYAN (GYAP)
KO (WHAK)

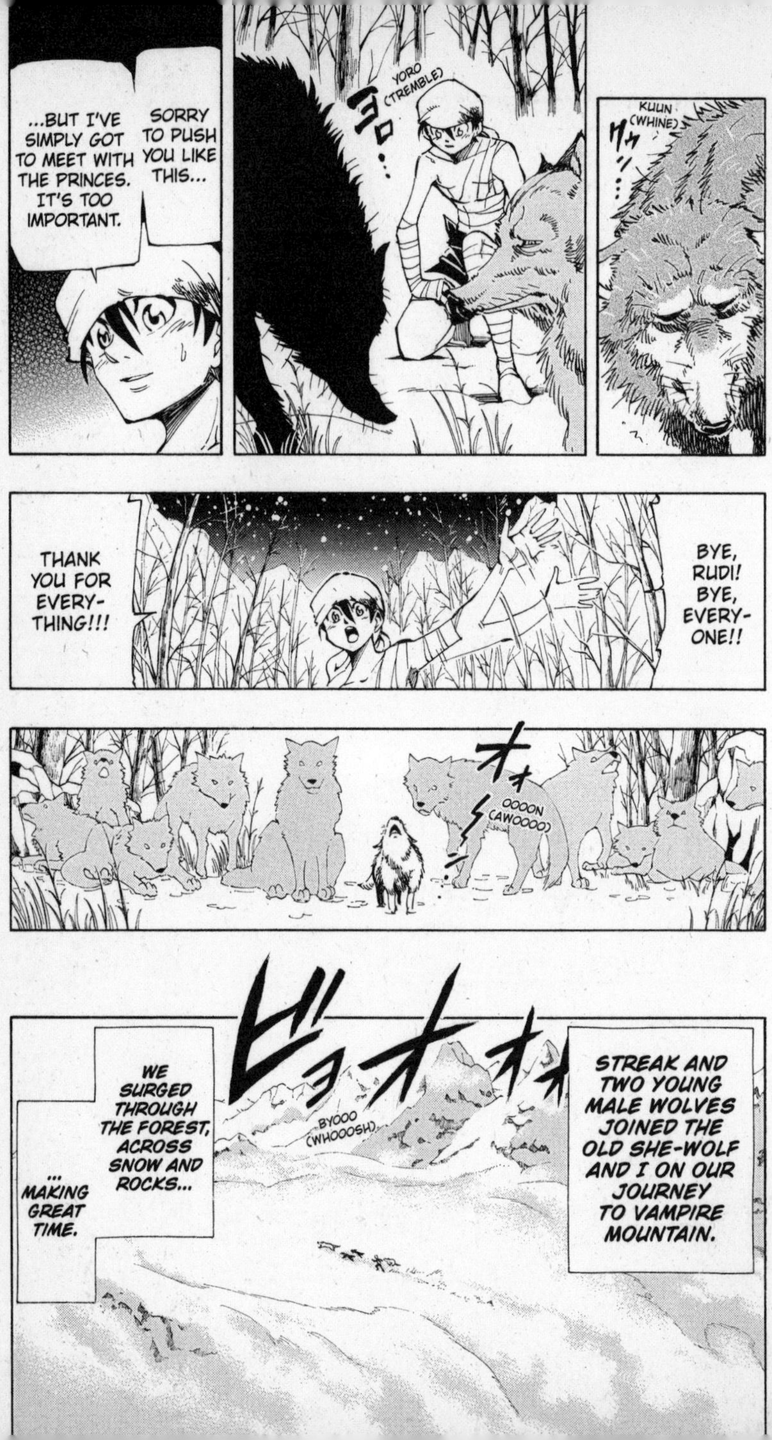
KUUN (WHINE)
YORO (TREMBLE)
SORRY TO PUSH YOU LIKE THIS...
...BUT I'VE SIMPLY GOT TO MEET WITH THE PRINCES. IT'S TOO IMPORTANT.
BYE, RUDI! BYE, EVERY-ONE!!
THANK YOU FOR EVERY-THING!!!
OOOON (AWOOOO)
BYOOO (WHOOOSH)
STREAK AND TWO YOUNG MALE WOLVES JOINED THE OLD SHE-WOLF AND I ON OUR JOURNEY TO VAMPIRE MOUNTAIN.
WE SURGED THROUGH THE FOREST, ACROSS SNOW AND ROCKS...
... MAKING GREAT TIME.

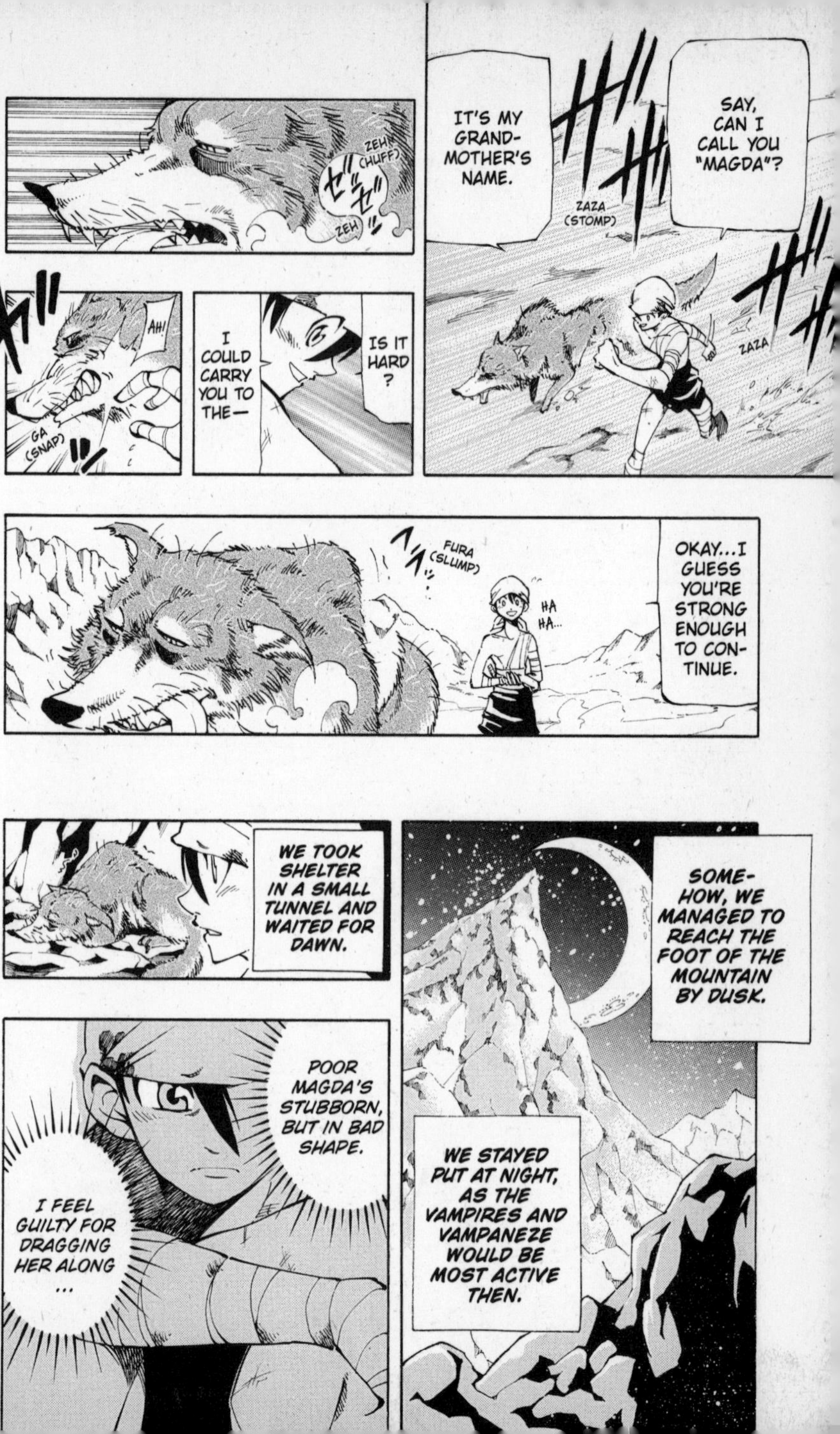
SAY, CAN I CALL YOU "MAGDA"?
ZAZA (STOMP)
IT'S MY GRAND-MOTHER'S NAME.
ZAZA
ZEH (HUFF)
ZEH
IS IT HARD?
I COULD CARRY YOU TO THE—
AH!
GA (SNAP)
OKAY...I GUESS YOU'RE STRONG ENOUGH TO CON-TINUE.
HA HA...
FURA (SLUMP)
SOME-HOW, WE MANAGED TO REACH THE FOOT OF THE MOUNTAIN BY DUSK.
WE STAYED PUT AT NIGHT, AS THE VAMPIRES AND VAMPANEZE WOULD BE MOST ACTIVE THEN.
WE TOOK SHELTER IN A SMALL TUNNEL AND WAITED FOR DAWN.
POOR MAGDA'S STUBBORN, BUT IN BAD SHAPE.
I FEEL GUILTY FOR DRAGGING HER ALONG...

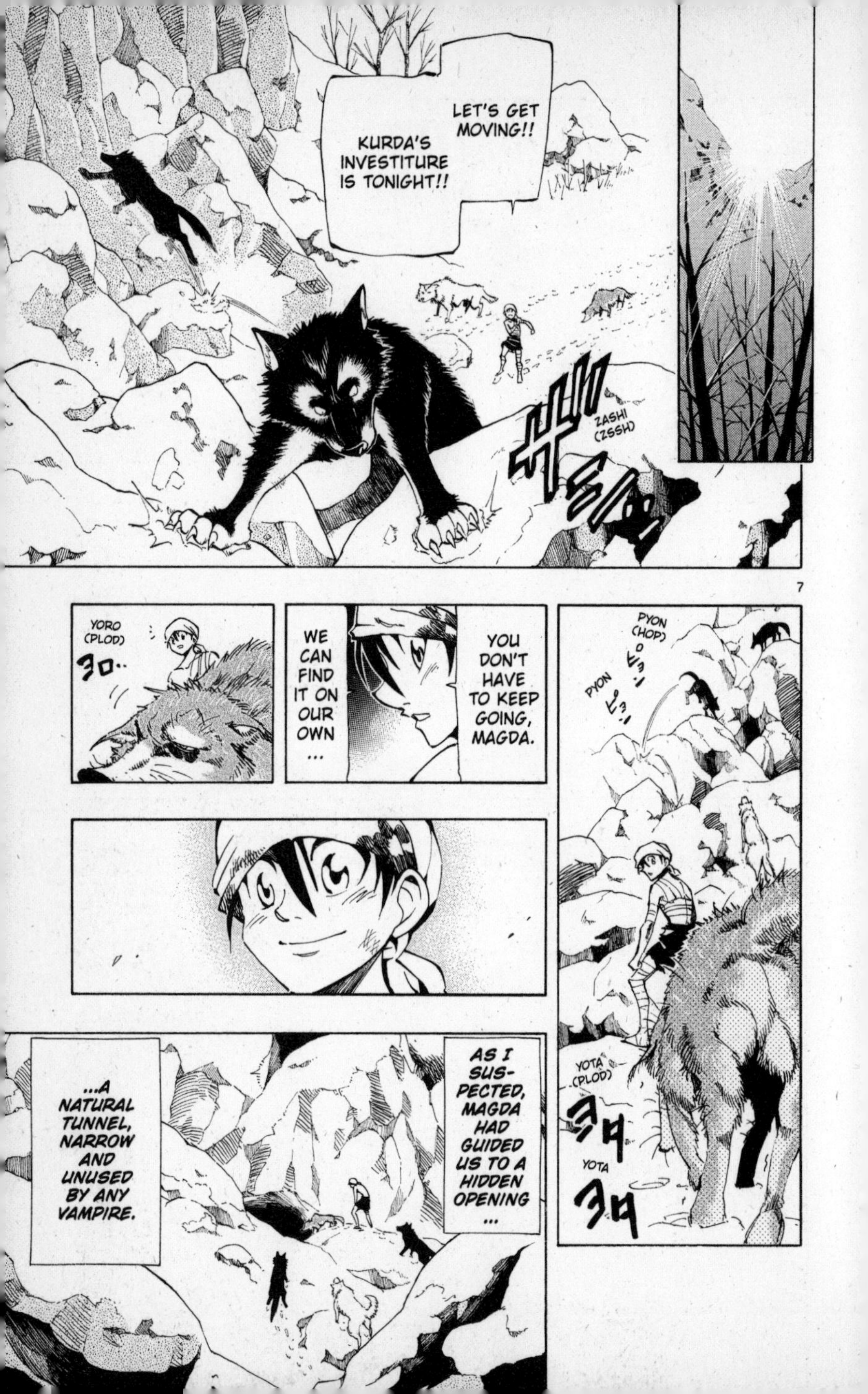
LET'S GET MOVING!!
KURDA'S INVESTITURE IS TONIGHT!!
ZASHI (ZSSH)
PYON (HOP)
PYON
YOTA (PLOD)
ヨタ
YOTA
ヨタ
YOU DON'T HAVE TO KEEP GOING, MAGDA.
WE CAN FIND IT ON OUR OWN...
YORO (PLOD)
ヨロ..
AS I SUSPECTED, MAGDA HAD GUIDED US TO A HIDDEN OPENING...
...A NATURAL TUNNEL, NARROW AND UNUSED BY ANY VAMPIRE.

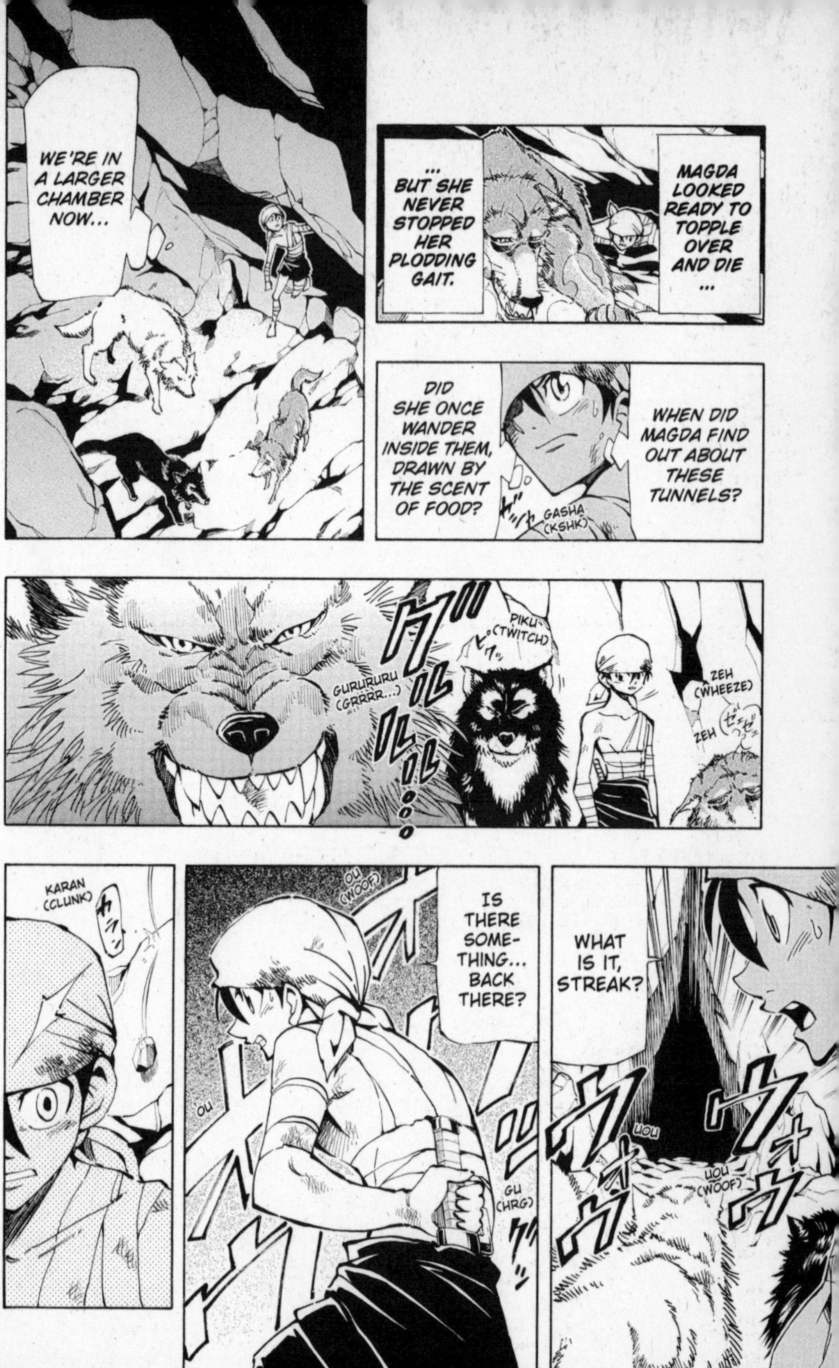

MAGDA LOOKED READY TO TOPPLE OVER AND DIE ...
... BUT SHE NEVER STOPPED HER PLODDING GAIT.
WHEN DID MAGDA FIND OUT ABOUT THESE TUNNELS?
DID SHE ONCE WANDER INSIDE THEM, DRAWN BY THE SCENT OF FOOD?
GASHA (KSHK)
WE'RE IN A LARGER CHAMBER NOW...
ZEH (WHEEZE)
ZEH
PIKU (TWITCH)
GURURURU (GRRRR...)
WHAT IS IT, STREAK?
UOU
UOU (WOOF)
IS THERE SOME-THING... BACK THERE?
OU (WOOF)
OU
GU (HRG)
KARAN (CLUNK)

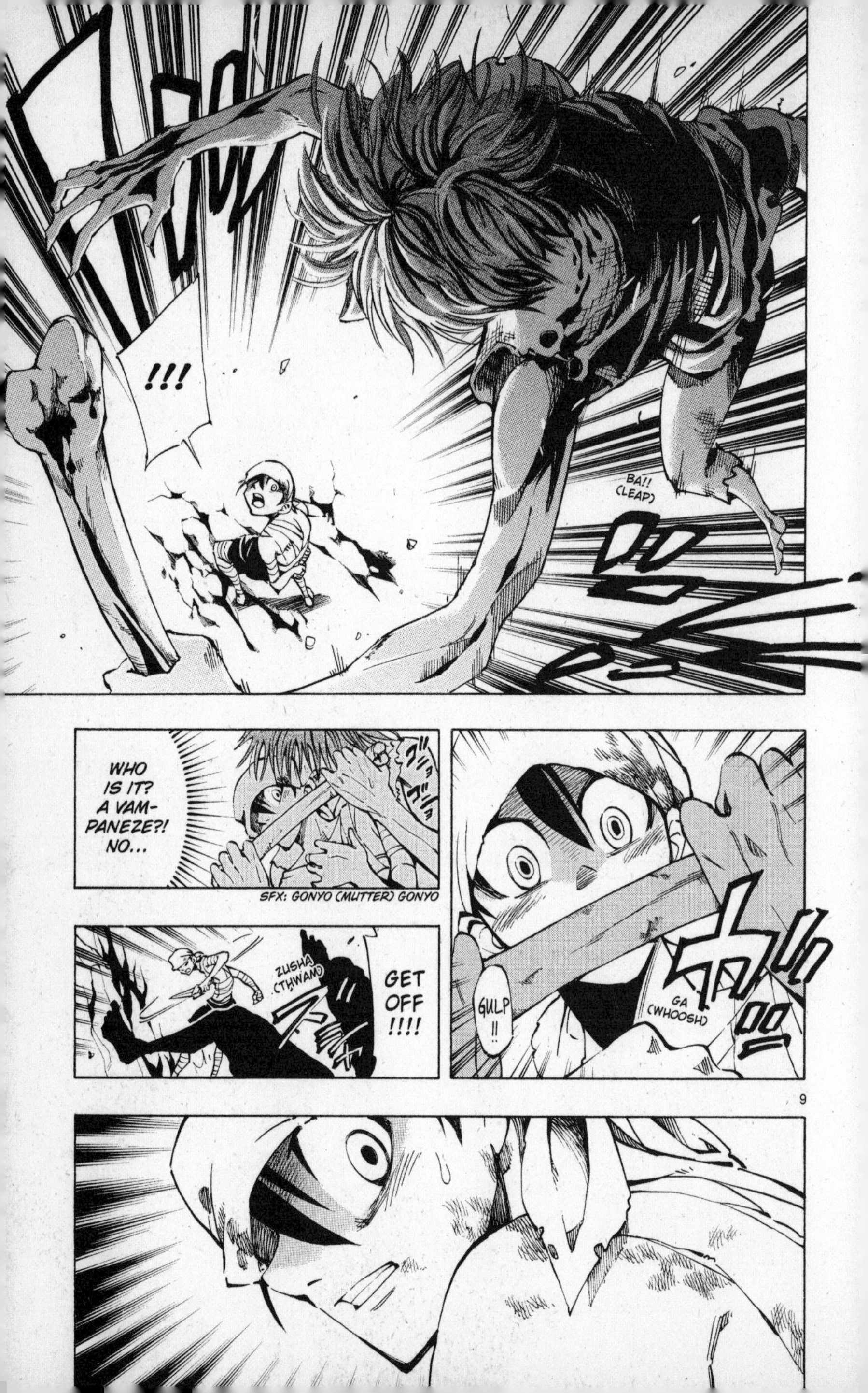
!!!
BA!! (LEAP)
GULP !!
GA (WHOOSH)
WHO IS IT? A VAMPANEZE?! NO...
SFX: GONYO (MUTTER) GONYO
GET OFF !!!!
ZUSHA (THWAM)

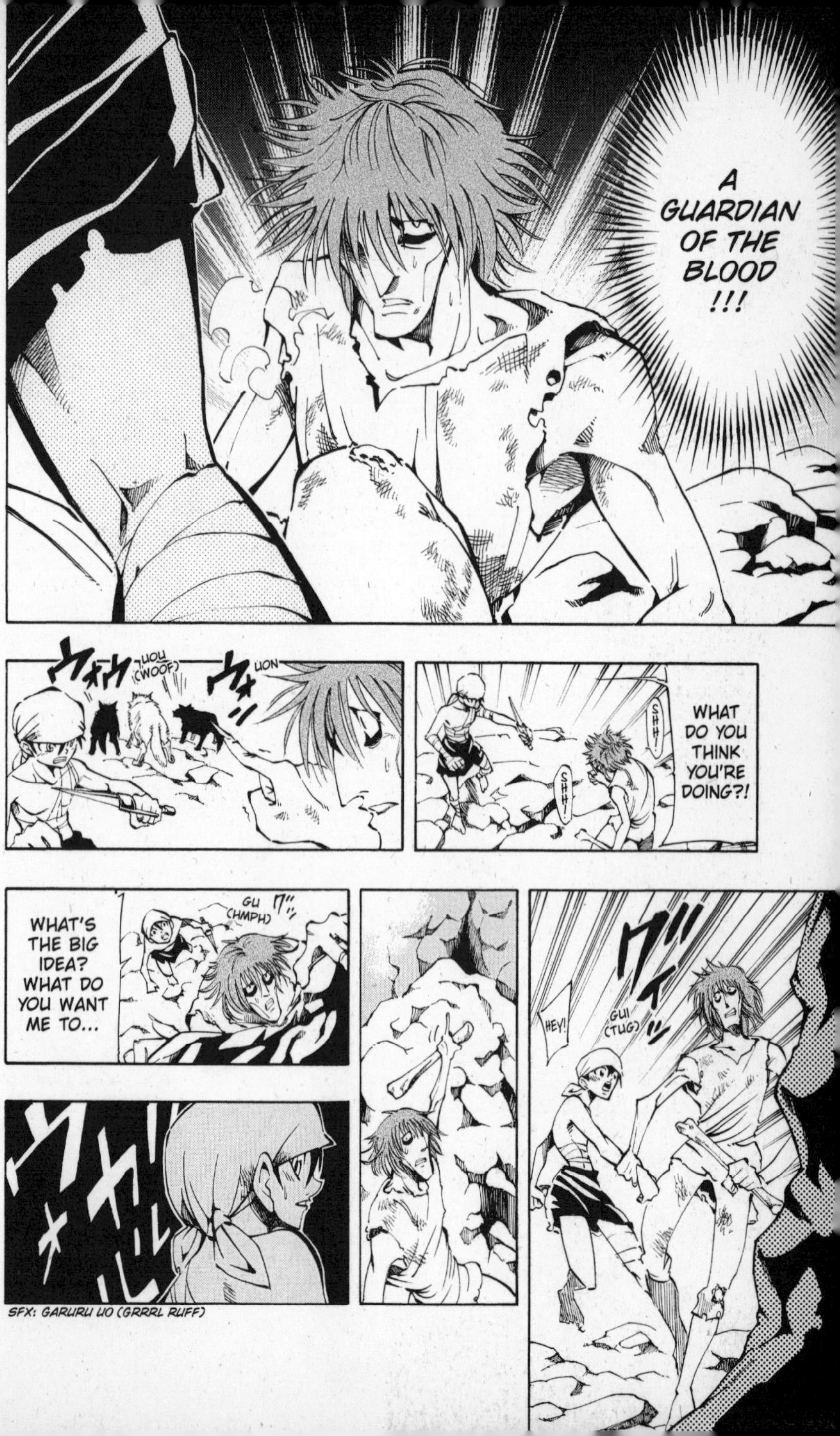
A GUARDIAN OF THE BLOOD!!!
WHAT DO YOU THINK YOU'RE DOING?!
SHH!
SHH!
UOU (WOOF)
UON
HEY!
GUI (TUG)
WHAT'S THE BIG IDEA? WHAT DO YOU WANT ME TO...
GU (HMPH)
SFX: GARURU UO (GRRRL RUFF)

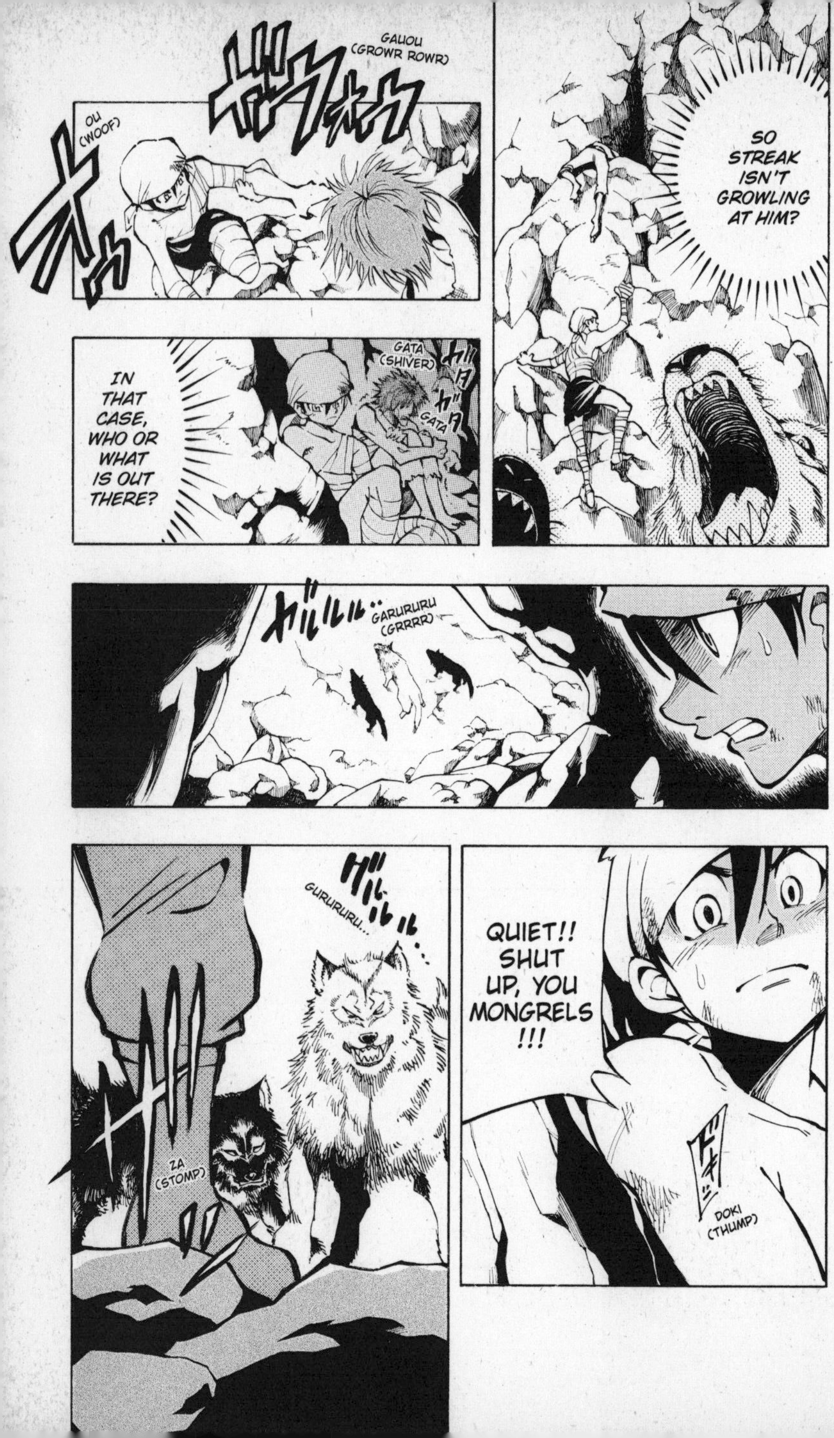
SO STREAK ISN'T GROWLING AT HIM?
GAUOU (GROWR ROWR)
OU (WOOF)
GATA (SHIVER) GATA
IN THAT CASE, WHO OR WHAT IS OUT THERE?
GARURURU (GRRRR)
QUIET!! SHUT UP, YOU MONGRELS!!!
DOKI (THUMP)
GURURURU...
ZA (STOMP)

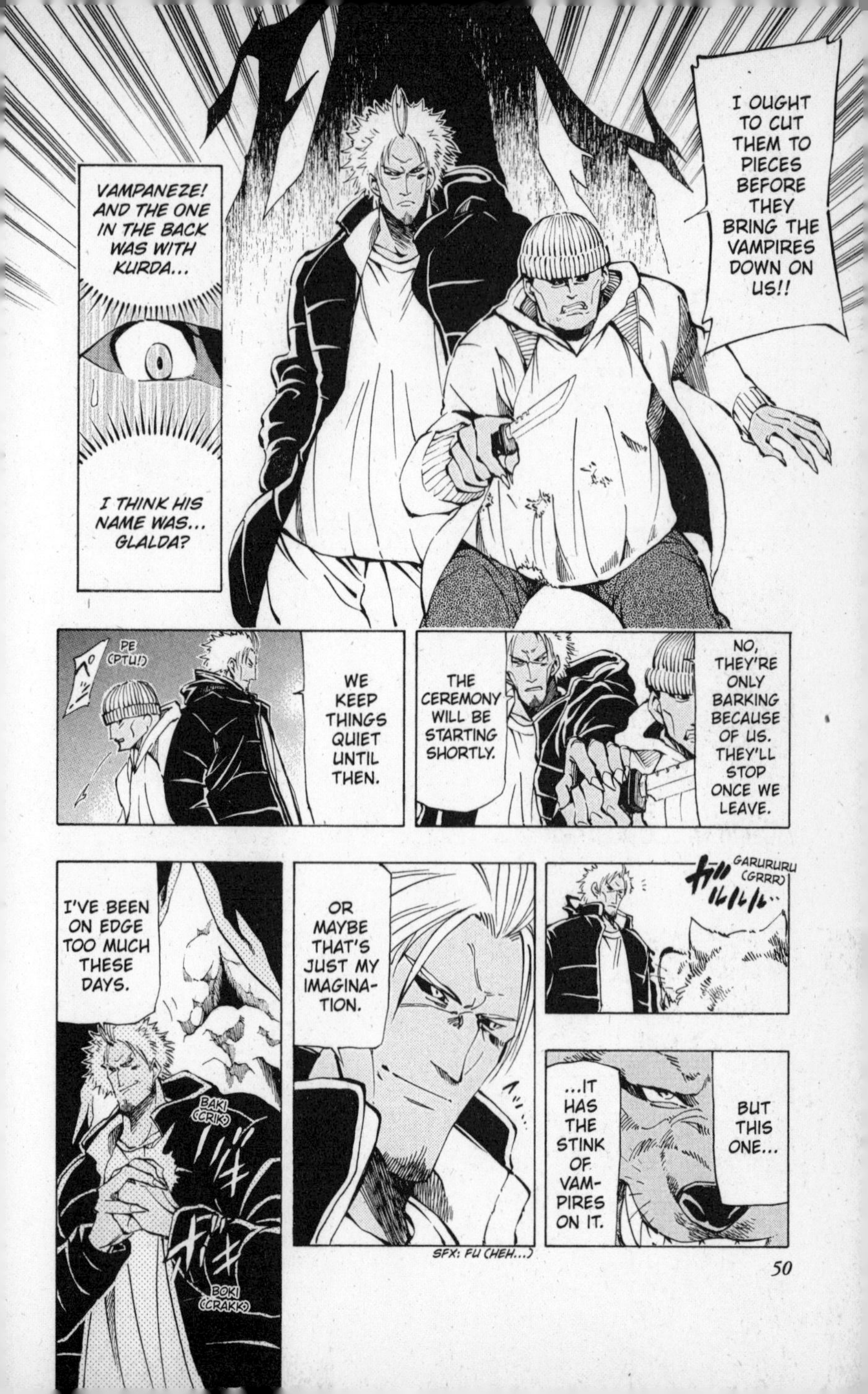
I OUGHT TO CUT THEM TO PIECES BEFORE THEY BRING THE VAMPIRES DOWN ON US!!
VAMPANEZE! AND THE ONE IN THE BACK WAS WITH KURDA...
I THINK HIS NAME WAS... GLALDA?
NO, THEY'RE ONLY BARKING BECAUSE OF US. THEY'LL STOP ONCE WE LEAVE.
THE CEREMONY WILL BE STARTING SHORTLY.
WE KEEP THINGS QUIET UNTIL THEN.
PE (PTU!)
GARURURU (GRRR)
BUT THIS ONE...
...IT HAS THE STINK OF VAMPIRES ON IT.
OR MAYBE THAT'S JUST MY IMAGINATION.
SFX: FU (HEH...)
I'VE BEEN ON EDGE TOO MUCH THESE DAYS.
BAKI (CRIK)
BOKI (CRAKK)

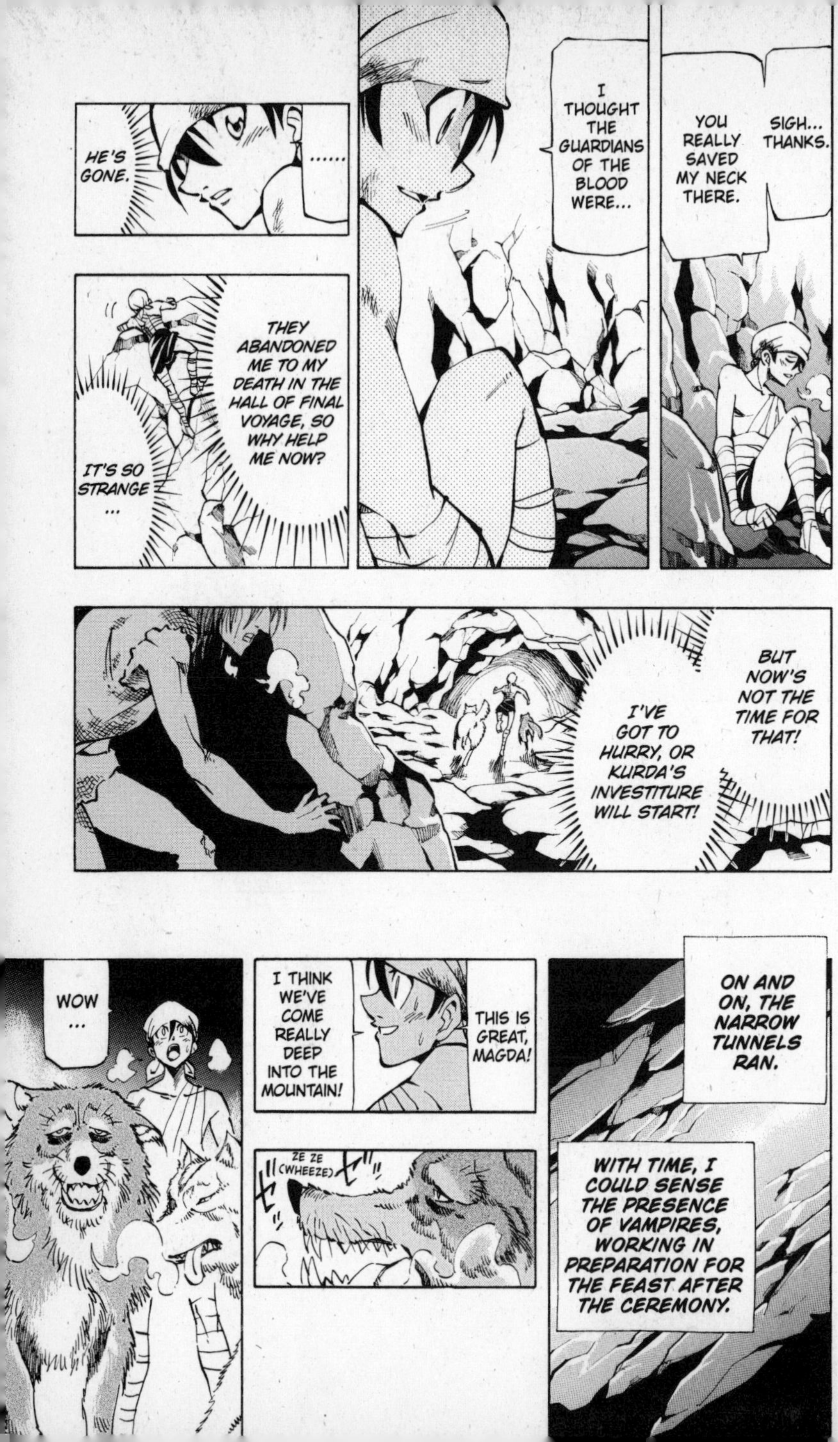
SIGH... THANKS.
YOU REALLY SAVED MY NECK THERE.
I THOUGHT THE GUARDIANS OF THE BLOOD WERE...
......
HE'S GONE.
THEY ABANDONED ME TO MY DEATH IN THE HALL OF FINAL VOYAGE, SO WHY HELP ME NOW?
IT'S SO STRANGE ...
BUT NOW'S NOT THE TIME FOR THAT!
I'VE GOT TO HURRY, OR KURDA'S INVESTITURE WILL START!
ON AND ON, THE NARROW TUNNELS RAN.
WITH TIME, I COULD SENSE THE PRESENCE OF VAMPIRES, WORKING IN PREPARATION FOR THE FEAST AFTER THE CEREMONY.
THIS IS GREAT, MAGDA!
I THINK WE'VE COME REALLY DEEP INTO THE MOUNTAIN!
ZE ZE (WHEEZE)
WOW ...

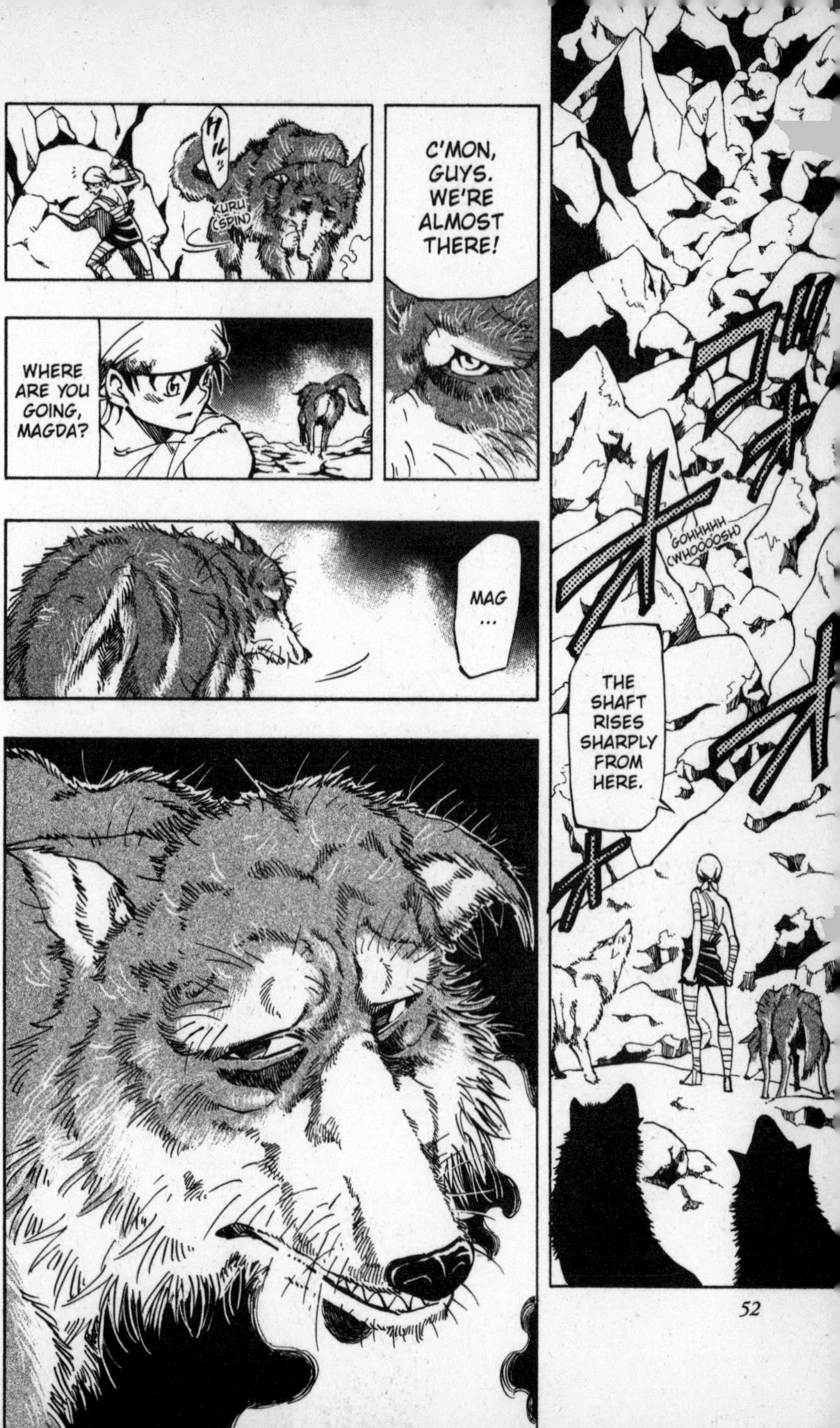
GOHHHHH (WHOOOOSH)
THE SHAFT RISES SHARPLY FROM HERE.
C'MON, GUYS. WE'RE ALMOST THERE!
KURU (SPIN)
WHERE ARE YOU GOING, MAGDA?
MAG ...

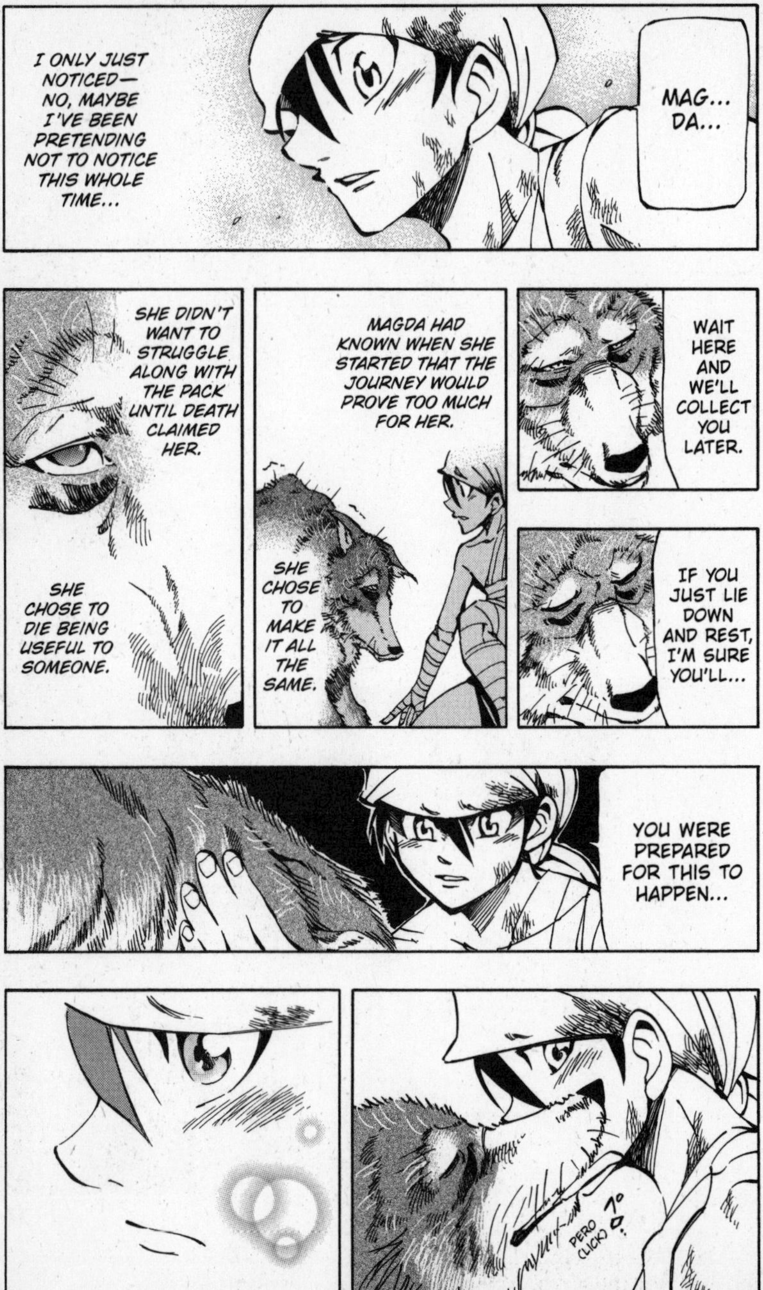
MAG... DA...
I ONLY JUST NOTICED— NO, MAYBE I'VE BEEN PRETENDING NOT TO NOTICE THIS WHOLE TIME...
WAIT HERE AND WE'LL COLLECT YOU LATER.
IF YOU JUST LIE DOWN AND REST, I'M SURE YOU'LL...
MAGDA HAD KNOWN WHEN SHE STARTED THAT THE JOURNEY WOULD PROVE TOO MUCH FOR HER.
SHE CHOSE TO MAKE IT ALL THE SAME.
SHE DIDN'T WANT TO STRUGGLE ALONG WITH THE PACK UNTIL DEATH CLAIMED HER.
SHE CHOSE TO DIE BEING USEFUL TO SOMEONE.
YOU WERE PREPARED FOR THIS TO HAPPEN...
PERO (CLICK)

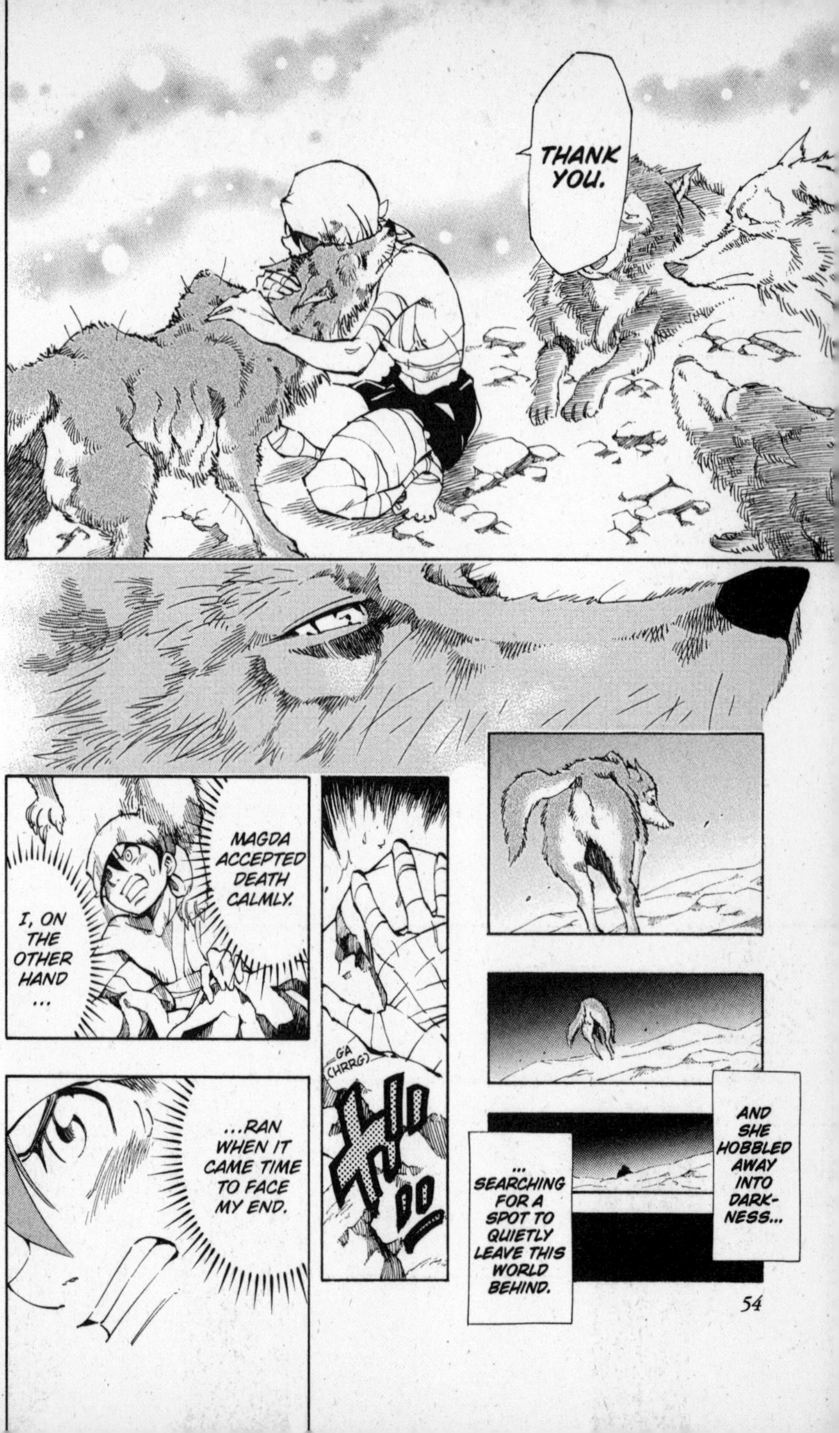
THANK YOU.
AND SHE HOBBLED AWAY INTO DARKNESS...
...SEARCHING FOR A SPOT TO QUIETLY LEAVE THIS WORLD BEHIND.
GA (HRRG)
MAGDA ACCEPTED DEATH CALMLY.
I, ON THE OTHER HAND...
...RAN WHEN IT CAME TIME TO FACE MY END.

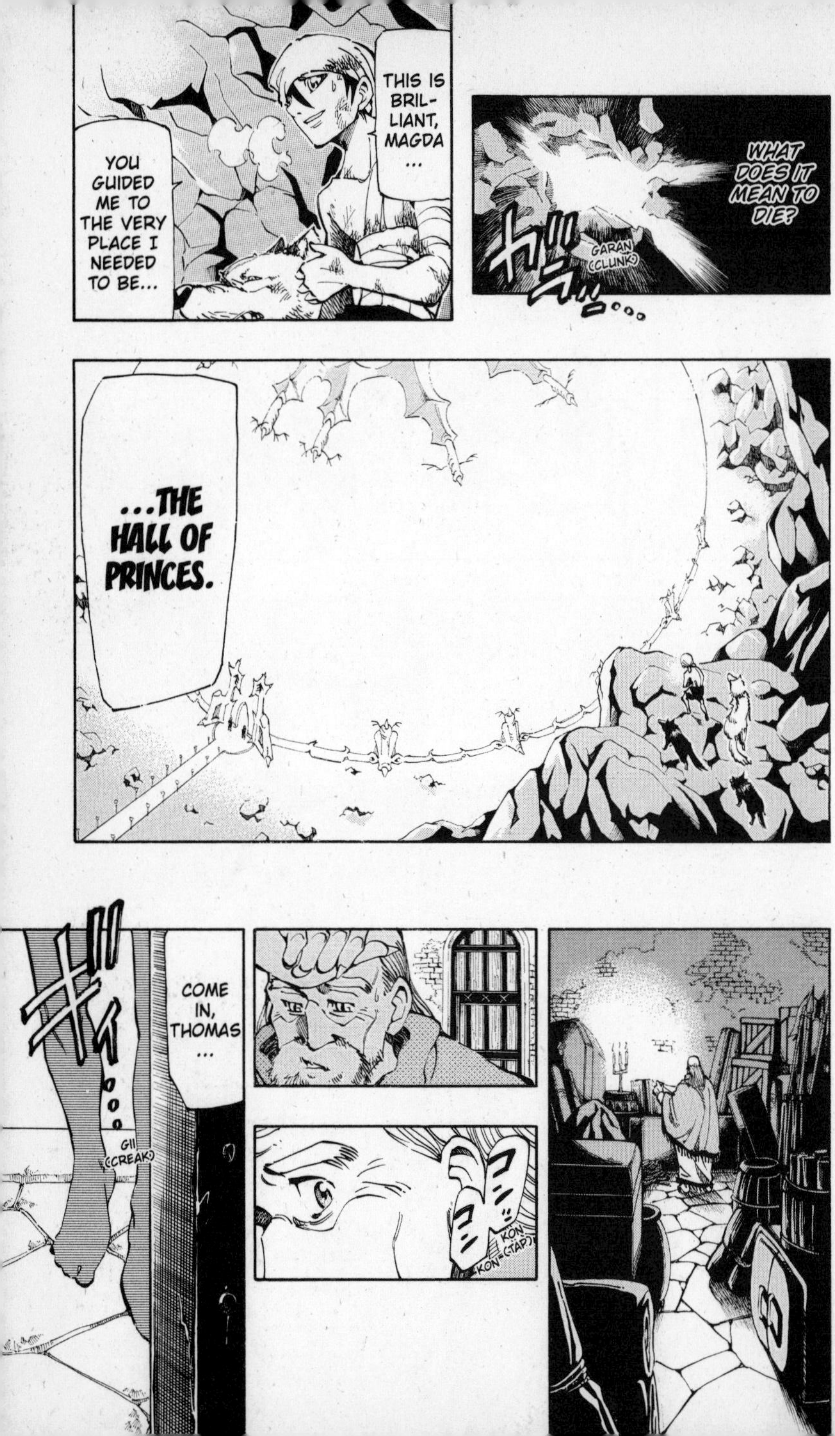
WHAT DOES IT MEAN TO DIE?
GARAN (CLUNK)
THIS IS BRIL-LIANT, MAGDA ...
YOU GUIDED ME TO THE VERY PLACE I NEEDED TO BE...
...THE HALL OF PRINCES.
KON KON (TAP)
COME IN, THOMAS ...
GII (CREAK)

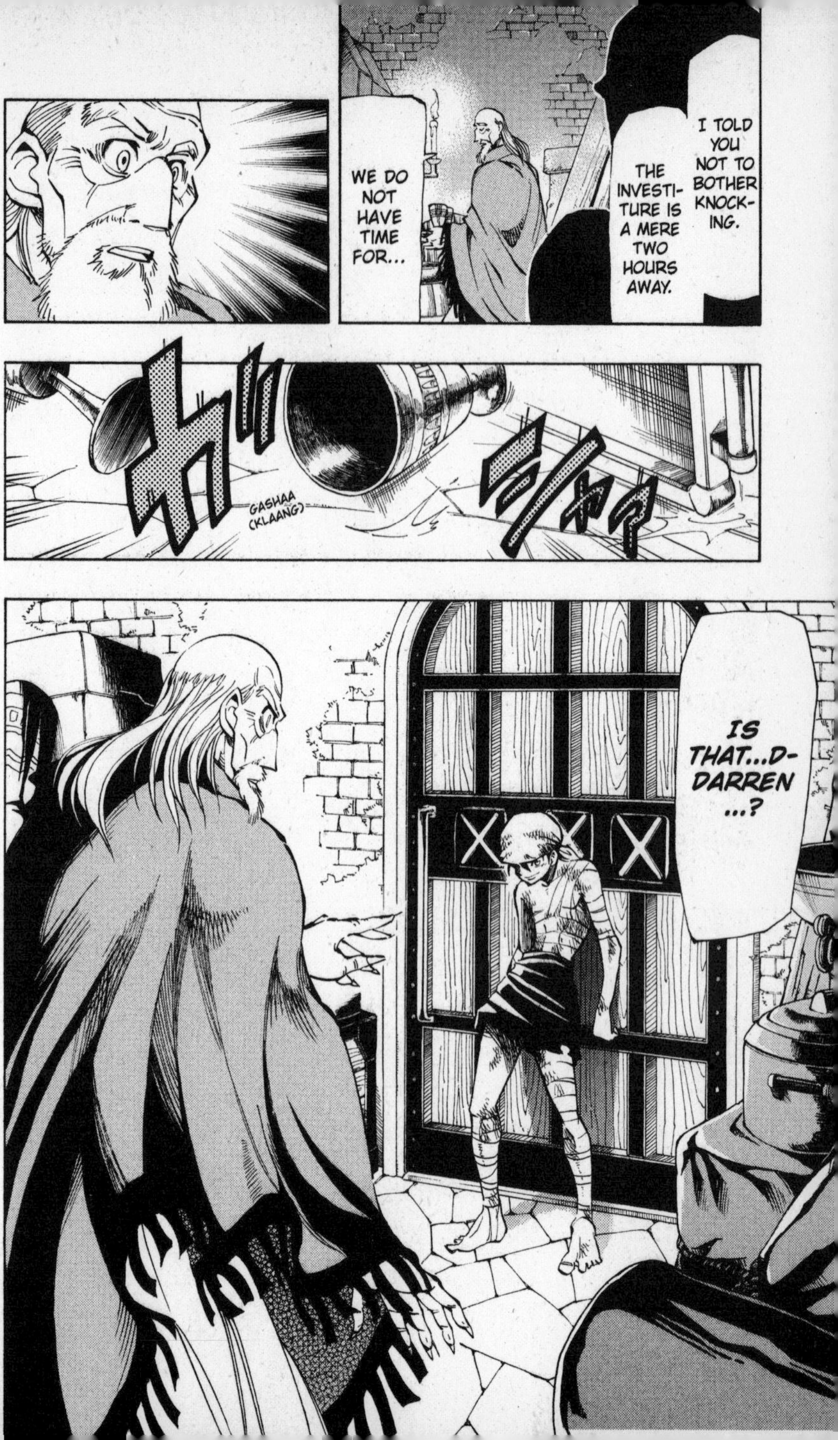
I TOLD YOU NOT TO BOTHER KNOCK-ING.
THE INVESTI-TURE IS A MERE TWO HOURS AWAY.
WE DO NOT HAVE TIME FOR...
GASHAA (KLAANG)
IS THAT...D-DARREN ...?

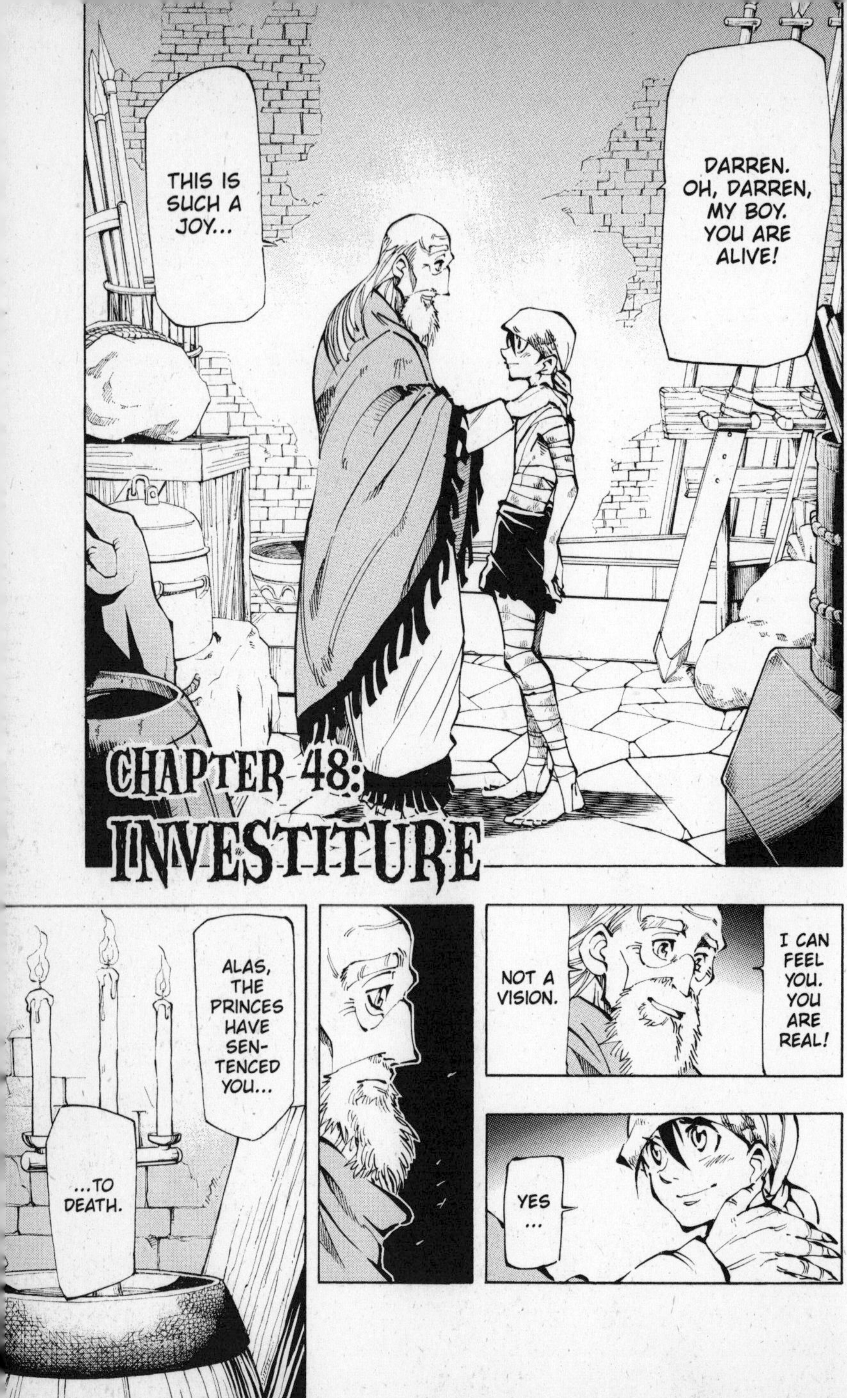
DARREN. OH, DARREN, MY BOY. YOU ARE ALIVE!
THIS IS SUCH A JOY...
CHAPTER 48: INVESTITURE
I CAN FEEL YOU. YOU ARE REAL!
NOT A VISION.
YES ...
ALAS, THE PRINCES HAVE SEN-TENCED YOU...
...TO DEATH.

YOUR TRAIL LED TO THE STREAM AND ENDED ABRUPTLY.

YOU FLED.

I FIGURED AS MUCH.

HOW DID YOU GET OUT?

I'M SORRY...

IT WAS A TERRIBLE MISTAKE.

BUT THAT'S GAVNER'S... WHY?

SU... (SHH)

AND I FENDED FOR MY LIFE WITH THIS.

I SWAM DOWN THE STREAM, OUT OF THE MOUNTAIN.

HE WAS MURDERED ...

GAVNER'S DEAD.

YOU'D BETTER STAY SITTING, SEBA.

MUR... DER...?

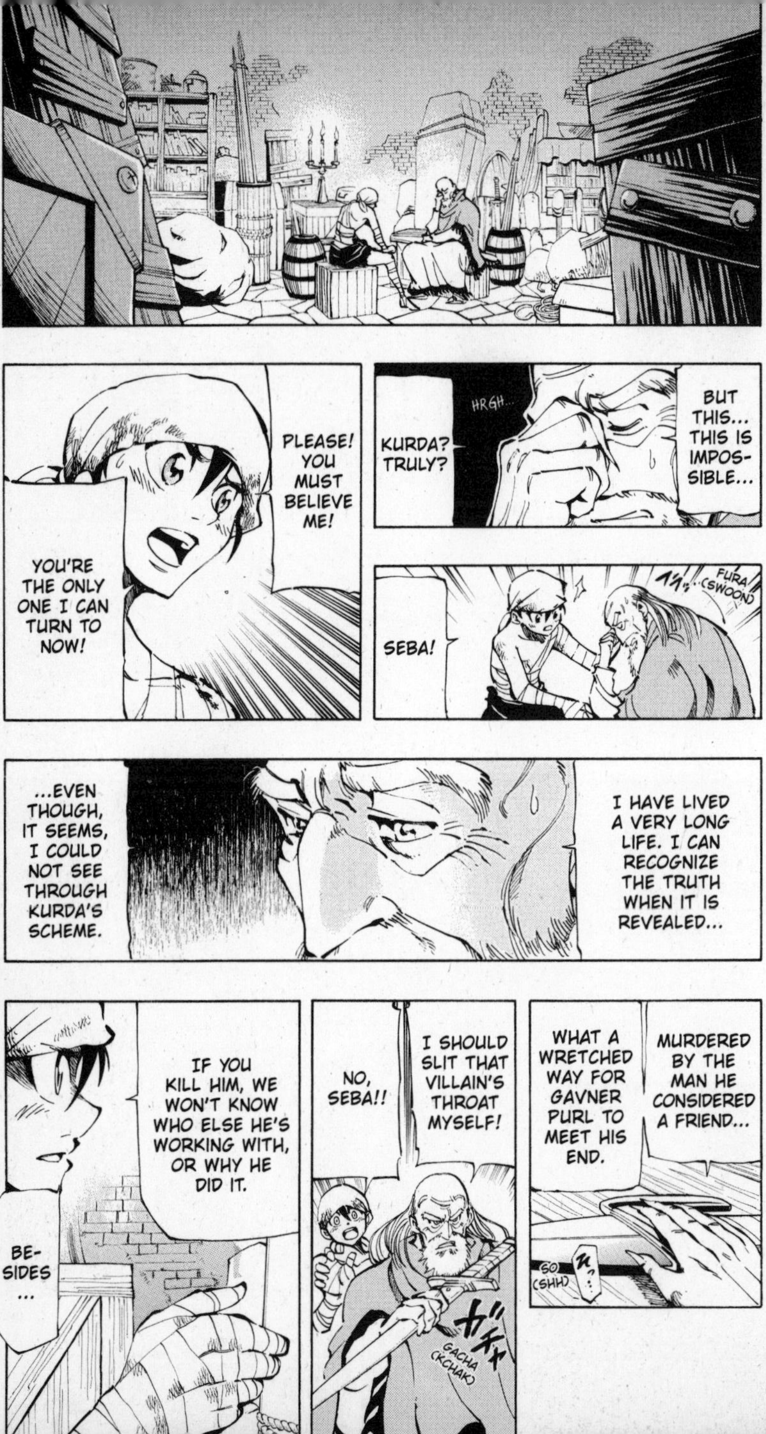

BUT THIS... THIS IS IMPOSSIBLE...
HRGH...
KURDA? TRULY?
FURA (SWOON)
SEBA!
PLEASE! YOU MUST BELIEVE ME!
YOU'RE THE ONLY ONE I CAN TURN TO NOW!
I HAVE LIVED A VERY LONG LIFE. I CAN RECOGNIZE THE TRUTH WHEN IT IS REVEALED...
...EVEN THOUGH, IT SEEMS, I COULD NOT SEE THROUGH KURDA'S SCHEME.
MURDERED BY THE MAN HE CONSIDERED A FRIEND...
WHAT A WRETCHED WAY FOR GAVNER PURL TO MEET HIS END.
SO (SHH)
I SHOULD SLIT THAT VILLAIN'S THROAT MYSELF!
NO, SEBA!!
GACHA (KCHAK)
IF YOU KILL HIM, WE WON'T KNOW WHO ELSE HE'S WORKING WITH, OR WHY HE DID IT.
BE- SIDES ...

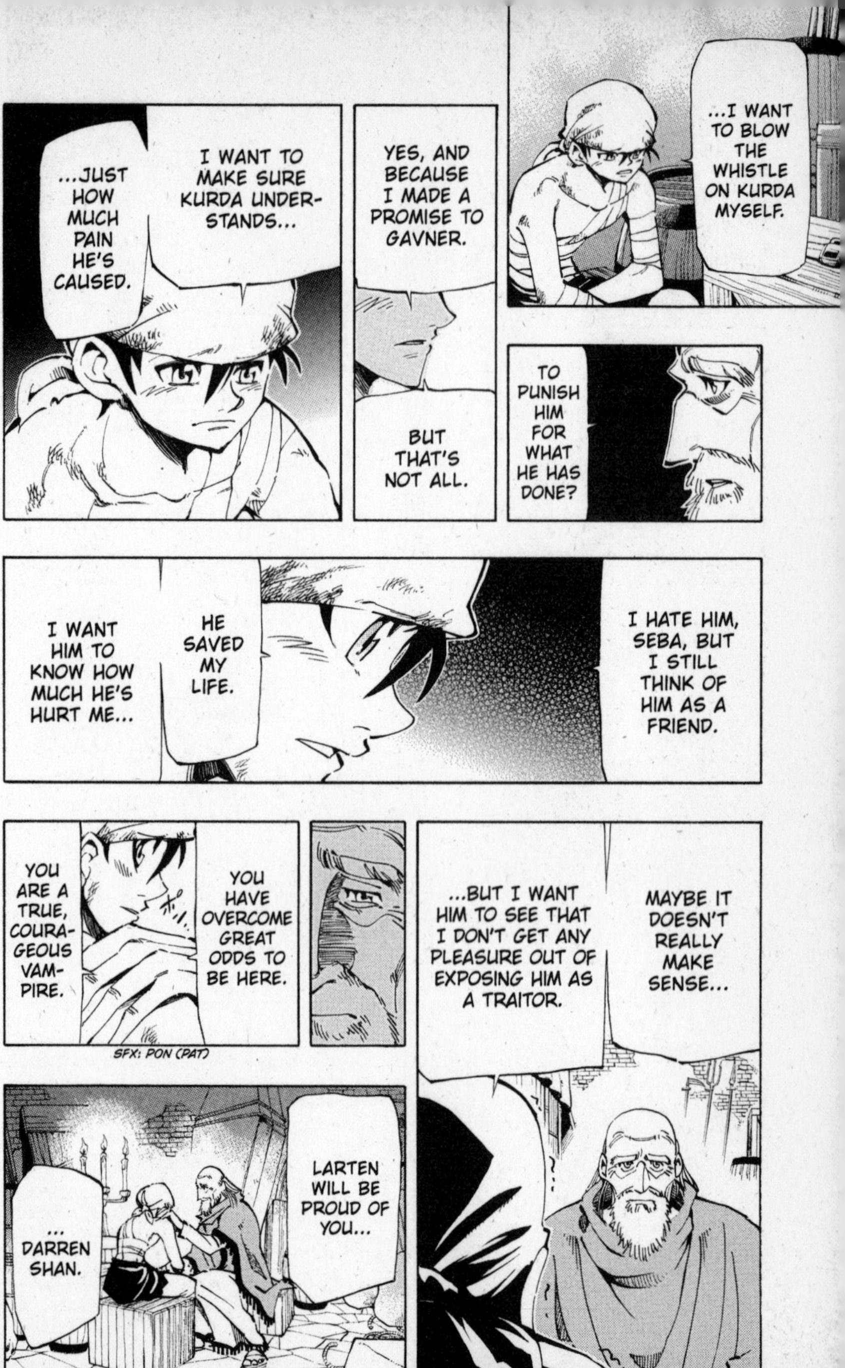
...I WANT TO BLOW THE WHISTLE ON KURDA MYSELF.
TO PUNISH HIM FOR WHAT HE HAS DONE?
YES, AND BECAUSE I MADE A PROMISE TO GAVNER.
BUT THAT'S NOT ALL.
I WANT TO MAKE SURE KURDA UNDERSTANDS...
...JUST HOW MUCH PAIN HE'S CAUSED.
I HATE HIM, SEBA, BUT I STILL THINK OF HIM AS A FRIEND.
HE SAVED MY LIFE.
I WANT HIM TO KNOW HOW MUCH HE'S HURT ME...
MAYBE IT DOESN'T REALLY MAKE SENSE...
...BUT I WANT HIM TO SEE THAT I DON'T GET ANY PLEASURE OUT OF EXPOSING HIM AS A TRAITOR.
YOU HAVE OVERCOME GREAT ODDS TO BE HERE.
YOU ARE A TRUE, COURAGEOUS VAMPIRE.
SFX: PON (PAT)
LARTEN WILL BE PROUD OF YOU...
...DARREN SHAN.

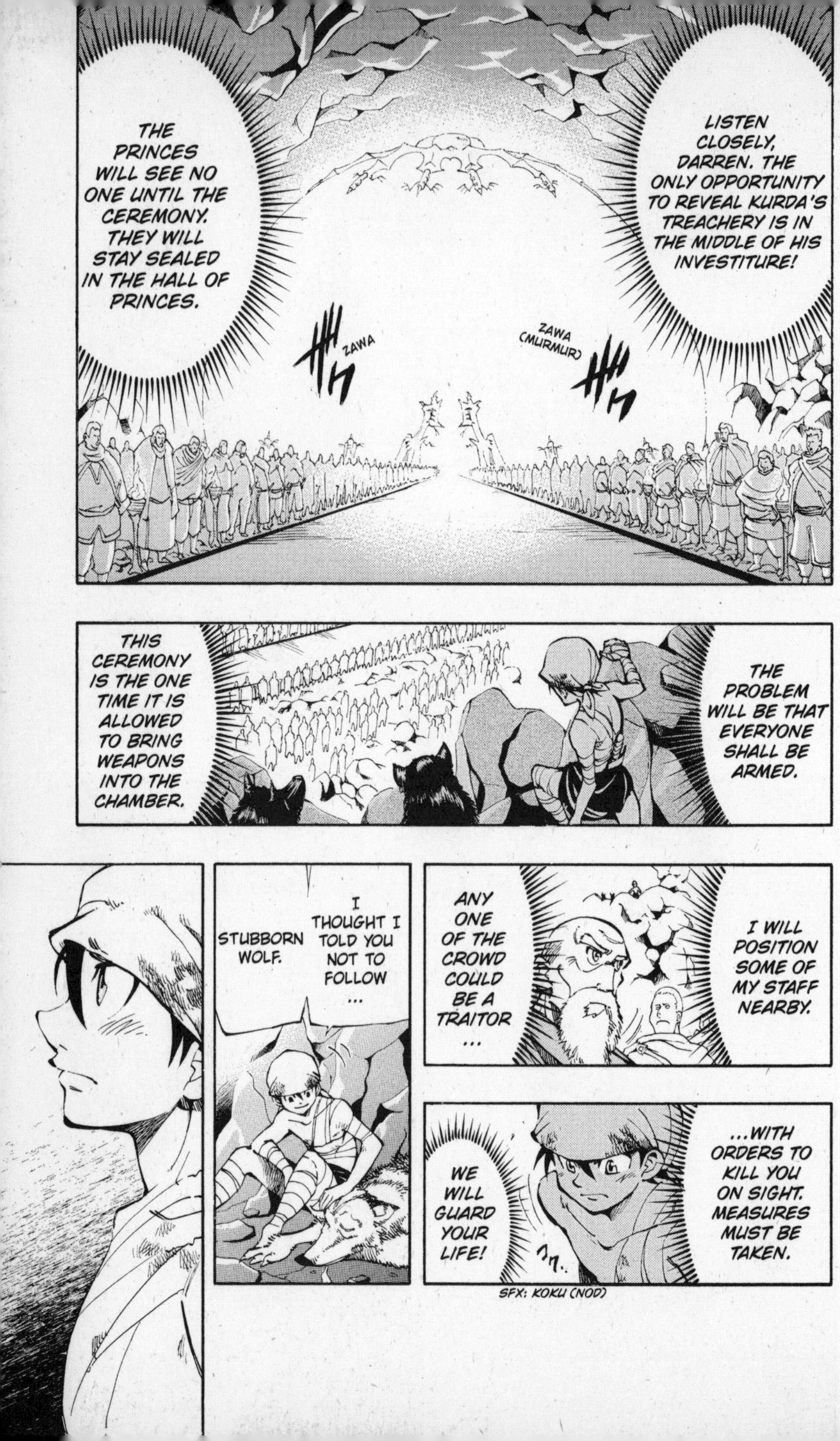
LISTEN CLOSELY, DARREN. THE ONLY OPPORTUNITY TO REVEAL KURDA'S TREACHERY IS IN THE MIDDLE OF HIS INVESTITURE!
THE PRINCES WILL SEE NO ONE UNTIL THE CEREMONY. THEY WILL STAY SEALED IN THE HALL OF PRINCES.
ZAWA (MURMUR)
ZAWA
THE PROBLEM WILL BE THAT EVERYONE SHALL BE ARMED.
THIS CEREMONY IS THE ONE TIME IT IS ALLOWED TO BRING WEAPONS INTO THE CHAMBER.
I WILL POSITION SOME OF MY STAFF NEARBY.
ANY ONE OF THE CROWD COULD BE A TRAITOR ...
...WITH ORDERS TO KILL YOU ON SIGHT. MEASURES MUST BE TAKEN.
WE WILL GUARD YOUR LIFE!
SFX: KOKU (NOD)
I THOUGHT I TOLD YOU NOT TO FOLLOW ...
STUBBORN WOLF.

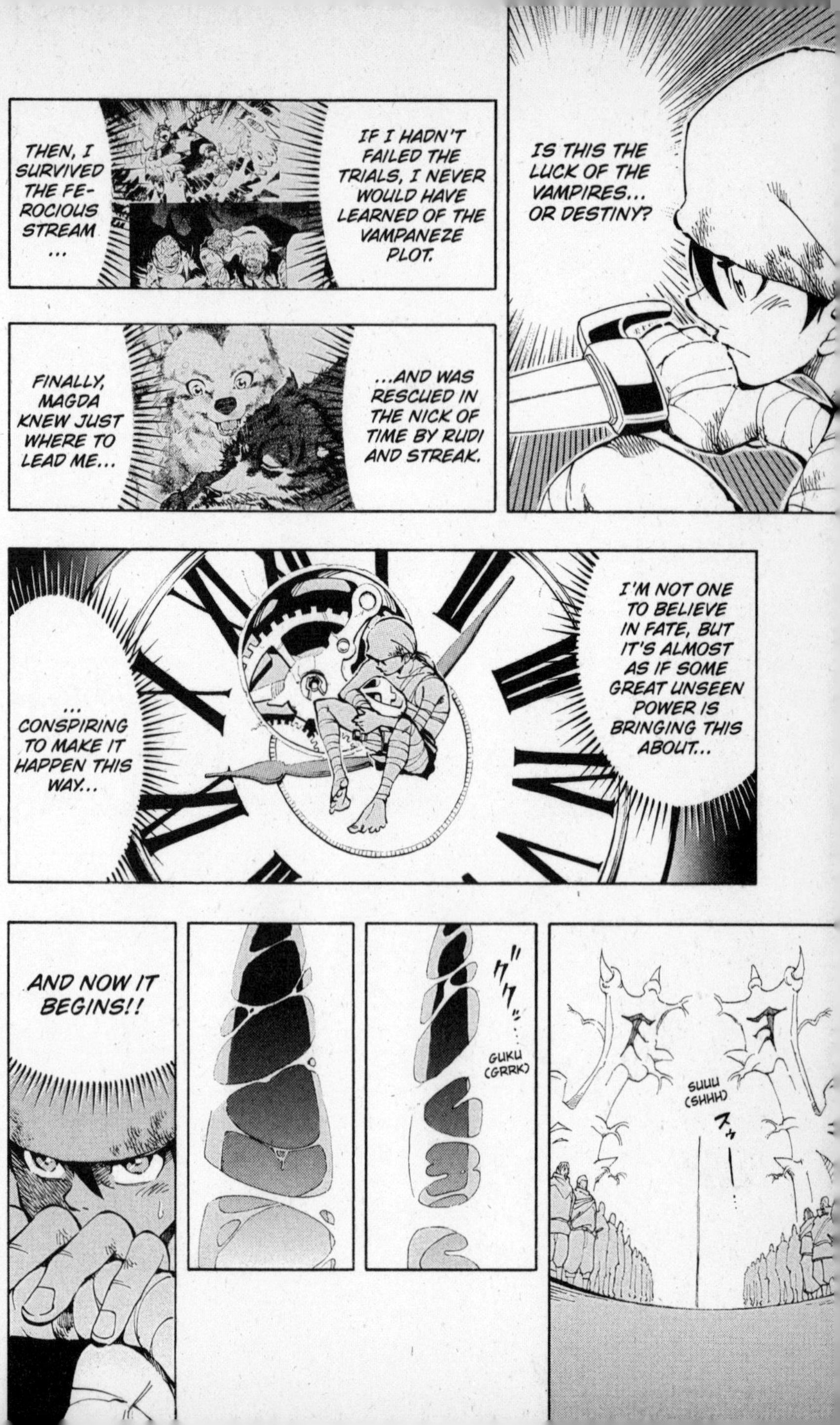
IS THIS THE LUCK OF THE VAMPIRES... OR DESTINY?
IF I HADN'T FAILED THE TRIALS, I NEVER WOULD HAVE LEARNED OF THE VAMPANEZE PLOT.
THEN, I SURVIVED THE FE-ROCIOUS STREAM ...
...AND WAS RESCUED IN THE NICK OF TIME BY RUDI AND STREAK.
FINALLY, MAGDA KNEW JUST WHERE TO LEAD ME...
I'M NOT ONE TO BELIEVE IN FATE, BUT IT'S ALMOST AS IF SOME GREAT UNSEEN POWER IS BRINGING THIS ABOUT...
... CONSPIRING TO MAKE IT HAPPEN THIS WAY...
SUUU (SHHH)
GUKU (GRRK)
AND NOW IT BEGINS!!

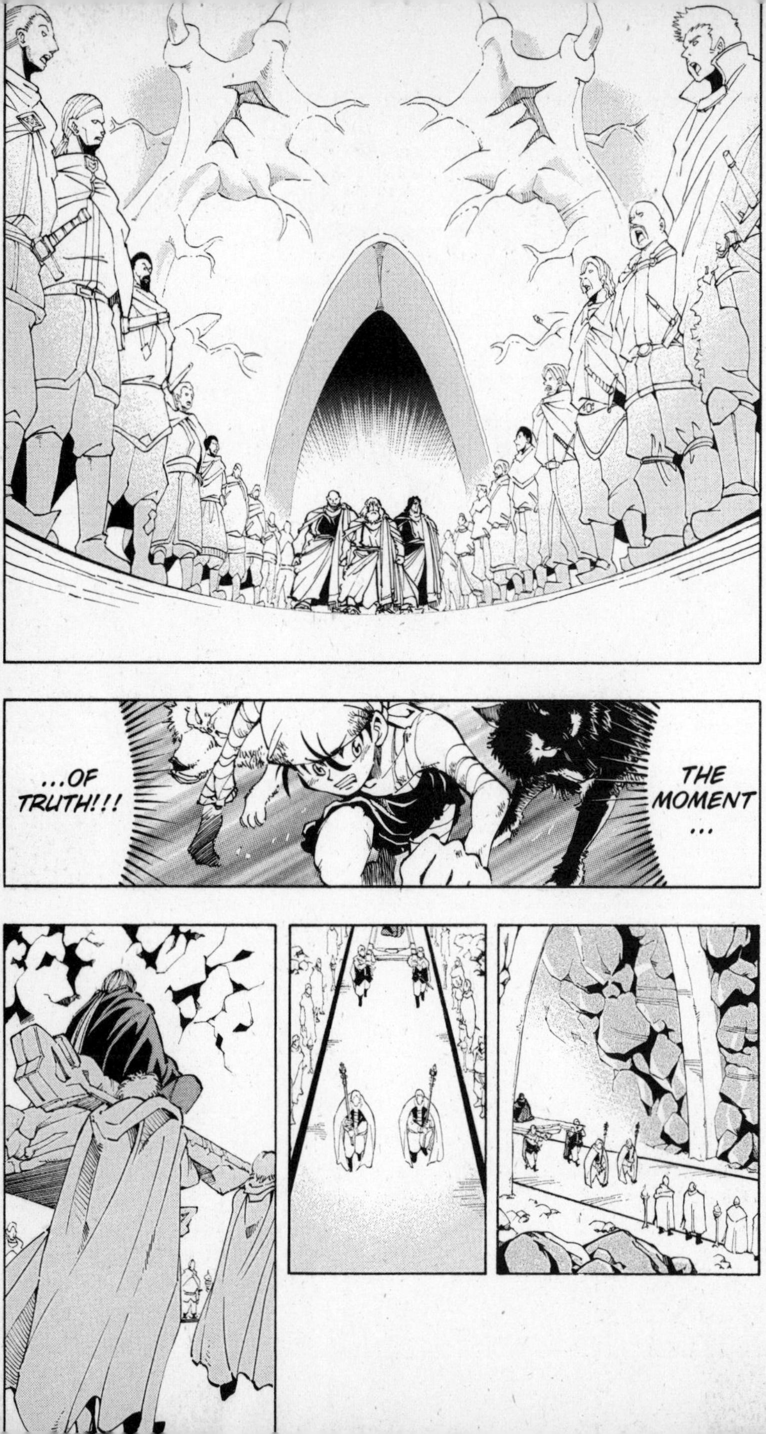
THE MOMENT ...
...OF TRUTH!!!

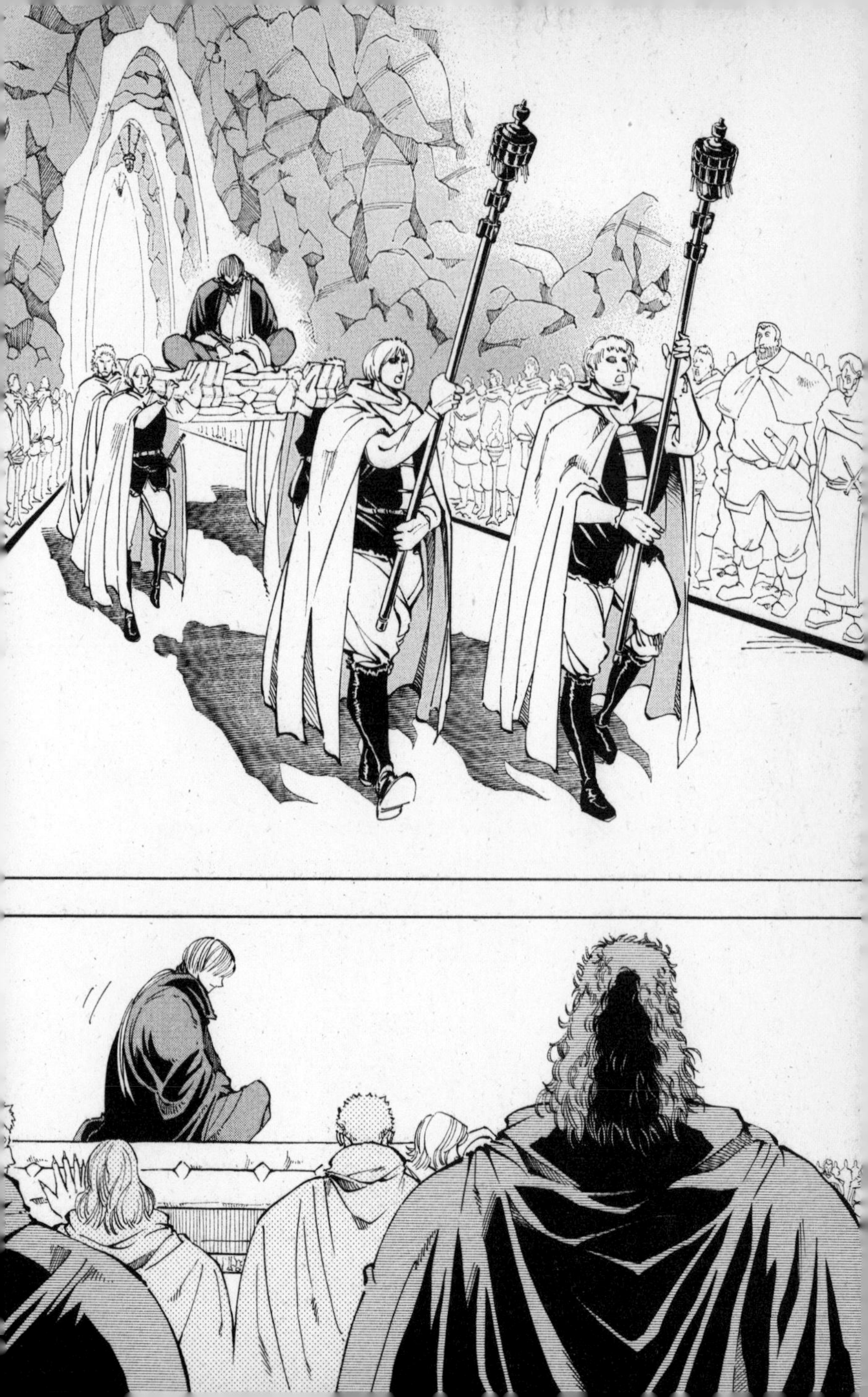

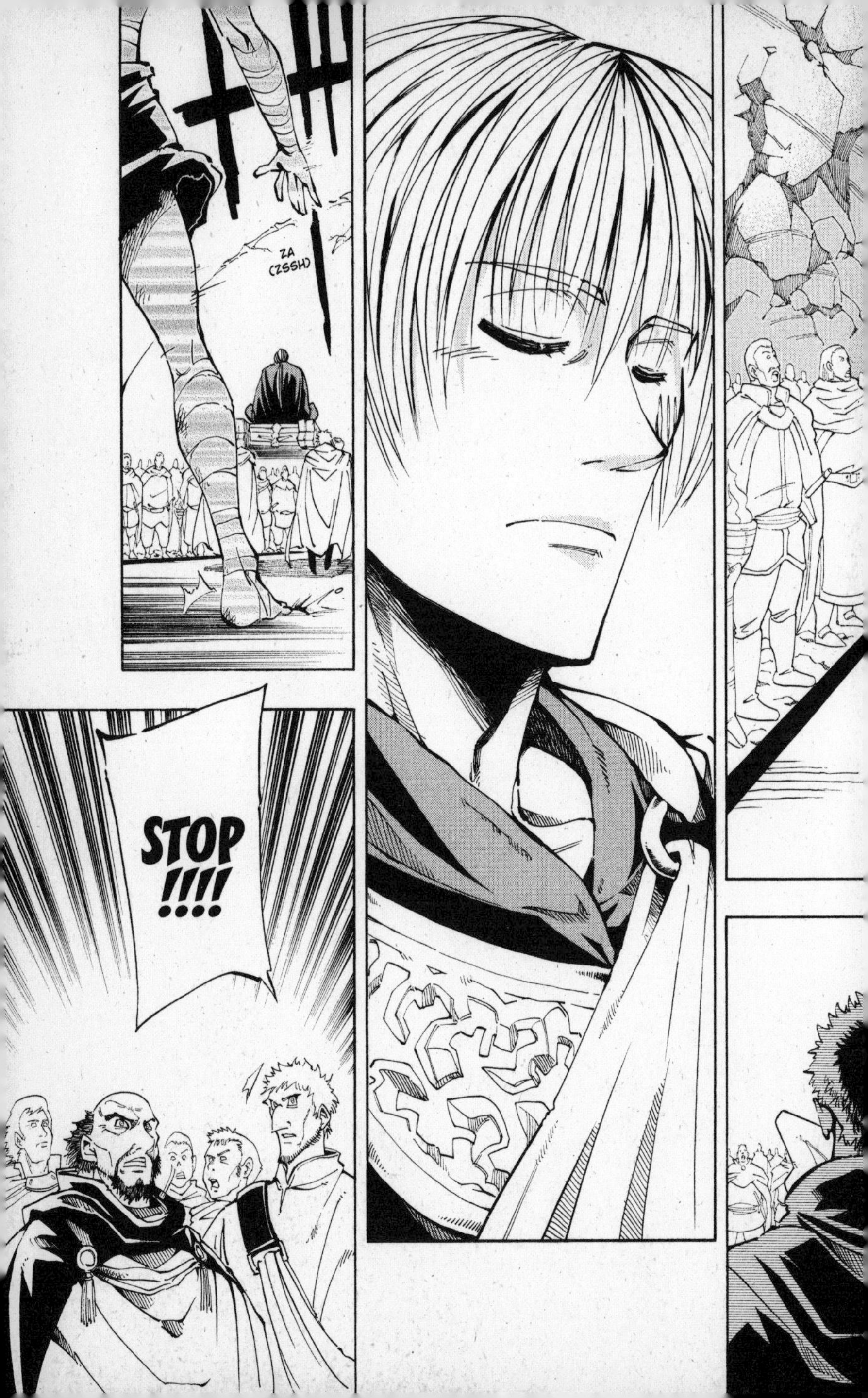

ZA (ZSSH)
STOP !!!!

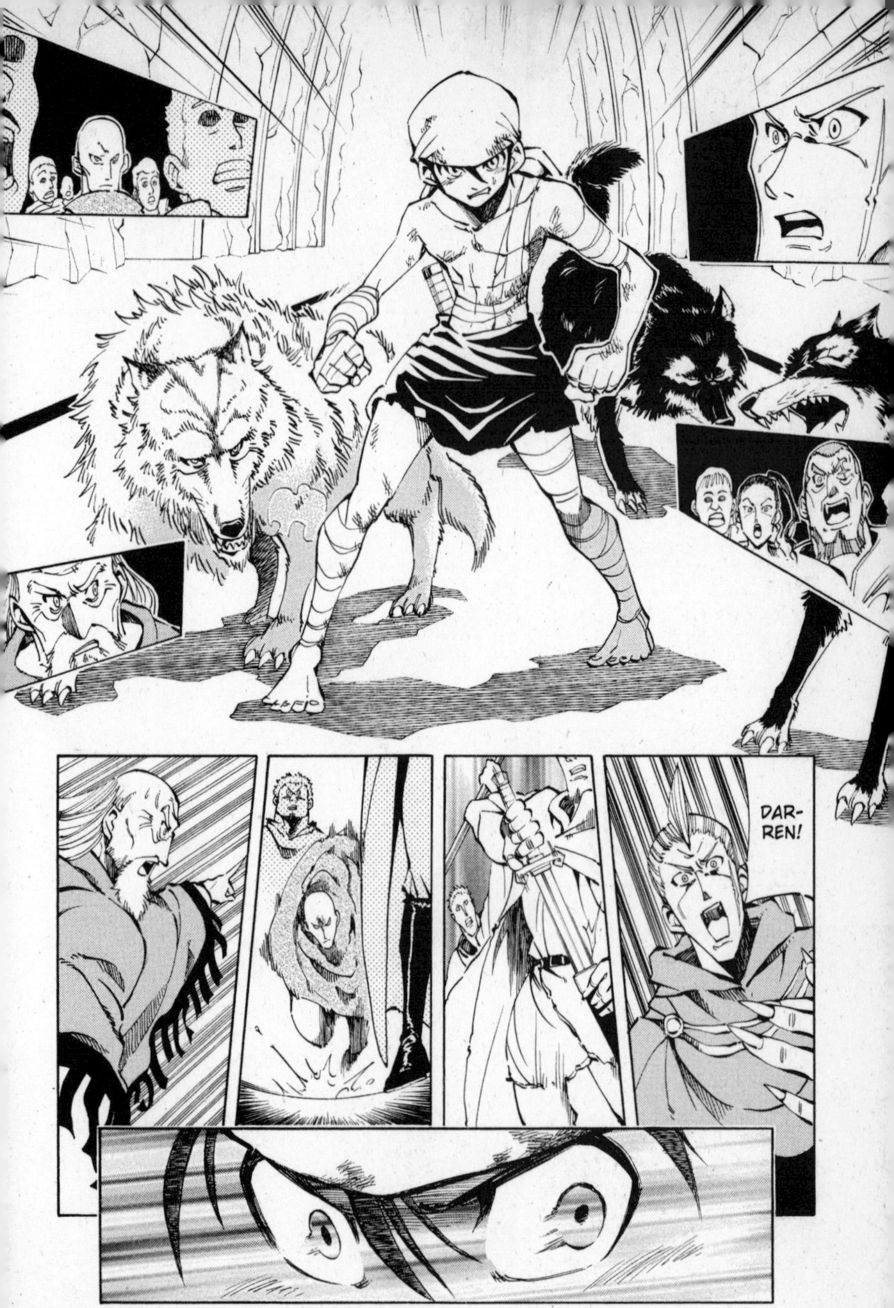
DAR-
REN!

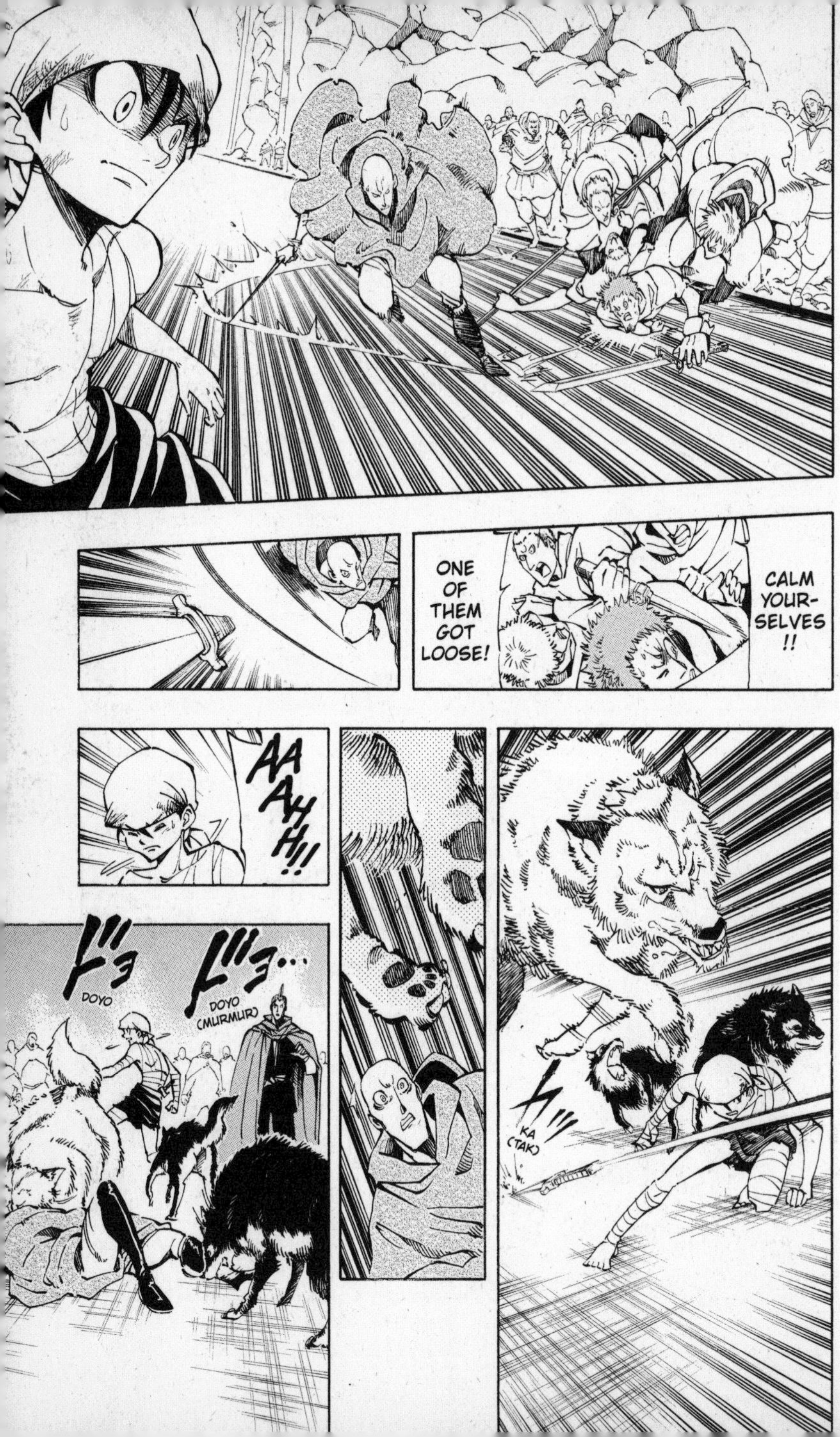
CALM YOURSELVES!!
ONE OF THEM GOT LOOSE!
KA (TAK)
AAAAH!!
ドョ…
DOYO (MURMUR)
ドョ
DOYO

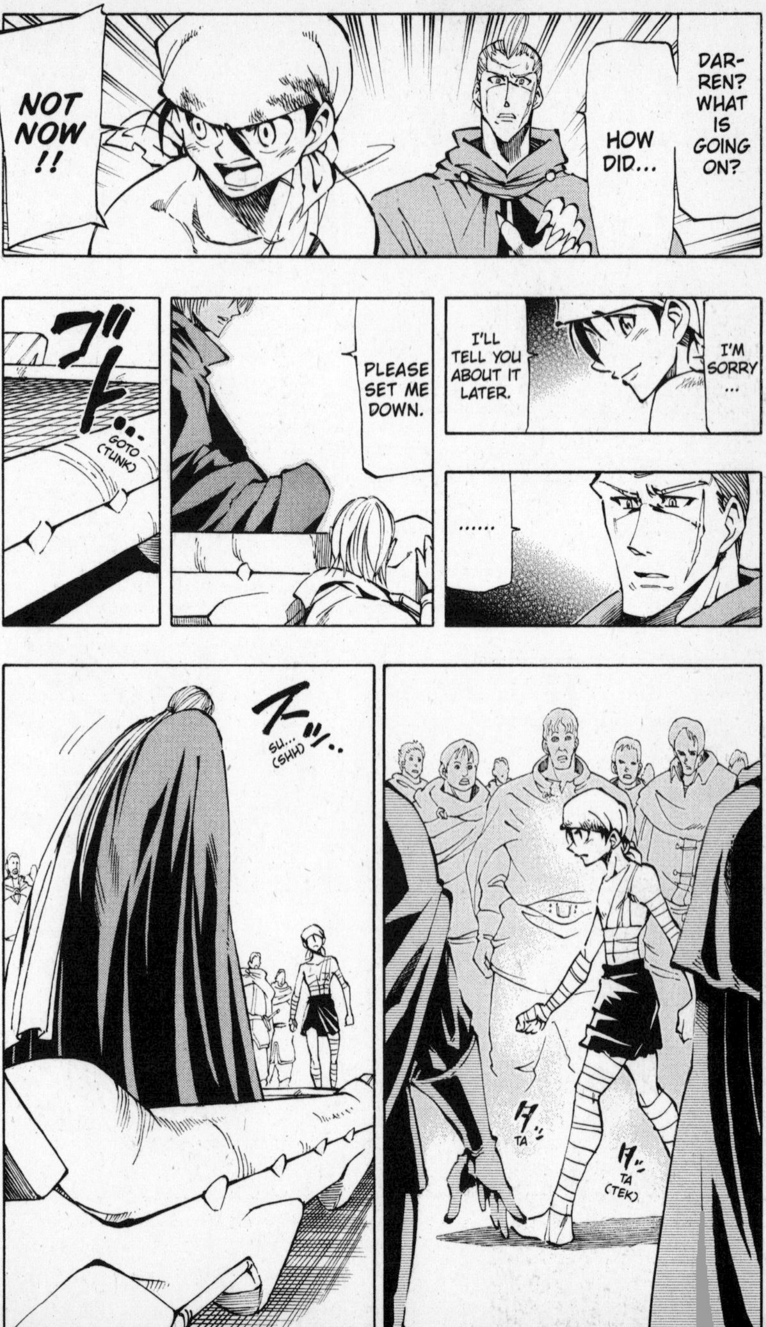
DAR-REN? WHAT IS GOING ON?
HOW DID...
NOT NOW!!
I'M SORRY...
I'LL TELL YOU ABOUT IT LATER.
......
PLEASE SET ME DOWN.
GOTO (TUNK)
TA
TA (TEK)
SU... (SHH)

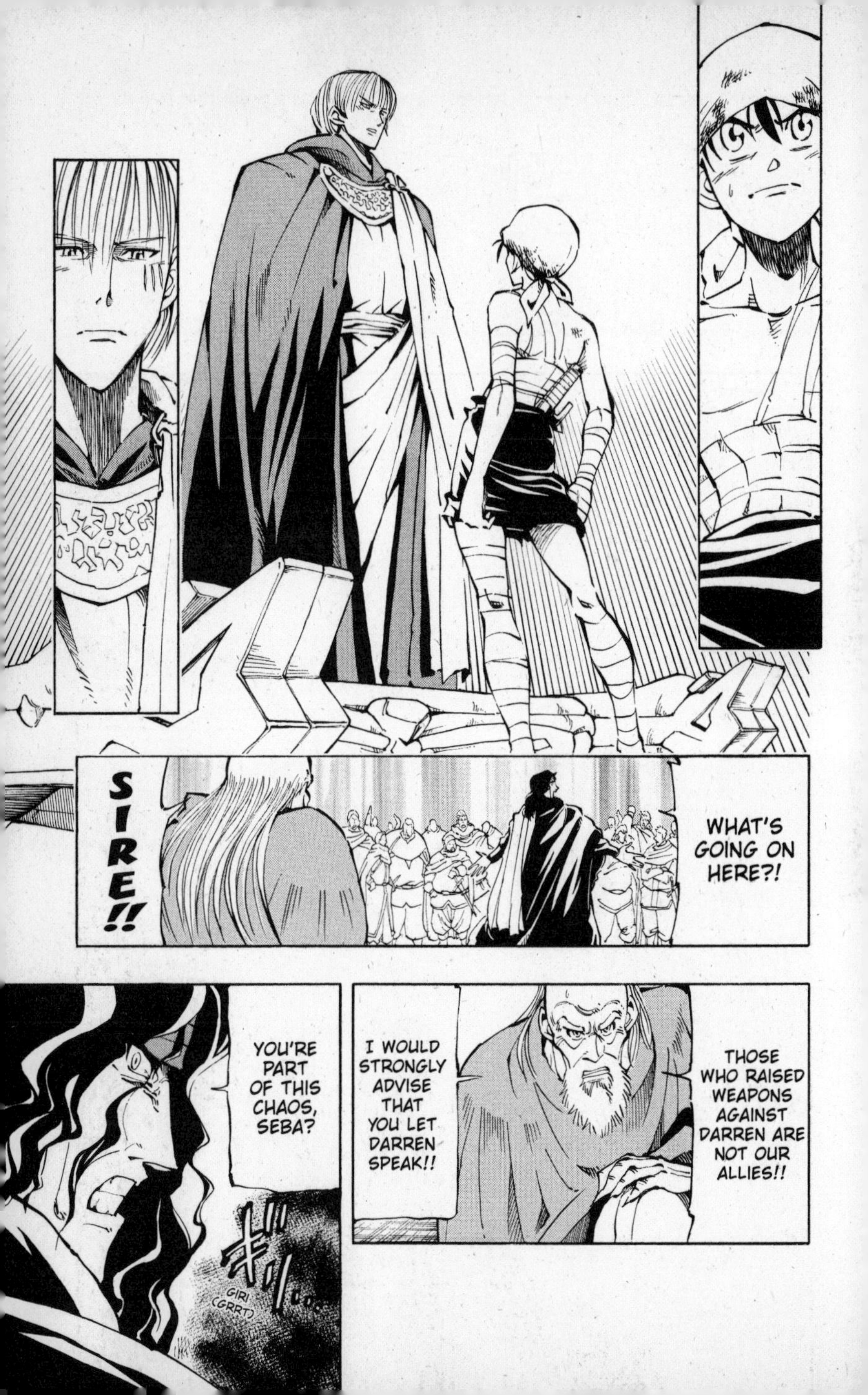
WHAT'S GOING ON HERE?!
SIRE!!
THOSE WHO RAISED WEAPONS AGAINST DARREN ARE NOT OUR ALLIES!!
I WOULD STRONGLY ADVISE THAT YOU LET DARREN SPEAK!!
YOU'RE PART OF THIS CHAOS, SEBA?
GIRI (GRRT)

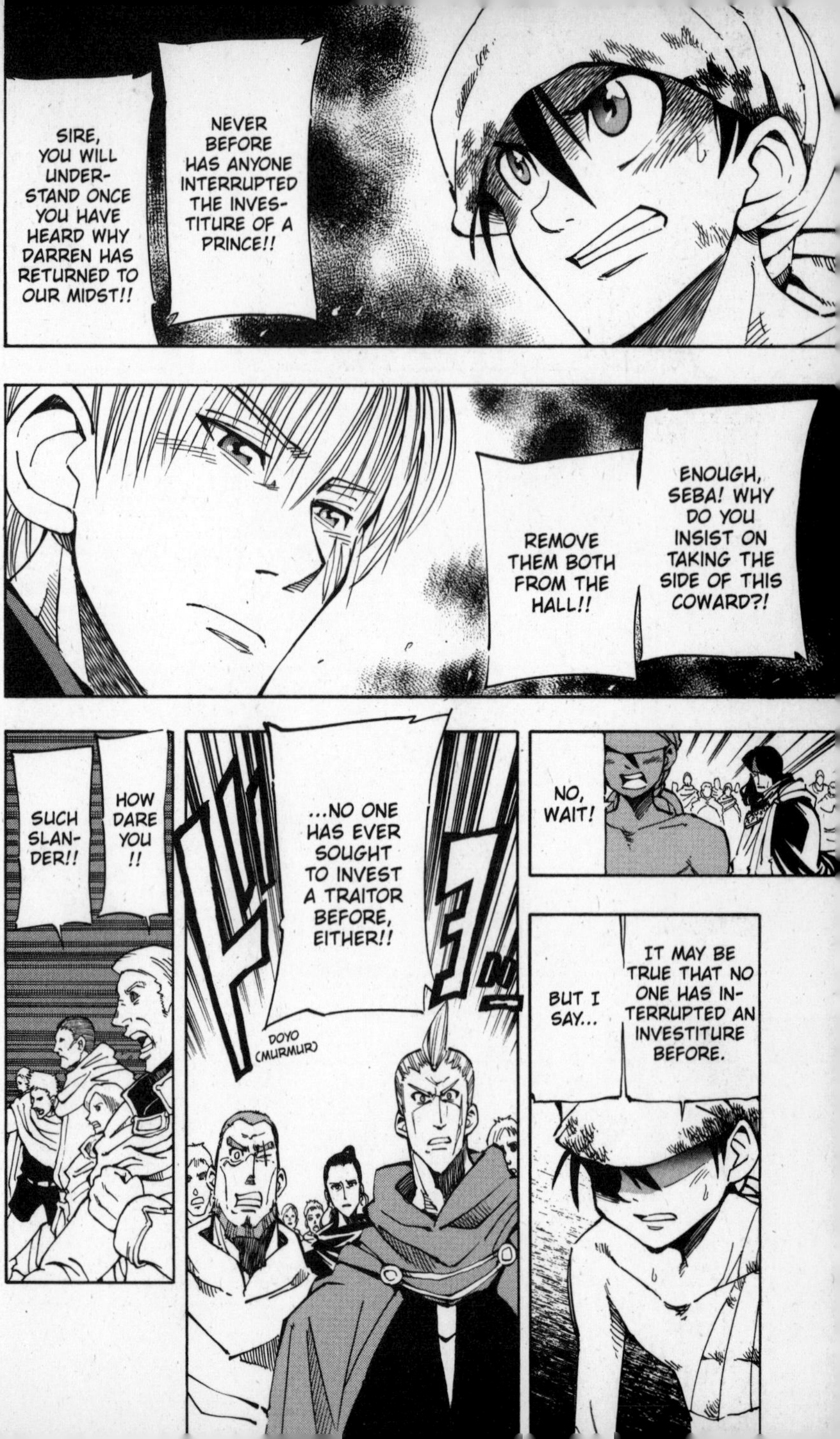
NEVER BEFORE HAS ANYONE INTERRUPTED THE INVESTITURE OF A PRINCE!!
SIRE, YOU WILL UNDERSTAND ONCE YOU HAVE HEARD WHY DARREN HAS RETURNED TO OUR MIDST!!
ENOUGH, SEBA! WHY DO YOU INSIST ON TAKING THE SIDE OF THIS COWARD?!
REMOVE THEM BOTH FROM THE HALL!!
NO, WAIT!
IT MAY BE TRUE THAT NO ONE HAS INTERRUPTED AN INVESTITURE BEFORE.
BUT I SAY...
...NO ONE HAS EVER SOUGHT TO INVEST A TRAITOR BEFORE, EITHER!!
DOYO (MURMUR)
HOW DARE YOU!!
SUCH SLANDER!!

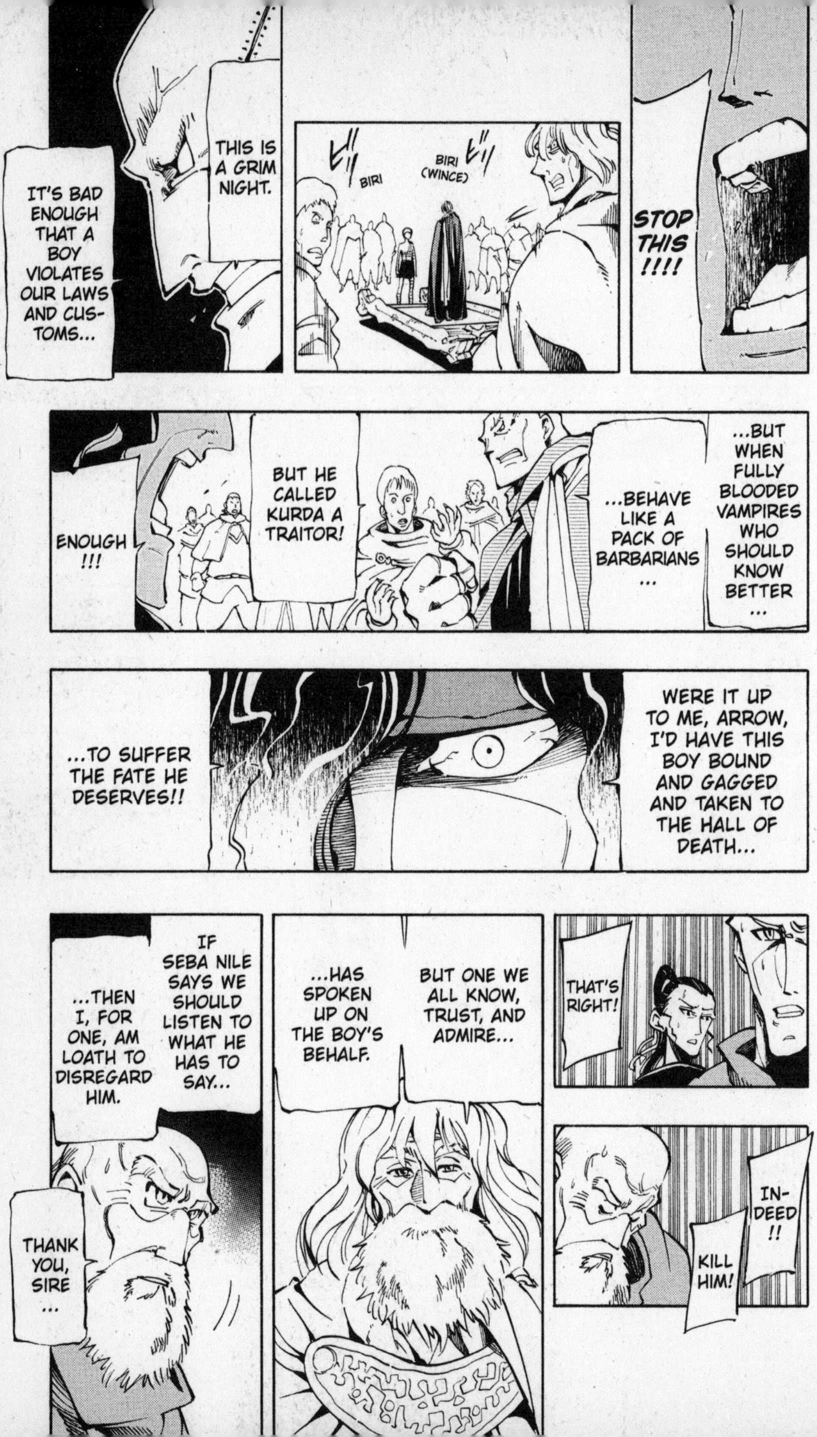
STOP THIS !!!!
BIRI (WINCE)
BIRI
THIS IS A GRIM NIGHT.
IT'S BAD ENOUGH THAT A BOY VIOLATES OUR LAWS AND CUSTOMS...
...BUT WHEN FULLY BLOODED VAMPIRES WHO SHOULD KNOW BETTER...
...BEHAVE LIKE A PACK OF BARBARIANS...
BUT HE CALLED KURDA A TRAITOR!
ENOUGH!!!
WERE IT UP TO ME, ARROW, I'D HAVE THIS BOY BOUND AND GAGGED AND TAKEN TO THE HALL OF DEATH...
...TO SUFFER THE FATE HE DESERVES!!
THAT'S RIGHT!
INDEED!!
KILL HIM!
BUT ONE WE ALL KNOW, TRUST, AND ADMIRE...
...HAS SPOKEN UP ON THE BOY'S BEHALF.
IF SEBA NILE SAYS WE SHOULD LISTEN TO WHAT HE HAS TO SAY...
...THEN I, FOR ONE, AM LOATH TO DISREGARD HIM.
THANK YOU, SIRE...

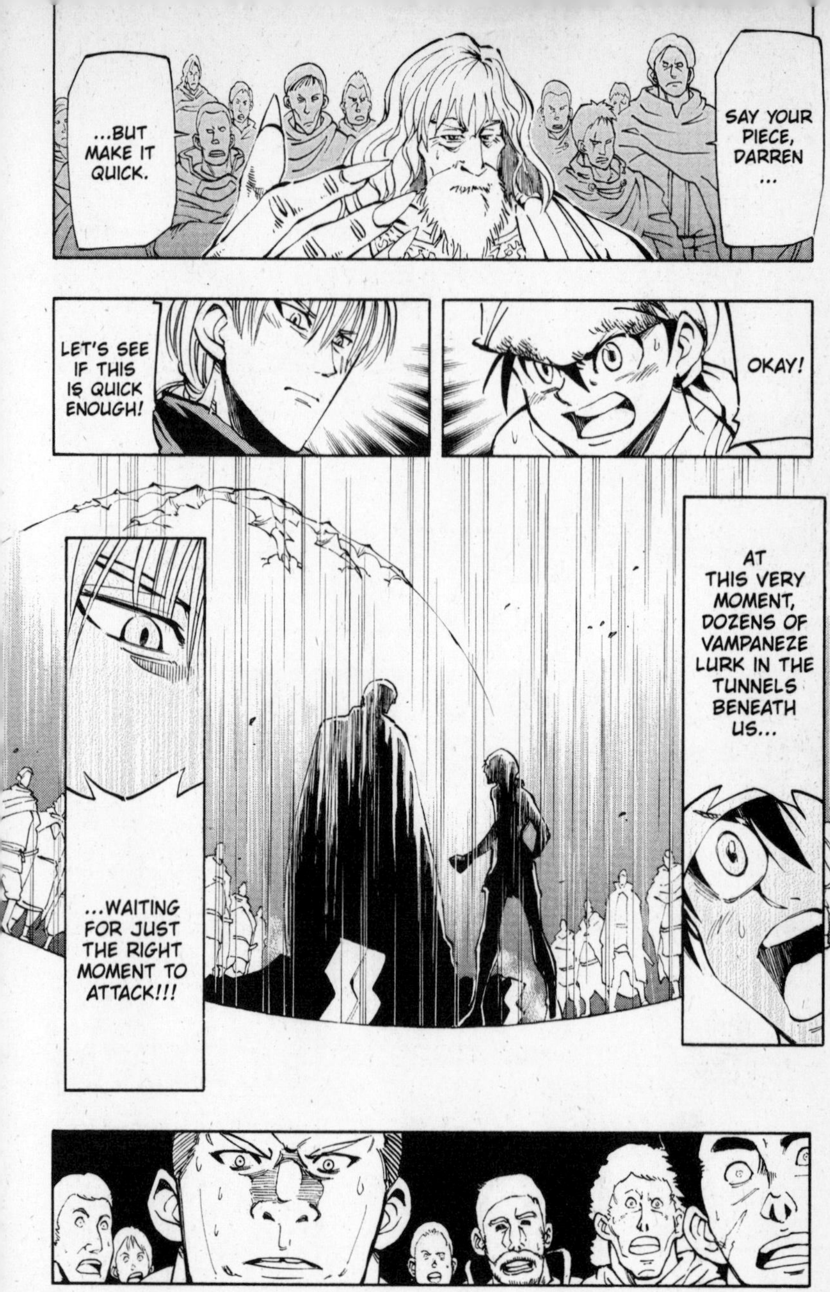
SAY YOUR PIECE, DARREN ...
...BUT MAKE IT QUICK.
OKAY!
LET'S SEE IF THIS IS QUICK ENOUGH!
AT THIS VERY MOMENT, DOZENS OF VAMPANEZE LURK IN THE TUNNELS BENEATH US...
...WAITING FOR JUST THE RIGHT MOMENT TO ATTACK!!!

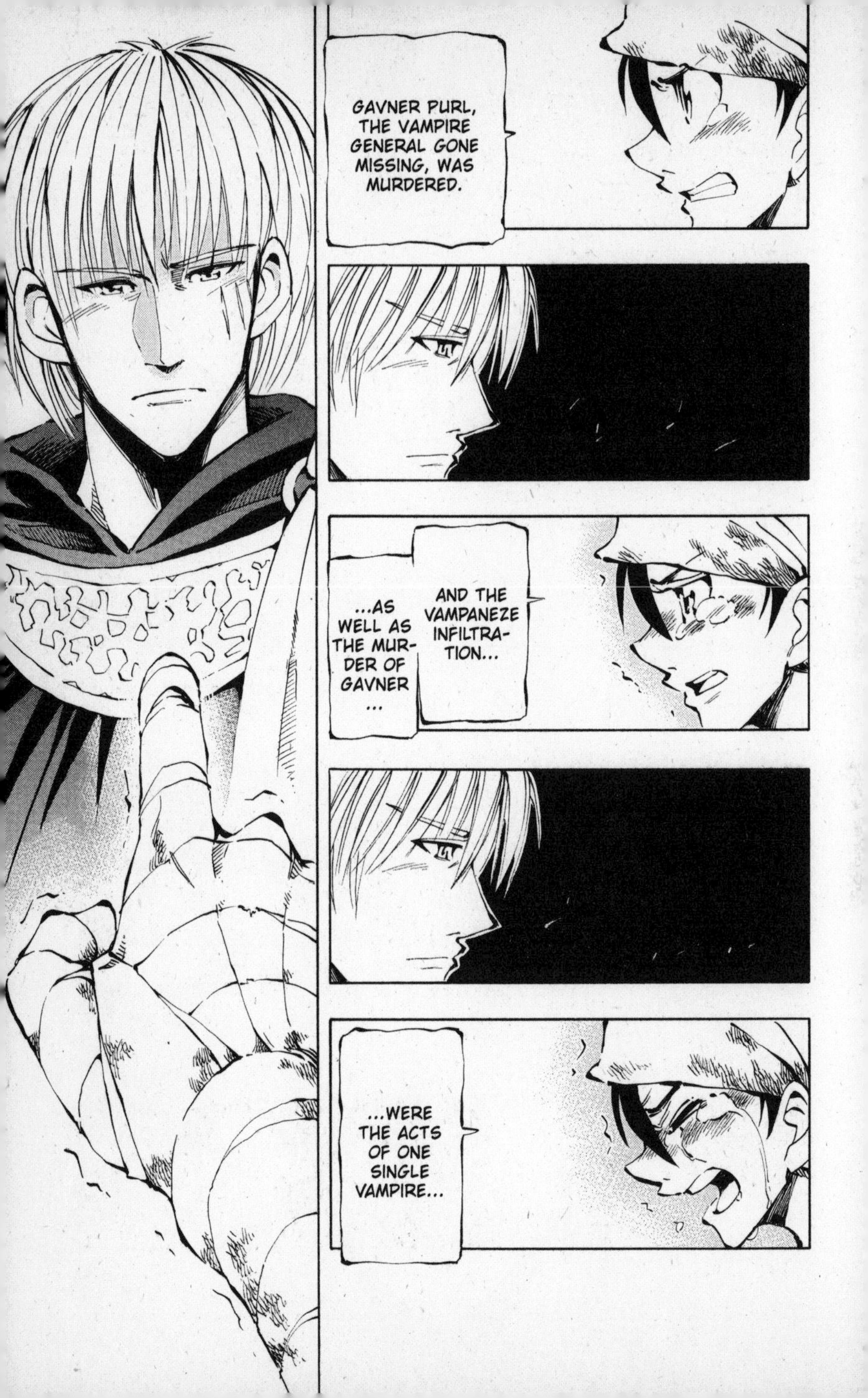
GAVNER PURL, THE VAMPIRE GENERAL GONE MISSING, WAS MURDERED.
AND THE VAMPANEZE INFILTRATION...
...AS WELL AS THE MURDER OF GAVNER ...
...WERE THE ACTS OF ONE SINGLE VAMPIRE...

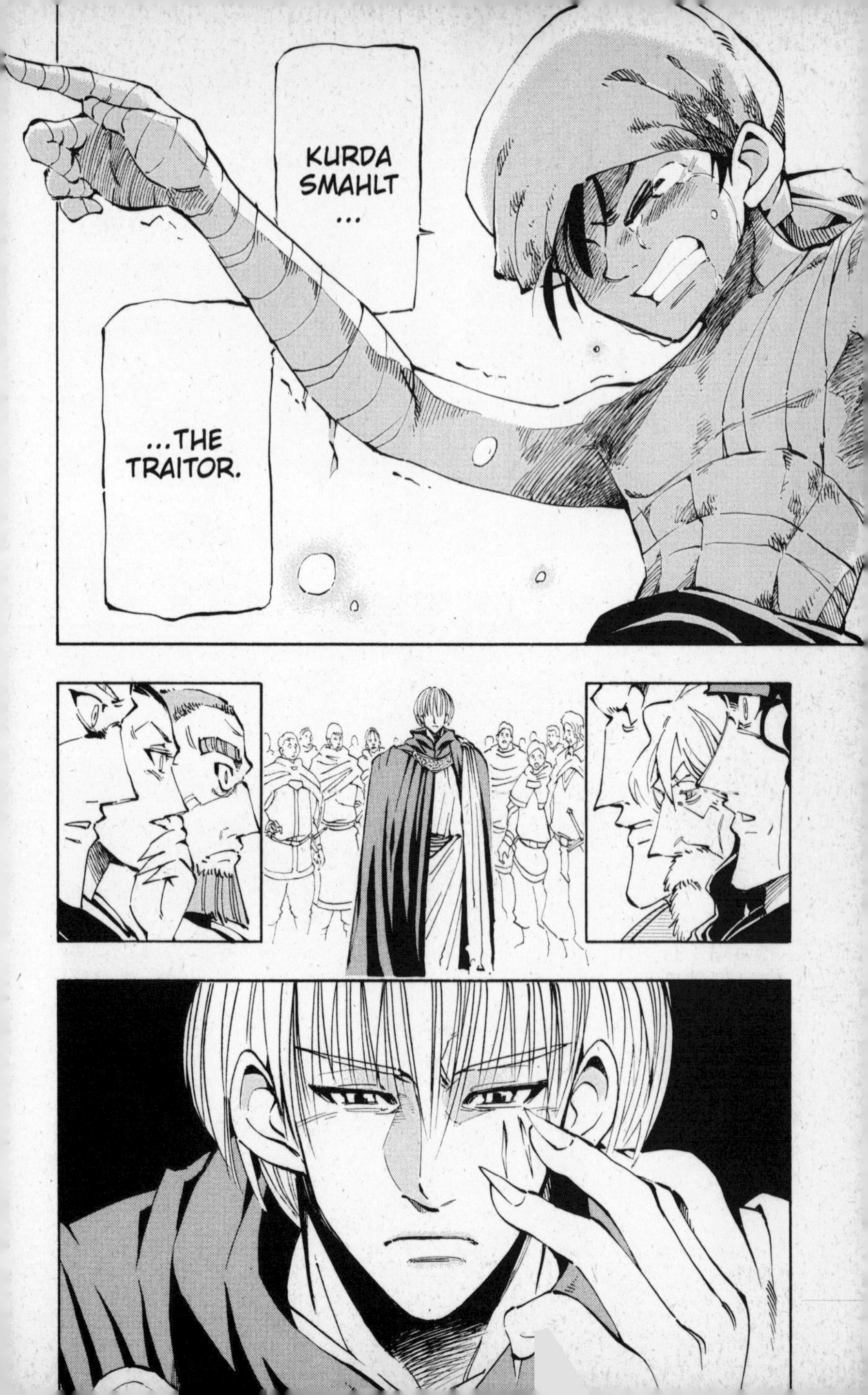
KURDA SMAHLT ...
...THE TRAITOR.

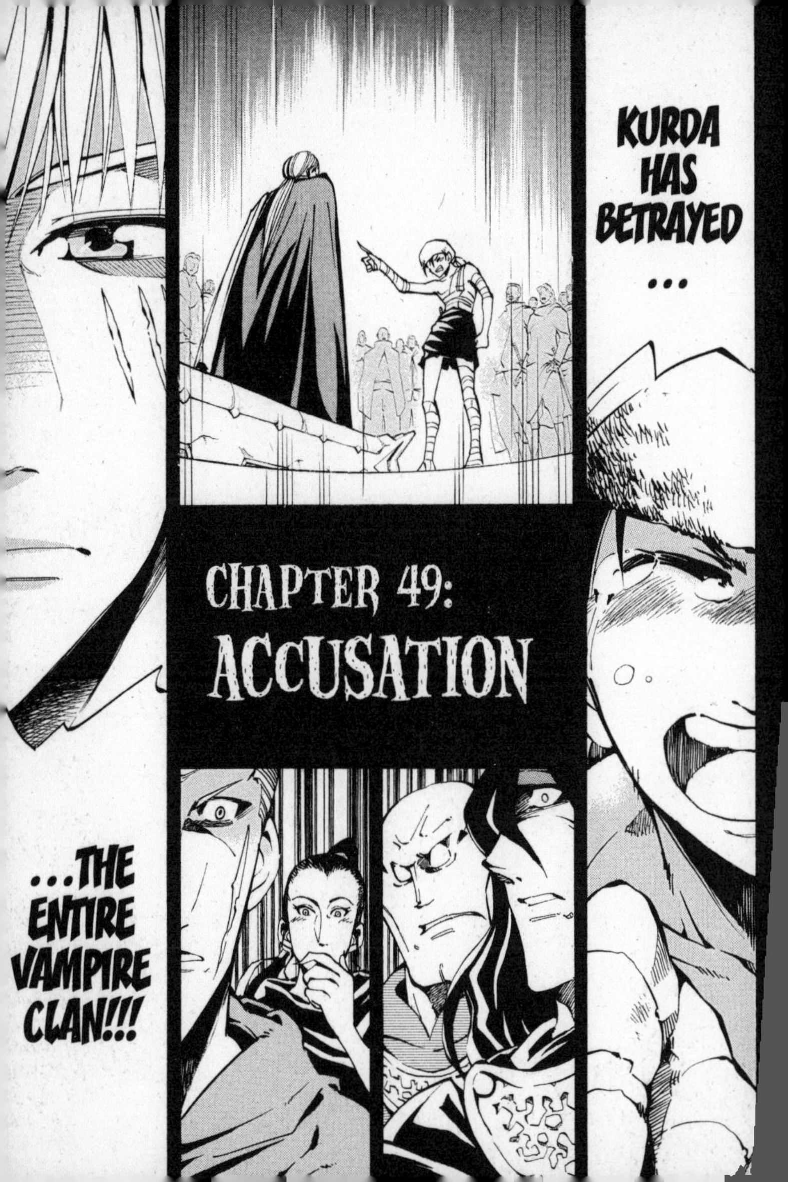
KURDA HAS BETRAYED ...
CHAPTER 49: ACCUSATION
...THE ENTIRE VAMPIRE CLAN!!!

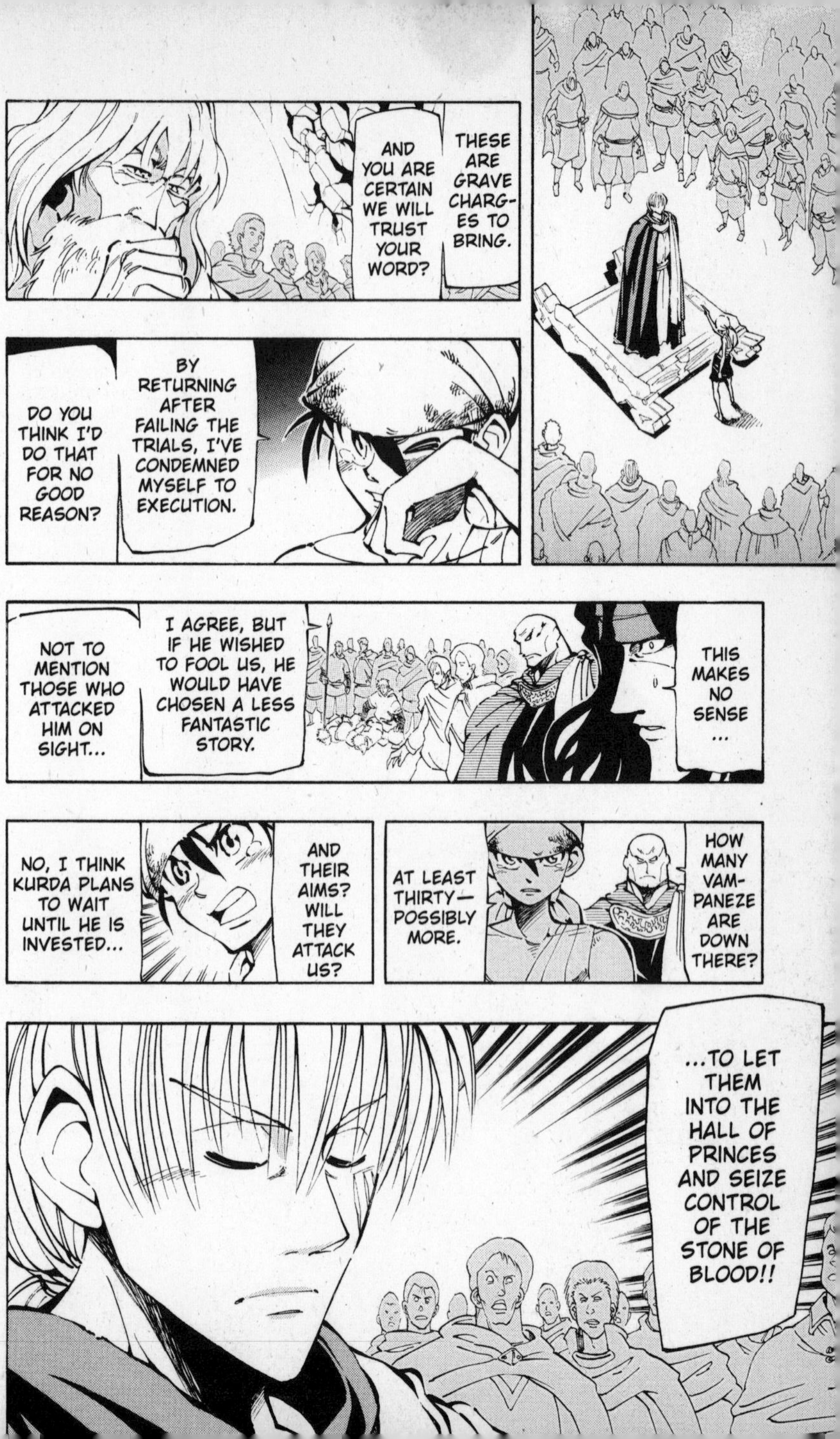
THESE ARE GRAVE CHARG-ES TO BRING.
AND YOU ARE CERTAIN WE WILL TRUST YOUR WORD?
BY RETURNING AFTER FAILING THE TRIALS, I'VE CONDEMNED MYSELF TO EXECUTION.
DO YOU THINK I'D DO THAT FOR NO GOOD REASON?
THIS MAKES NO SENSE ...
I AGREE, BUT IF HE WISHED TO FOOL US, HE WOULD HAVE CHOSEN A LESS FANTASTIC STORY.
NOT TO MENTION THOSE WHO ATTACKED HIM ON SIGHT...
HOW MANY VAM-PANEZE ARE DOWN THERE?
AT LEAST THIRTY— POSSIBLY MORE.
AND THEIR AIMS? WILL THEY ATTACK US?
NO, I THINK KURDA PLANS TO WAIT UNTIL HE IS INVESTED...
...TO LET THEM INTO THE HALL OF PRINCES AND SEIZE CONTROL OF THE STONE OF BLOOD!!

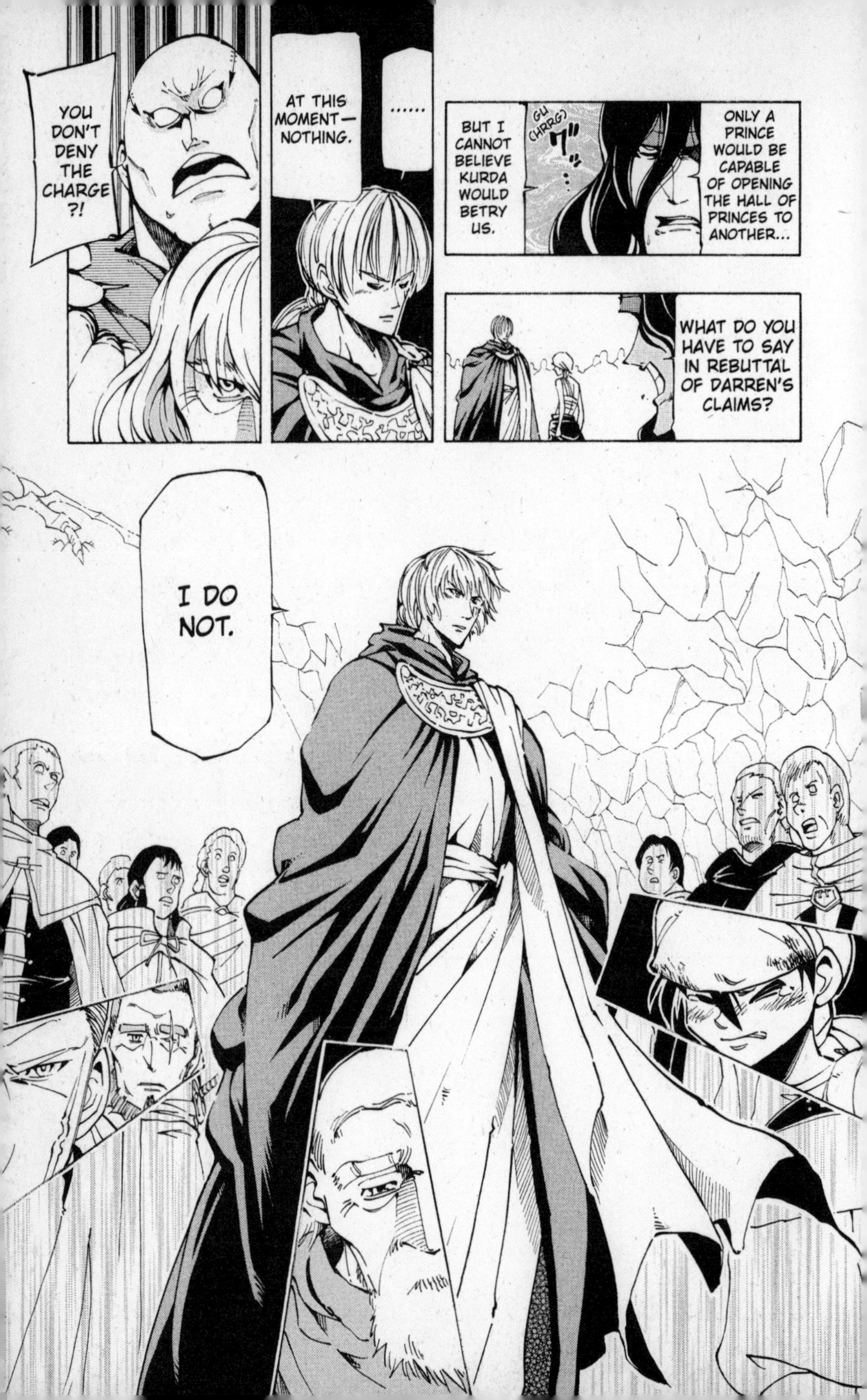

ONLY A PRINCE WOULD BE CAPABLE OF OPENING THE HALL OF PRINCES TO ANOTHER...
GU (HRRG)
BUT I CANNOT BELIEVE KURDA WOULD BETRY US.
WHAT DO YOU HAVE TO SAY IN REBUTTAL OF DARREN'S CLAIMS?
......
AT THIS MOMENT—NOTHING.
YOU DON'T DENY THE CHARGE?!
I DO NOT.

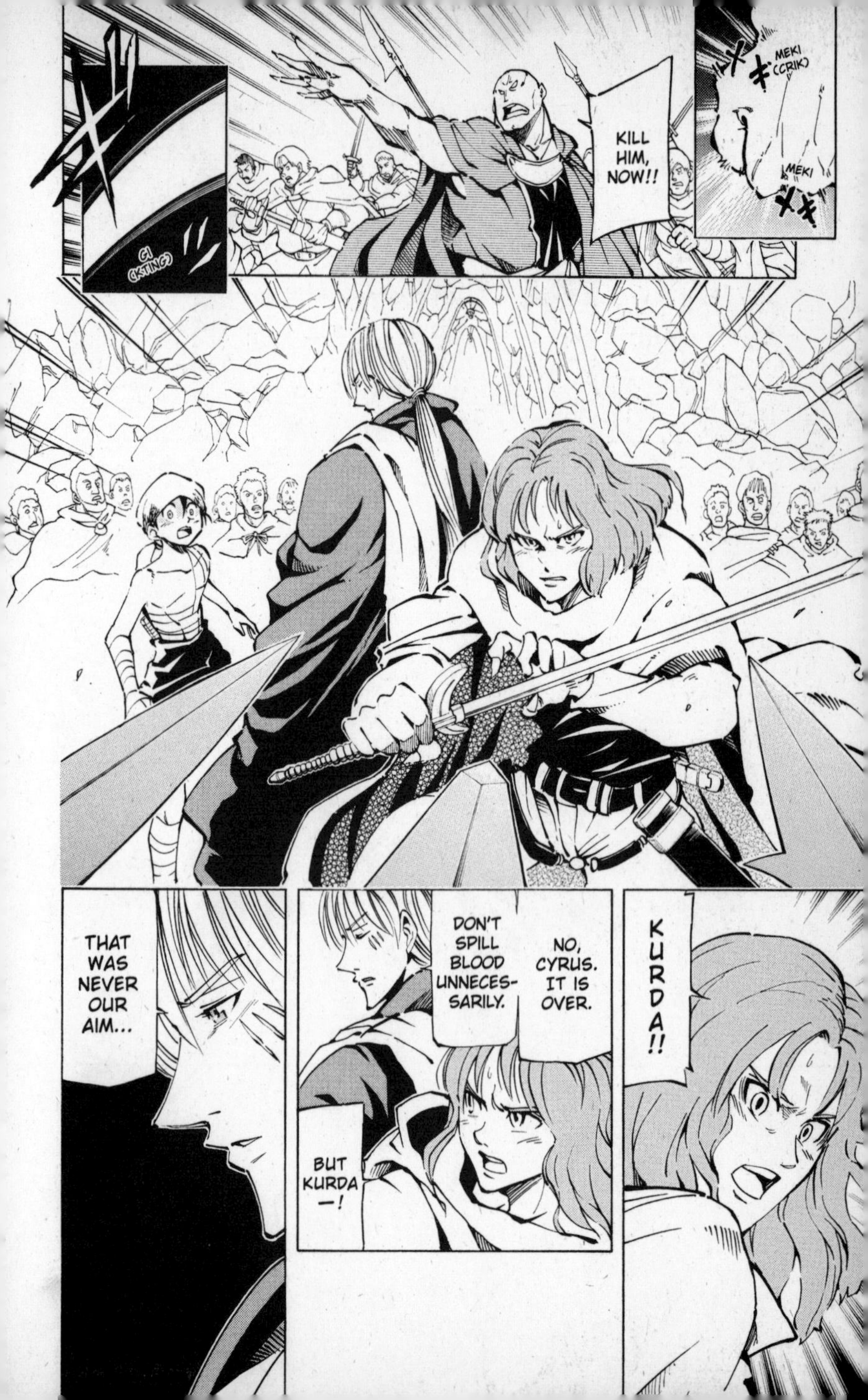
MEKI (CRIK)
MEKI
KILL HIM, NOW!!
CI (KTING)
KURDA!!
NO, CYRUS. IT IS OVER.
DON'T SPILL BLOOD UNNECES-SARILY.
BUT KURDA—!
THAT WAS NEVER OUR AIM...

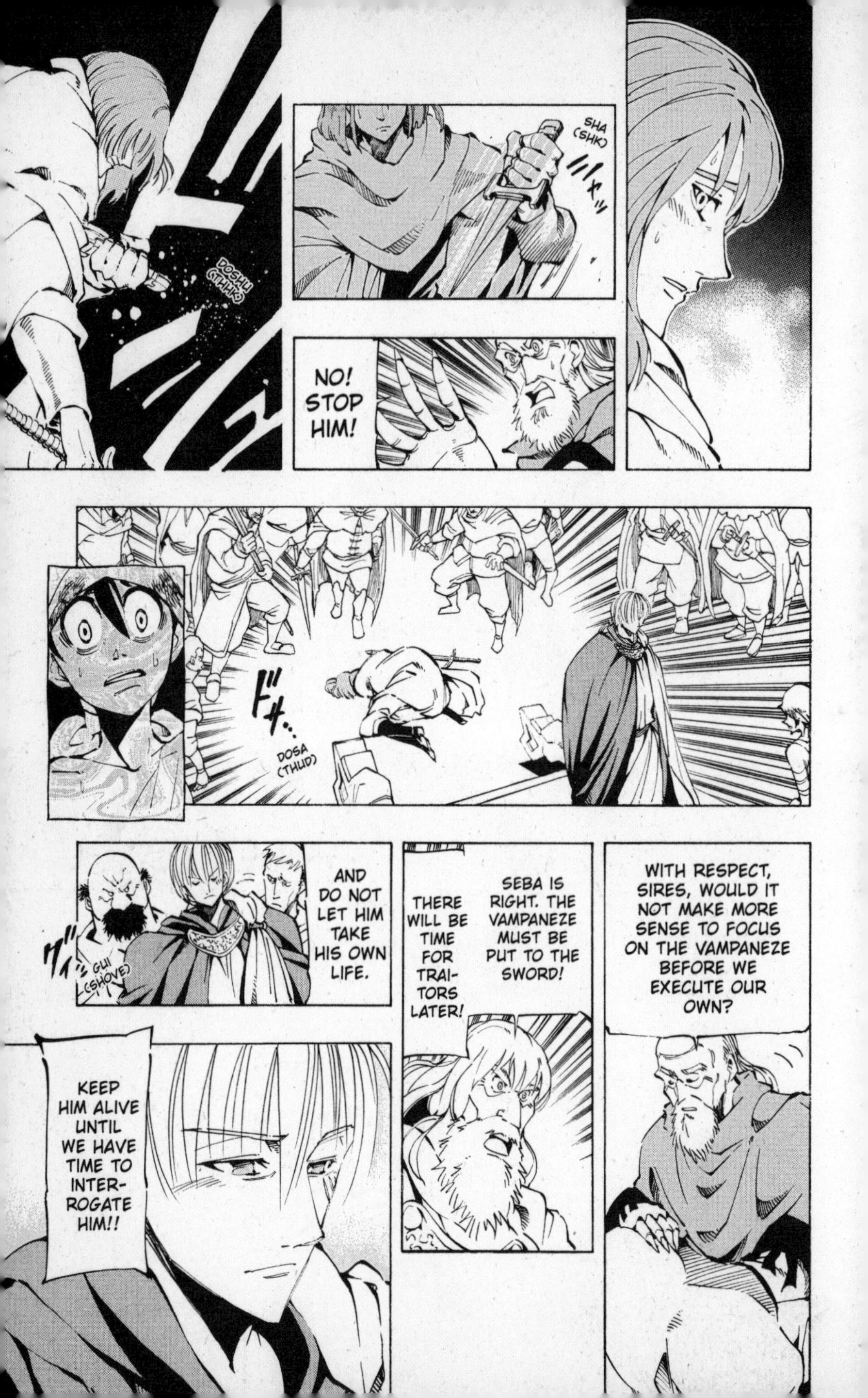
SHA (SHK)
NO! STOP HIM!
DOSHU (THUK)
DOSA (THUD)
WITH RESPECT, SIRES, WOULD IT NOT MAKE MORE SENSE TO FOCUS ON THE VAMPANEZE BEFORE WE EXECUTE OUR OWN?
SEBA IS RIGHT. THE VAMPANEZE MUST BE PUT TO THE SWORD!
THERE WILL BE TIME FOR TRAI-TORS LATER!
AND DO NOT LET HIM TAKE HIS OWN LIFE.
GUI (SHOVE)
KEEP HIM ALIVE UNTIL WE HAVE TIME TO INTER-ROGATE HIM!!

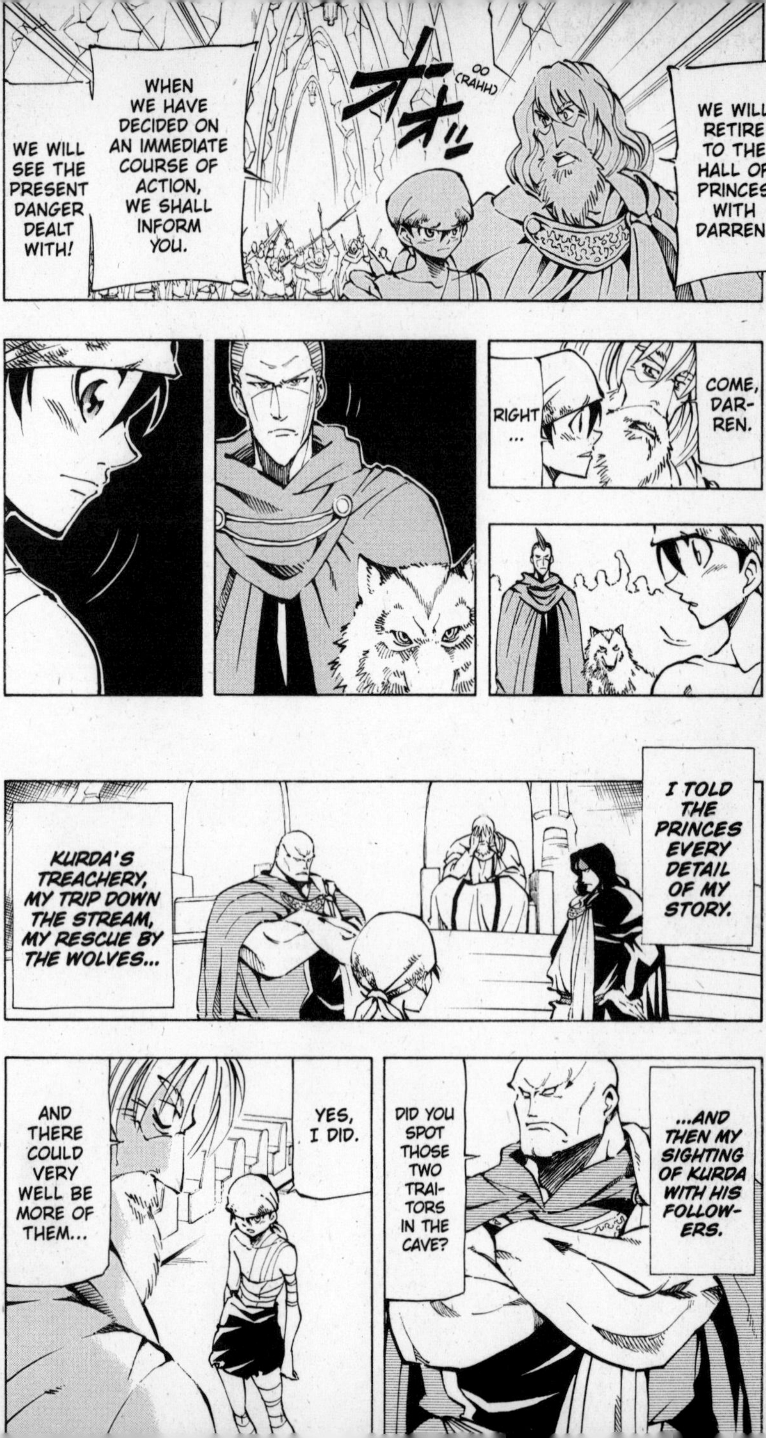

WE WILL RETIRE TO THE HALL OF PRINCES WITH DARREN!
オオッ
OO (RAHH)
WHEN WE HAVE DECIDED ON AN IMMEDIATE COURSE OF ACTION, WE SHALL INFORM YOU.
WE WILL SEE THE PRESENT DANGER DEALT WITH!
COME, DAR-REN.
RIGHT...
I TOLD THE PRINCES EVERY DETAIL OF MY STORY.
KURDA'S TREACHERY, MY TRIP DOWN THE STREAM, MY RESCUE BY THE WOLVES...
...AND THEN MY SIGHTING OF KURDA WITH HIS FOLLOW-ERS.
DID YOU SPOT THOSE TWO TRAI-TORS IN THE CAVE?
YES, I DID.
AND THERE COULD VERY WELL BE MORE OF THEM...

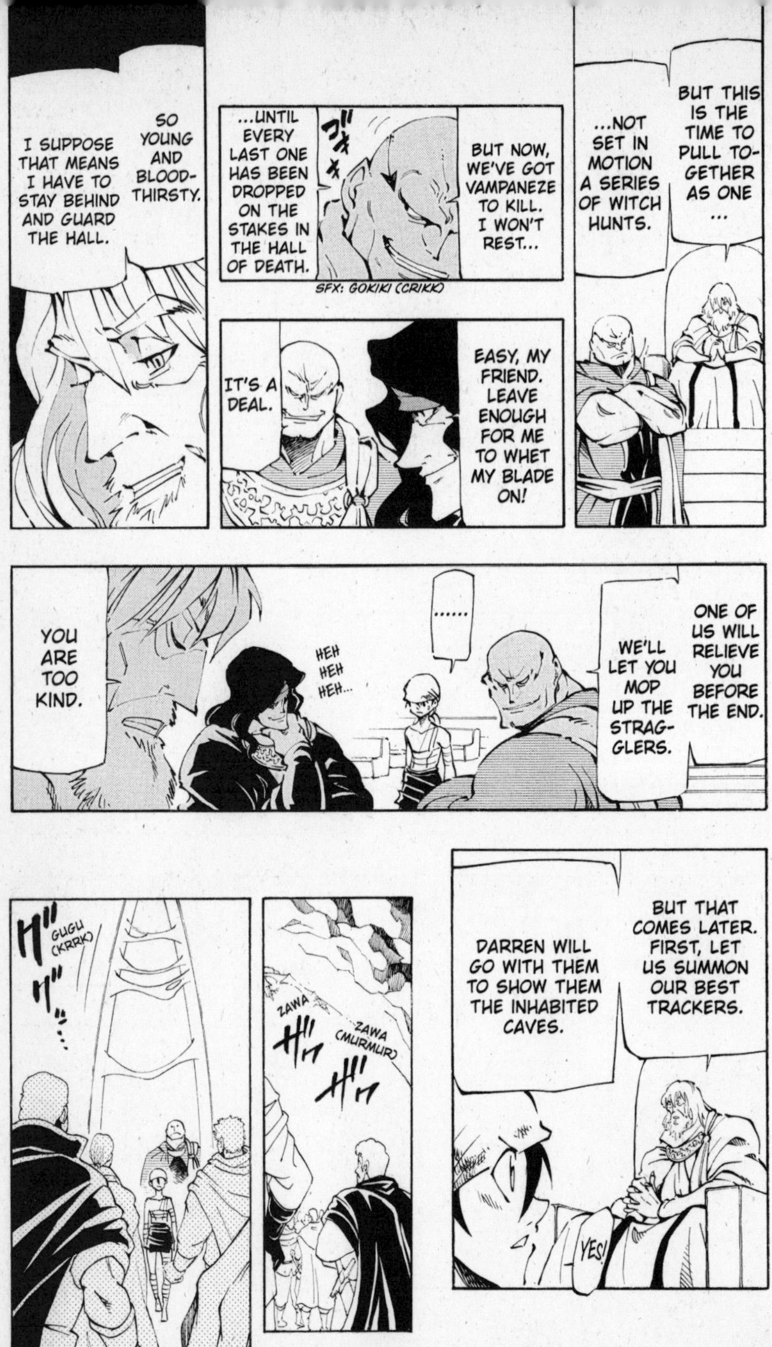
BUT THIS IS THE TIME TO PULL TO-GETHER AS ONE ...
...NOT SET IN MOTION A SERIES OF WITCH HUNTS.
BUT NOW, WE'VE GOT VAMPANEZE TO KILL. I WON'T REST...
...UNTIL EVERY LAST ONE HAS BEEN DROPPED ON THE STAKES IN THE HALL OF DEATH.
SFX: GOKIKI (CRIKK)
EASY, MY FRIEND. LEAVE ENOUGH FOR ME TO WHET MY BLADE ON!
IT'S A DEAL.
SO YOUNG AND BLOOD-THIRSTY.
I SUPPOSE THAT MEANS I HAVE TO STAY BEHIND AND GUARD THE HALL.
ONE OF US WILL RELIEVE YOU BEFORE THE END.
WE'LL LET YOU MOP UP THE STRAG-GLERS.
......
HEH HEH HEH...
YOU ARE TOO KIND.
BUT THAT COMES LATER. FIRST, LET US SUMMON OUR BEST TRACKERS.
DARREN WILL GO WITH THEM TO SHOW THEM THE INHABITED CAVES.
YES!
ZAWA
ZAWA (MURMUR)
GUGU (KRRK)

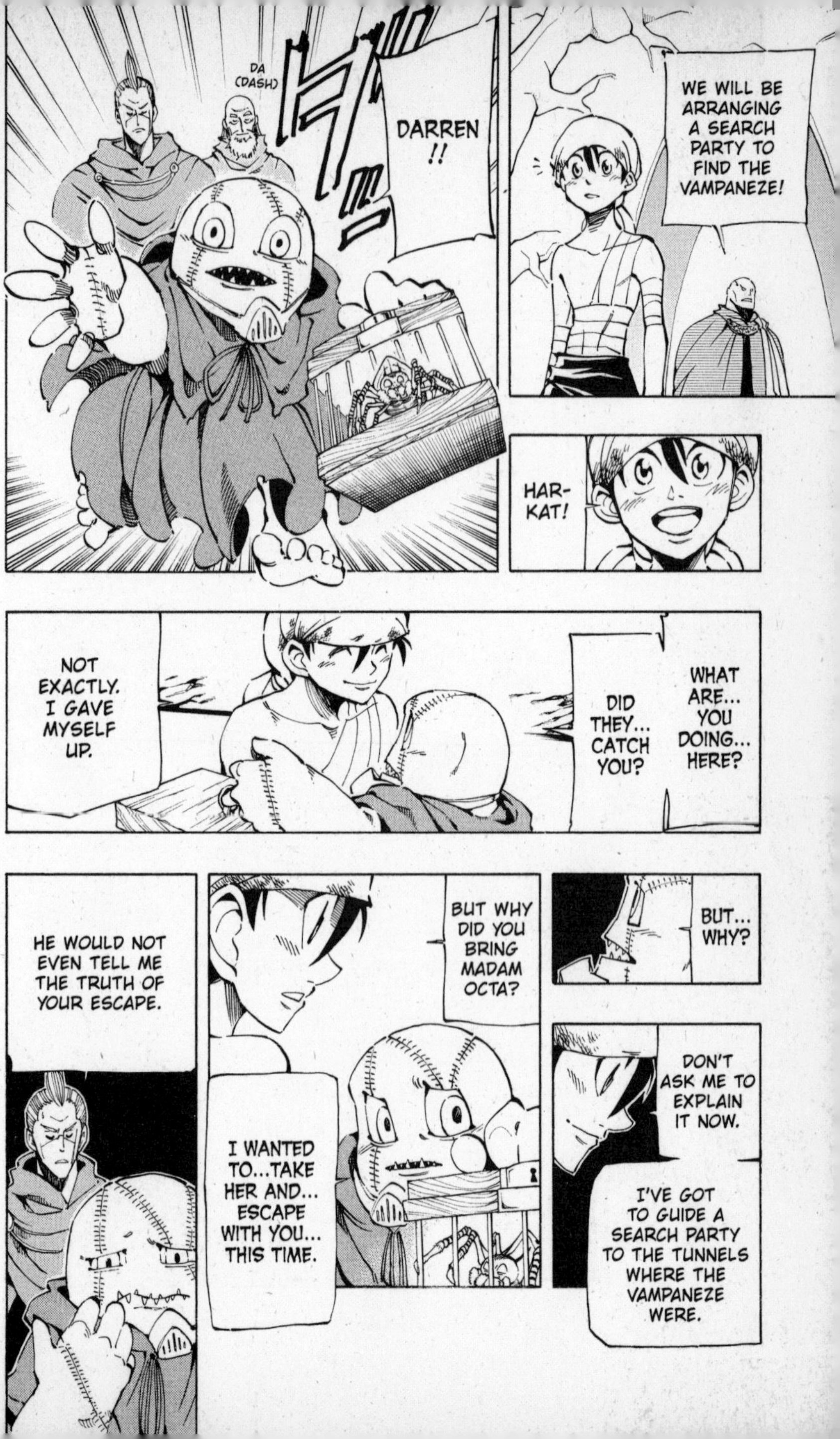
WE WILL BE ARRANGING A SEARCH PARTY TO FIND THE VAMPANEZE!
HAR-KAT!
DA (DASH)
DARREN !!
WHAT ARE... YOU DOING... HERE?
DID THEY... CATCH YOU?
NOT EXACTLY. I GAVE MYSELF UP.
BUT... WHY?
DON'T ASK ME TO EXPLAIN IT NOW.
I'VE GOT TO GUIDE A SEARCH PARTY TO THE TUNNELS WHERE THE VAMPANEZE WERE.
BUT WHY DID YOU BRING MADAM OCTA?
I WANTED TO...TAKE HER AND... ESCAPE WITH YOU... THIS TIME.
HE WOULD NOT EVEN TELL ME THE TRUTH OF YOUR ESCAPE.

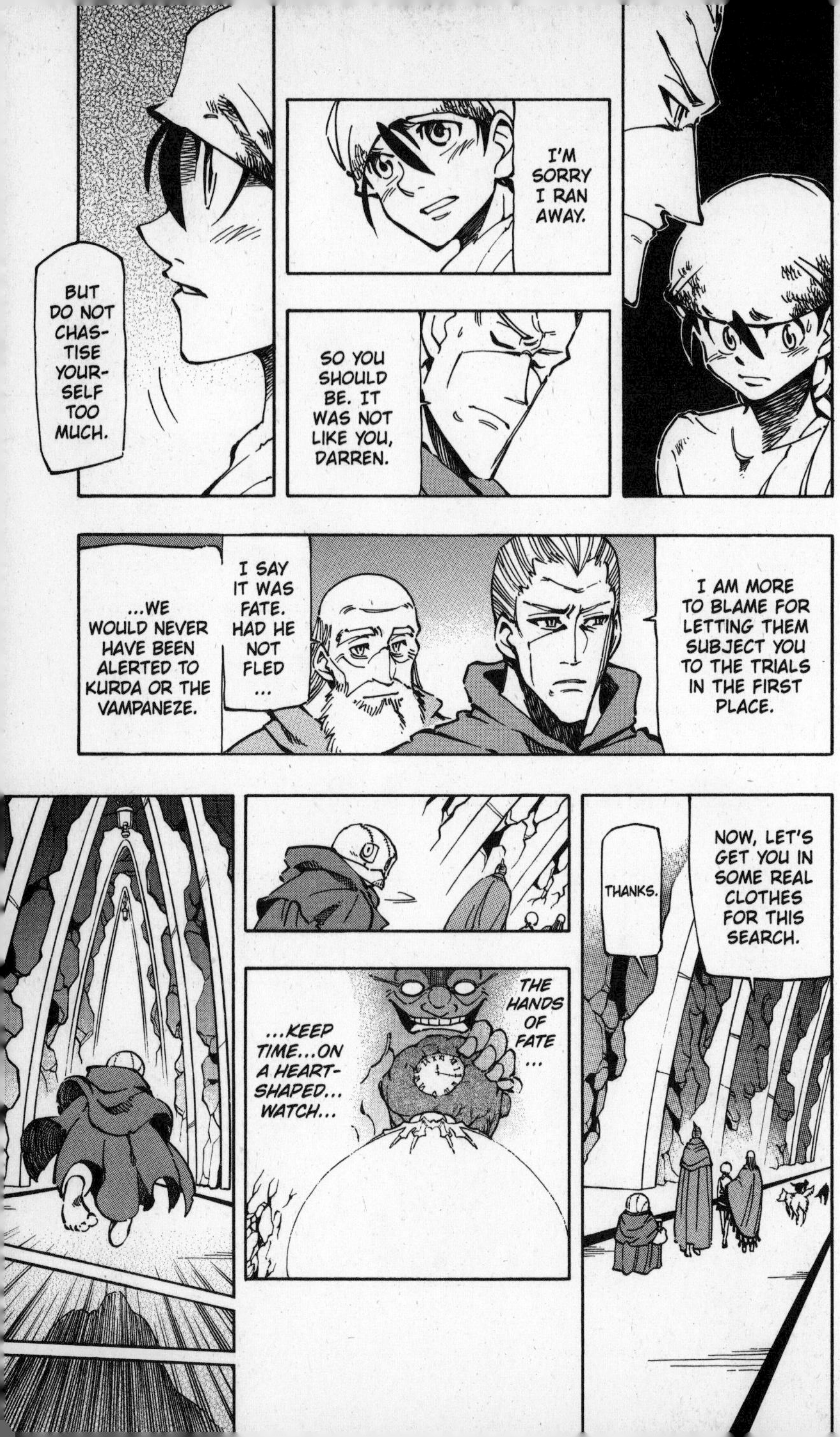
I'M SORRY I RAN AWAY.
SO YOU SHOULD BE. IT WAS NOT LIKE YOU, DARREN.
BUT DO NOT CHASTISE YOUR-SELF TOO MUCH.
I AM MORE TO BLAME FOR LETTING THEM SUBJECT YOU TO THE TRIALS IN THE FIRST PLACE.
I SAY IT WAS FATE. HAD HE NOT FLED ...
...WE WOULD NEVER HAVE BEEN ALERTED TO KURDA OR THE VAMPANEZE.
NOW, LET'S GET YOU IN SOME REAL CLOTHES FOR THIS SEARCH.
THANKS.
THE HANDS OF FATE ...
...KEEP TIME...ON A HEART-SHAPED... WATCH...

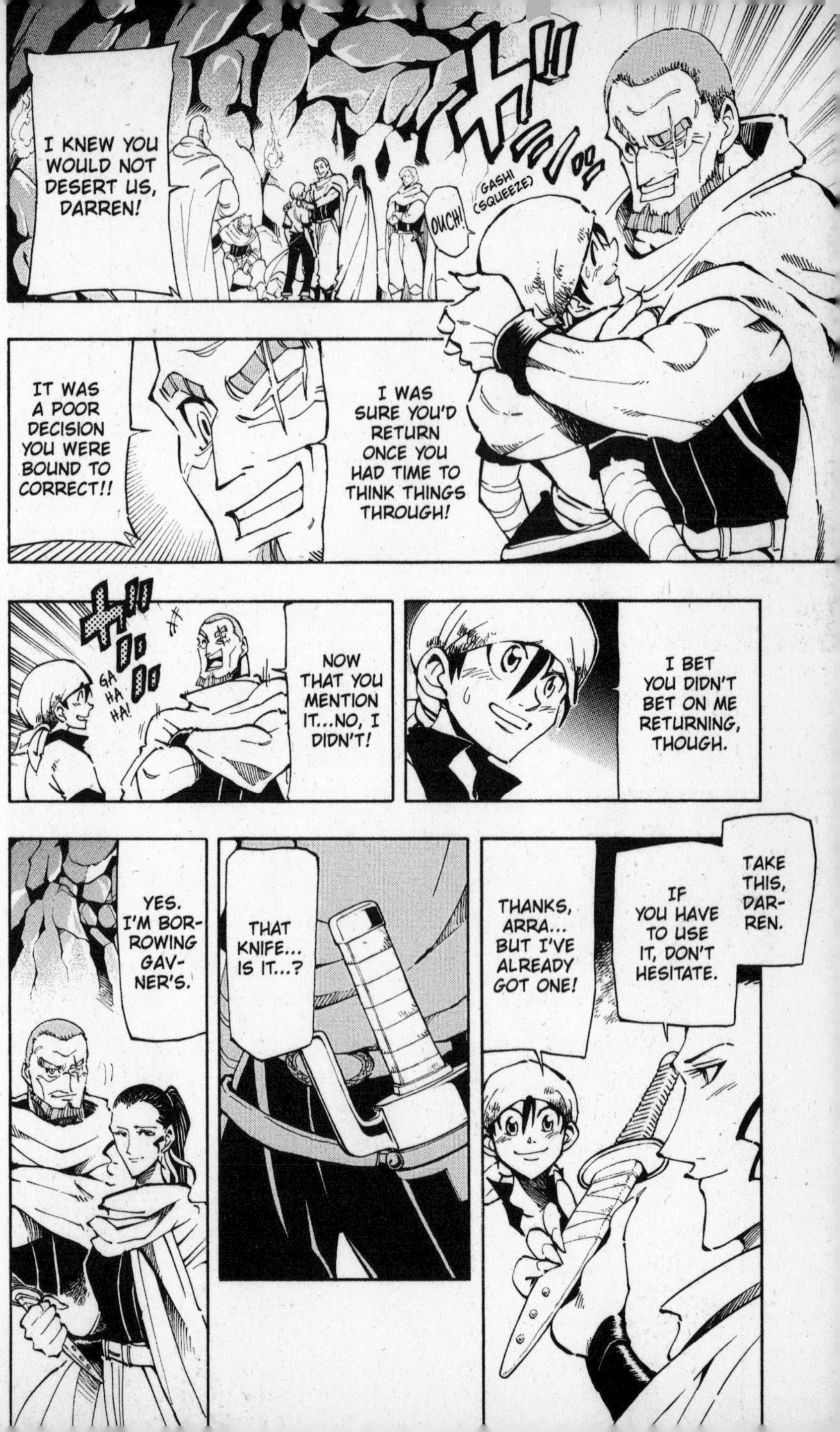
GASHI (SQUEEZE)
I KNEW YOU WOULD NOT DESERT US, DARREN!
OUCH!
I WAS SURE YOU'D RETURN ONCE YOU HAD TIME TO THINK THINGS THROUGH!
IT WAS A POOR DECISION YOU WERE BOUND TO CORRECT!!
I BET YOU DIDN'T BET ON ME RETURNING, THOUGH.
NOW THAT YOU MENTION IT...NO, I DIDN'T!
GA HA HA!
TAKE THIS, DAR-REN.
IF YOU HAVE TO USE IT, DON'T HESITATE.
THANKS, ARRA... BUT I'VE ALREADY GOT ONE!
THAT KNIFE... IS IT...?
YES. I'M BOR-ROWING GAV-NER'S.

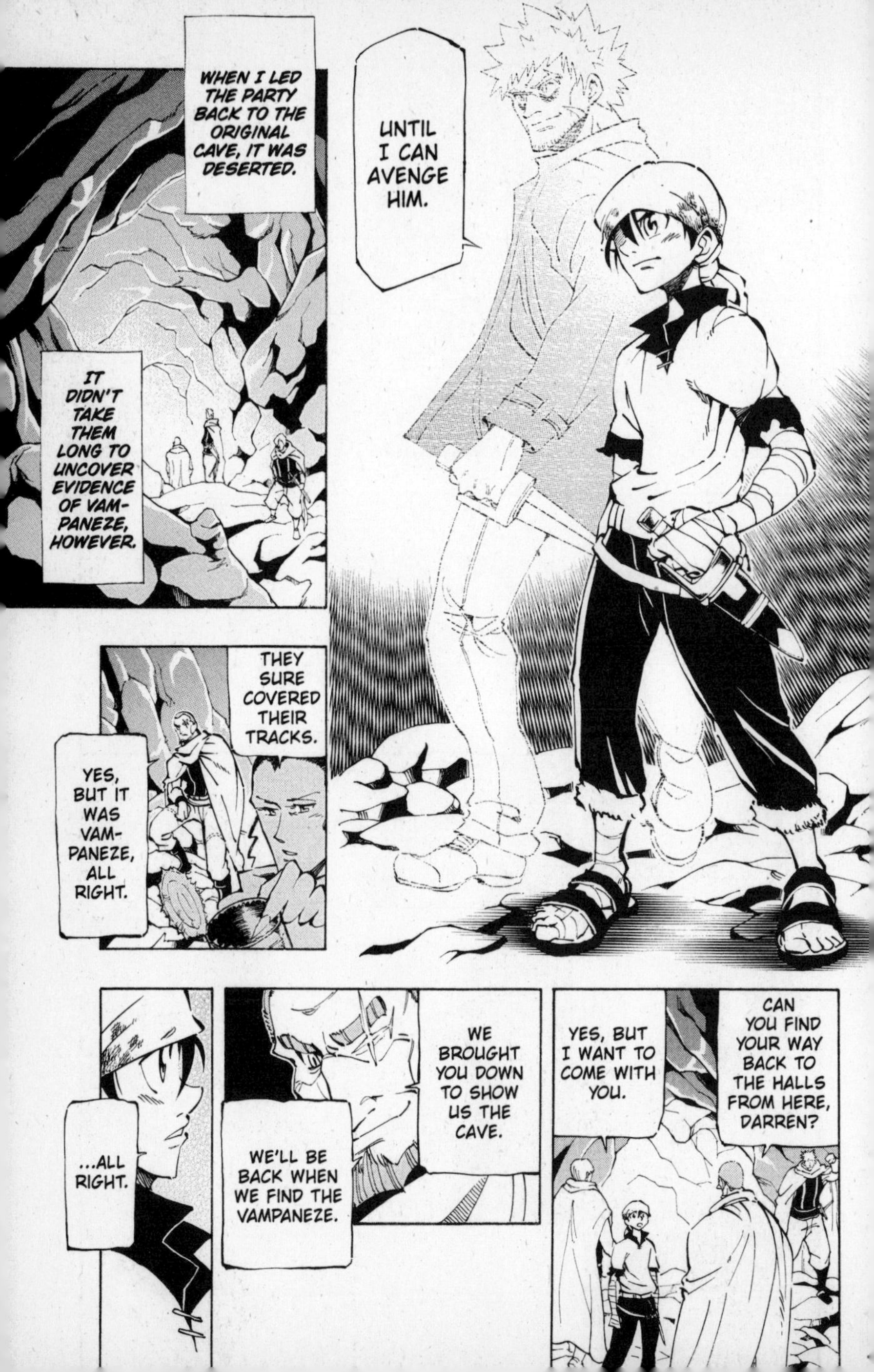
UNTIL I CAN AVENGE HIM.
WHEN I LED THE PARTY BACK TO THE ORIGINAL CAVE, IT WAS DESERTED.
IT DIDN'T TAKE THEM LONG TO UNCOVER EVIDENCE OF VAM-PANEZE, HOWEVER.
THEY SURE COVERED THEIR TRACKS.
YES, BUT IT WAS VAM-PANEZE, ALL RIGHT.
CAN YOU FIND YOUR WAY BACK TO THE HALLS FROM HERE, DARREN?
YES, BUT I WANT TO COME WITH YOU.
WE BROUGHT YOU DOWN TO SHOW US THE CAVE.
WE'LL BE BACK WHEN WE FIND THE VAMPANEZE.
...ALL RIGHT.

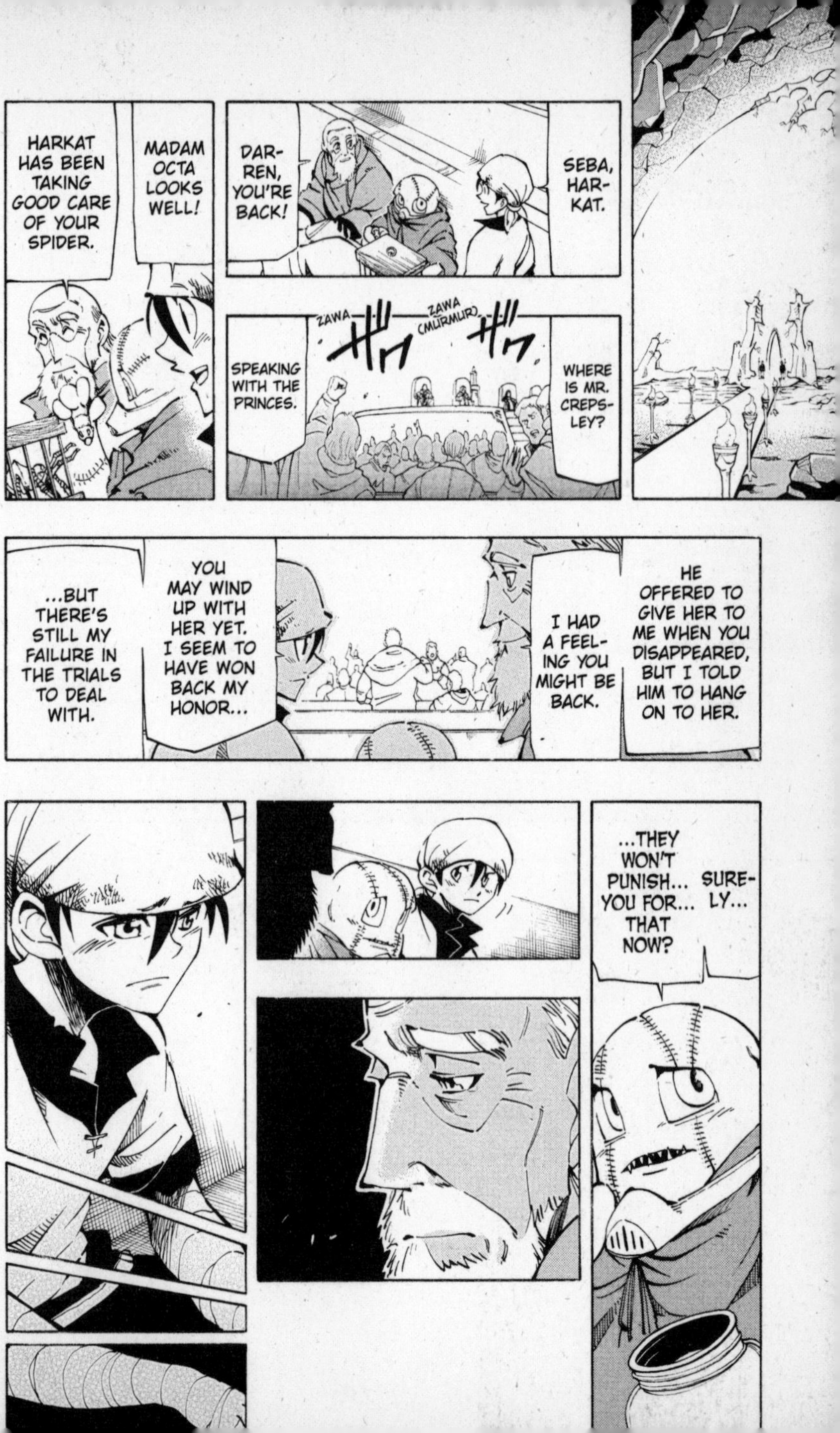
SEBA, HAR-KAT.
DAR-REN, YOU'RE BACK!
ZAWA
ZAWA (MURMUR)
WHERE IS MR. CREPS-LEY?
SPEAKING WITH THE PRINCES.
MADAM OCTA LOOKS WELL!
HARKAT HAS BEEN TAKING GOOD CARE OF YOUR SPIDER.
HE OFFERED TO GIVE HER TO ME WHEN YOU DISAPPEARED, BUT I TOLD HIM TO HANG ON TO HER.
I HAD A FEEL-ING YOU MIGHT BE BACK.
YOU MAY WIND UP WITH HER YET. I SEEM TO HAVE WON BACK MY HONOR...
...BUT THERE'S STILL MY FAILURE IN THE TRIALS TO DEAL WITH.
SURE-LY...
...THEY WON'T PUNISH... YOU FOR... THAT NOW?

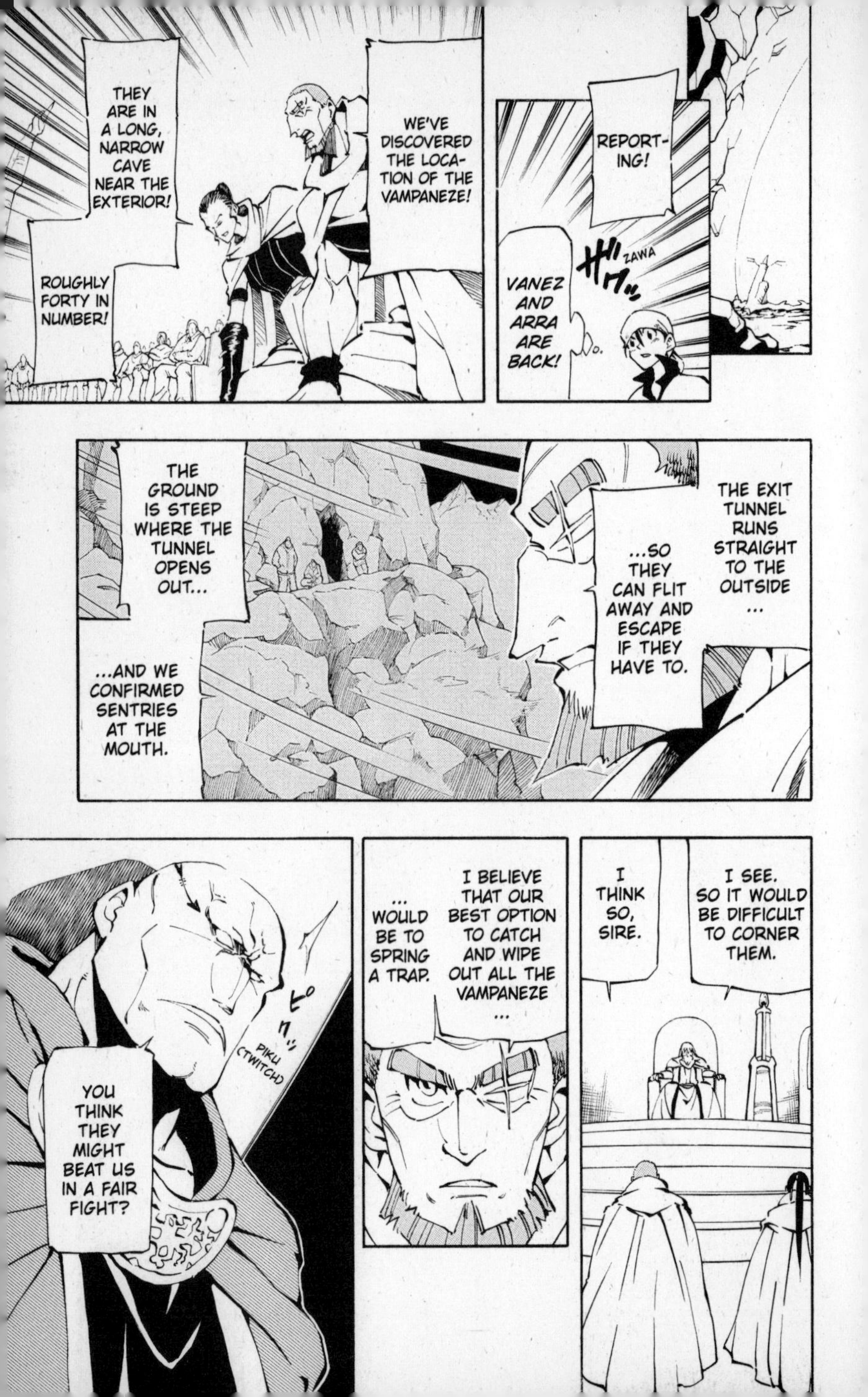
REPORTING!
ZAWA
VANEZ AND ARRA ARE BACK!
WE'VE DISCOVERED THE LOCATION OF THE VAMPANEZE!
THEY ARE IN A LONG, NARROW CAVE NEAR THE EXTERIOR!
ROUGHLY FORTY IN NUMBER!
THE EXIT TUNNEL RUNS STRAIGHT TO THE OUTSIDE ...
...SO THEY CAN FLIT AWAY AND ESCAPE IF THEY HAVE TO.
THE GROUND IS STEEP WHERE THE TUNNEL OPENS OUT...
...AND WE CONFIRMED SENTRIES AT THE MOUTH.
I SEE. SO IT WOULD BE DIFFICULT TO CORNER THEM.
I THINK SO, SIRE.
I BELIEVE THAT OUR BEST OPTION TO CATCH AND WIPE OUT ALL THE VAMPANEZE ...
... WOULD BE TO SPRING A TRAP.
PIKU (TWITCH)
YOU THINK THEY MIGHT BEAT US IN A FAIR FIGHT?

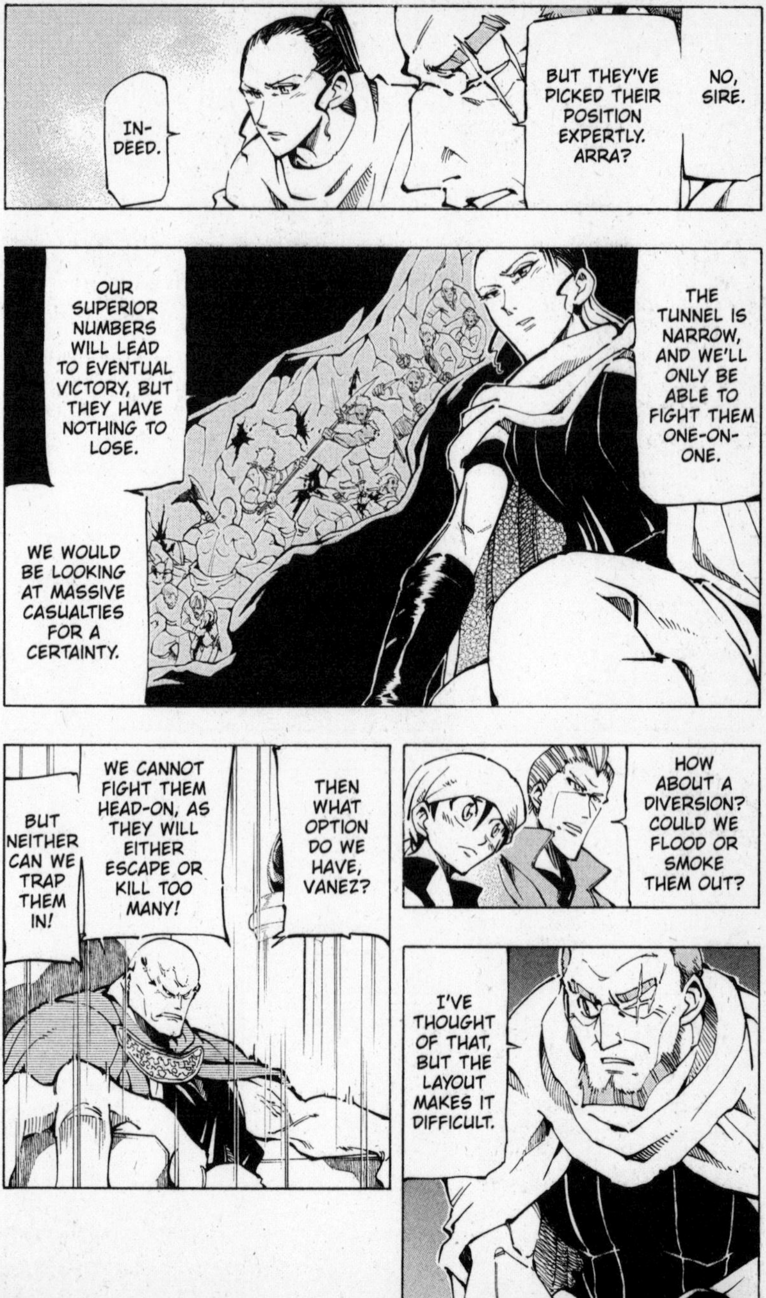
NO, SIRE.
BUT THEY'VE PICKED THEIR POSITION EXPERTLY. ARRA?
IN-DEED.
THE TUNNEL IS NARROW, AND WE'LL ONLY BE ABLE TO FIGHT THEM ONE-ON-ONE.
OUR SUPERIOR NUMBERS WILL LEAD TO EVENTUAL VICTORY, BUT THEY HAVE NOTHING TO LOSE.
WE WOULD BE LOOKING AT MASSIVE CASUALTIES FOR A CERTAINTY.
HOW ABOUT A DIVERSION? COULD WE FLOOD OR SMOKE THEM OUT?
I'VE THOUGHT OF THAT, BUT THE LAYOUT MAKES IT DIFFICULT.
THEN WHAT OPTION DO WE HAVE, VANEZ?
WE CANNOT FIGHT THEM HEAD-ON, AS THEY WILL EITHER ESCAPE OR KILL TOO MANY!
BUT NEITHER CAN WE TRAP THEM IN!

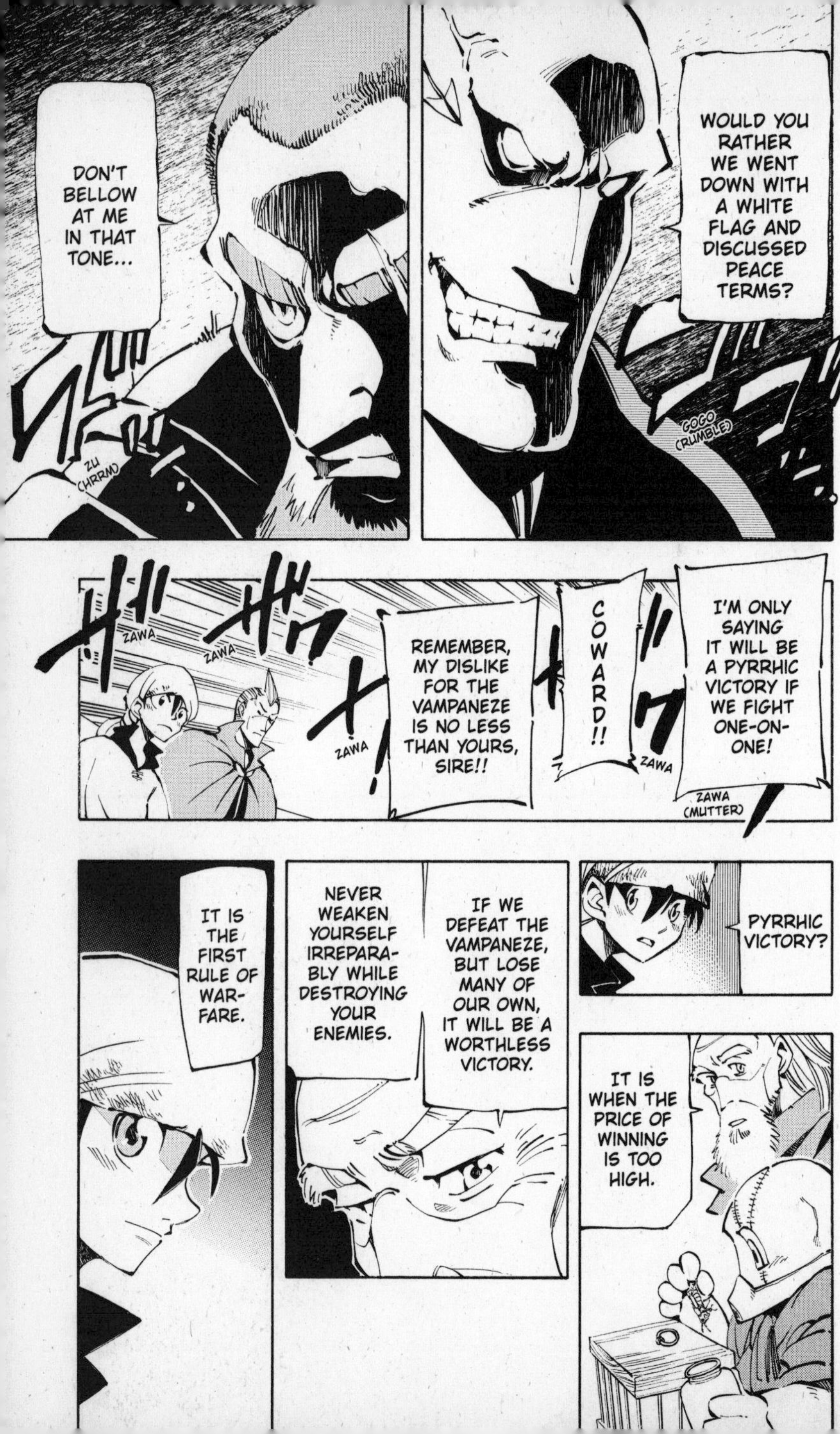
WOULD YOU RATHER WE WENT DOWN WITH A WHITE FLAG AND DISCUSSED PEACE TERMS?
GOGO (RUMBLE)
DON'T BELLOW AT ME IN THAT TONE...
ZU (HRRM)
I'M ONLY SAYING IT WILL BE A PYRRHIC VICTORY IF WE FIGHT ONE-ON-ONE!
ZAWA (MUTTER)
ZAWA
COWARD!!
REMEMBER, MY DISLIKE FOR THE VAMPANEZE IS NO LESS THAN YOURS, SIRE!!
ZAWA
ZAWA
ZAWA
PYRRHIC VICTORY?
IT IS WHEN THE PRICE OF WINNING IS TOO HIGH.
IF WE DEFEAT THE VAMPANEZE, BUT LOSE MANY OF OUR OWN, IT WILL BE A WORTHLESS VICTORY.
NEVER WEAKEN YOURSELF IRREPARABLY WHILE DESTROYING YOUR ENEMIES.
IT IS THE FIRST RULE OF WARFARE.

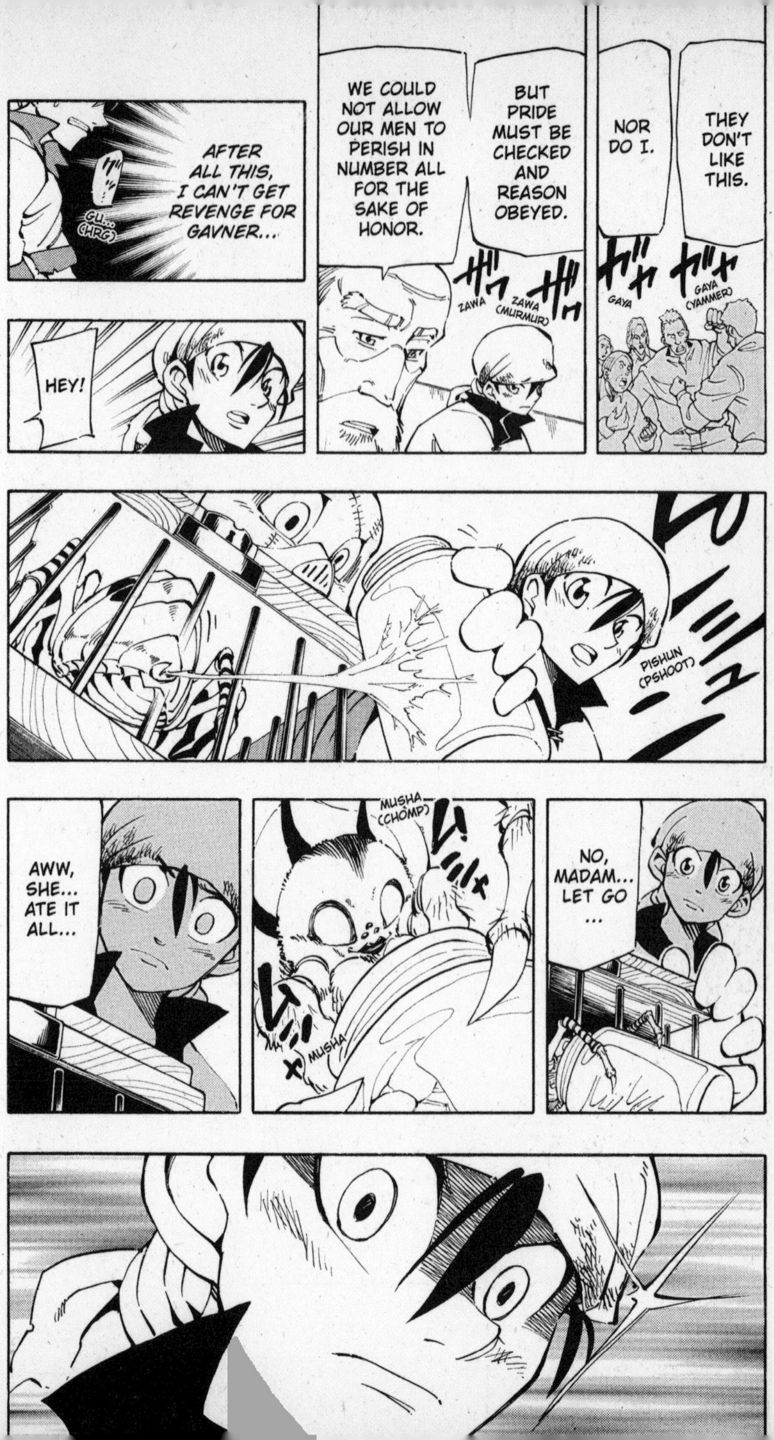

THEY DON'T LIKE THIS.
NOR DO I.
GAYA
GAYA (YAMMER)
WE COULD NOT ALLOW OUR MEN TO PERISH IN NUMBER ALL FOR THE SAKE OF HONOR.
BUT PRIDE MUST BE CHECKED AND REASON OBEYED.
ZAWA (MURMUR)
ZAWA
AFTER ALL THIS, I CAN'T GET REVENGE FOR GAVNER...
GU... (HRG)
HEY!
PISHUN (PSHOOT)
NO, MADAM... LET GO ...
MUSHA (CHOMP)
MUSHA
AWW, SHE... ATE IT ALL...

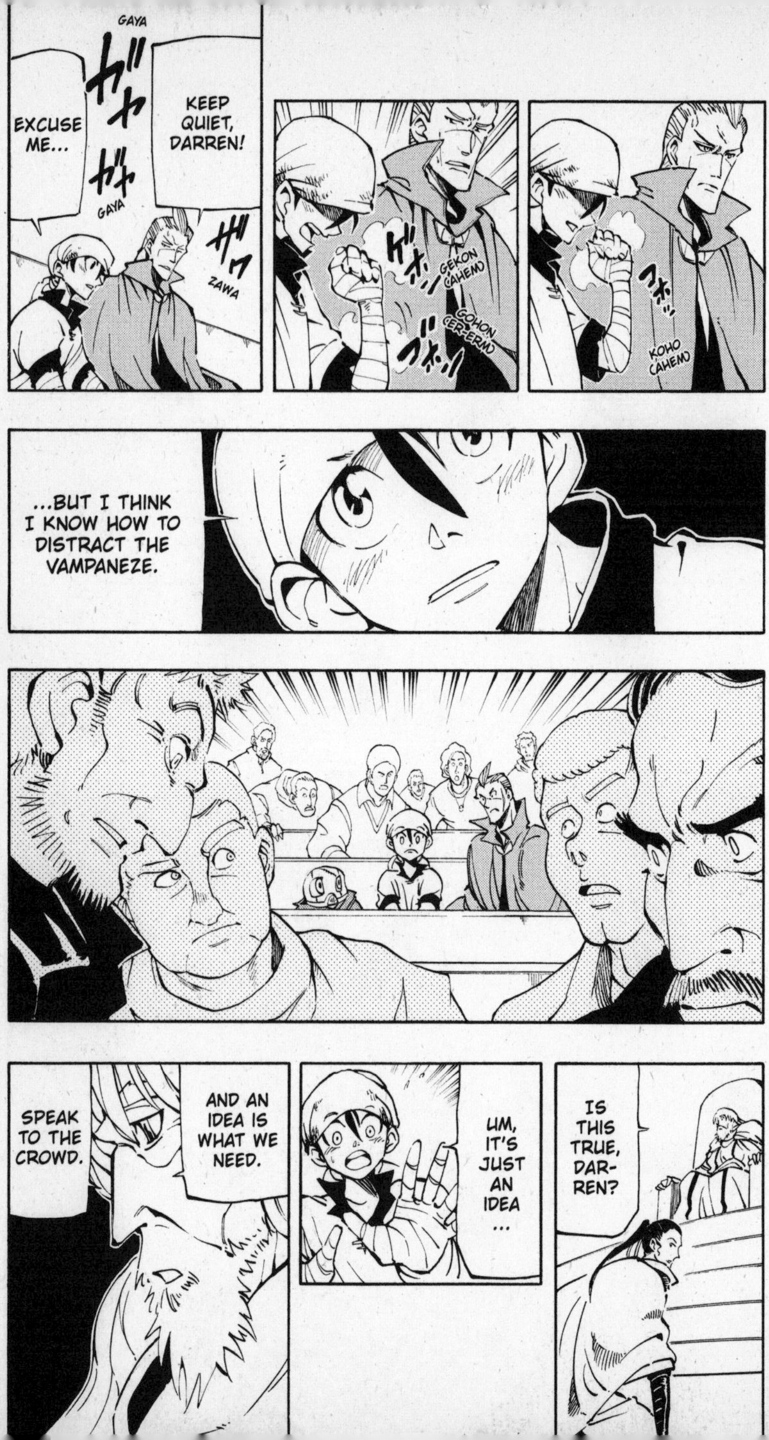
KOHO (AHEM)
GEKON (AHEM)
GOHON (ER-ERM)
KEEP QUIET, DARREN!
GAYA
EXCUSE ME...
GAYA
ZAWA
...BUT I THINK I KNOW HOW TO DISTRACT THE VAMPANEZE.
IS THIS TRUE, DAR-REN?
UM, IT'S JUST AN IDEA ...
AND AN IDEA IS WHAT WE NEED.
SPEAK TO THE CROWD.

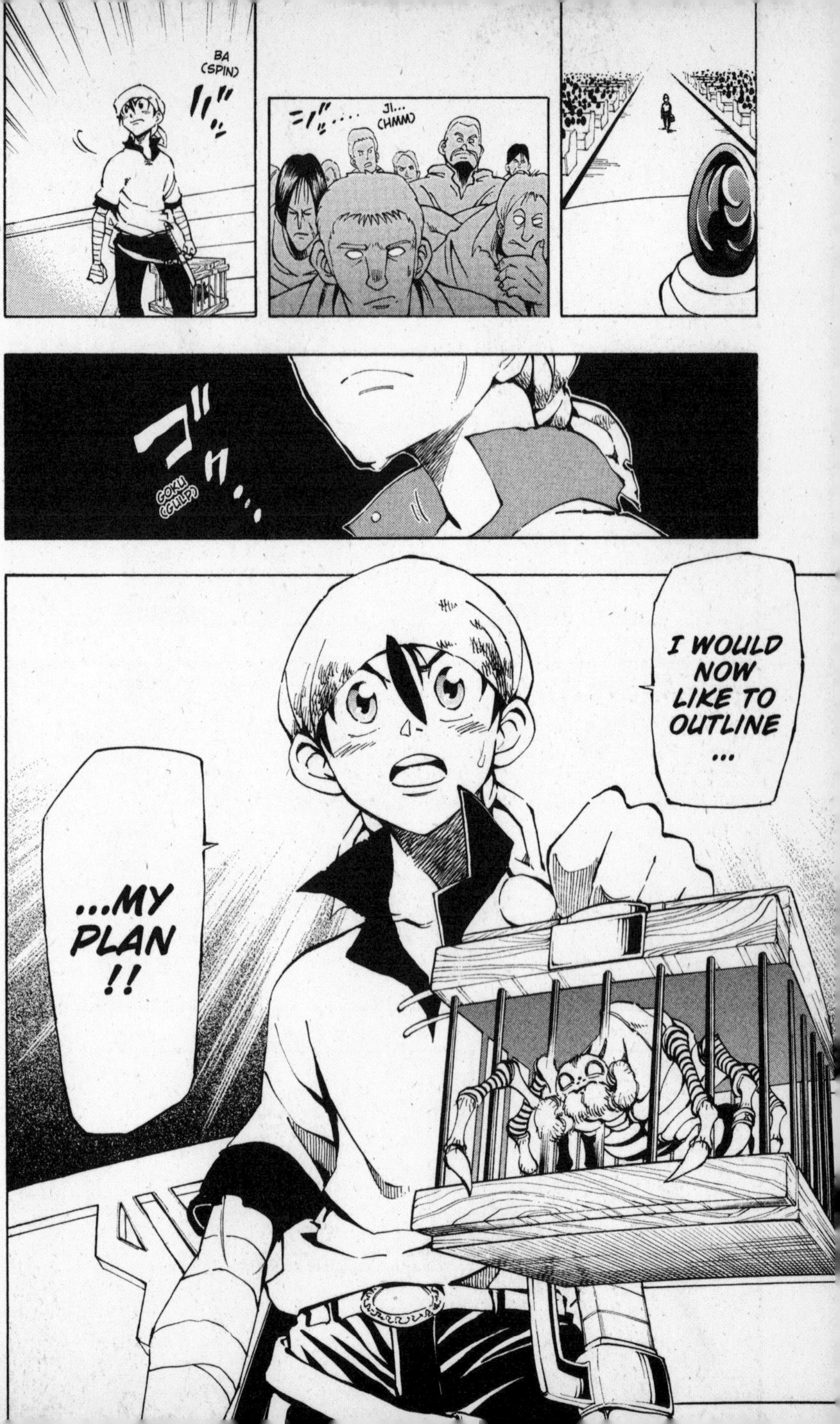
JI... (HMM)
BA (SPIN)
GOKU (GULP)
I WOULD NOW LIKE TO OUTLINE ...
...MY PLAN !!

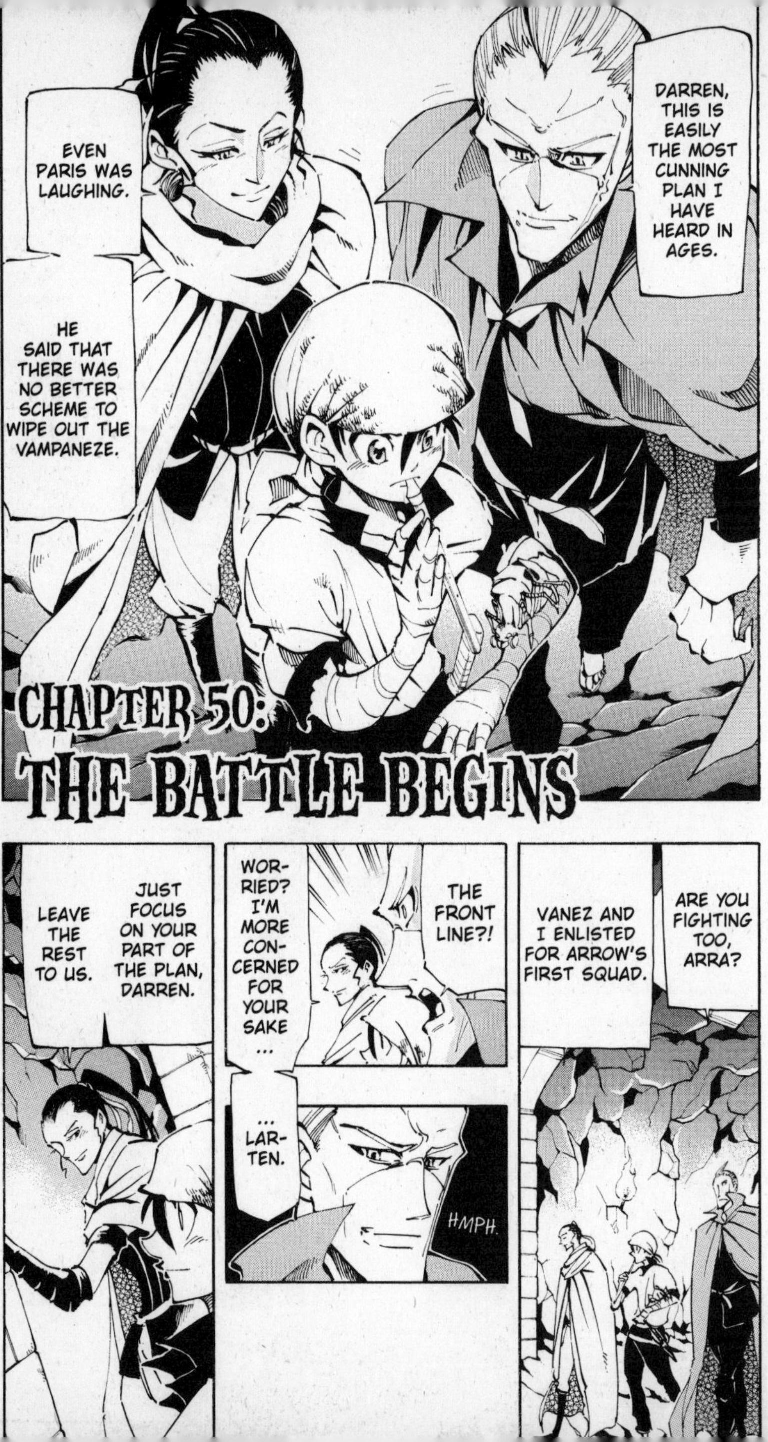
DARREN, THIS IS EASILY THE MOST CUNNING PLAN I HAVE HEARD IN AGES.
EVEN PARIS WAS LAUGHING.
HE SAID THAT THERE WAS NO BETTER SCHEME TO WIPE OUT THE VAMPANEZE.
CHAPTER 50: THE BATTLE BEGINS
ARE YOU FIGHTING TOO, ARRA?
VANEZ AND I ENLISTED FOR ARROW'S FIRST SQUAD.
THE FRONT LINE?!
WORRIED? I'M MORE CONCERNED FOR YOUR SAKE ...
... LARTEN.
HMPH.
JUST FOCUS ON YOUR PART OF THE PLAN, DARREN.
LEAVE THE REST TO US.

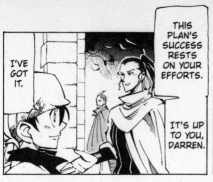

SEBA AND I SHALL WORK WITHIN THE TUNNEL.
YOU WILL START FROM THE OUT-SIDE.
BE CAREFUL, DARREN.
THIS PLAN'S SUCCESS RESTS ON YOUR EFFORTS.
IT'S UP TO YOU, DARREN.
I'VE GOT IT.
LUCK TO YOU.
YOU TOO, ARRA.
KOSO (SNEAK)
THAT'S THE MOUTH OF THE TUNNEL THE VAMPANEZE ARE IN.
BUT NOW THE SUN IS SHINING ON IT.
SFX: DOKI (BA-BUMP) DOKI
WE MUST ATTACK BY DAY TO PREVENT THEM FROM ESCAPING!
AND I'M THE ONLY HALF-VAMPIRE, CAPABLE OF MOVING UNDER DAYLIGHT.

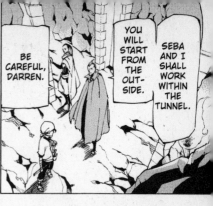

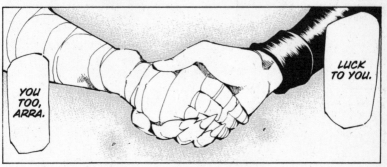

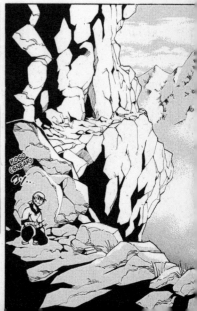

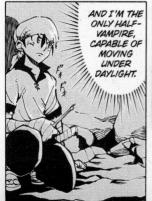

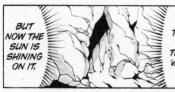

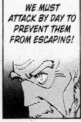

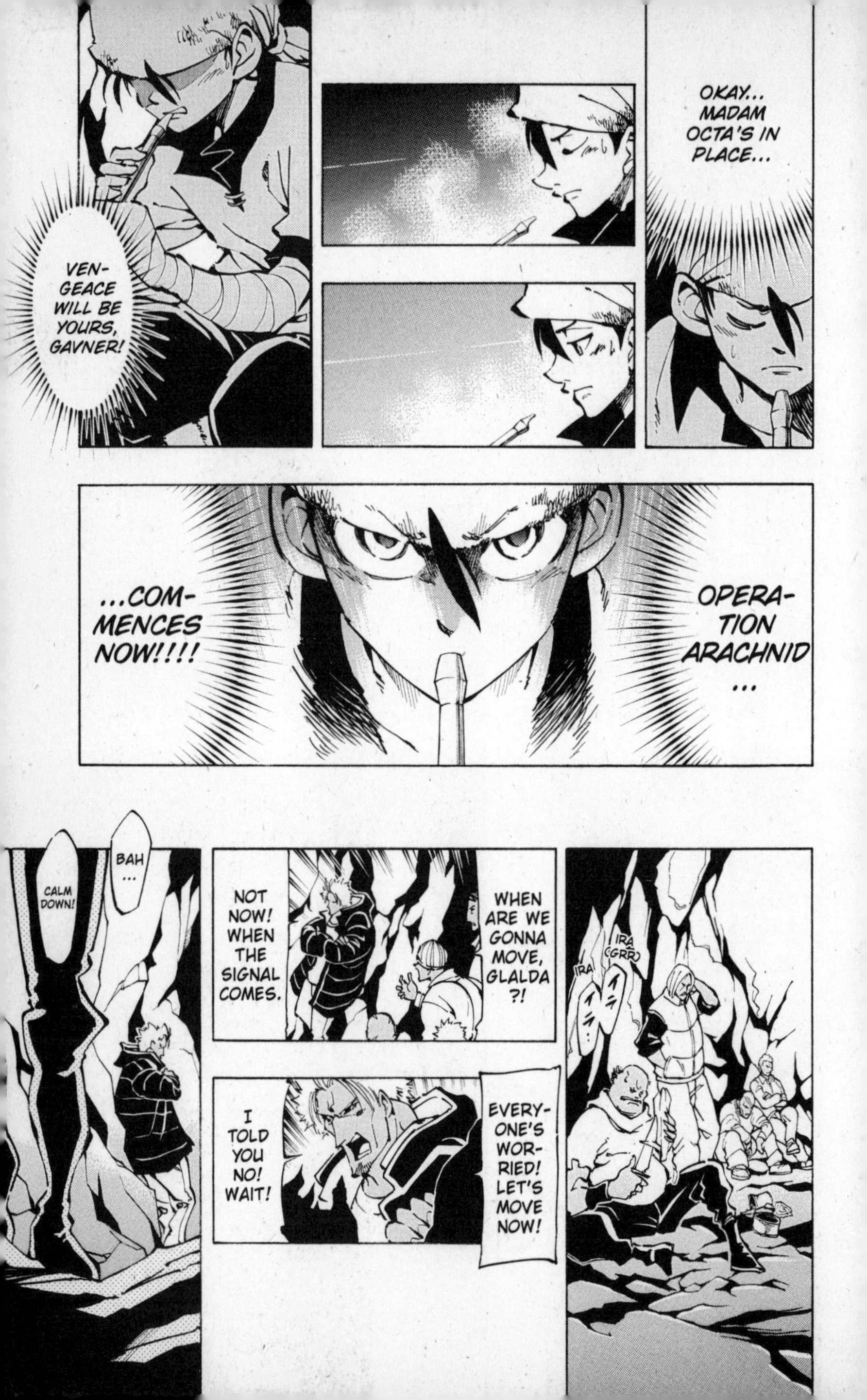
OKAY... MADAM OCTA'S IN PLACE...
VENGEACE WILL BE YOURS, GAVNER!
OPERATION ARACHNID ...
...COMMENCES NOW!!!!
IRA (GRR)
IRA
WHEN ARE WE GONNA MOVE, GLALDA?!
NOT NOW! WHEN THE SIGNAL COMES.
EVERYONE'S WORRIED! LET'S MOVE NOW!
I TOLD YOU NO! WAIT!
BAH ...
CALM DOWN!

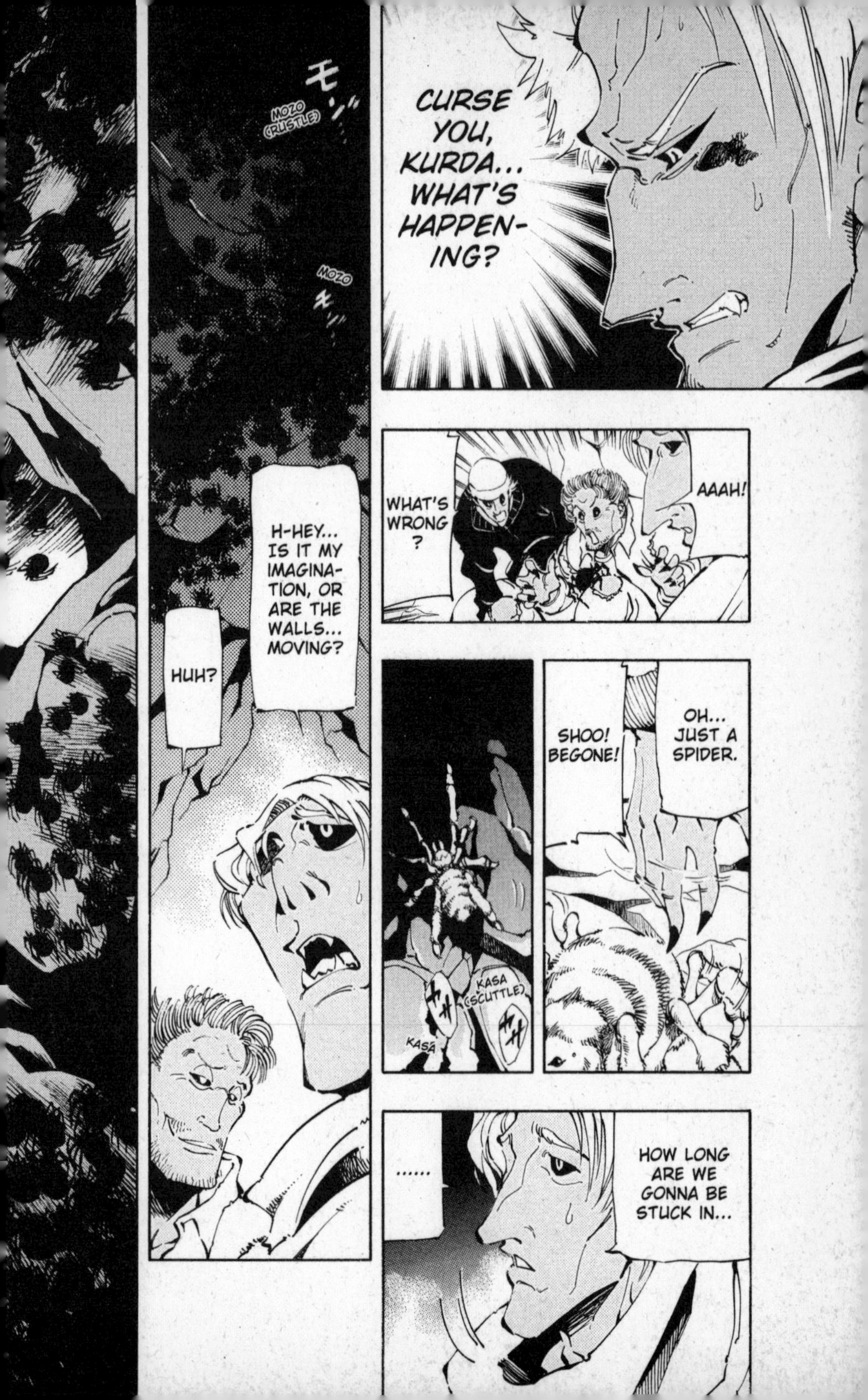
CURSE YOU, KURDA... WHAT'S HAPPENING?
AAAH!
WHAT'S WRONG?
OH... JUST A SPIDER.
SHOO! BEGONE!
KASA (SCUTTLE)
KASA
HOW LONG ARE WE GONNA BE STUCK IN...
......
MOZO (RUSTLE)
MOZO
H-HEY... IS IT MY IMAGINATION, OR ARE THE WALLS... MOVING?
HUH?

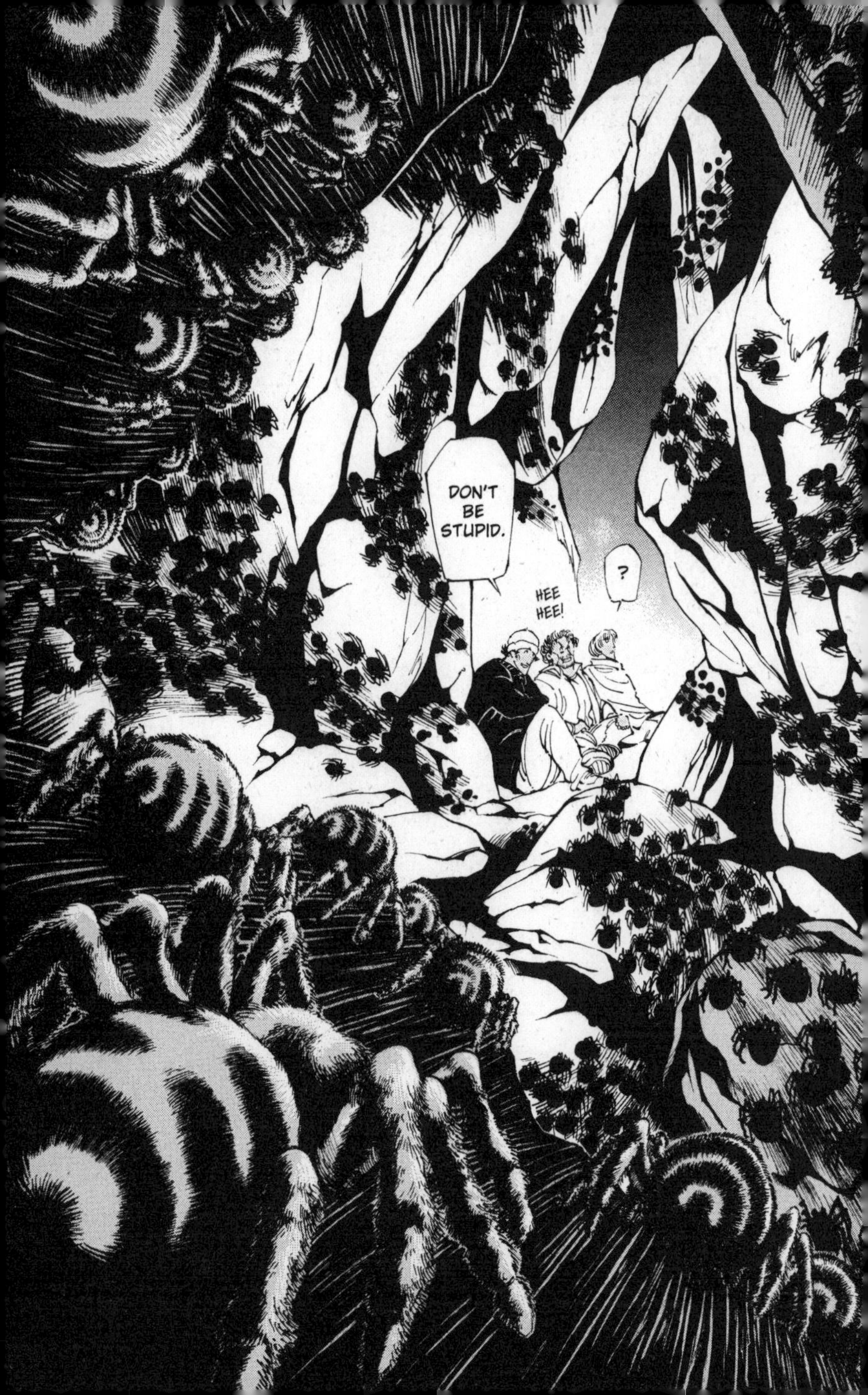
?
HEE HEE!
DON'T BE STUPID.

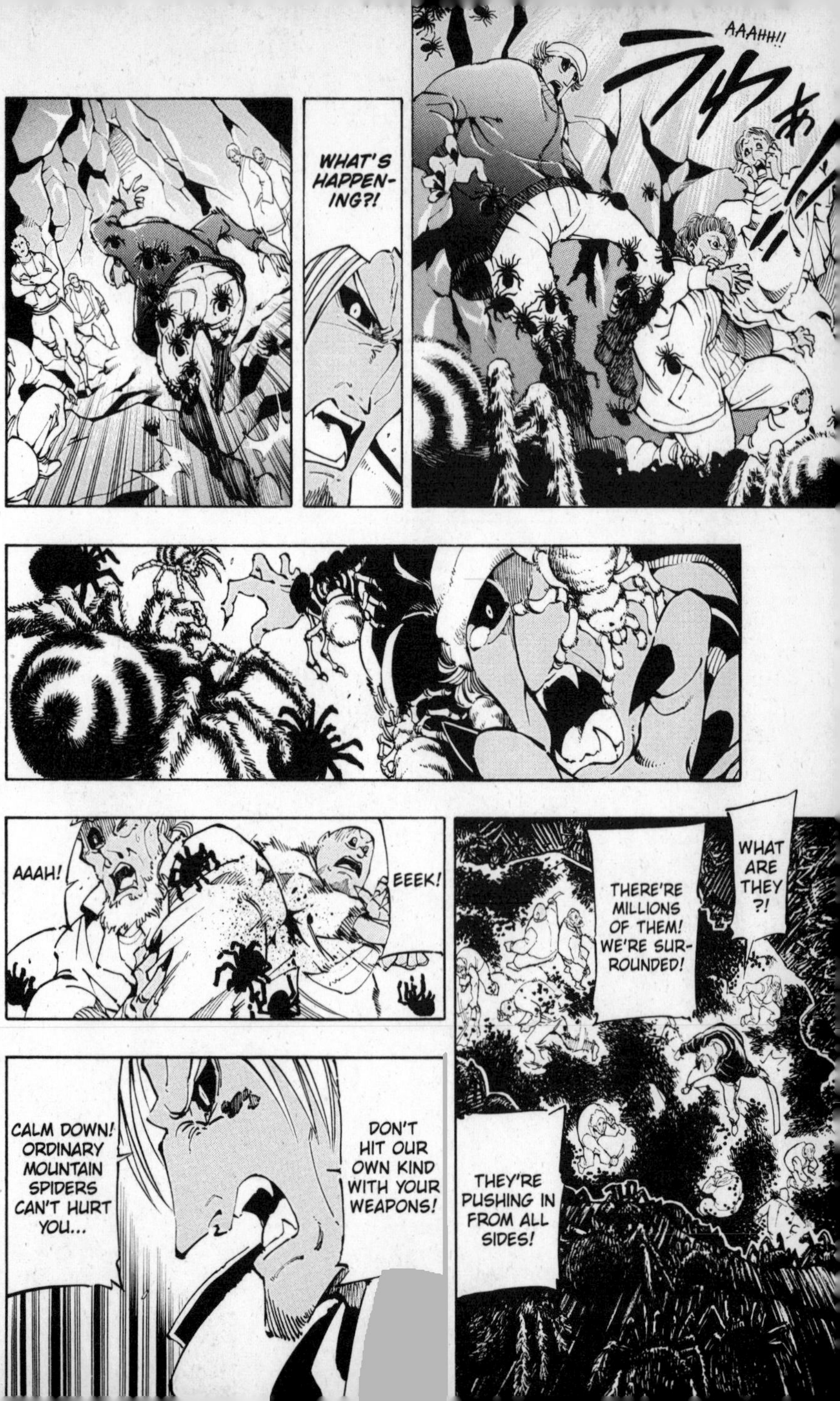
AAAHH!!
WHAT'S HAPPEN-ING?!
WHAT ARE THEY ?!
THERE'RE MILLIONS OF THEM! WE'RE SUR-ROUNDED!
THEY'RE PUSHING IN FROM ALL SIDES!
EEEK!
AAAH!
DON'T HIT OUR OWN KIND WITH YOUR WEAPONS!
CALM DOWN! ORDINARY MOUNTAIN SPIDERS CAN'T HURT YOU...

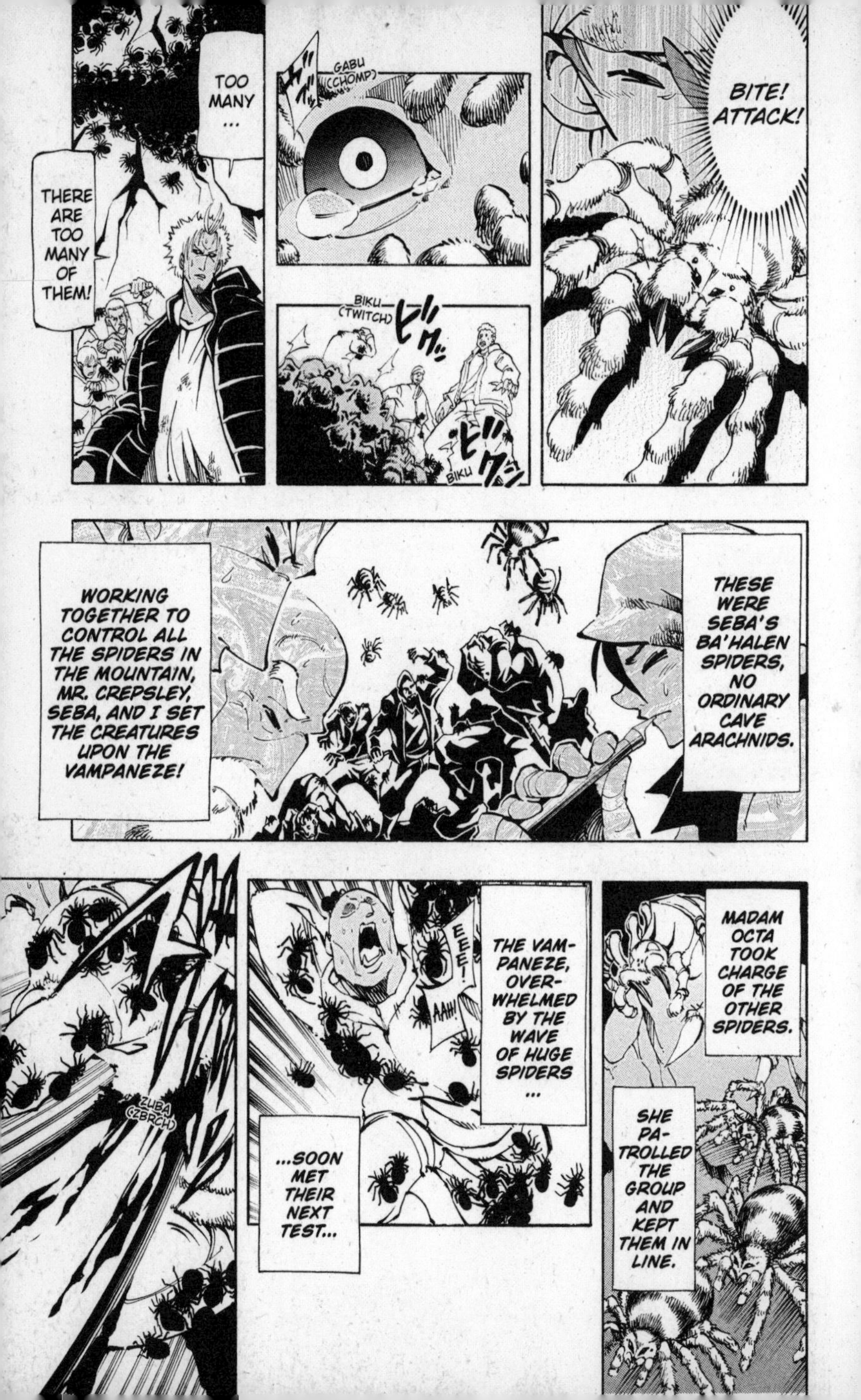
BITE! ATTACK!
GABU (CHOMP)
BIKU (TWITCH)
BIKU
TOO MANY ...
THERE ARE TOO MANY OF THEM!
THESE WERE SEBA'S BA'HALEN SPIDERS, NO ORDINARY CAVE ARACHNIDS.
WORKING TOGETHER TO CONTROL ALL THE SPIDERS IN THE MOUNTAIN, MR. CREPSLEY, SEBA, AND I SET THE CREATURES UPON THE VAMPANEZE!
MADAM OCTA TOOK CHARGE OF THE OTHER SPIDERS.
SHE PATROLLED THE GROUP AND KEPT THEM IN LINE.
THE VAMPANEZE, OVERWHELMED BY THE WAVE OF HUGE SPIDERS ...
EEE!
AAH!
...SOON MET THEIR NEXT TEST...
ZUBA (ZBRCH)

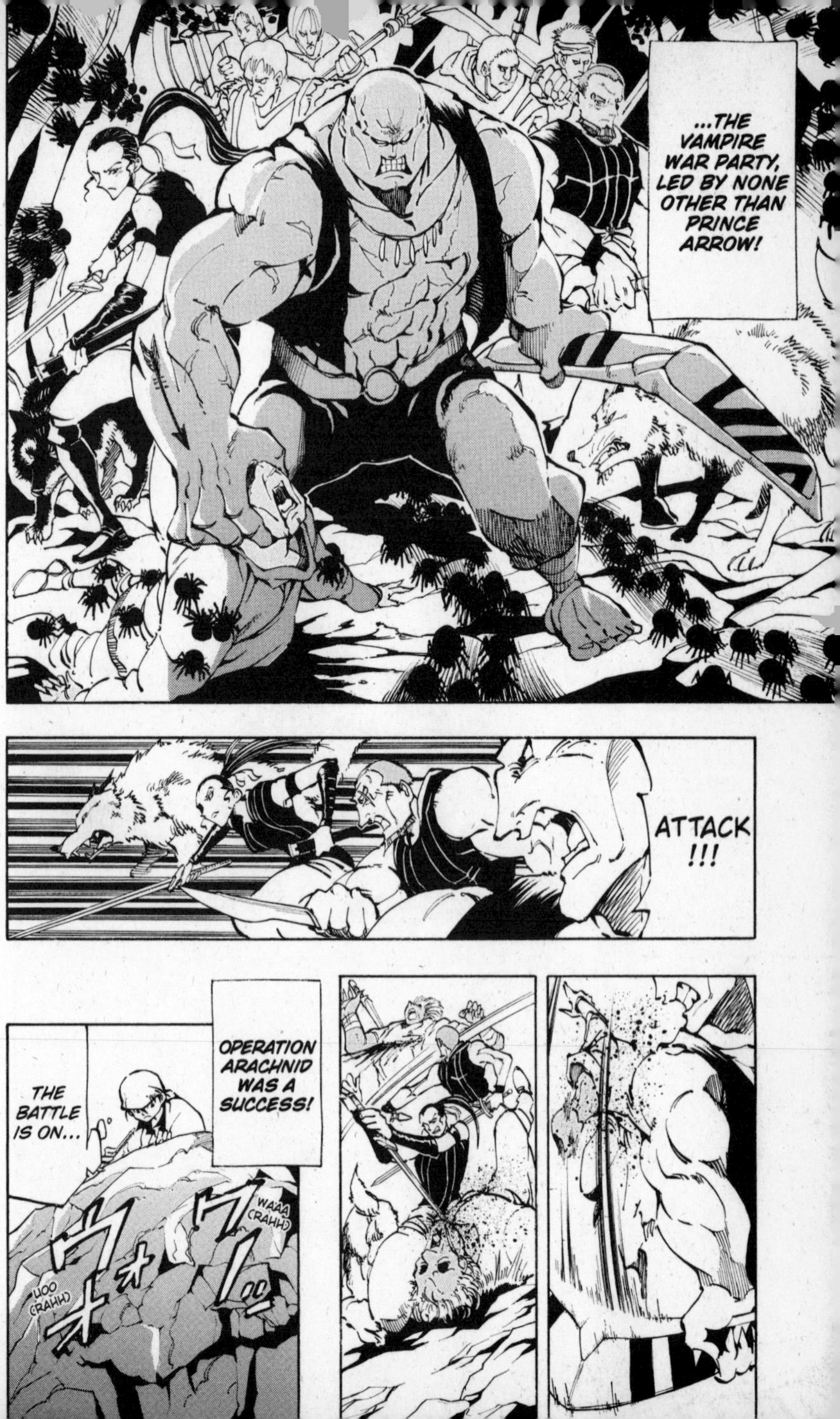
...THE VAMPIRE WAR PARTY, LED BY NONE OTHER THAN PRINCE ARROW!
ATTACK !!!
OPERATION ARACHNID WAS A SUCCESS!
THE BATTLE IS ON...
WAAA (RAHH)
UOO (RAHH)

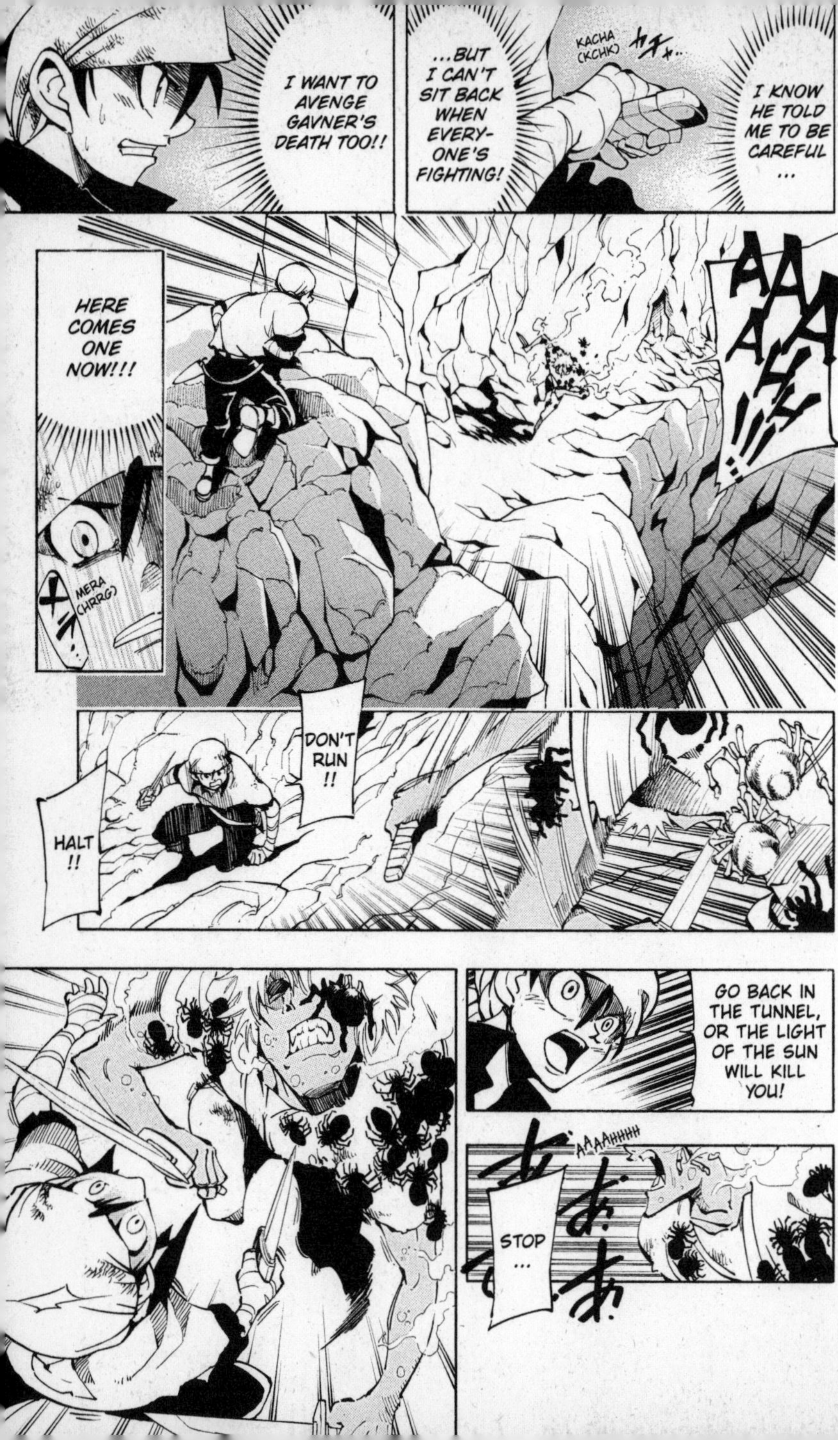
I KNOW HE TOLD ME TO BE CAREFUL ...
KACHA (KCHK)
...BUT I CAN'T SIT BACK WHEN EVERY-ONE'S FIGHTING!
I WANT TO AVENGE GAVNER'S DEATH TOO!!
AAAAHH!!!!
HERE COMES ONE NOW!!!
MERA (HRRG)
DON'T RUN !!
HALT !!
GO BACK IN THE TUNNEL, OR THE LIGHT OF THE SUN WILL KILL YOU!
AAAAHHHH
STOP ...

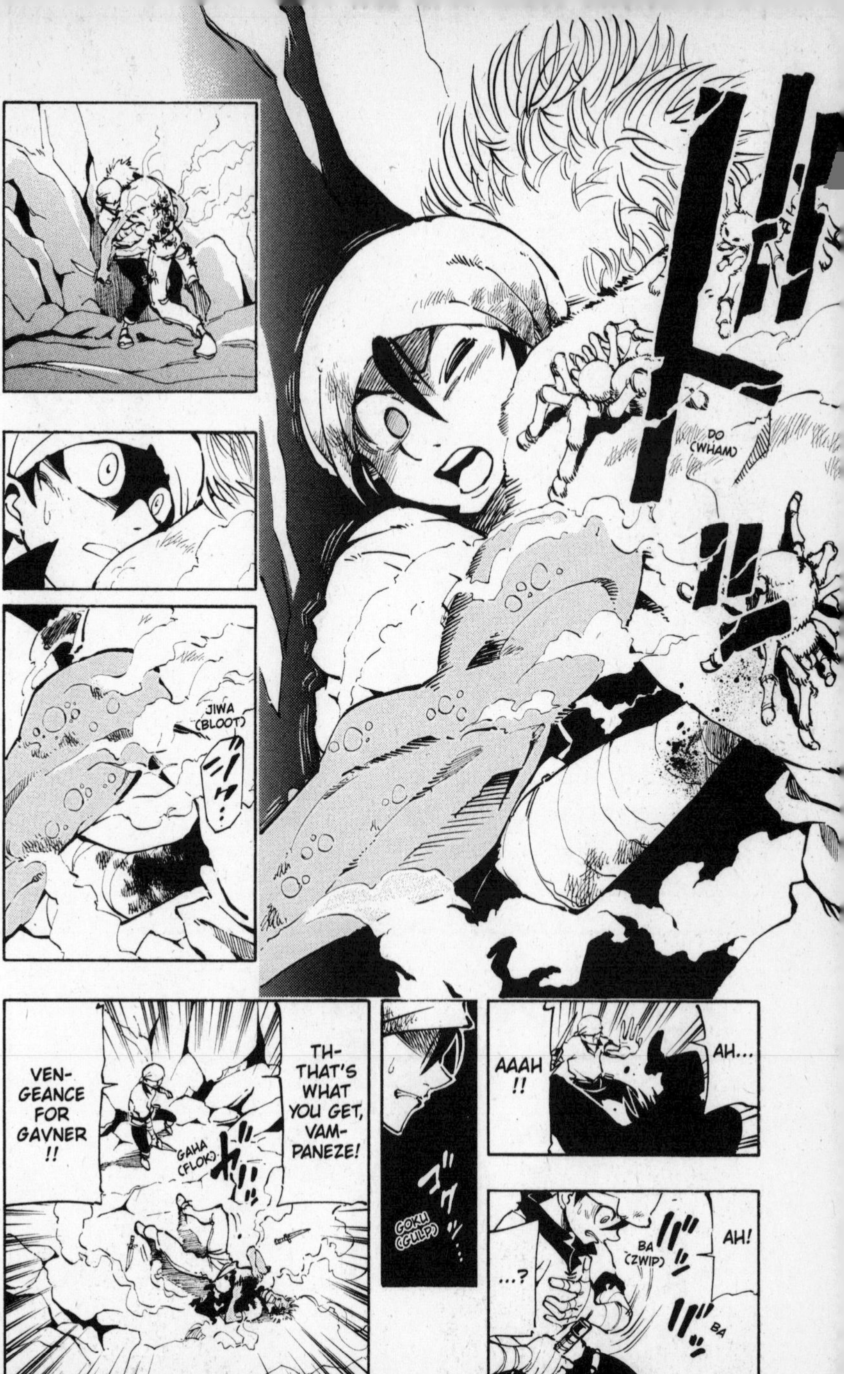
DO (WHAM)
JIWA (BLOOT)
AH...
AAAH !!
AH!
BA (ZWIP)
...?
BA
GOKU (GULP)
TH-THAT'S WHAT YOU GET, VAMPANEZE!
VENGEANCE FOR GAVNER !!
GAHA (FLOK)

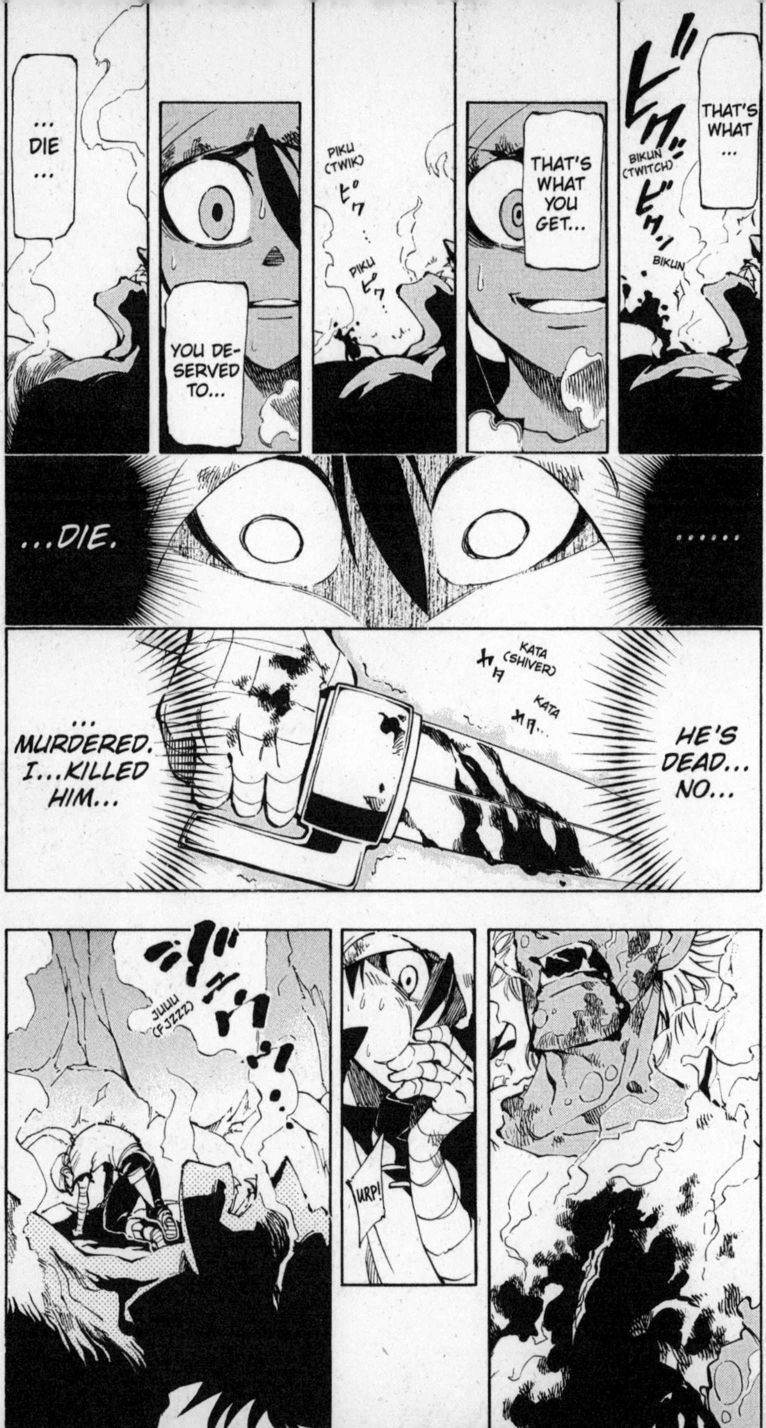
THAT'S WHAT ...
BIKUN (TWITCH)
BIKUN
THAT'S WHAT YOU GET...
PIKU (TWIK)
PIKU
YOU DE-SERVED TO...
... DIE ...
......
...DIE.
HE'S DEAD... NO...
KATA (SHIVER)
KATA
... MURDERED. I...KILLED HIM...
URP!
JUUU (FJZZZ)

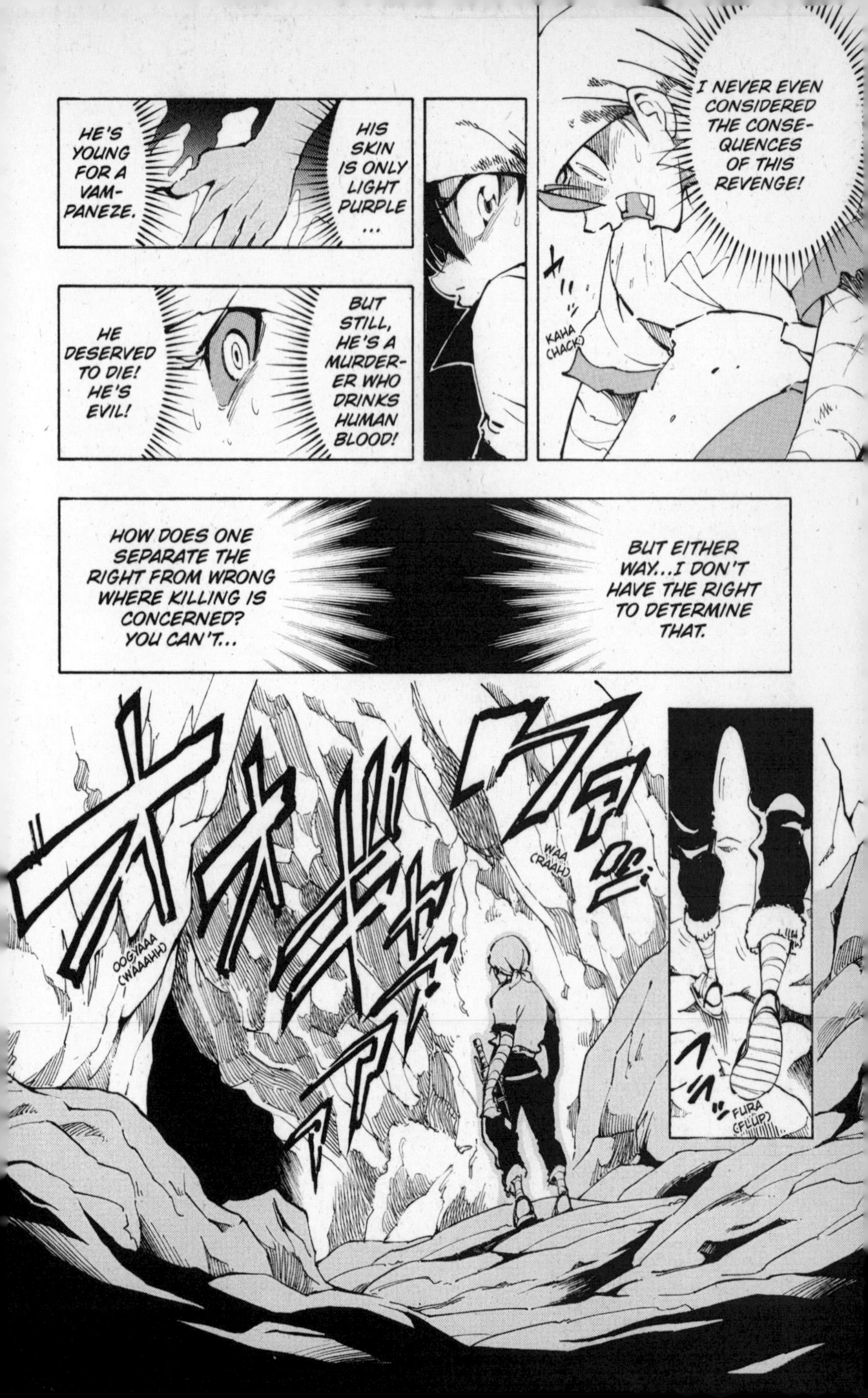
I NEVER EVEN CONSIDERED THE CONSE-QUENCES OF THIS REVENGE!
KAHA (HACK)
HIS SKIN IS ONLY LIGHT PURPLE ...
HE'S YOUNG FOR A VAM-PANEZE.
BUT STILL, HE'S A MURDER-ER WHO DRINKS HUMAN BLOOD!
HE DESERVED TO DIE! HE'S EVIL!
BUT EITHER WAY...I DON'T HAVE THE RIGHT TO DETERMINE THAT.
HOW DOES ONE SEPARATE THE RIGHT FROM WRONG WHERE KILLING IS CONCERNED? YOU CAN'T...
FURA (FLUP)
WAA (RAAH)
OOGYAAA (WAAAHH)

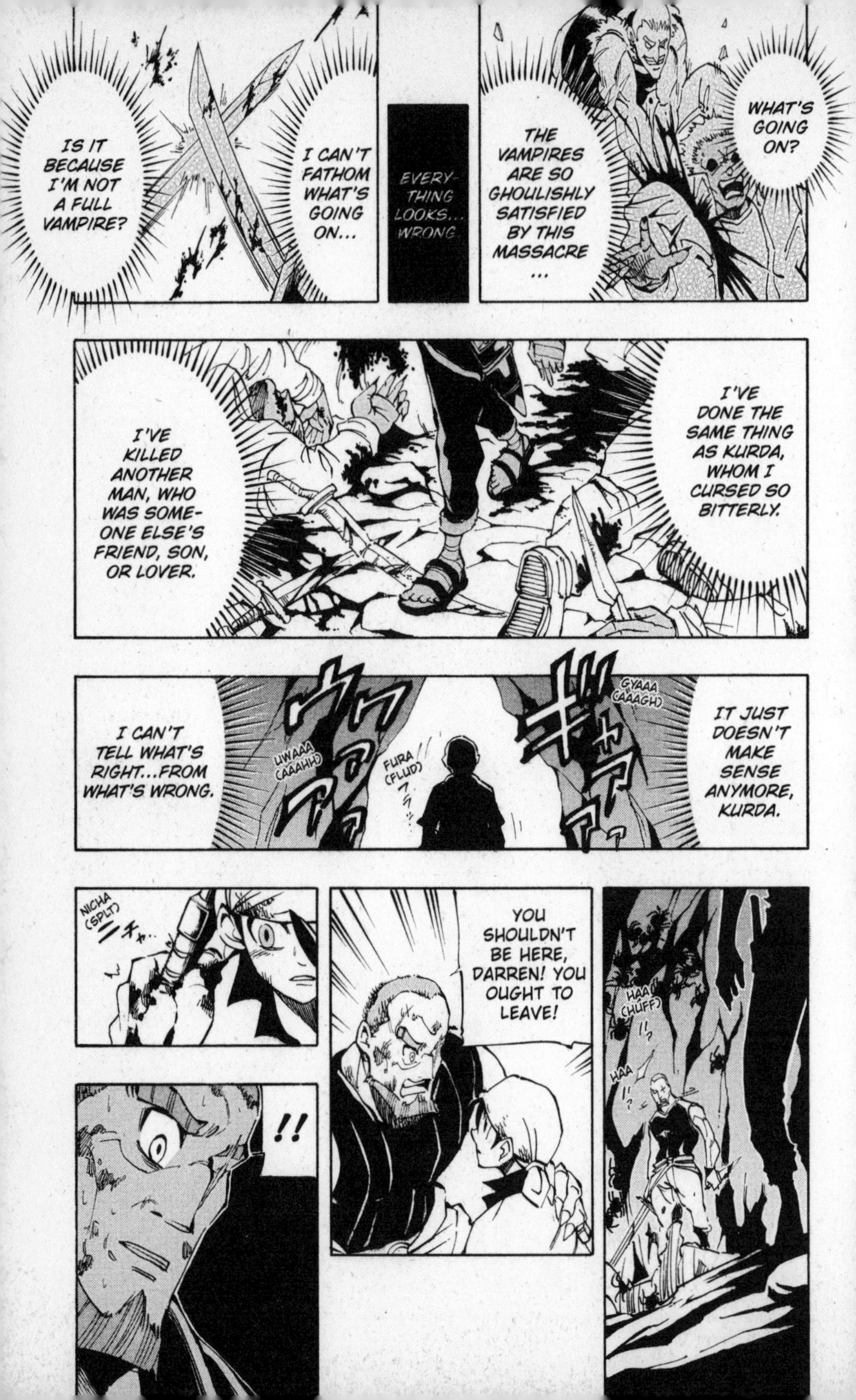

WHAT'S GOING ON?
THE VAMPIRES ARE SO GHOULISHLY SATISFIED BY THIS MASSACRE...
EVERYTHING LOOKS... WRONG.
I CAN'T FATHOM WHAT'S GOING ON...
IS IT BECAUSE I'M NOT A FULL VAMPIRE?
I'VE DONE THE SAME THING AS KURDA, WHOM I CURSED SO BITTERLY.
I'VE KILLED ANOTHER MAN, WHO WAS SOMEONE ELSE'S FRIEND, SON, OR LOVER.
IT JUST DOESN'T MAKE SENSE ANYMORE, KURDA.
GYAAA (AAAGH)
FURA (FLUD)
UWAAA (AAAHH)
I CAN'T TELL WHAT'S RIGHT...FROM WHAT'S WRONG.
HAA (HUFF)
!!
HAA
!?
YOU SHOULDN'T BE HERE, DARREN! YOU OUGHT TO LEAVE!
NICHA (SPLT)
!!

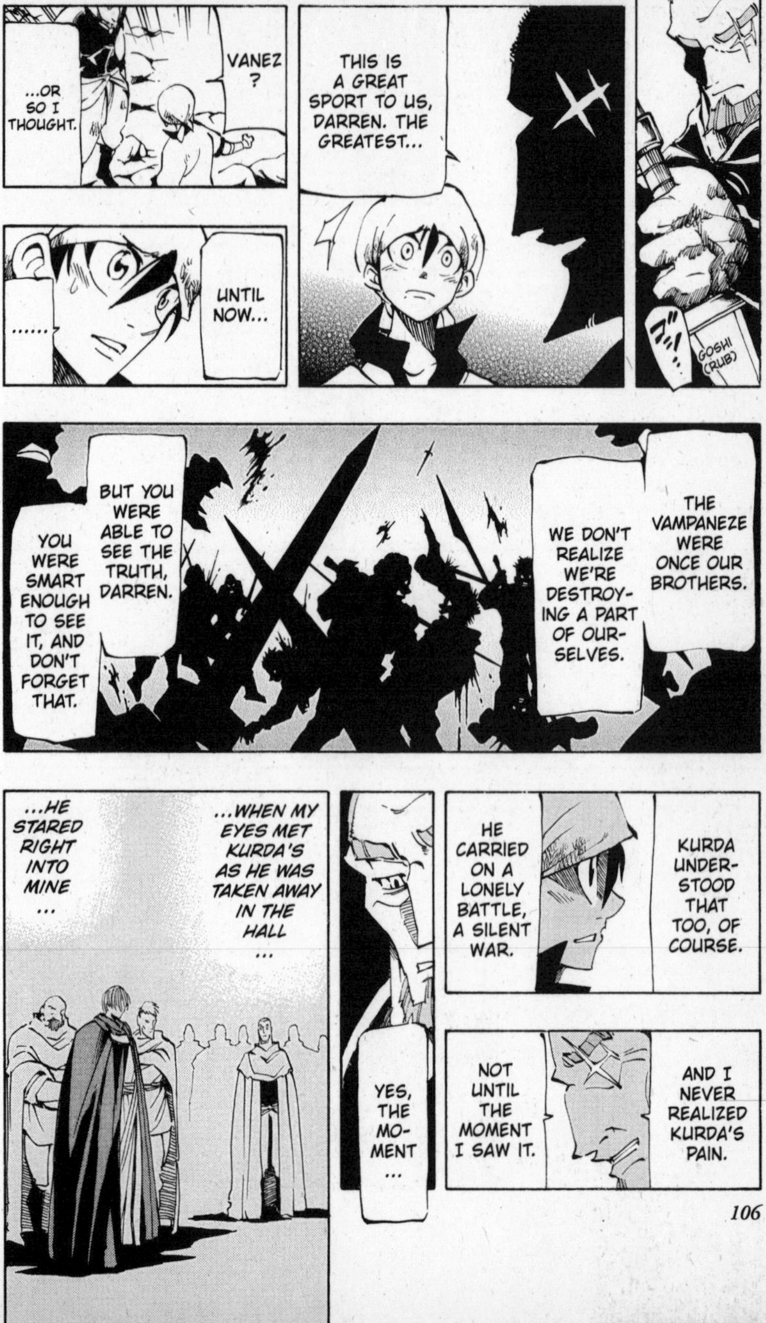
GOSHI (RUB)
THIS IS A GREAT SPORT TO US, DARREN. THE GREATEST...
VANEZ ?
...OR SO I THOUGHT.
UNTIL NOW...
......
THE VAMPANEZE WERE ONCE OUR BROTHERS.
WE DON'T REALIZE WE'RE DESTROYING A PART OF OURSELVES.
BUT YOU WERE ABLE TO SEE THE TRUTH, DARREN.
YOU WERE SMART ENOUGH TO SEE IT, AND DON'T FORGET THAT.
KURDA UNDERSTOOD THAT TOO, OF COURSE.
HE CARRIED ON A LONELY BATTLE, A SILENT WAR.
AND I NEVER REALIZED KURDA'S PAIN.
NOT UNTIL THE MOMENT I SAW IT.
YES, THE MOMENT...
...WHEN MY EYES MET KURDA'S AS HE WAS TAKEN AWAY IN THE HALL...
...HE STARED RIGHT INTO MINE...

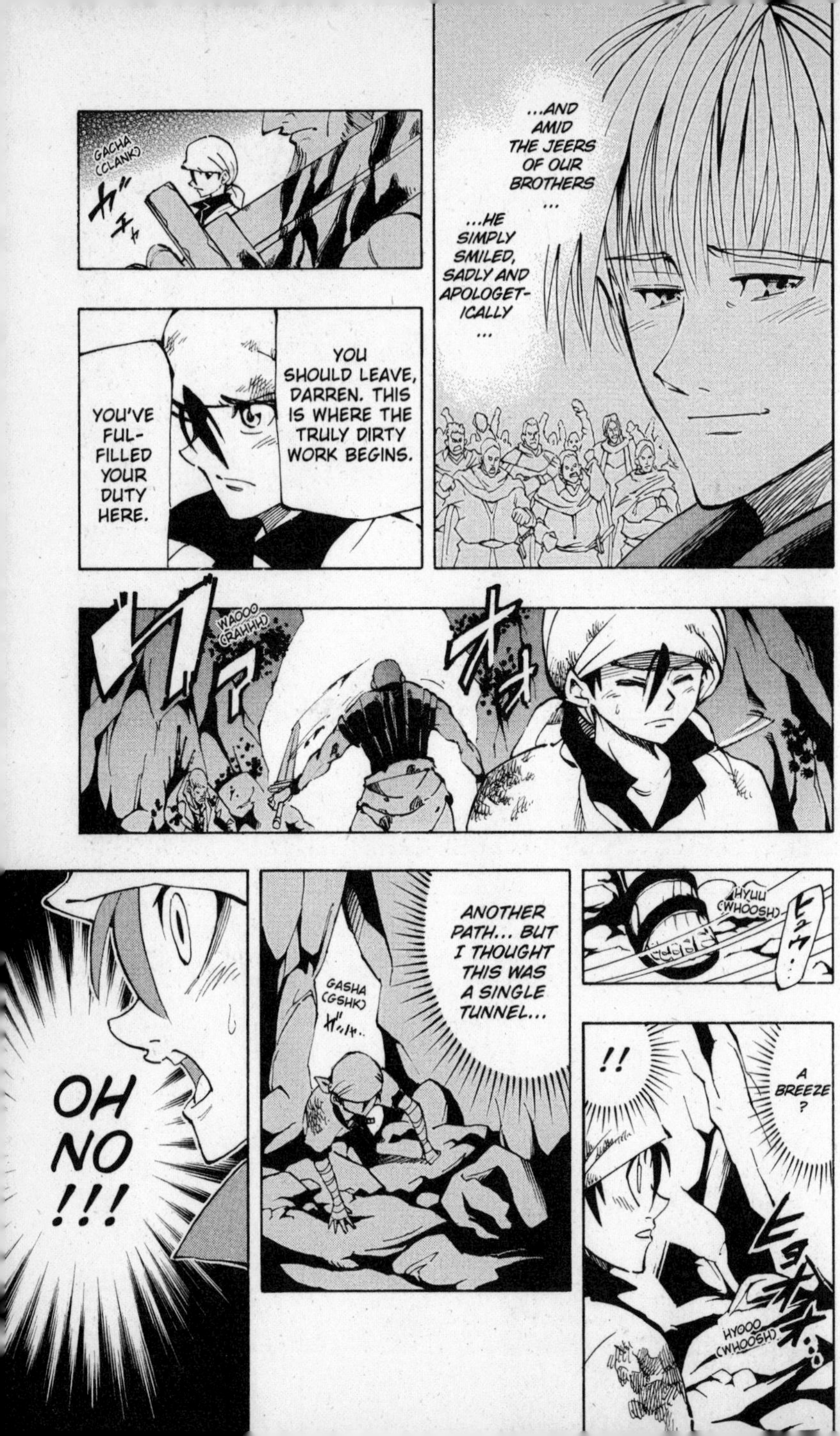
...AND AMID THE JEERS OF OUR BROTHERS ...
...HE SIMPLY SMILED, SADLY AND APOLOGETICALLY ...
GACHA (CLANK)
YOU SHOULD LEAVE, DARREN. THIS IS WHERE THE TRULY DIRTY WORK BEGINS.
YOU'VE FULFILLED YOUR DUTY HERE.
WAOOO (RAHHH)
HYUU (WHOOSH)
!!
A BREEZE ?
HYOOO (WHOOSH)
ANOTHER PATH... BUT I THOUGHT THIS WAS A SINGLE TUNNEL...
GASHA (GSHK)
OH NO !!!

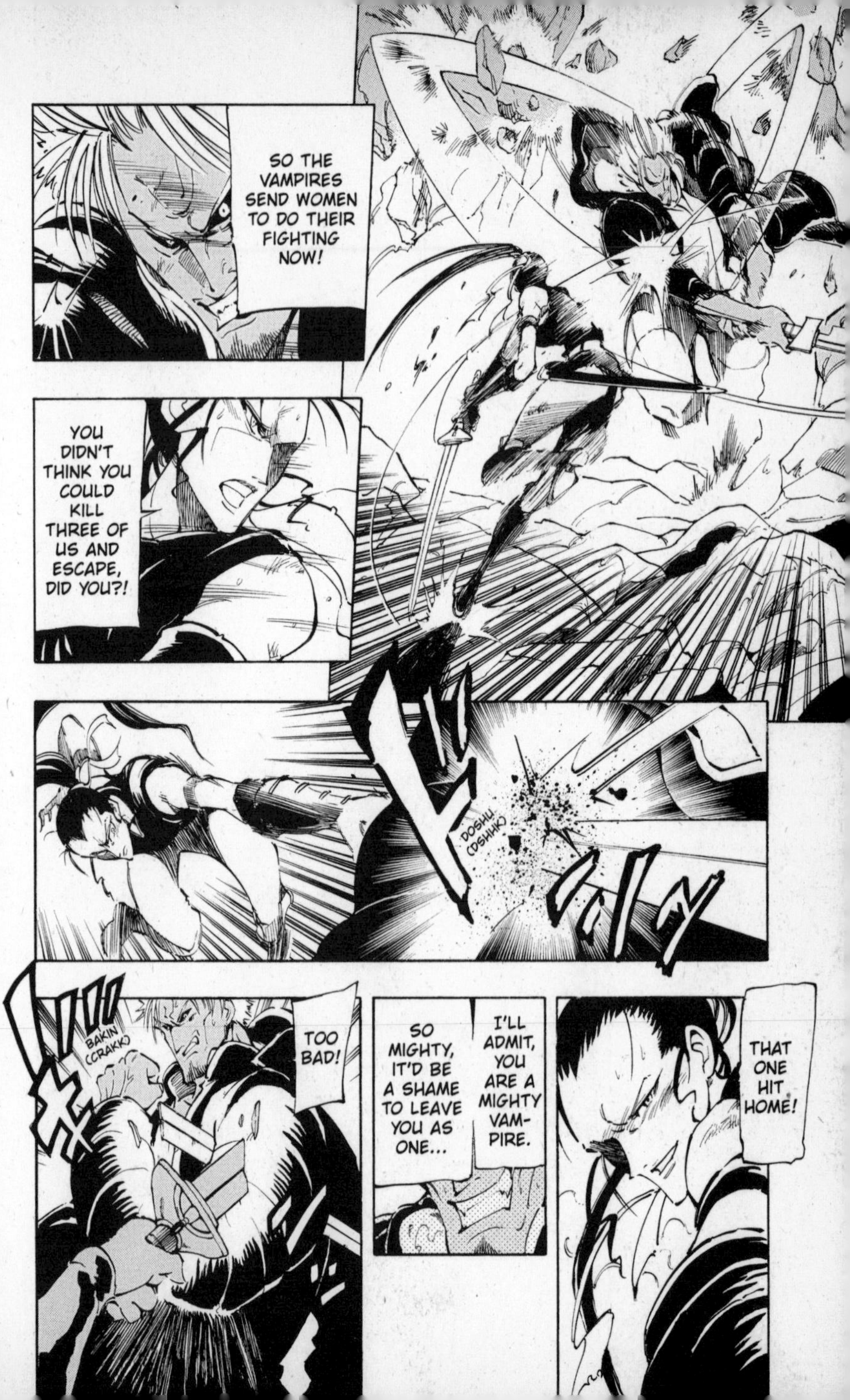
SO THE VAMPIRES SEND WOMEN TO DO THEIR FIGHTING NOW!
YOU DIDN'T THINK YOU COULD KILL THREE OF US AND ESCAPE, DID YOU?!
DOSHU (DSHHK)
THAT ONE HIT HOME!
I'LL ADMIT, YOU ARE A MIGHTY VAM-PIRE.
SO MIGHTY, IT'D BE A SHAME TO LEAVE YOU AS ONE...
TOO BAD!
BAKIN (CRAKK)

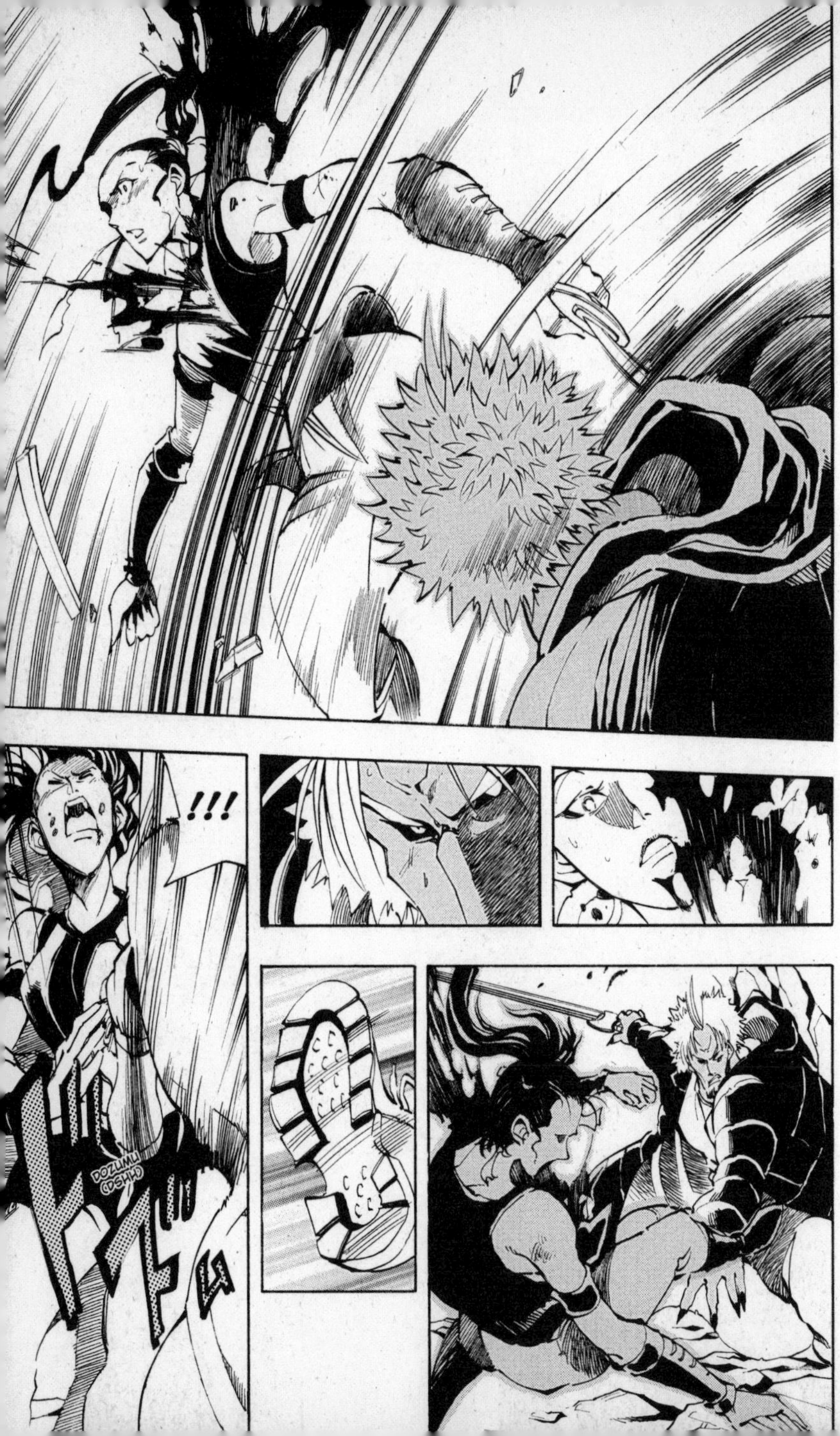

!!!
DOZUMU
(DSHD)

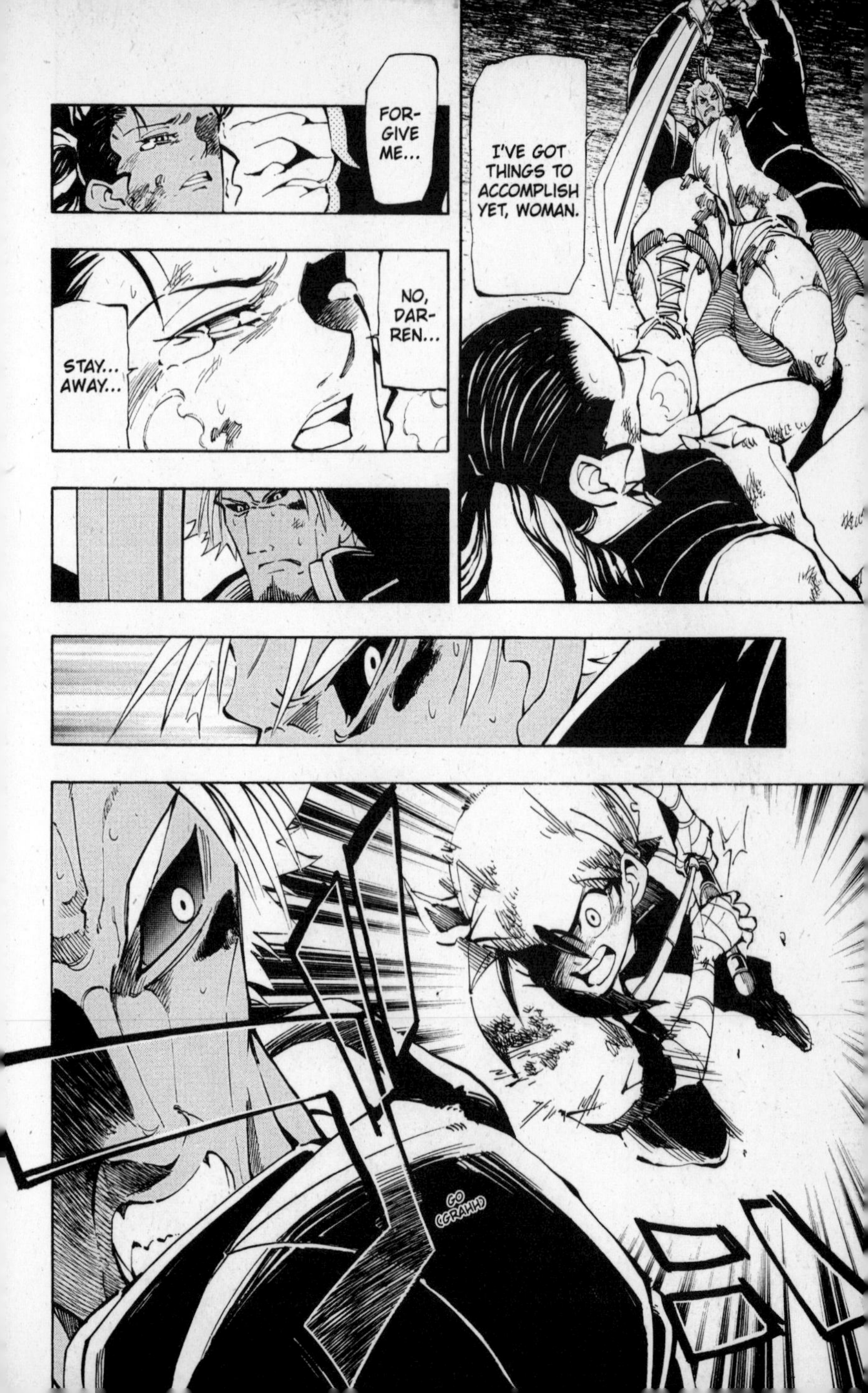
I'VE GOT THINGS TO ACCOMPLISH YET, WOMAN.
FOR-GIVE ME...
NO, DAR-REN...
STAY... AWAY...
GO (GRAHH)

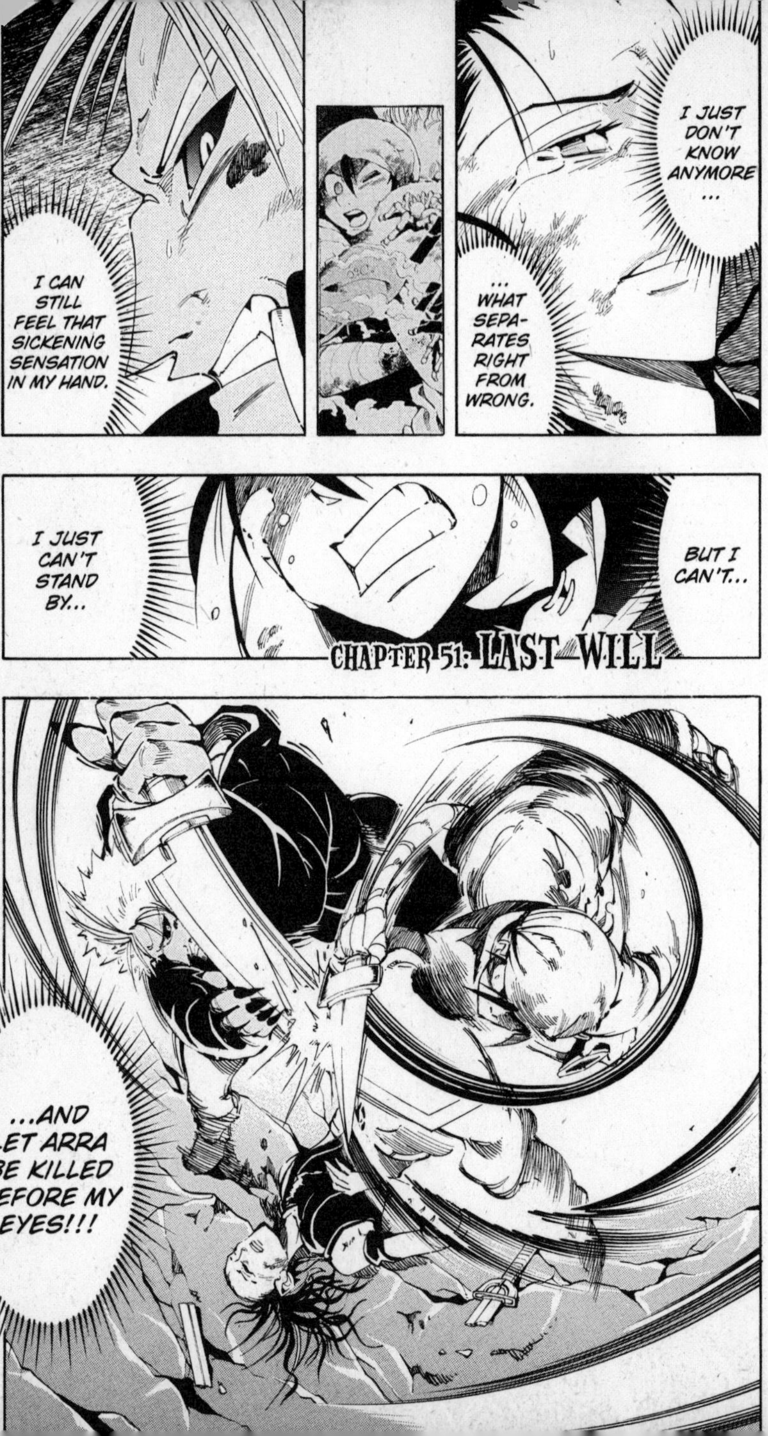
I JUST DON'T KNOW ANYMORE ...
... WHAT SEPA-RATES RIGHT FROM WRONG.
I CAN STILL FEEL THAT SICKENING SENSATION IN MY HAND.
BUT I CAN'T...
I JUST CAN'T STAND BY...
CHAPTER 51: LAST WILL
...AND LET ARRA BE KILLED BEFORE MY EYES!!!

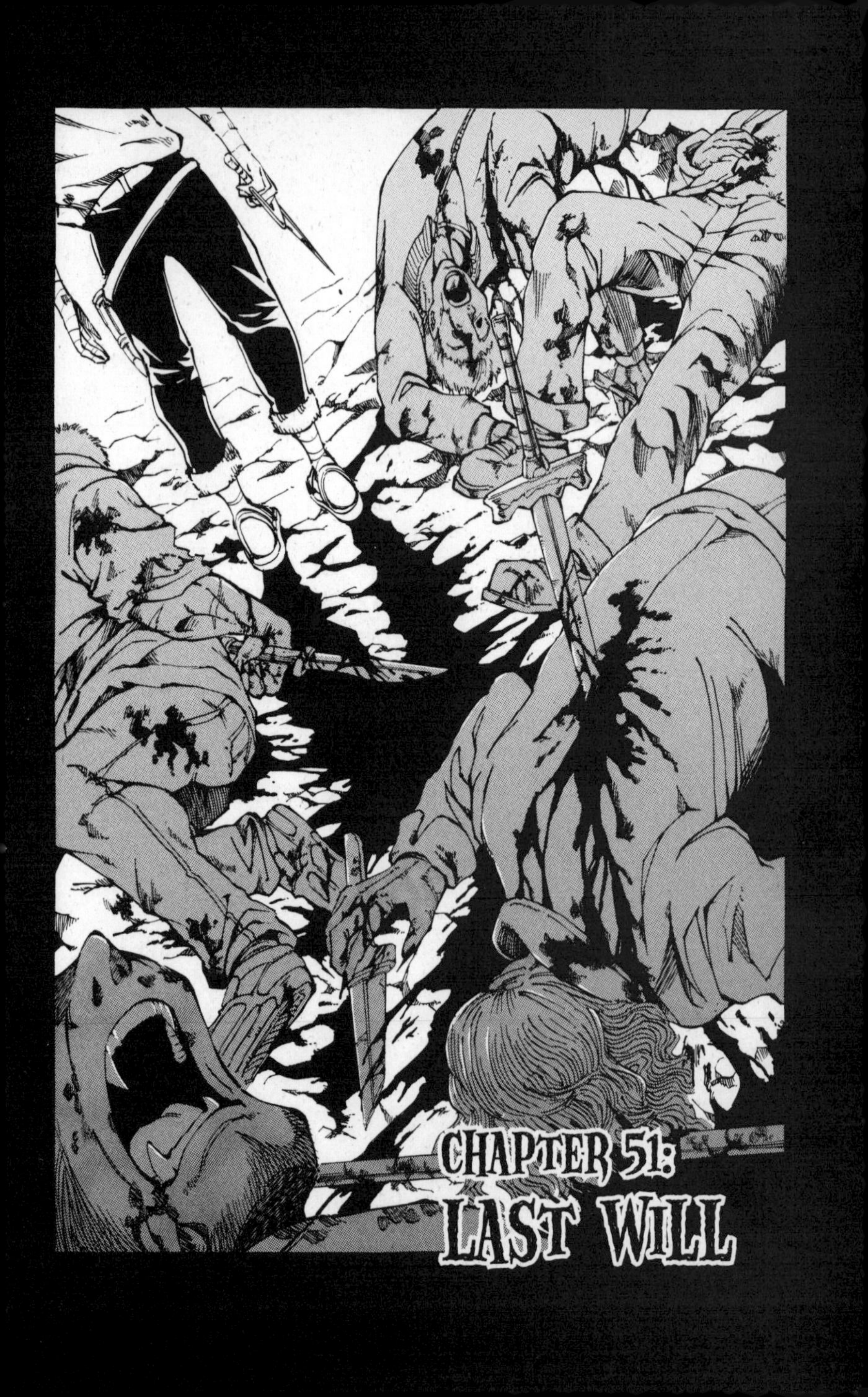

CHAPTER 51: LAST WILL

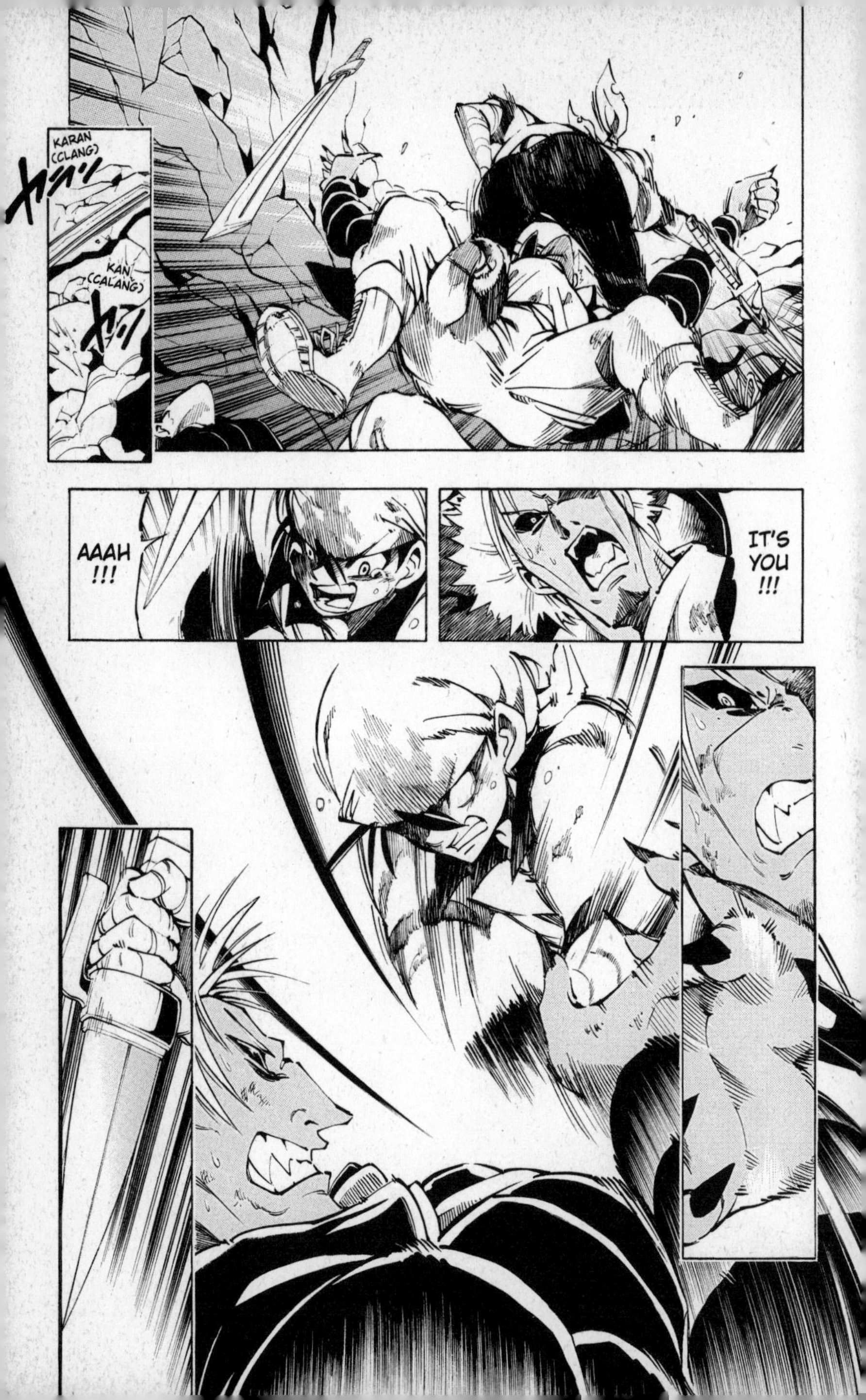
KARAN (CLANG)
KAN (CALANG)
IT'S YOU !!!
AAAH !!!

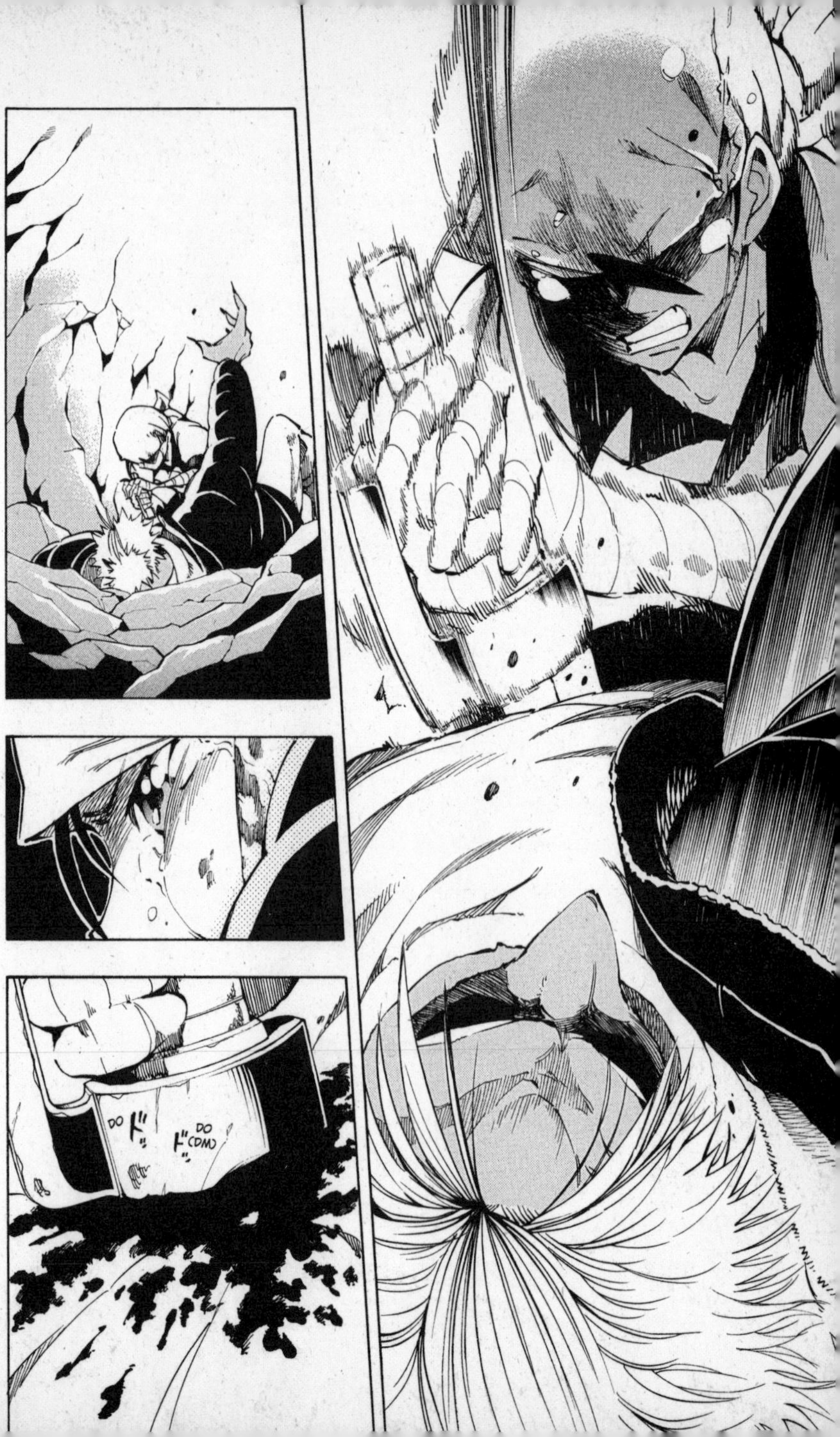
DO ド" DO ド" (DM)

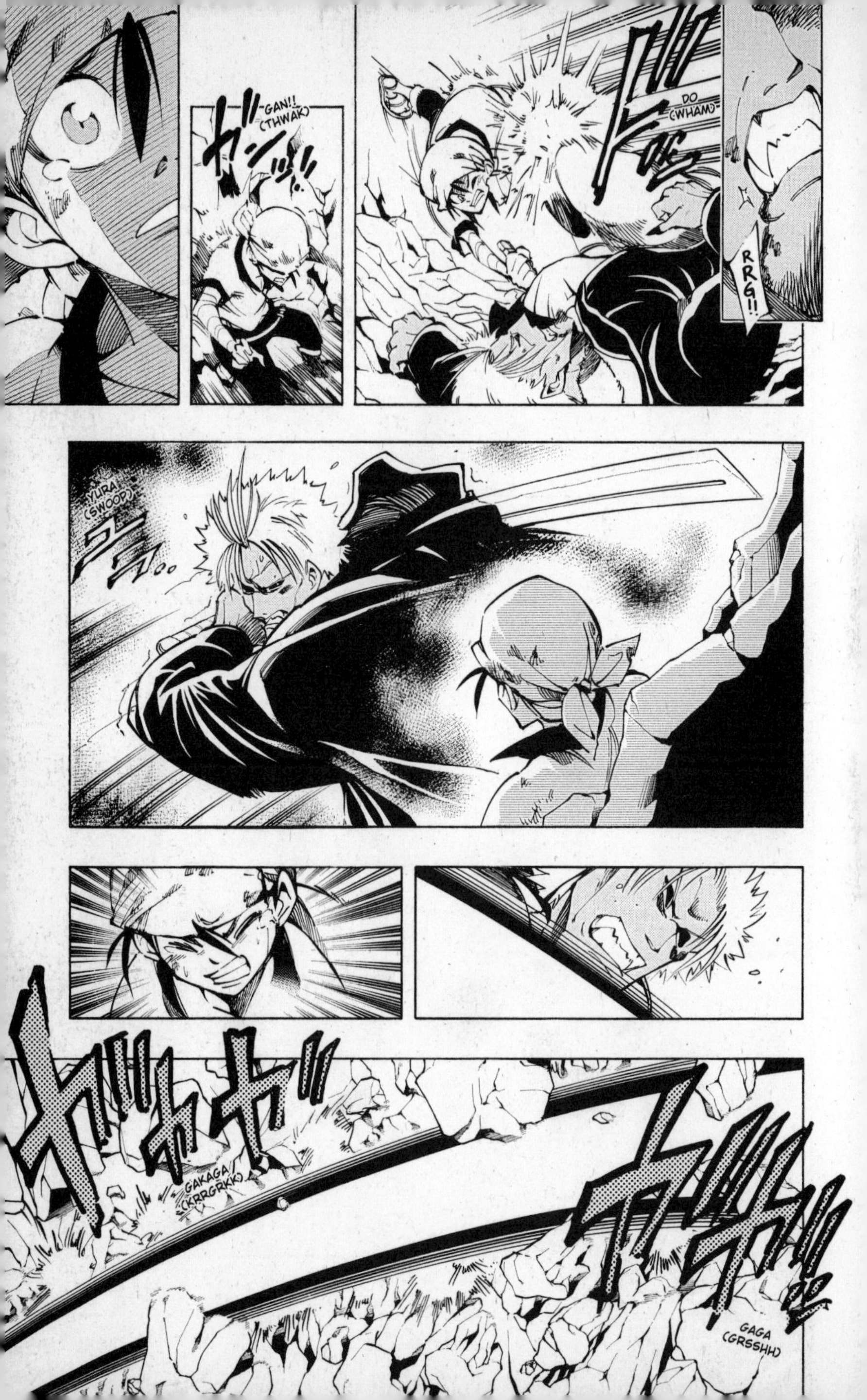
RRG!!
DO (WHAM)
GAN!! (THWAK)
YURA (SWOOP)
GAGA (GRSSHH)
GAKAGA (KRRGRKK)

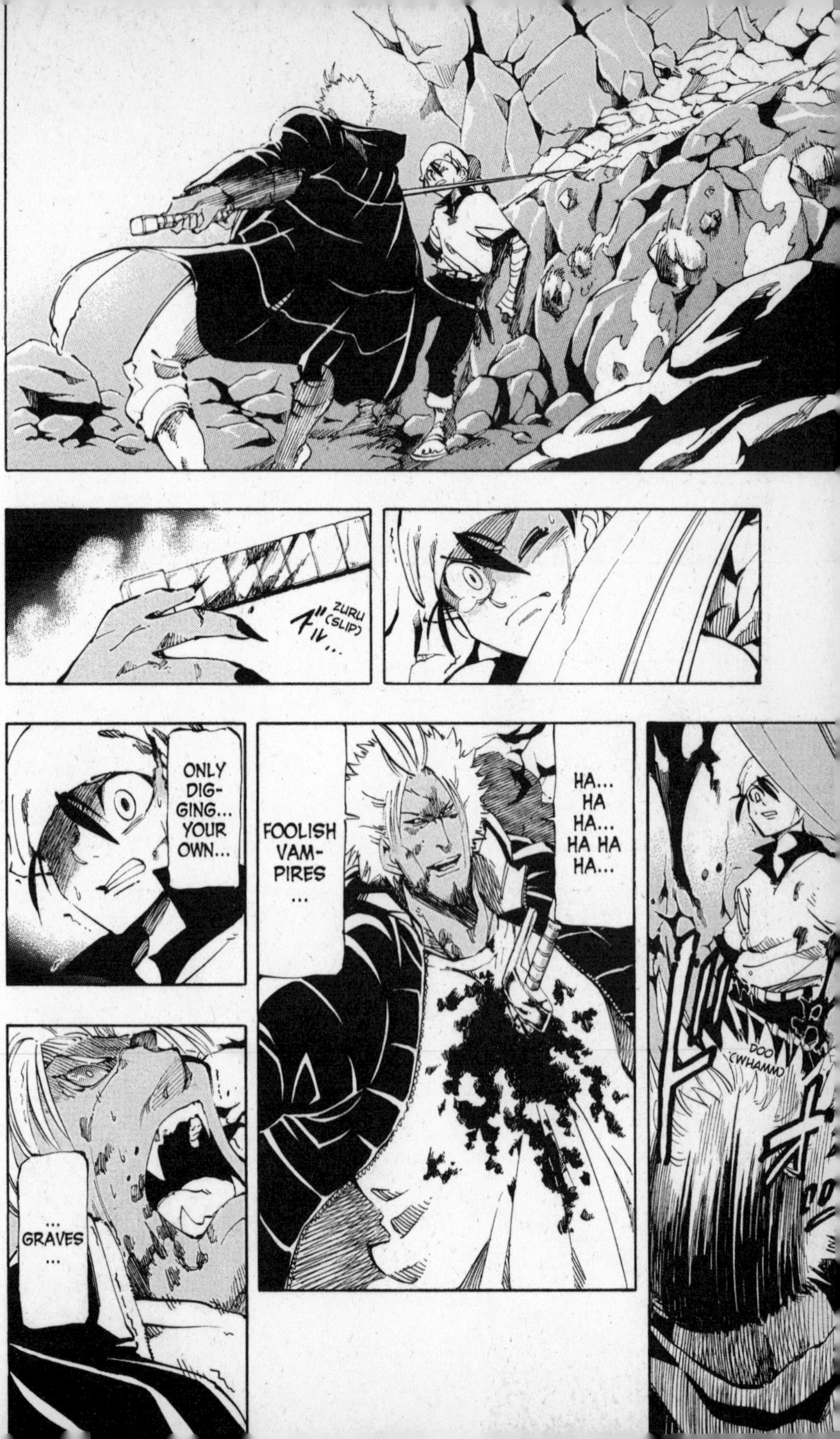
ZURU (SLIP)
ズル...
DOO (WHAMM)
HA... HA HA... HA HA HA...
FOOLISH VAMPIRES ...
ONLY DIGGING... YOUR OWN...
... GRAVES ...

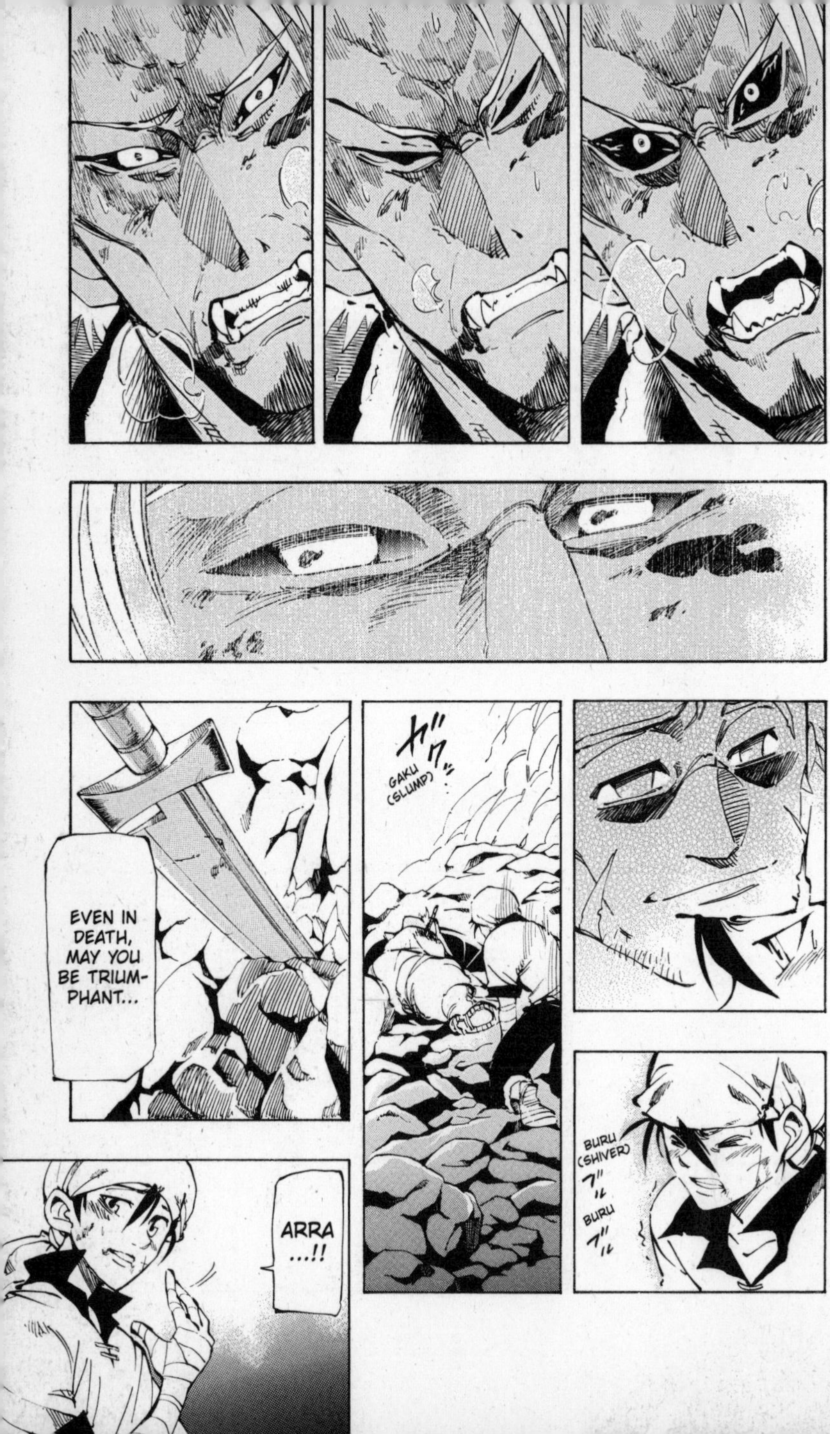
BURU (SHIVER)
ブル
BURU
ブル
ガク
GAKU (SLUMP)
EVEN IN DEATH, MAY YOU BE TRIUMPHANT...
ARRA ...!!

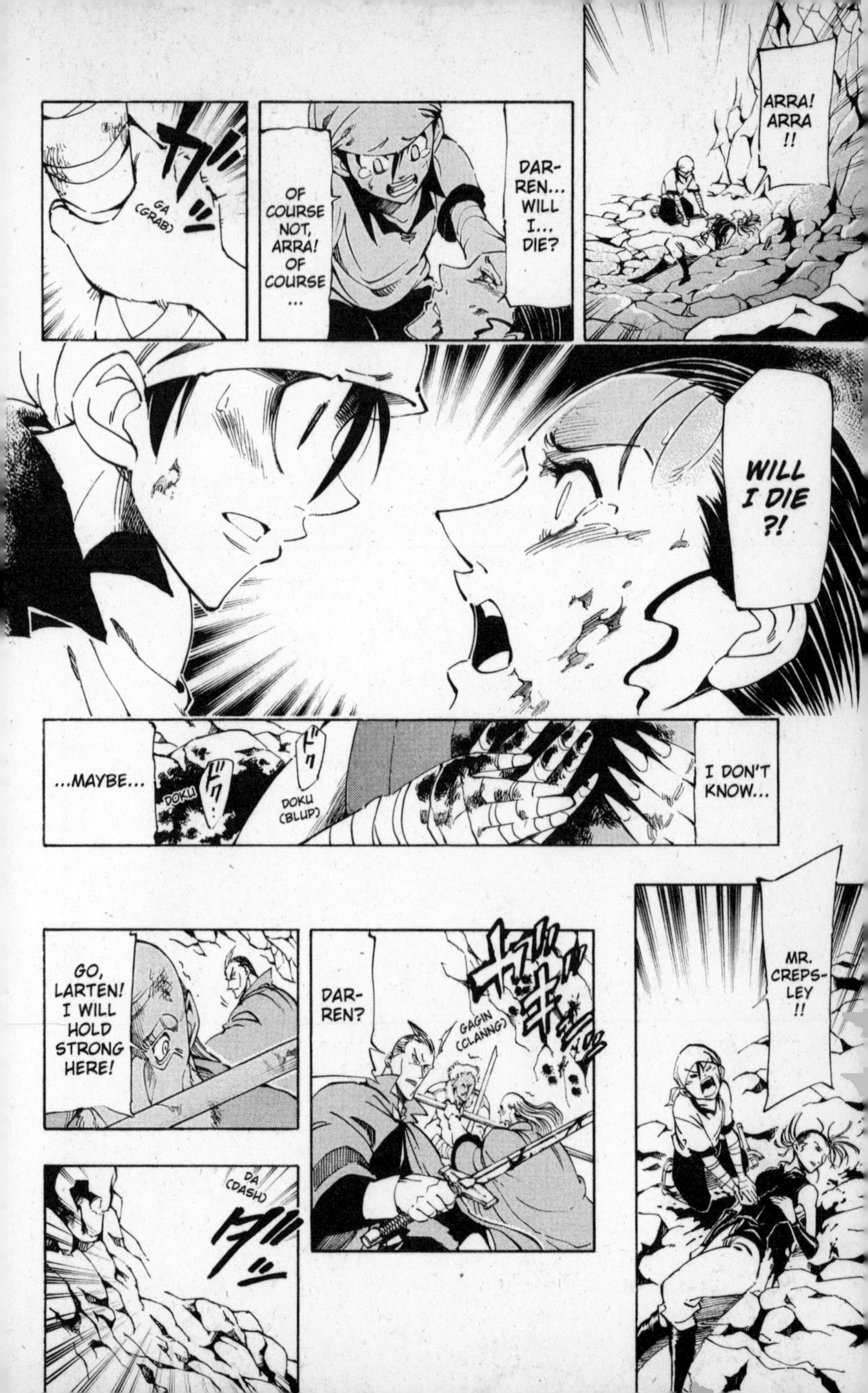

ARRA! ARRA !!
DAR-REN... WILL I... DIE?
OF COURSE NOT, ARRA! OF COURSE ...
GA (GRAB)
WILL I DIE ?!
I DON'T KNOW...
DOKU (BLUP)
DOKU
...MAYBE...
MR. CREPS-LEY !!
DAR-REN?
GAGIN (CLANNG)
GO, LARTEN! I WILL HOLD STRONG HERE!
DA (DASH)

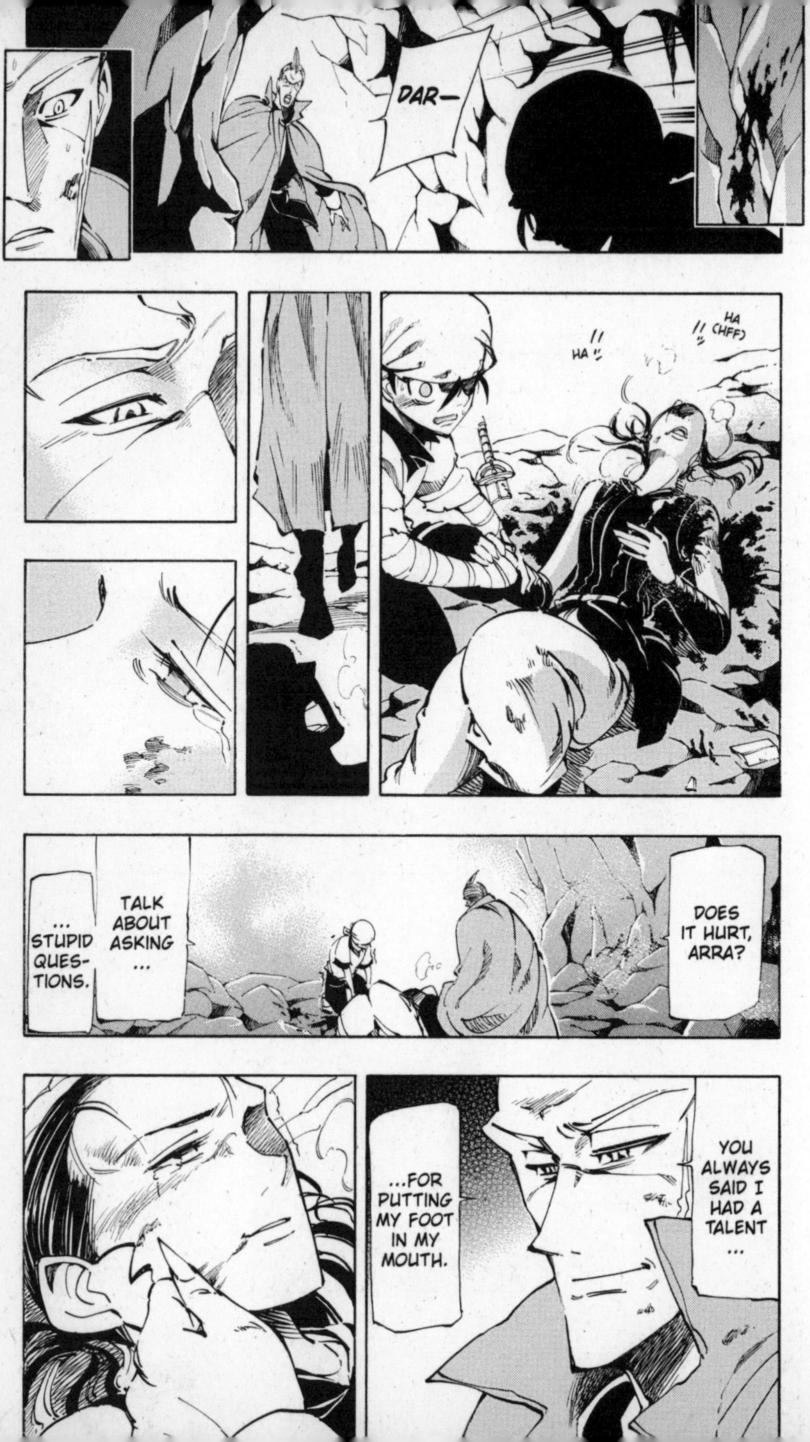
DAR—
HA (HFF)
!!
HA !!
DOES IT HURT, ARRA?
TALK ABOUT ASKING ...
... STUPID QUES-TIONS.
YOU ALWAYS SAID I HAD A TALENT ...
...FOR PUTTING MY FOOT IN MY MOUTH.

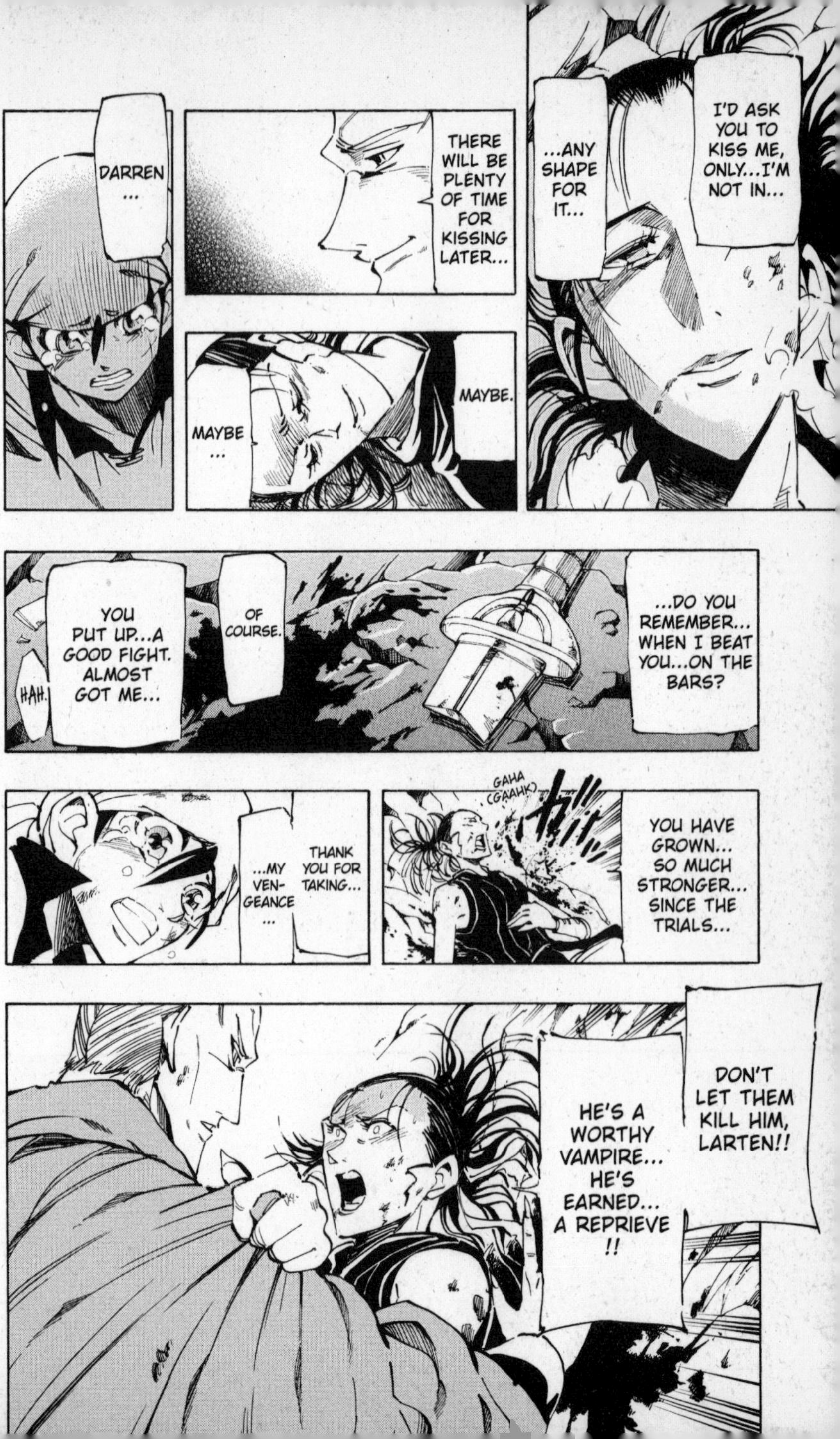
I'D ASK YOU TO KISS ME, ONLY...I'M NOT IN...
...ANY SHAPE FOR IT...
THERE WILL BE PLENTY OF TIME FOR KISSING LATER...
MAYBE.
MAYBE ...
DARREN ...
...DO YOU REMEMBER... WHEN I BEAT YOU...ON THE BARS?
OF COURSE.
YOU PUT UP...A GOOD FIGHT. ALMOST GOT ME...
HAH.
YOU HAVE GROWN... SO MUCH STRONGER... SINCE THE TRIALS...
GAHA (GAAHK)
THANK YOU FOR TAKING...
...MY VEN-GEANCE ...
DON'T LET THEM KILL HIM, LARTEN!!
HE'S A WORTHY VAMPIRE... HE'S EARNED... A REPRIEVE !!

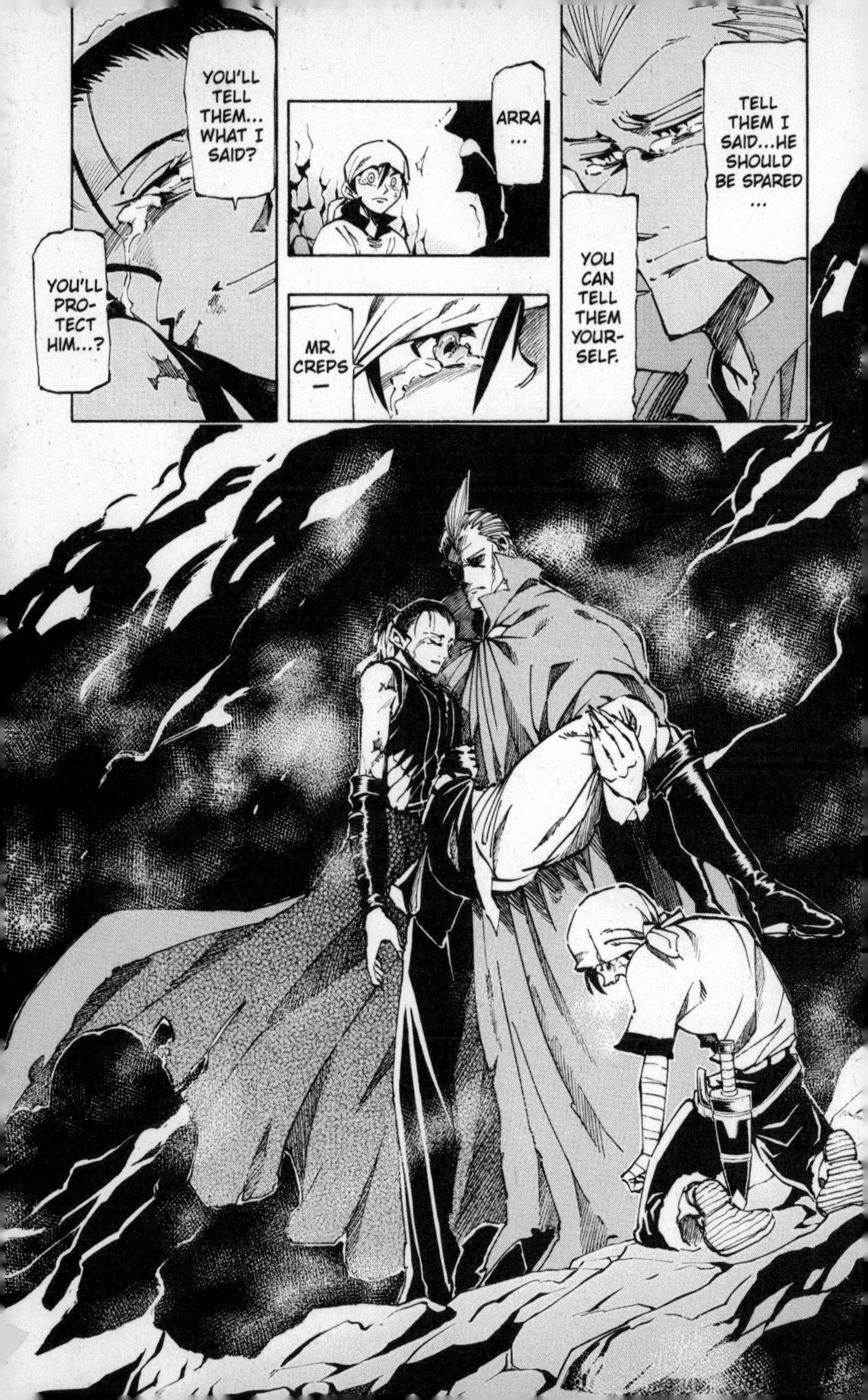
TELL THEM I SAID...HE SHOULD BE SPARED ...
YOU CAN TELL THEM YOURSELF.
ARRA ...
MR. CREPS —
YOU'LL TELL THEM... WHAT I SAID?
YOU'LL PROTECT HIM...?

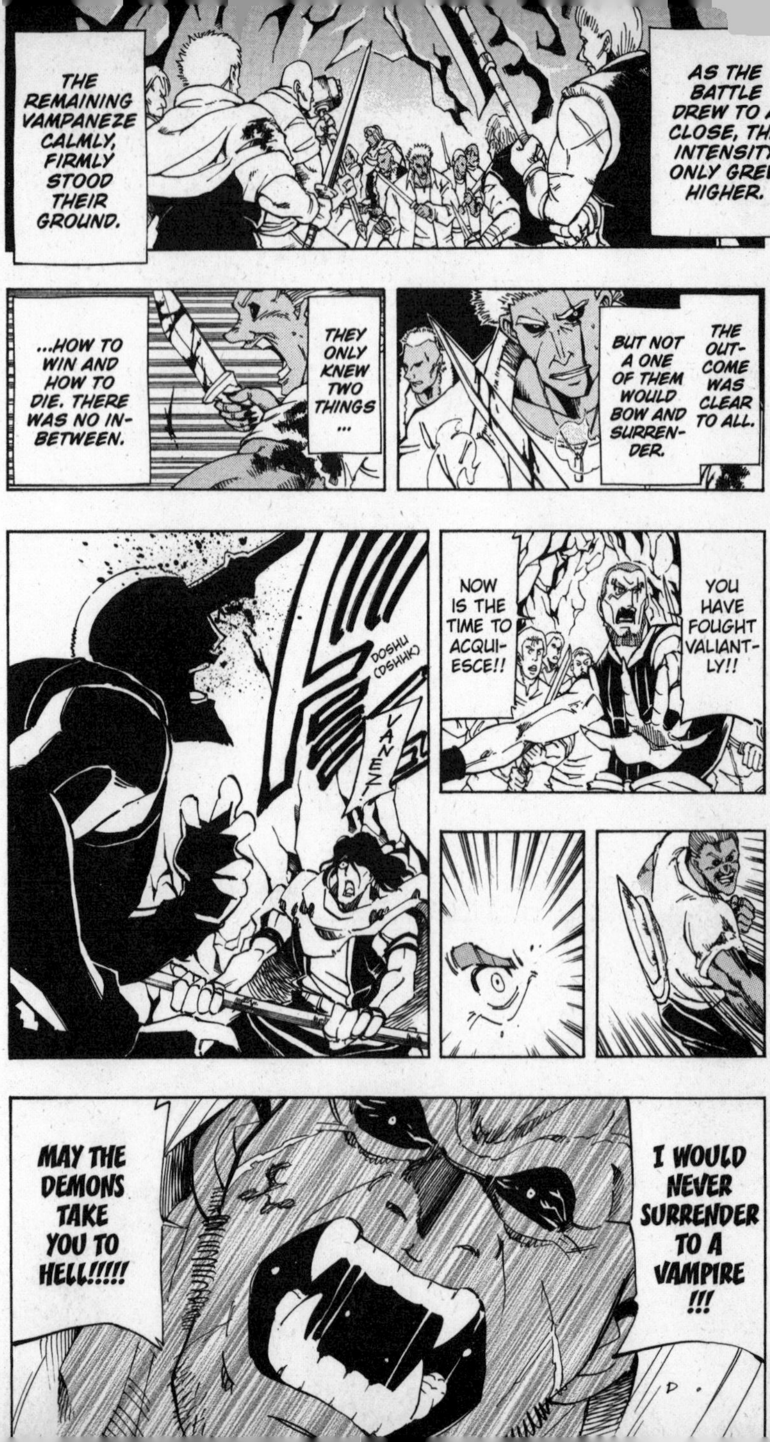
AS THE BATTLE DREW TO A CLOSE, THE INTENSITY ONLY GREW HIGHER.
THE REMAINING VAMPANEZE CALMLY, FIRMLY STOOD THEIR GROUND.
THE OUTCOME WAS CLEAR TO ALL.
BUT NOT A ONE OF THEM WOULD BOW AND SURRENDER.
THEY ONLY KNEW TWO THINGS...
...HOW TO WIN AND HOW TO DIE. THERE WAS NO IN-BETWEEN.
YOU HAVE FOUGHT VALIANTLY!!
NOW IS THE TIME TO ACQUIESCE!!
DOSHU (DSHHK)
VANEZ!
I WOULD NEVER SURRENDER TO A VAMPIRE!!!
MAY THE DEMONS TAKE YOU TO HELL!!!!!

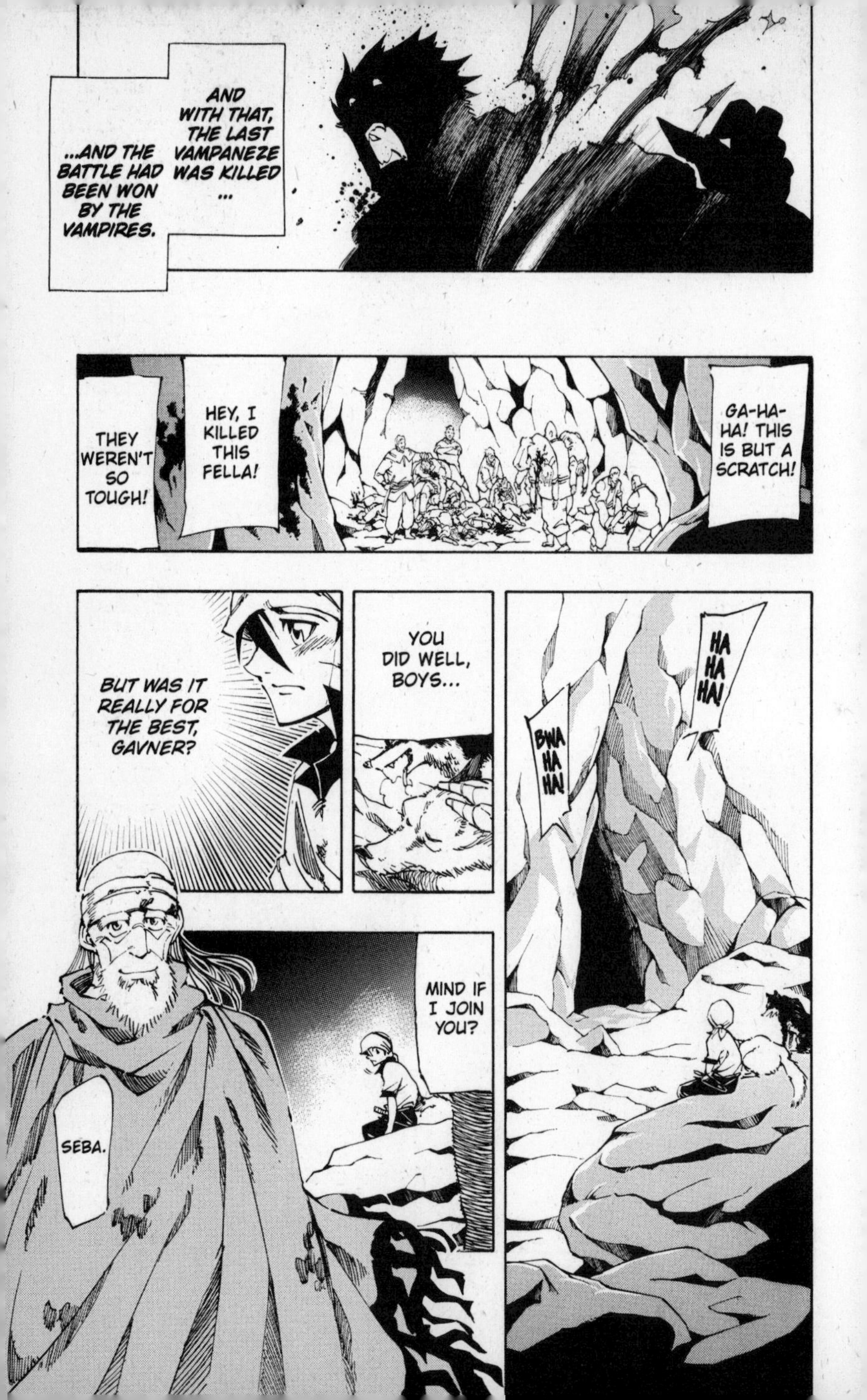
AND WITH THAT, THE LAST VAMPANEZE WAS KILLED ...
...AND THE BATTLE HAD BEEN WON BY THE VAMPIRES.
GA-HA-HA! THIS IS BUT A SCRATCH!
HEY, I KILLED THIS FELLA!
THEY WEREN'T SO TOUGH!
HA HA HA!
BWA HA HA!
YOU DID WELL, BOYS...
BUT WAS IT REALLY FOR THE BEST, GAVNER?
MIND IF I JOIN YOU?
SEBA.

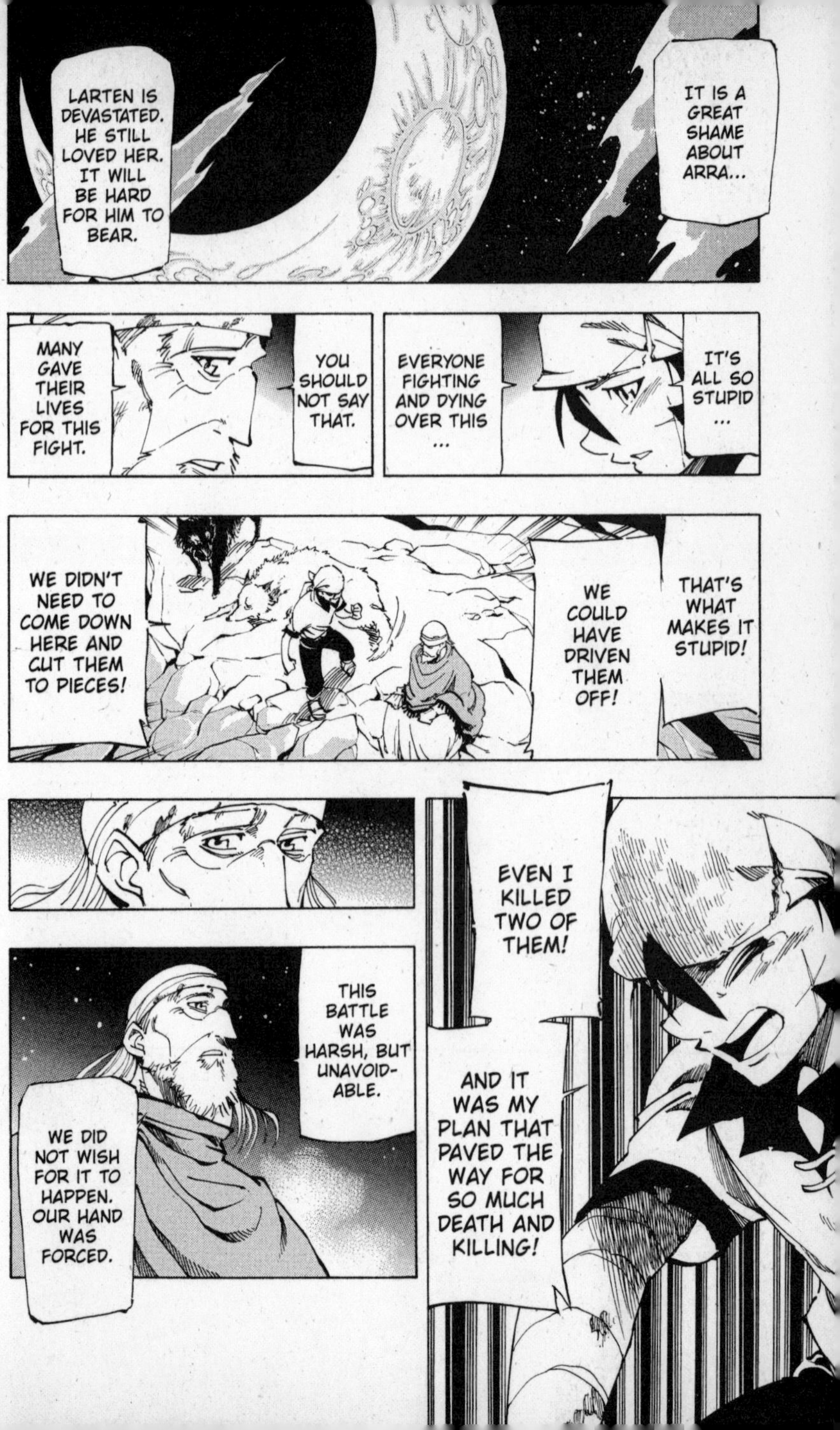
IT IS A GREAT SHAME ABOUT ARRA...
LARTEN IS DEVASTATED. HE STILL LOVED HER. IT WILL BE HARD FOR HIM TO BEAR.
IT'S ALL SO STUPID ...
EVERYONE FIGHTING AND DYING OVER THIS ...
YOU SHOULD NOT SAY THAT.
MANY GAVE THEIR LIVES FOR THIS FIGHT.
THAT'S WHAT MAKES IT STUPID!
WE COULD HAVE DRIVEN THEM OFF!
WE DIDN'T NEED TO COME DOWN HERE AND CUT THEM TO PIECES!
EVEN I KILLED TWO OF THEM!
AND IT WAS MY PLAN THAT PAVED THE WAY FOR SO MUCH DEATH AND KILLING!
THIS BATTLE WAS HARSH, BUT UNAVOID-ABLE.
WE DID NOT WISH FOR IT TO HAPPEN. OUR HAND WAS FORCED.

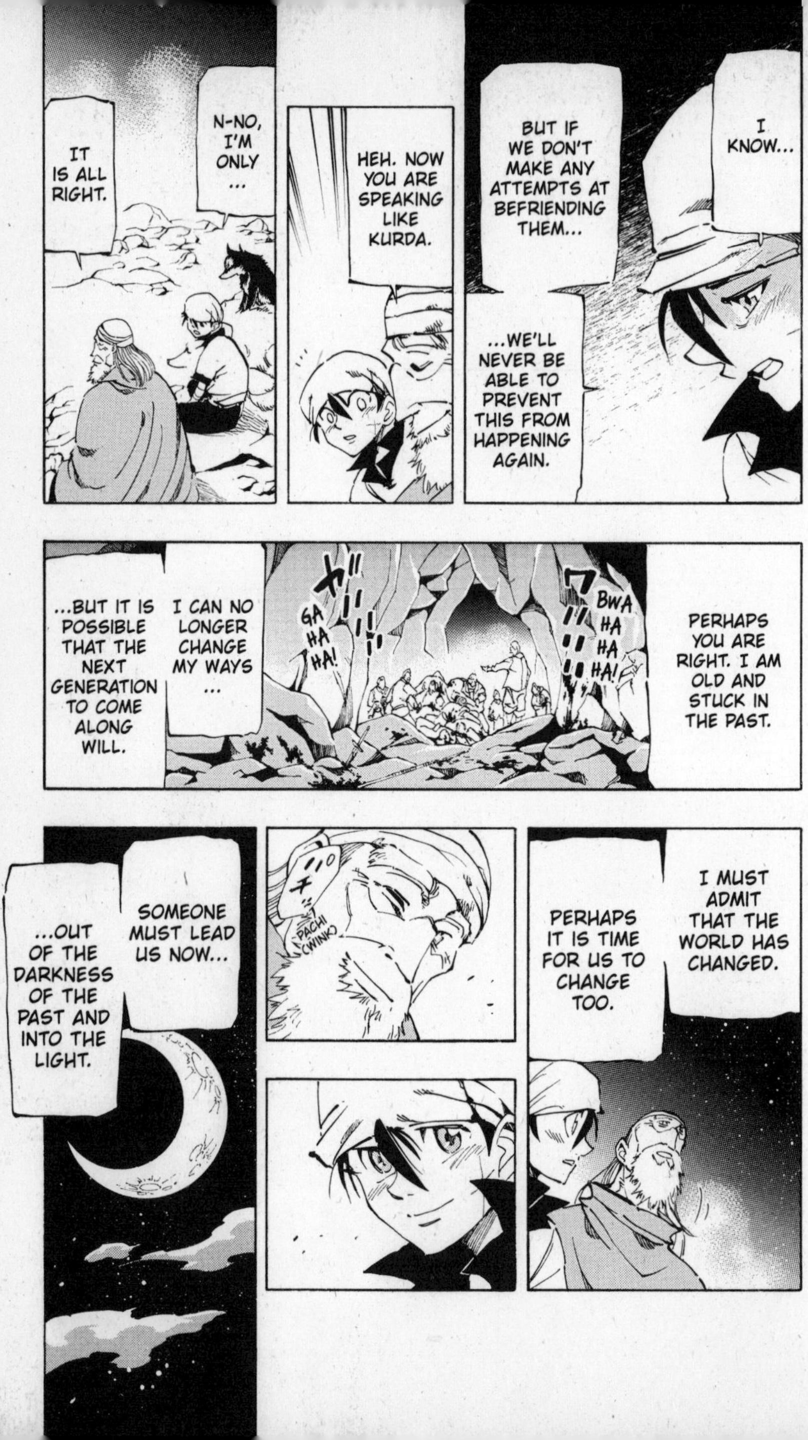
I KNOW...
BUT IF WE DON'T MAKE ANY ATTEMPTS AT BEFRIENDING THEM...
...WE'LL NEVER BE ABLE TO PREVENT THIS FROM HAPPENING AGAIN.
HEH. NOW YOU ARE SPEAKING LIKE KURDA.
N-NO, I'M ONLY ...
IT IS ALL RIGHT.
PERHAPS YOU ARE RIGHT. I AM OLD AND STUCK IN THE PAST.
BWA HA HA HA!
GA HA HA HA!
I CAN NO LONGER CHANGE MY WAYS ...
...BUT IT IS POSSIBLE THAT THE NEXT GENERATION TO COME ALONG WILL.
I MUST ADMIT THAT THE WORLD HAS CHANGED.
PERHAPS IT IS TIME FOR US TO CHANGE TOO.
PACHI (WINK)
SOMEONE MUST LEAD US NOW...
...OUT OF THE DARKNESS OF THE PAST AND INTO THE LIGHT.

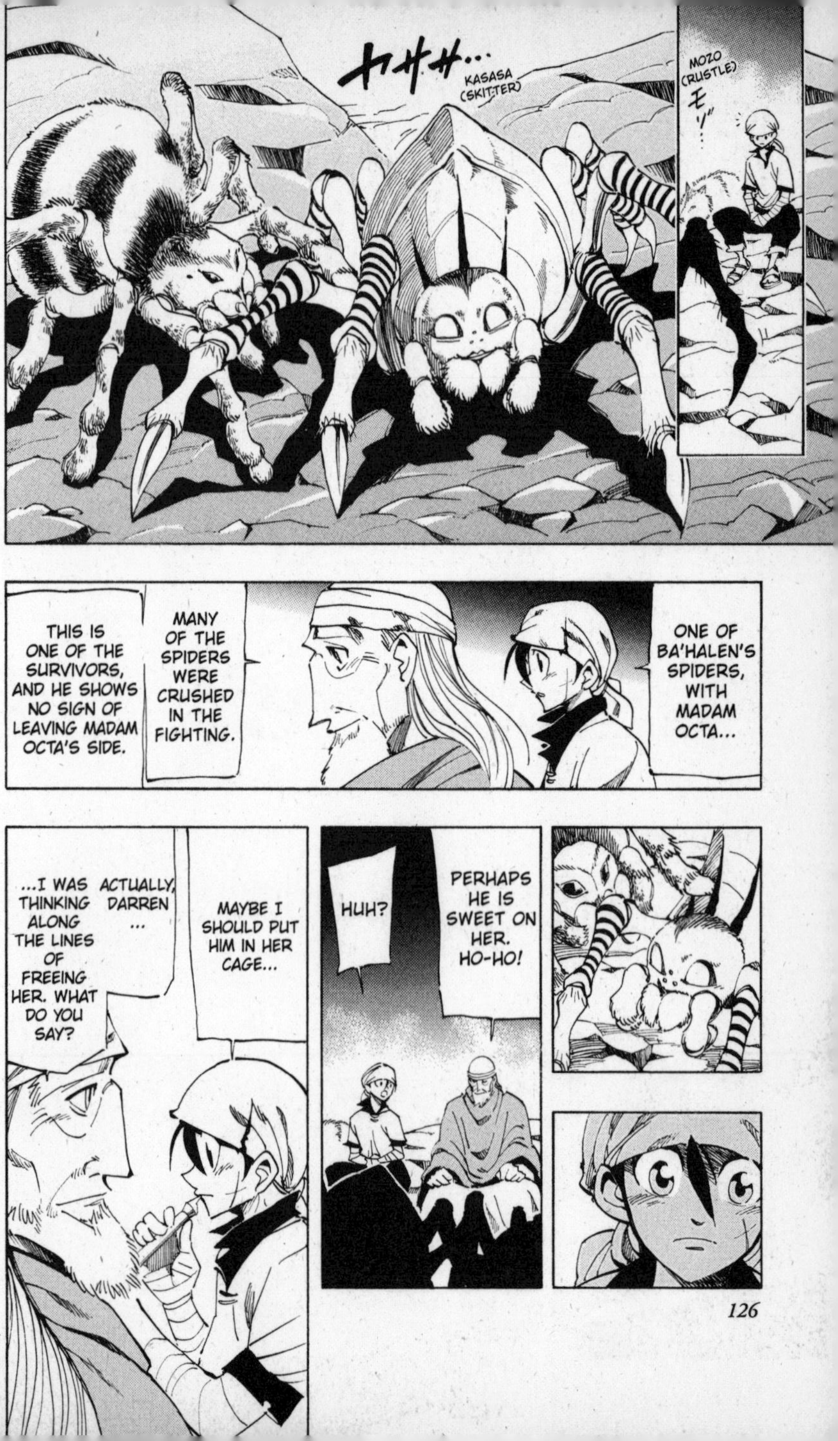

MOZO (RUSTLE)
モゾ…
カサササ…
KASASA (SKITTER)
ONE OF BA'HALEN'S SPIDERS, WITH MADAM OCTA...
MANY OF THE SPIDERS WERE CRUSHED IN THE FIGHTING.
THIS IS ONE OF THE SURVIVORS, AND HE SHOWS NO SIGN OF LEAVING MADAM OCTA'S SIDE.
PERHAPS HE IS SWEET ON HER. HO-HO!
HUH?
MAYBE I SHOULD PUT HIM IN HER CAGE...
ACTUALLY, DARREN...
...I WAS THINKING ALONG THE LINES OF FREEING HER. WHAT DO YOU SAY?

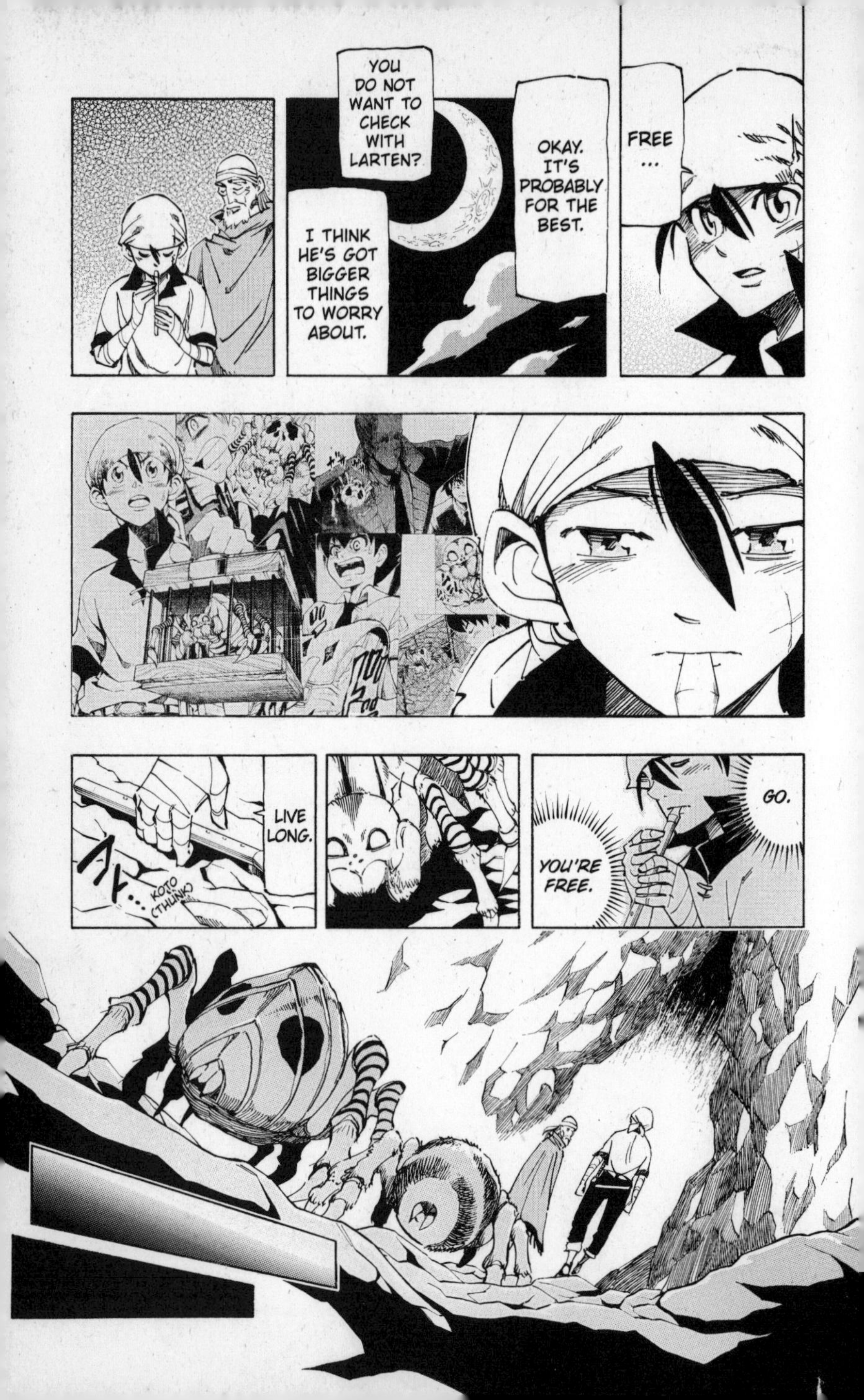
FREE ...
OKAY. IT'S PROBABLY FOR THE BEST.
YOU DO NOT WANT TO CHECK WITH LARTEN?
I THINK HE'S GOT BIGGER THINGS TO WORRY ABOUT.
GO.
YOU'RE FREE.
LIVE LONG.
KOTO (THUNK)

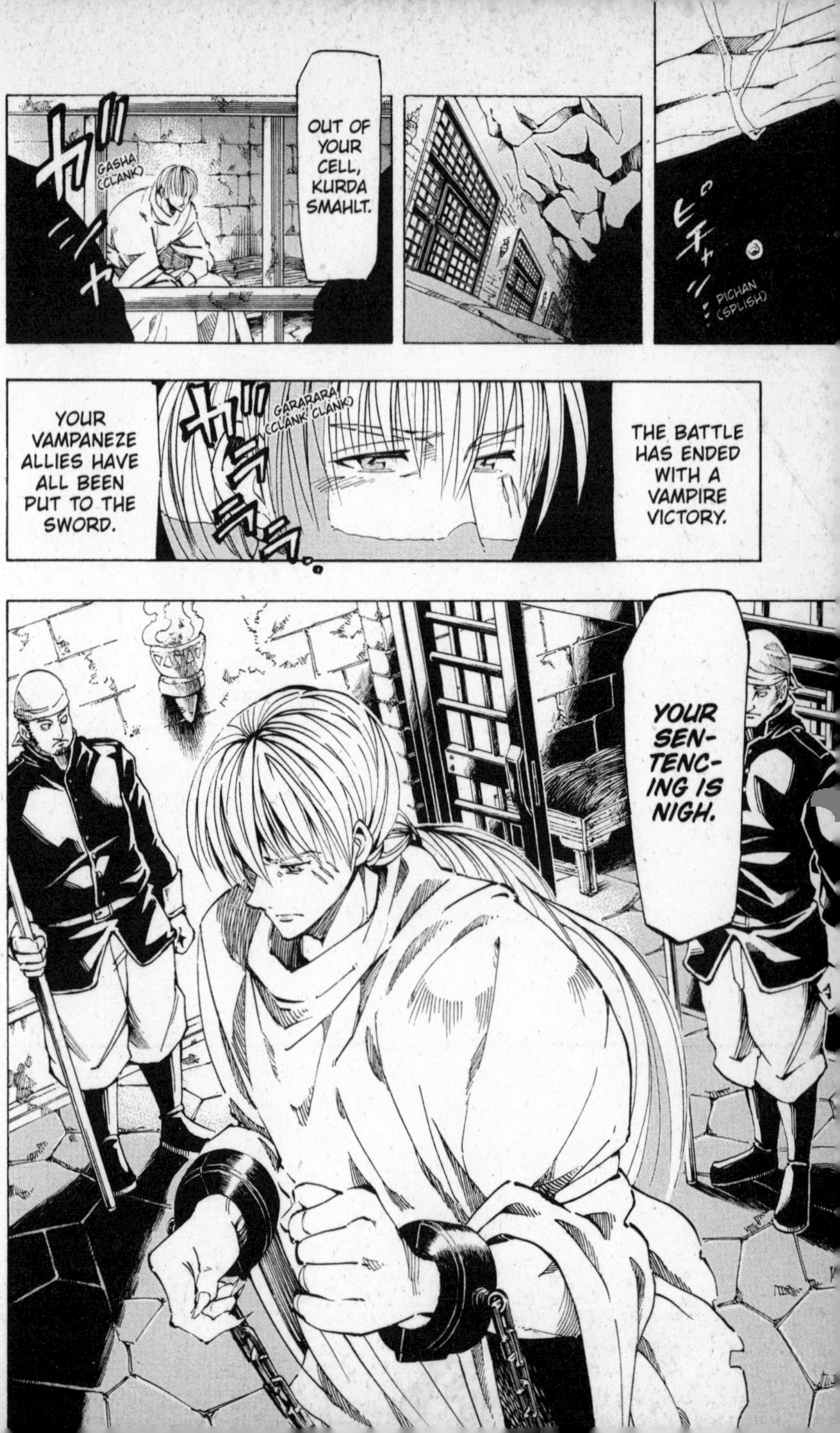
PICHAN (SPLISH)
OUT OF YOUR CELL, KURDA SMAHLT.
GASHA (CLANK)
THE BATTLE HAS ENDED WITH A VAMPIRE VICTORY.
GARARARA (CLANK CLANK)
YOUR VAMPANEZE ALLIES HAVE ALL BEEN PUT TO THE SWORD.
YOUR SEN-TENC-ING IS NIGH.

CHAPTER 52:
KURDA'S CONFESSION

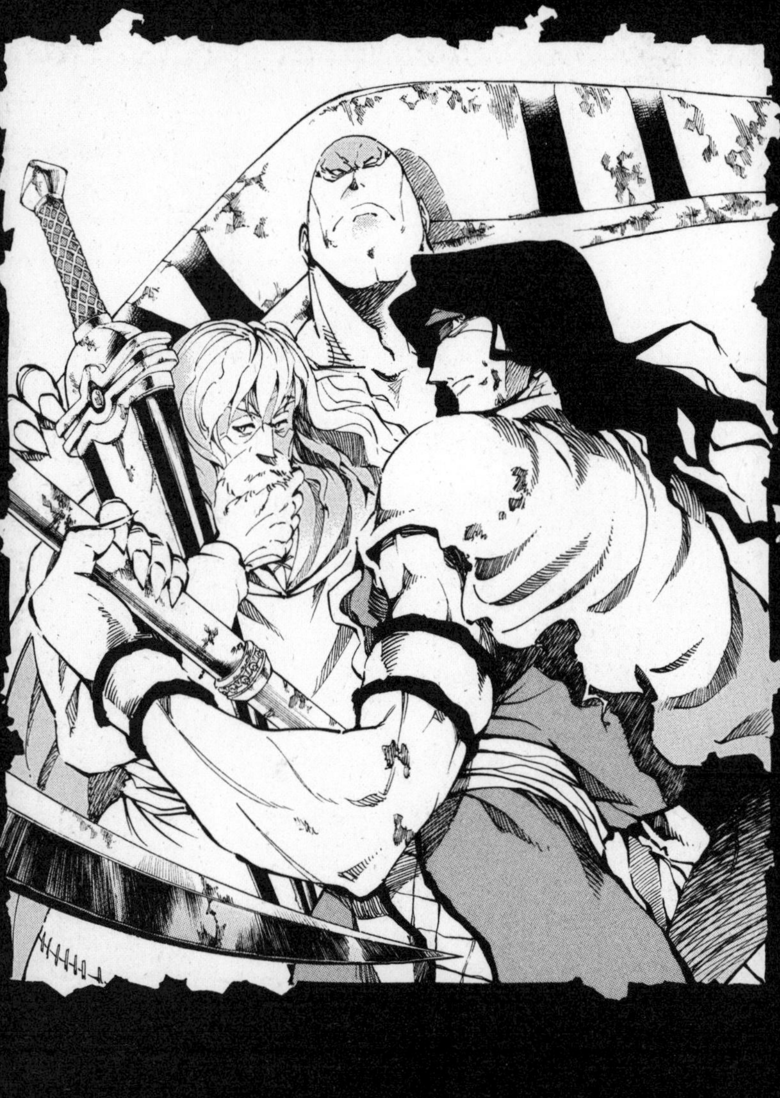

PASA
(FLAP)

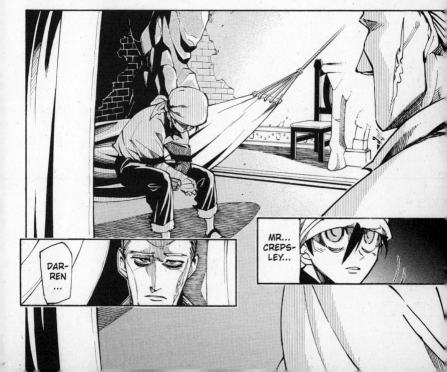

MR...
CREPS-
LEY...

DAR-
REN
...

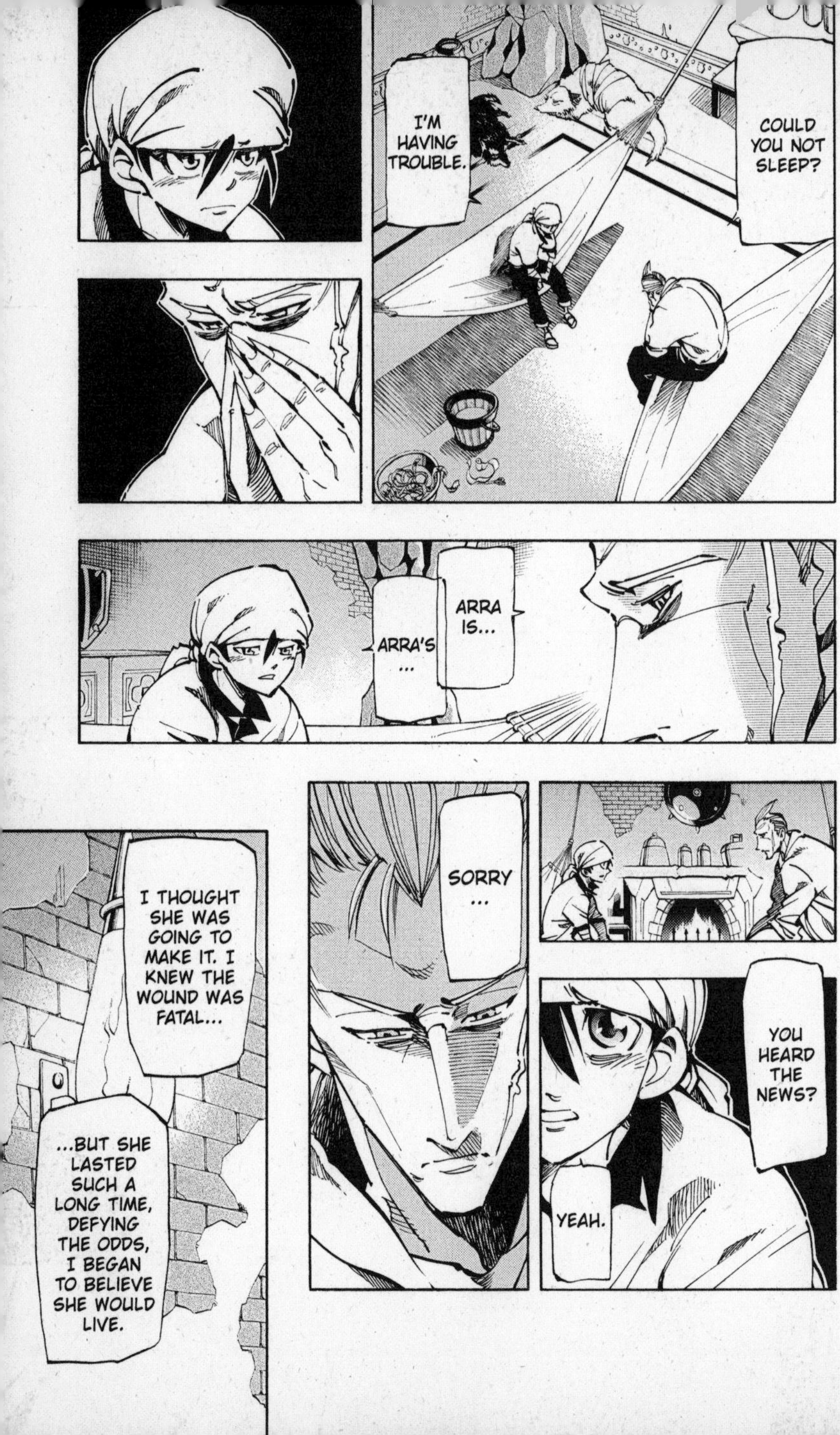
COULD YOU NOT SLEEP?
I'M HAVING TROUBLE.
ARRA IS...
ARRA'S ...
YOU HEARD THE NEWS?
YEAH.
SORRY ...
I THOUGHT SHE WAS GOING TO MAKE IT. I KNEW THE WOUND WAS FATAL...
...BUT SHE LASTED SUCH A LONG TIME, DEFYING THE ODDS, I BEGAN TO BELIEVE SHE WOULD LIVE.

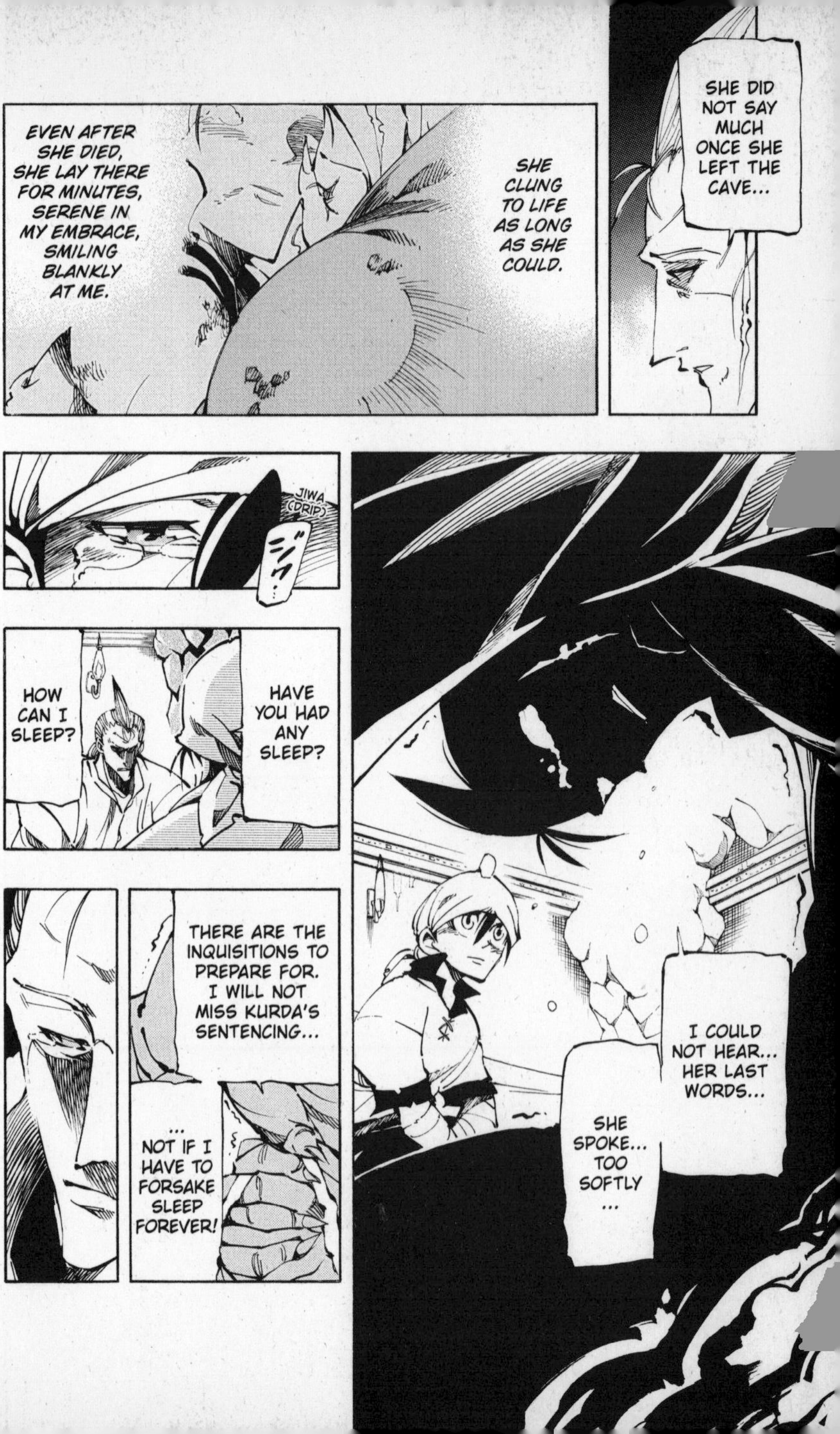
SHE DID NOT SAY MUCH ONCE SHE LEFT THE CAVE...
SHE CLUNG TO LIFE AS LONG AS SHE COULD.
EVEN AFTER SHE DIED, SHE LAY THERE FOR MINUTES, SERENE IN MY EMBRACE, SMILING BLANKLY AT ME.
I COULD NOT HEAR... HER LAST WORDS...
SHE SPOKE... TOO SOFTLY ...
JIWA (DRIP)
ジワ…
HAVE YOU HAD ANY SLEEP?
HOW CAN I SLEEP?
THERE ARE THE INQUISITIONS TO PREPARE FOR. I WILL NOT MISS KURDA'S SENTENCING...
... NOT IF I HAVE TO FORSAKE SLEEP FOREVER!

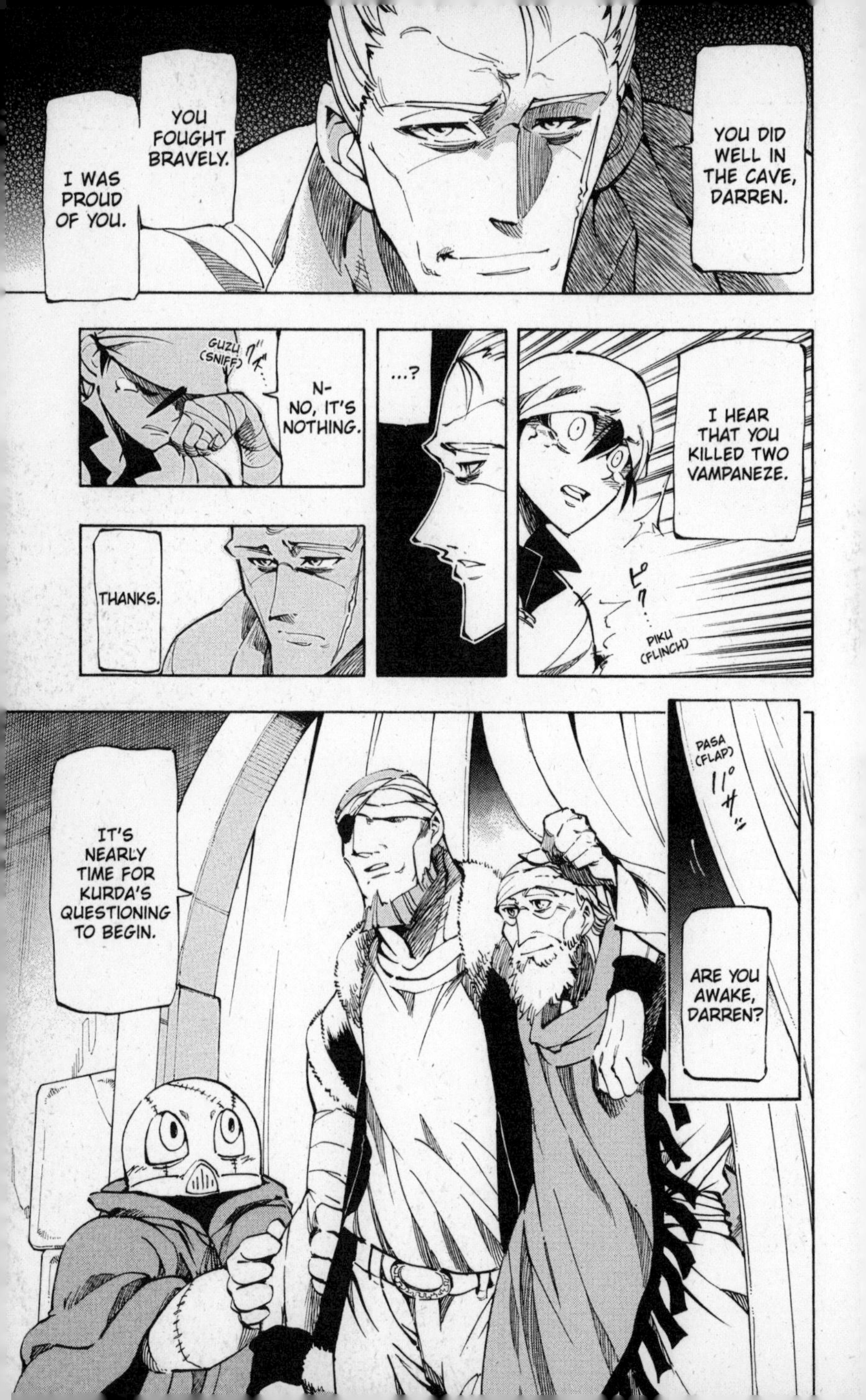

YOU DID WELL IN THE CAVE, DARREN.
YOU FOUGHT BRAVELY.
I WAS PROUD OF YOU.
I HEAR THAT YOU KILLED TWO VAMPANEZE.
PIKU (FLINCH)
...?
N- NO, IT'S NOTHING.
GUZU (SNIFF)
THANKS.
PASA (FLAP)
ARE YOU AWAKE, DARREN?
IT'S NEARLY TIME FOR KURDA'S QUESTIONING TO BEGIN.

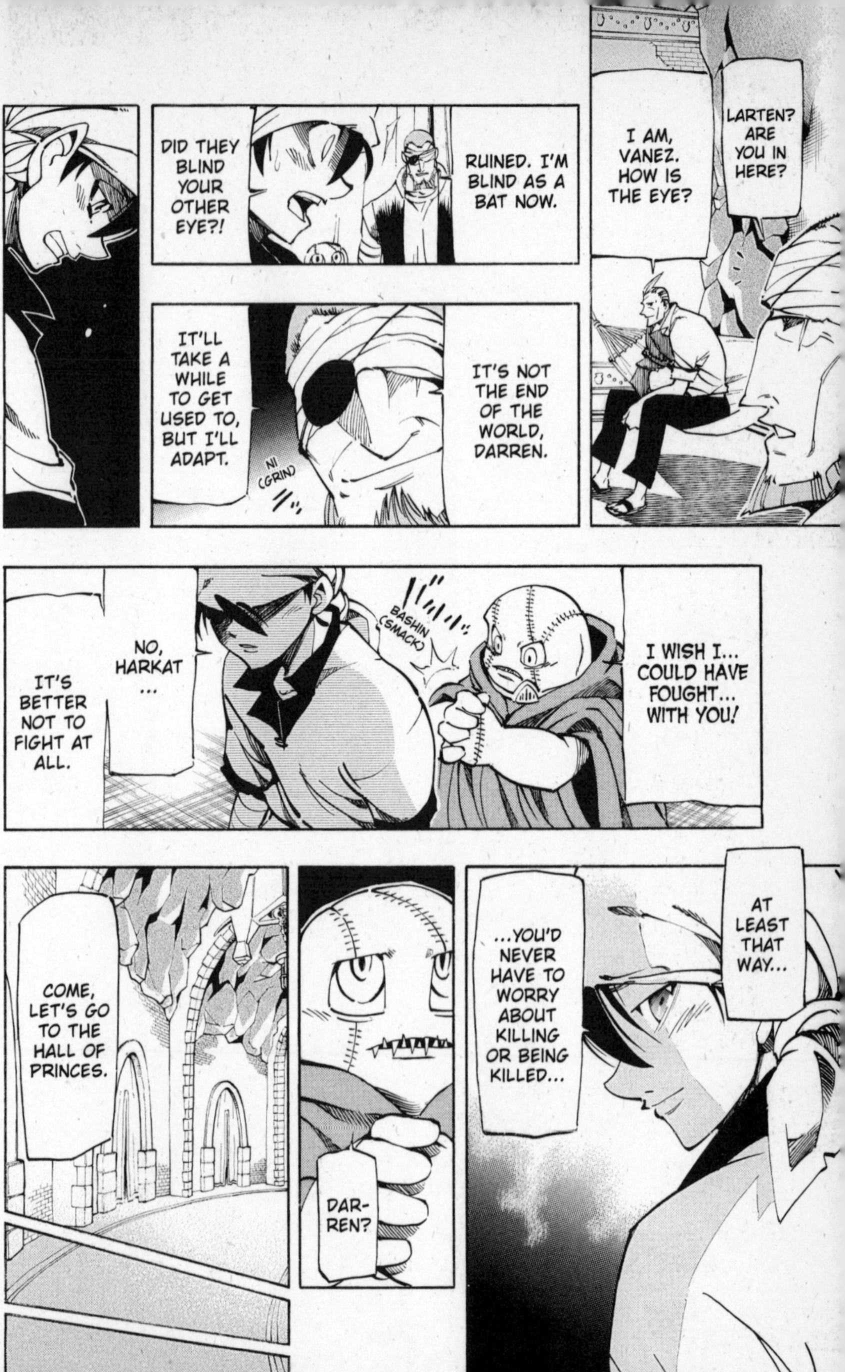

LARTEN? ARE YOU IN HERE?
I AM, VANEZ. HOW IS THE EYE?
RUINED. I'M BLIND AS A BAT NOW.
DID THEY BLIND YOUR OTHER EYE?!
IT'S NOT THE END OF THE WORLD, DARREN.
IT'LL TAKE A WHILE TO GET USED TO, BUT I'LL ADAPT.
NI (GRIN)
I WISH I... COULD HAVE FOUGHT... WITH YOU!
BASHIN (SMACK)
NO, HARKAT ...
IT'S BETTER NOT TO FIGHT AT ALL.
AT LEAST THAT WAY...
...YOU'D NEVER HAVE TO WORRY ABOUT KILLING OR BEING KILLED...
DAR-REN?
COME, LET'S GO TO THE HALL OF PRINCES.

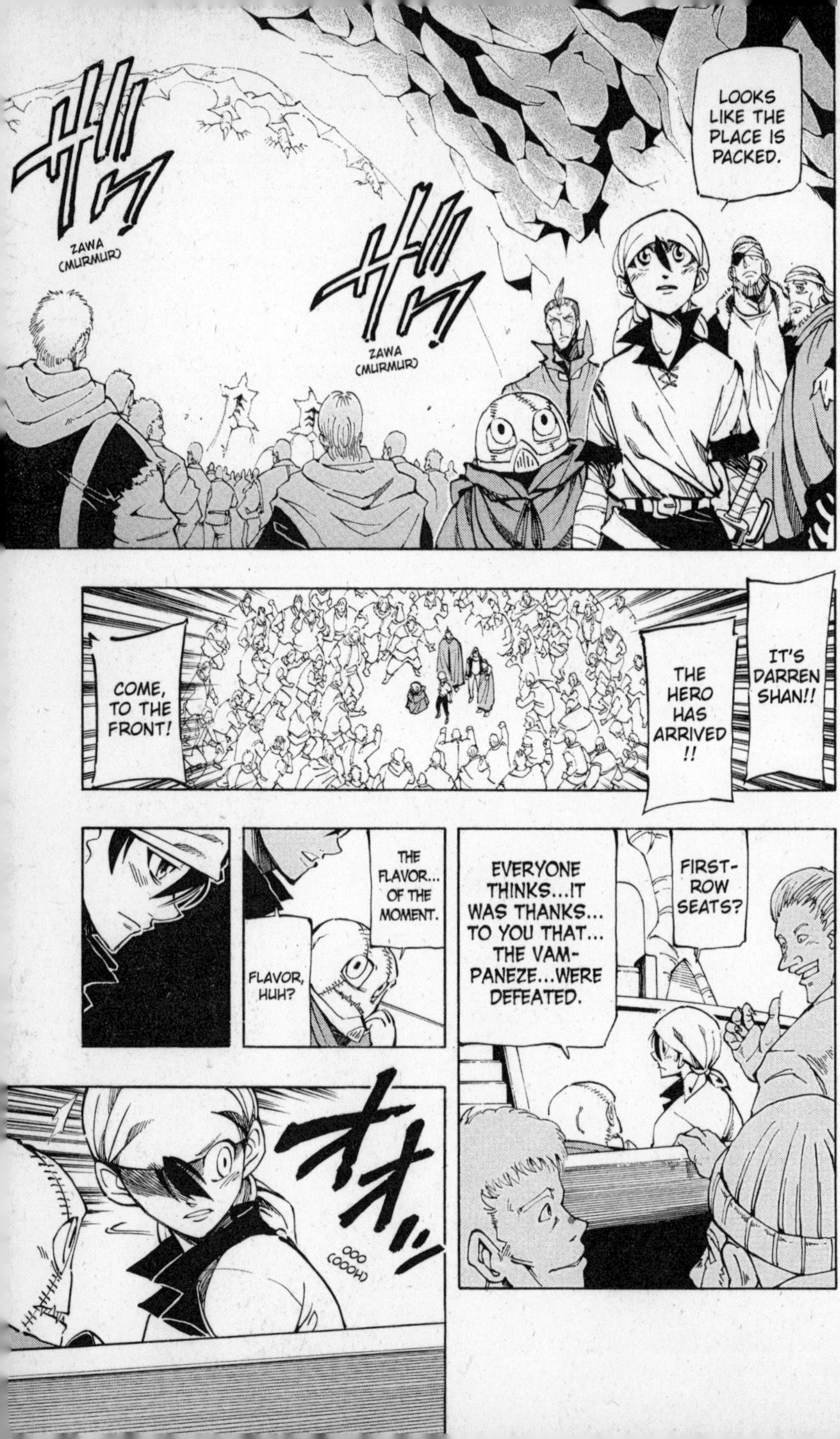
LOOKS LIKE THE PLACE IS PACKED.
ZAWA (MURMUR)
ZAWA (MURMUR)
IT'S DARREN SHAN!!
THE HERO HAS ARRIVED!!
COME, TO THE FRONT!
FIRST-ROW SEATS?
EVERYONE THINKS...IT WAS THANKS... TO YOU THAT... THE VAM-PANEZE...WERE DEFEATED.
THE FLAVOR... OF THE MOMENT.
FLAVOR, HUH?
OOO (OOOH)

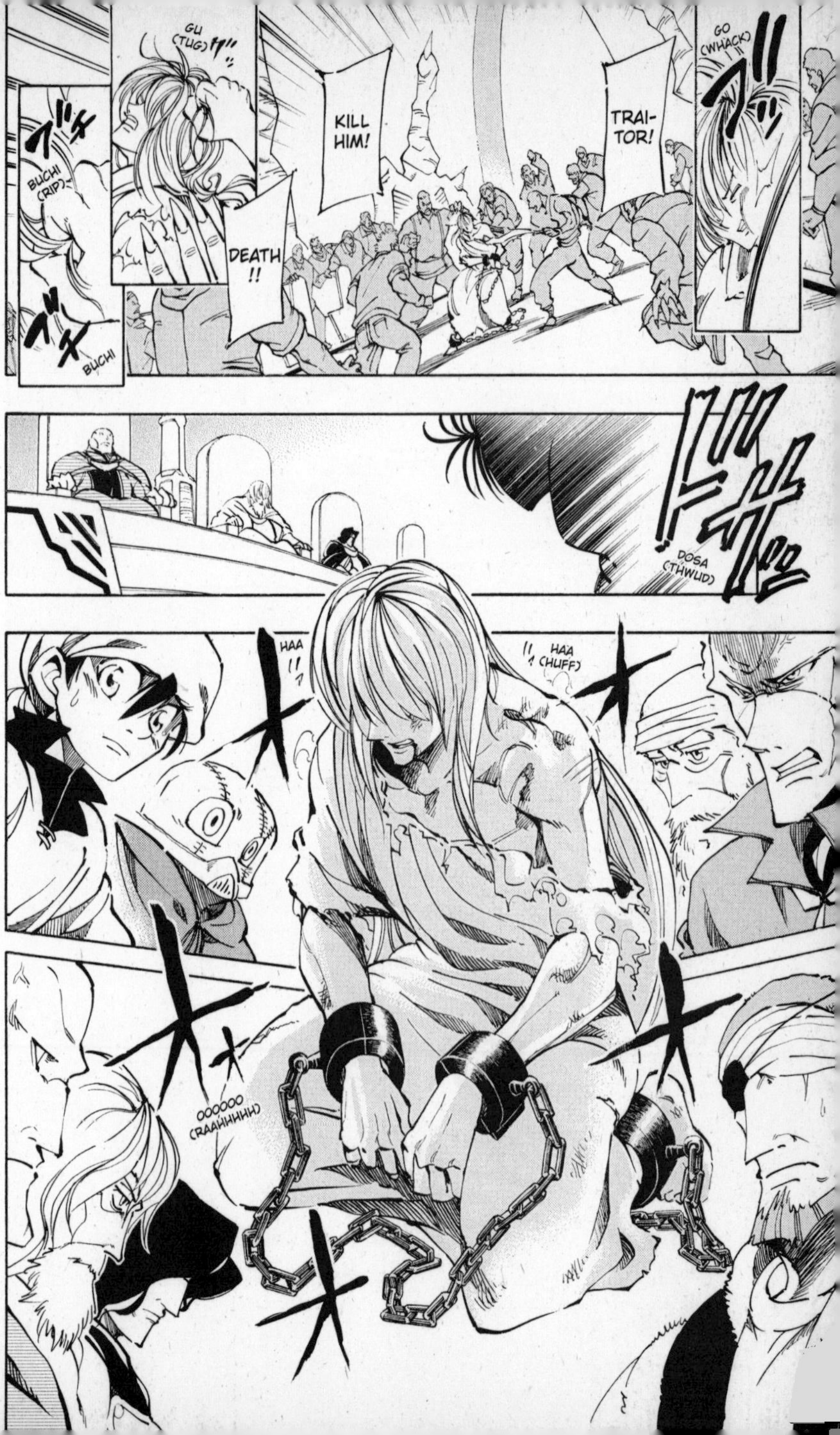
GO (WHACK)
TRAI-TOR!
KILL HIM!
DEATH !!
GU (TUG)
BUCHI (RIP)
BUCHI
DOSA (THWUD)
!! HAA (CHUFF)
HAA !!
OOOOOO (RAAHHHHH)

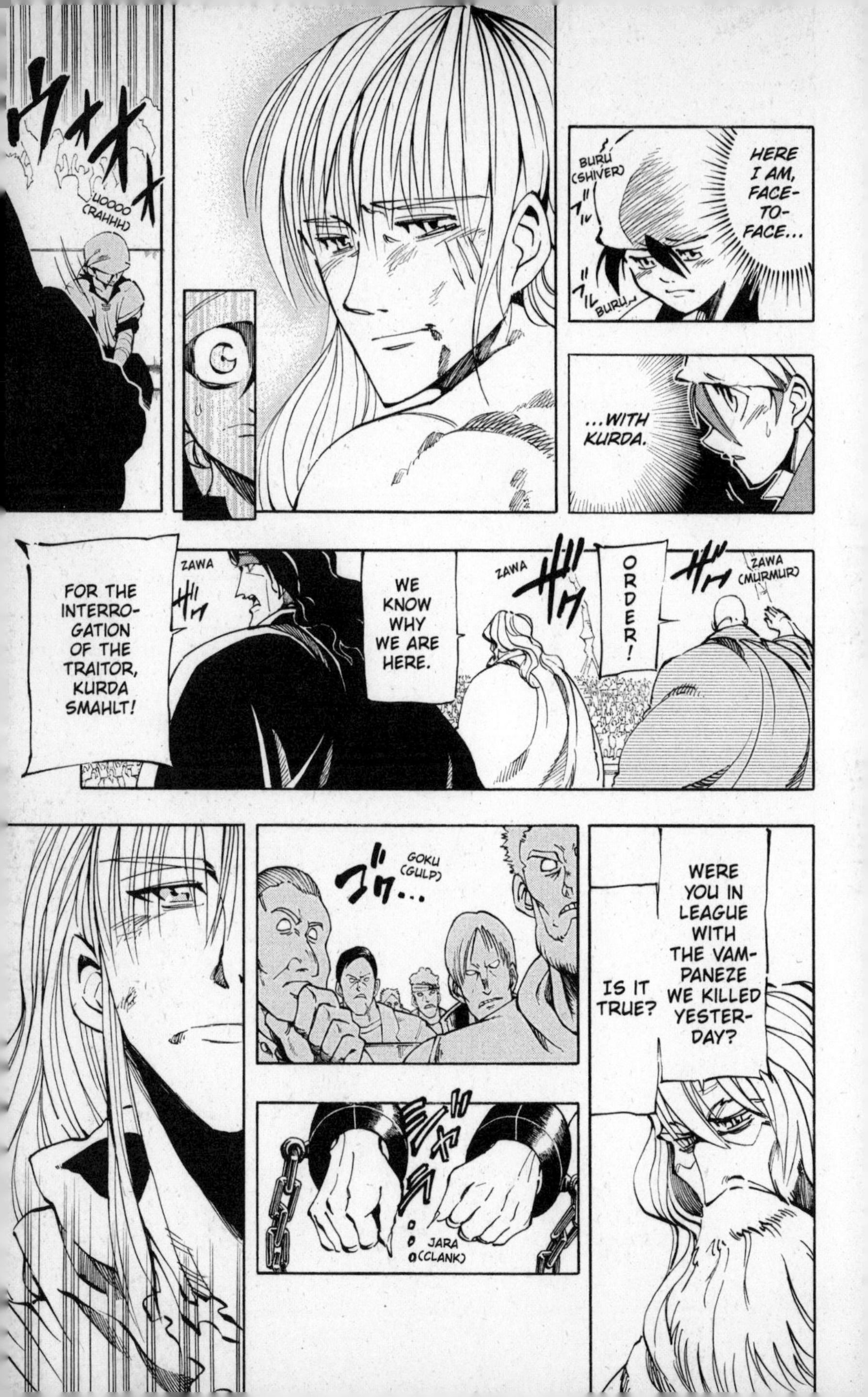
BURU (SHIVER)
HERE I AM, FACE-TO-FACE...
BURU
...WITH KURDA.
UOOOO (RAHHH)
ZAWA (MURMUR)
ORDER!
ZAWA
WE KNOW WHY WE ARE HERE.
ZAWA
FOR THE INTERROGATION OF THE TRAITOR, KURDA SMAHLT!
WERE YOU IN LEAGUE WITH THE VAMPANEZE WE KILLED YESTERDAY?
IS IT TRUE?
GOKU (GULP)
JARA (CLANK)

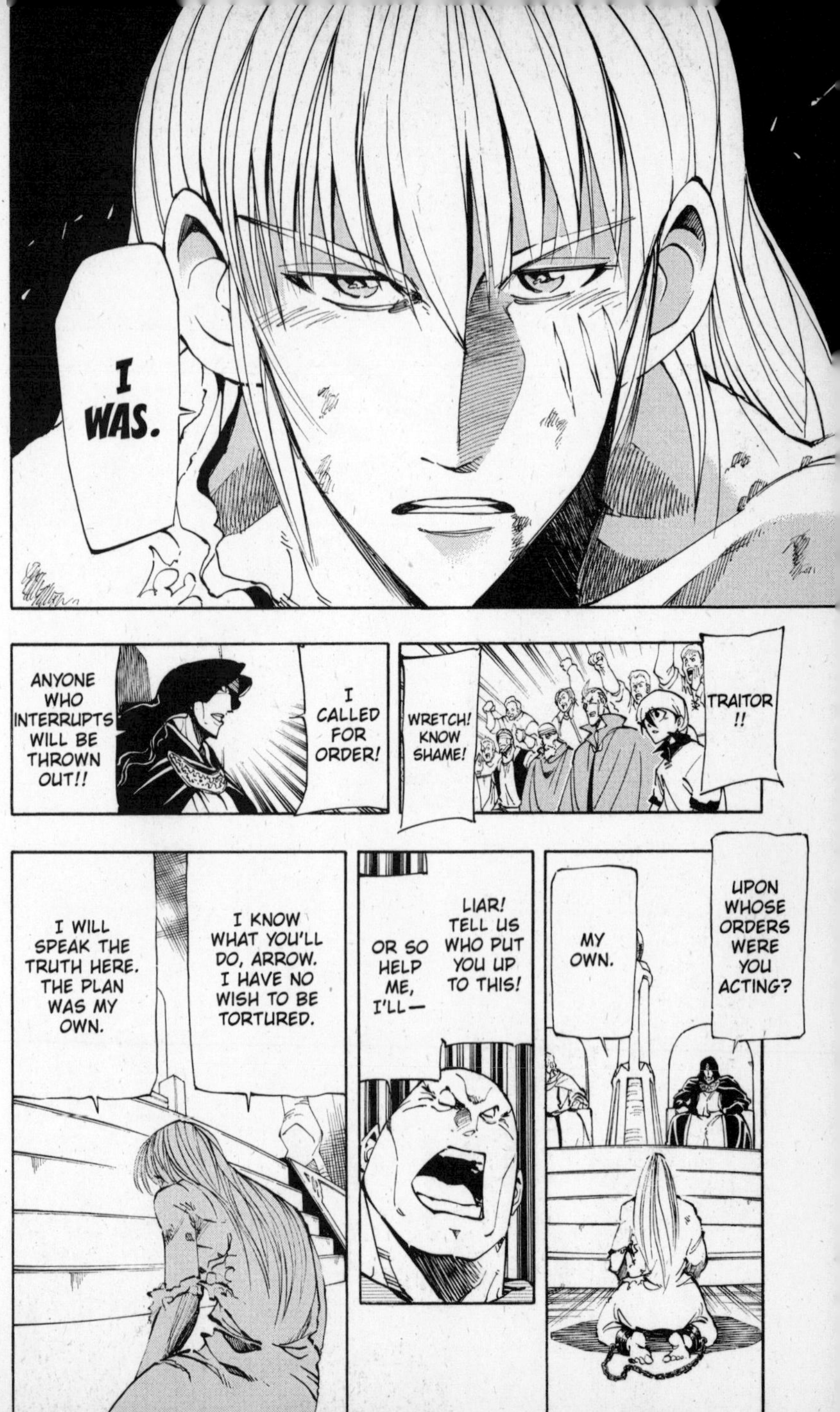
I WAS.
TRAITOR !!
WRETCH! KNOW SHAME!
I CALLED FOR ORDER!
ANYONE WHO INTERRUPTS WILL BE THROWN OUT!!
UPON WHOSE ORDERS WERE YOU ACTING?
MY OWN.
LIAR! TELL US WHO PUT YOU UP TO THIS!
OR SO HELP ME, I'LL—
I KNOW WHAT YOU'LL DO, ARROW. I HAVE NO WISH TO BE TORTURED.
I WILL SPEAK THE TRUTH HERE. THE PLAN WAS MY OWN.

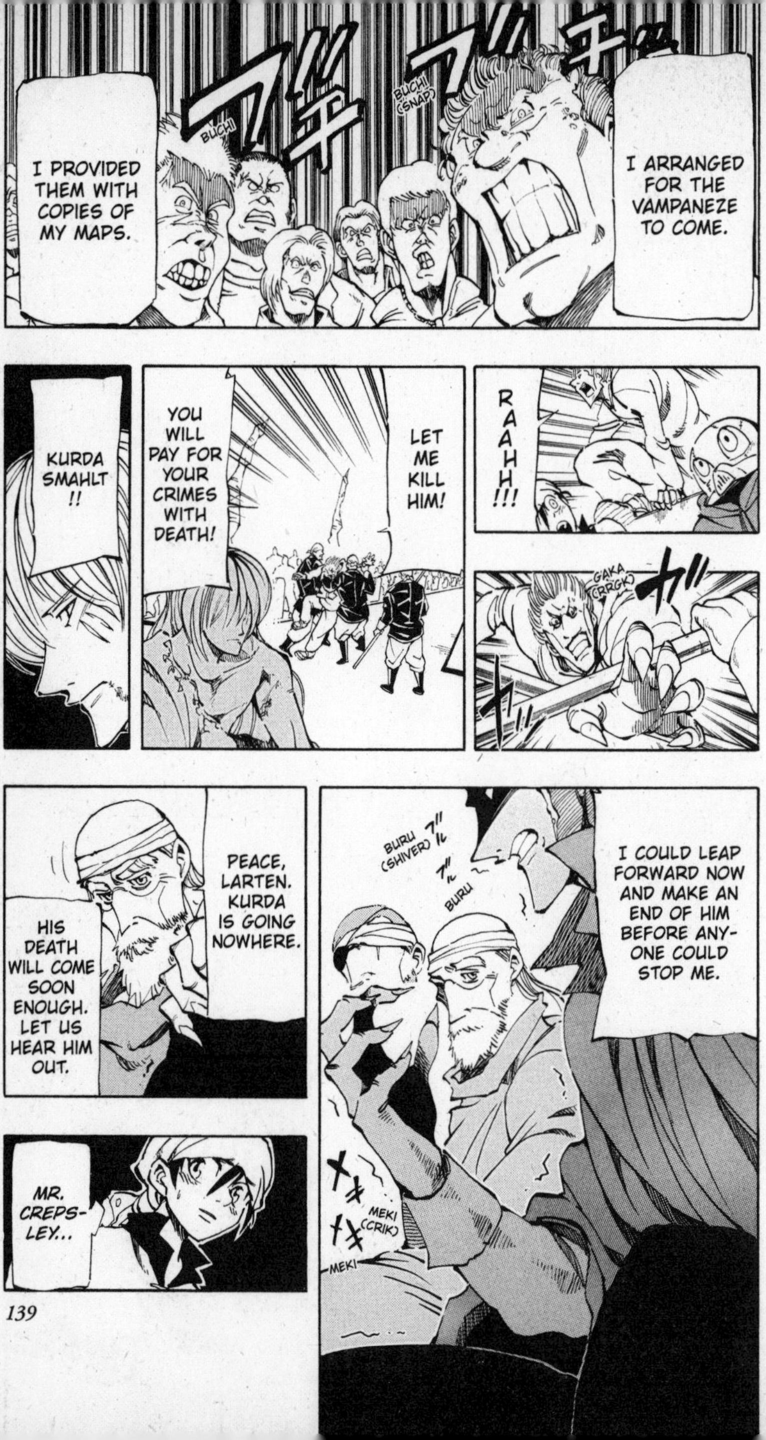
I ARRANGED FOR THE VAMPANEZE TO COME.
BUCHI (SNAP)
BUCHI
I PROVIDED THEM WITH COPIES OF MY MAPS.
RAAHH!!!
GAKA (CRRGK)
LET ME KILL HIM!
YOU WILL PAY FOR YOUR CRIMES WITH DEATH!
KURDA SMAHLT !!
I COULD LEAP FORWARD NOW AND MAKE AN END OF HIM BEFORE ANY-ONE COULD STOP ME.
BURU (SHIVER)
BURU
MEKI (CRIK)
MEKI
PEACE, LARTEN. KURDA IS GOING NOWHERE.
HIS DEATH WILL COME SOON ENOUGH. LET US HEAR HIM OUT.
MR. CREPS-LEY...

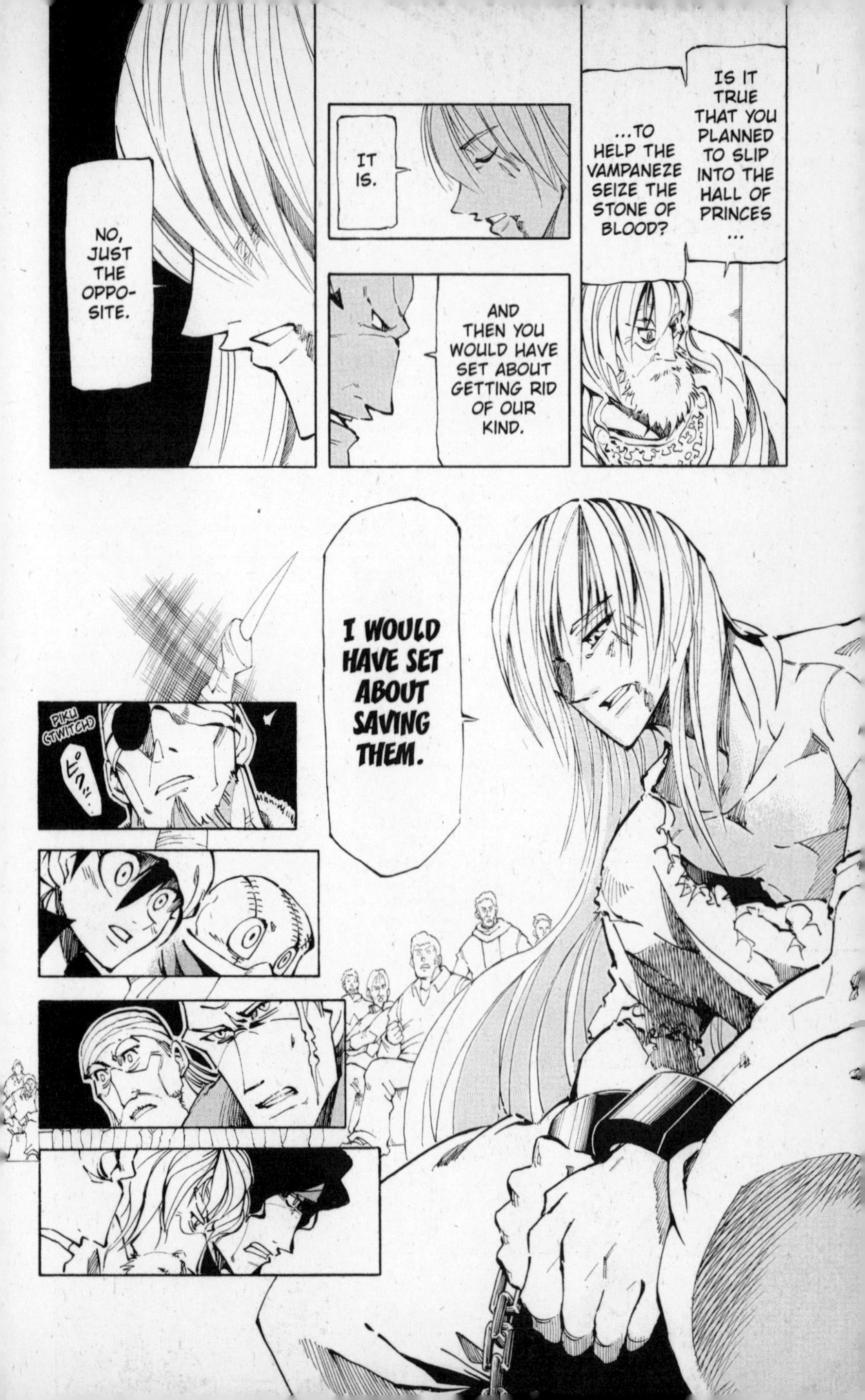

IS IT TRUE THAT YOU PLANNED TO SLIP INTO THE HALL OF PRINCES ...
...TO HELP THE VAMPANEZE SEIZE THE STONE OF BLOOD?
IT IS.
AND THEN YOU WOULD HAVE SET ABOUT GETTING RID OF OUR KIND.
NO, JUST THE OPPO-SITE.
I WOULD HAVE SET ABOUT SAVING THEM.
PIKU (TWITCH)

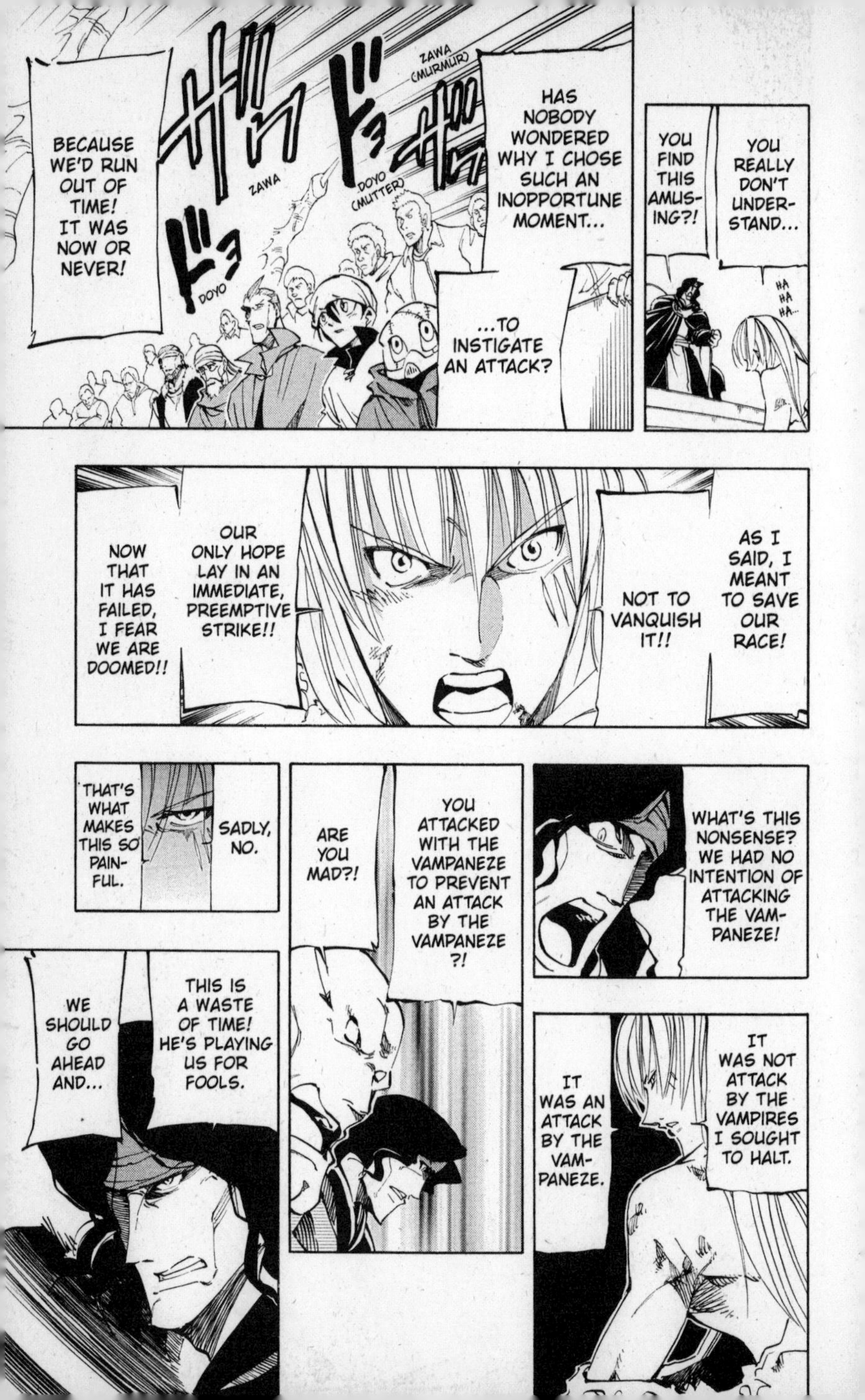
YOU REALLY DON'T UNDER-STAND...
YOU FIND THIS AMUS-ING?!
HA HA HA...
HAS NOBODY WONDERED WHY I CHOSE SUCH AN INOPPORTUNE MOMENT...
...TO INSTIGATE AN ATTACK?
ZAWA (MURMUR)
DOYO (MUTTER)
ZAWA
DOYO
BECAUSE WE'D RUN OUT OF TIME! IT WAS NOW OR NEVER!
AS I SAID, I MEANT TO SAVE OUR RACE!
NOT TO VANQUISH IT!!
OUR ONLY HOPE LAY IN AN IMMEDIATE, PREEMPTIVE STRIKE!!
NOW THAT IT HAS FAILED, I FEAR WE ARE DOOMED!!
WHAT'S THIS NONSENSE? WE HAD NO INTENTION OF ATTACKING THE VAM-PANEZE!
IT WAS NOT ATTACK BY THE VAMPIRES I SOUGHT TO HALT.
IT WAS AN ATTACK BY THE VAM-PANEZE.
YOU ATTACKED WITH THE VAMPANEZE TO PREVENT AN ATTACK BY THE VAMPANEZE ?!
ARE YOU MAD?!
SADLY, NO.
THAT'S WHAT MAKES THIS SO PAIN-FUL.
THIS IS A WASTE OF TIME! HE'S PLAYING US FOR FOOLS.
WE SHOULD GO AHEAD AND...

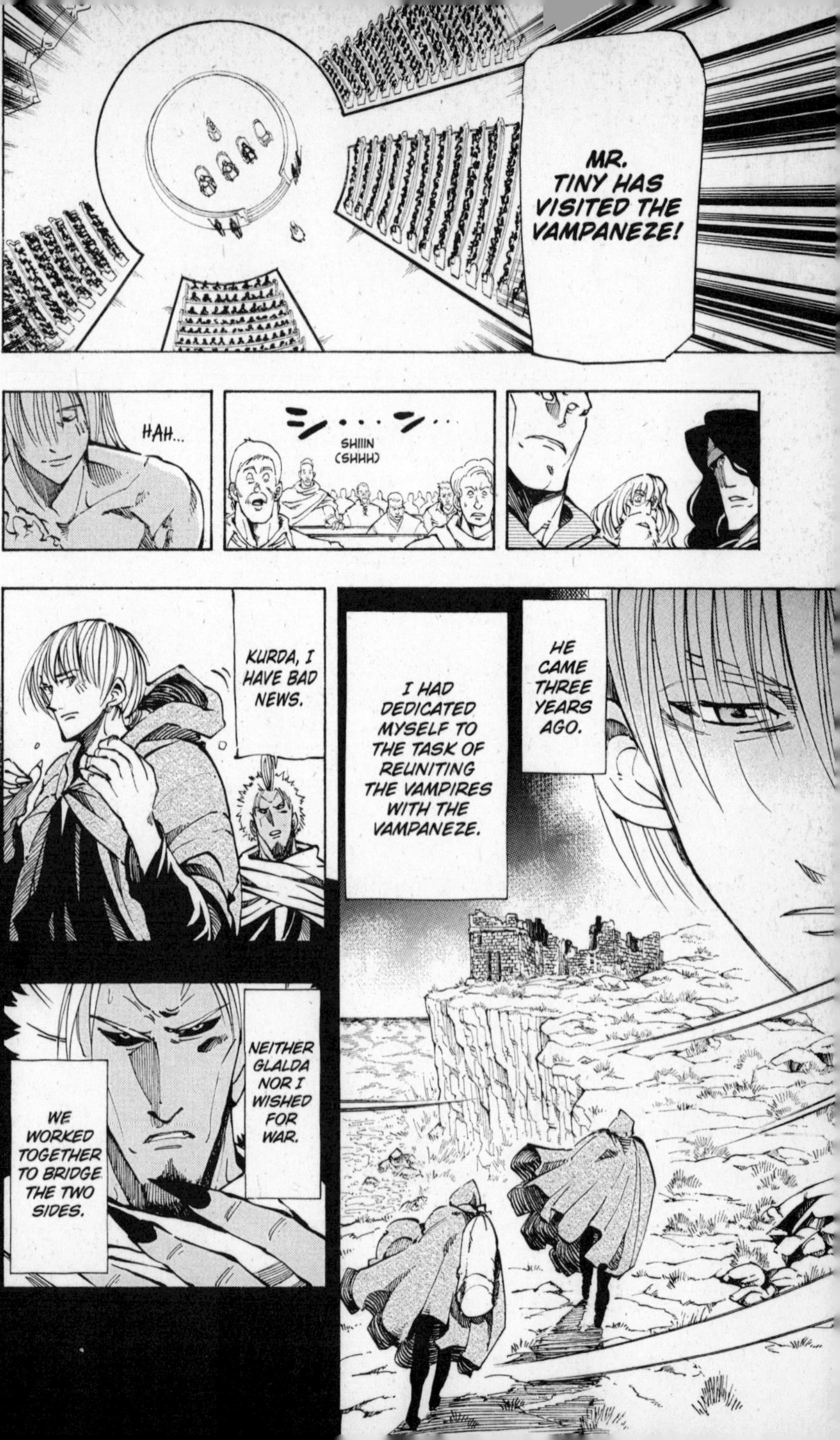
MR. TINY HAS VISITED THE VAMPANEZE!
SHIIIN (SHHH)
HAH...
HE CAME THREE YEARS AGO.
I HAD DEDICATED MYSELF TO THE TASK OF REUNITING THE VAMPIRES WITH THE VAMPANEZE.
KURDA, I HAVE BAD NEWS.
NEITHER GLALDA NOR I WISHED FOR WAR.
WE WORKED TOGETHER TO BRIDGE THE TWO SIDES.

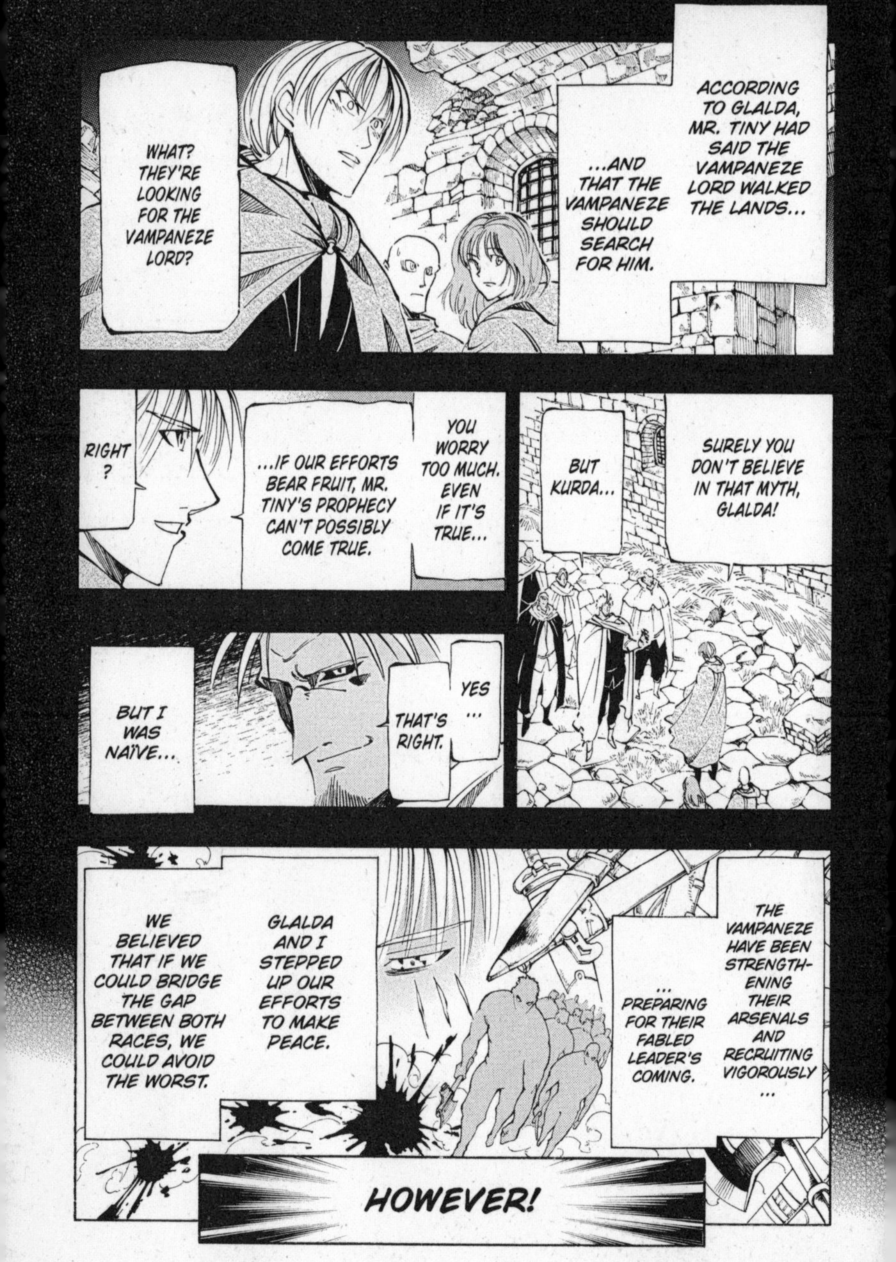
ACCORDING TO GLALDA, MR. TINY HAD SAID THE VAMPANEZE LORD WALKED THE LANDS...
...AND THAT THE VAMPANEZE SHOULD SEARCH FOR HIM.
WHAT? THEY'RE LOOKING FOR THE VAMPANEZE LORD?
SURELY YOU DON'T BELIEVE IN THAT MYTH, GLALDA!
BUT KURDA...
YOU WORRY TOO MUCH. EVEN IF IT'S TRUE...
...IF OUR EFFORTS BEAR FRUIT, MR. TINY'S PROPHECY CAN'T POSSIBLY COME TRUE.
RIGHT ?
YES ...
THAT'S RIGHT.
BUT I WAS NAÏVE...
THE VAMPANEZE HAVE BEEN STRENGTH-ENING THEIR ARSENALS AND RECRUITING VIGOROUSLY ...
... PREPARING FOR THEIR FABLED LEADER'S COMING.
GLALDA AND I STEPPED UP OUR EFFORTS TO MAKE PEACE.
WE BELIEVED THAT IF WE COULD BRIDGE THE GAP BETWEEN BOTH RACES, WE COULD AVOID THE WORST.
HOWEVER!

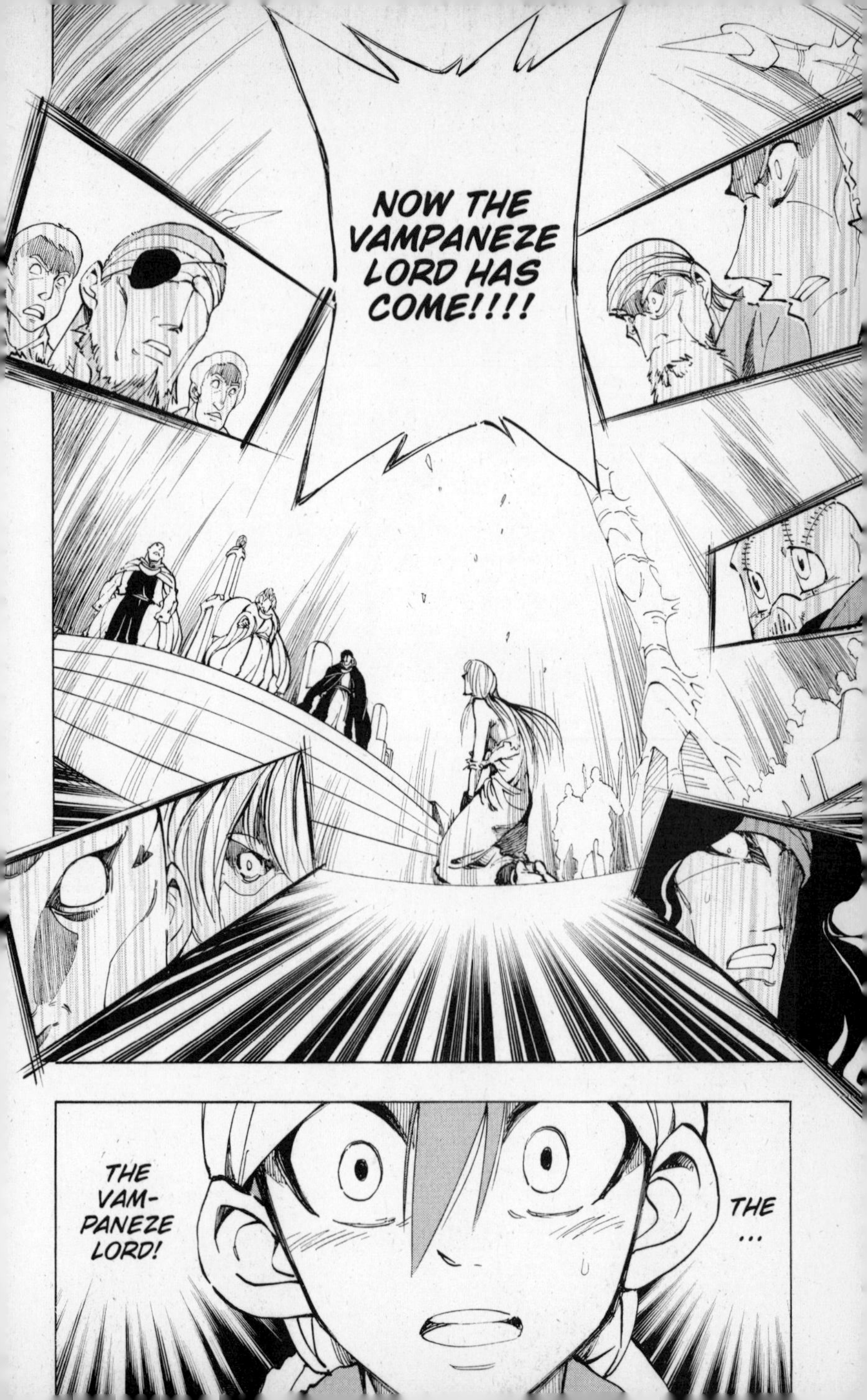
NOW THE VAMPANEZE LORD HAS COME!!!!
THE ...
THE VAM-PANEZE LORD!

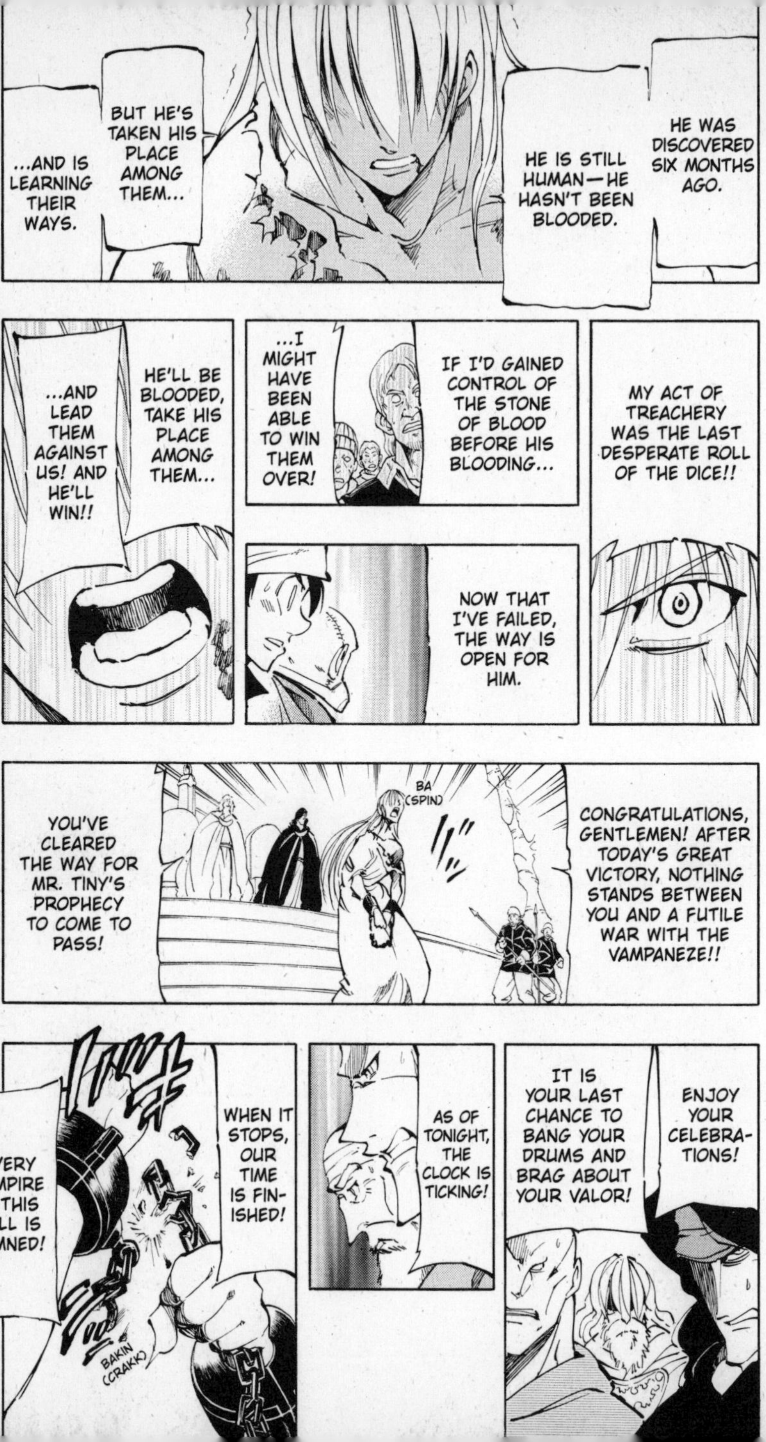
HE WAS DISCOVERED SIX MONTHS AGO.
HE IS STILL HUMAN—HE HASN'T BEEN BLOODED.
BUT HE'S TAKEN HIS PLACE AMONG THEM...
...AND IS LEARNING THEIR WAYS.
MY ACT OF TREACHERY WAS THE LAST DESPERATE ROLL OF THE DICE!!
IF I'D GAINED CONTROL OF THE STONE OF BLOOD BEFORE HIS BLOODING...
...I MIGHT HAVE BEEN ABLE TO WIN THEM OVER!
NOW THAT I'VE FAILED, THE WAY IS OPEN FOR HIM.
HE'LL BE BLOODED, TAKE HIS PLACE AMONG THEM...
...AND LEAD THEM AGAINST US! AND HE'LL WIN!!
CONGRATULATIONS, GENTLEMEN! AFTER TODAY'S GREAT VICTORY, NOTHING STANDS BETWEEN YOU AND A FUTILE WAR WITH THE VAMPANEZE!!
BA (SPIN)
YOU'VE CLEARED THE WAY FOR MR. TINY'S PROPHECY TO COME TO PASS!
ENJOY YOUR CELEBRATIONS!
IT IS YOUR LAST CHANCE TO BANG YOUR DRUMS AND BRAG ABOUT YOUR VALOR!
AS OF TONIGHT, THE CLOCK IS TICKING!
WHEN IT STOPS, OUR TIME IS FINISHED!
EVERY VAMPIRE IN THIS HALL IS DAMNED!
BAKIN (CRAKK)

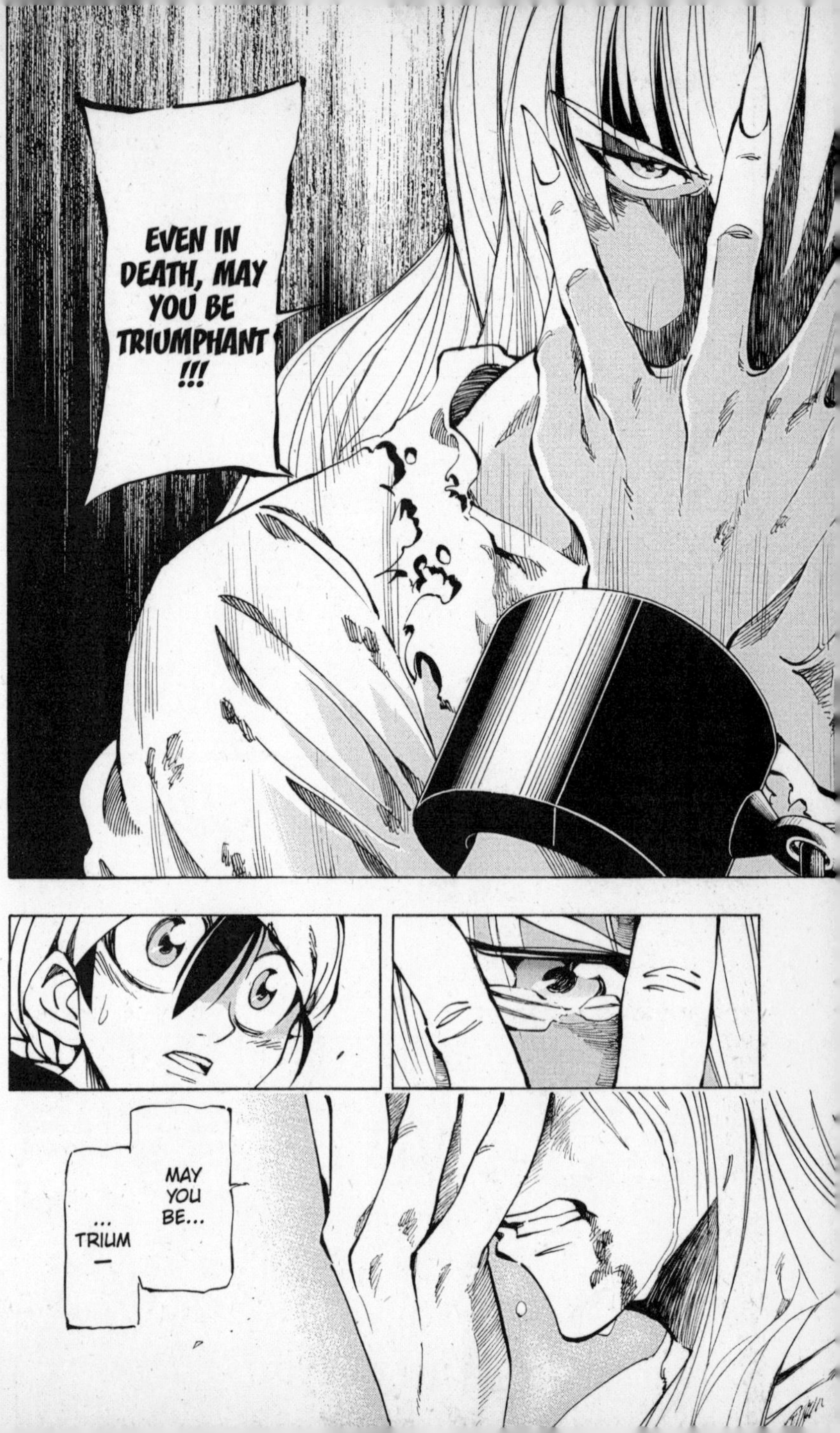
EVEN IN DEATH, MAY YOU BE TRIUMPHANT!!!
MAY YOU BE...
...TRIUM—

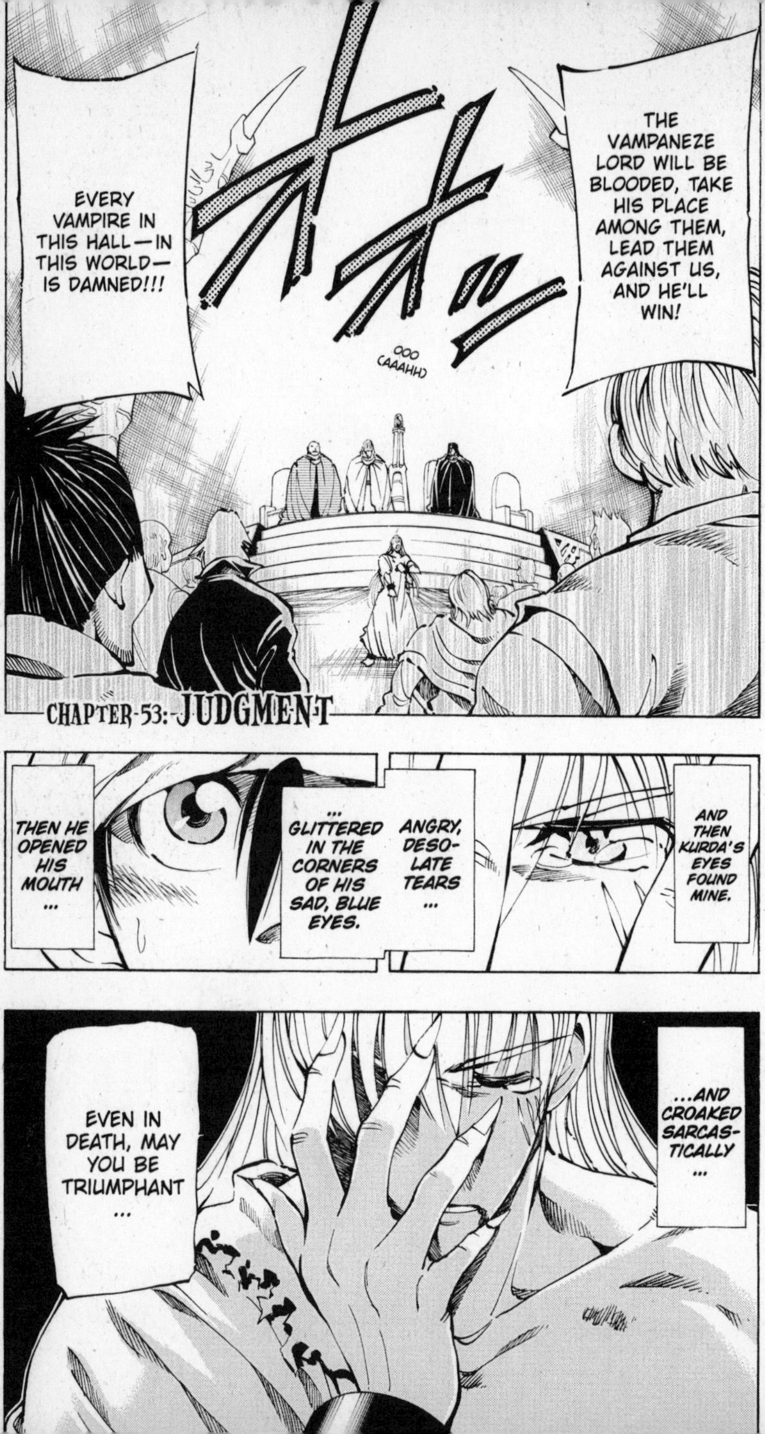
THE VAMPANEZE LORD WILL BE BLOODED, TAKE HIS PLACE AMONG THEM, LEAD THEM AGAINST US, AND HE'LL WIN!
OOO (AAAHH)
EVERY VAMPIRE IN THIS HALL—IN THIS WORLD—IS DAMNED!!!
CHAPTER 53: JUDGMENT
AND THEN KURDA'S EYES FOUND MINE.
ANGRY, DESO-LATE TEARS ...
... GLITTERED IN THE CORNERS OF HIS SAD, BLUE EYES.
THEN HE OPENED HIS MOUTH ...
...AND CROAKED SARCAS-TICALLY ...
EVEN IN DEATH, MAY YOU BE TRIUMPHANT ...

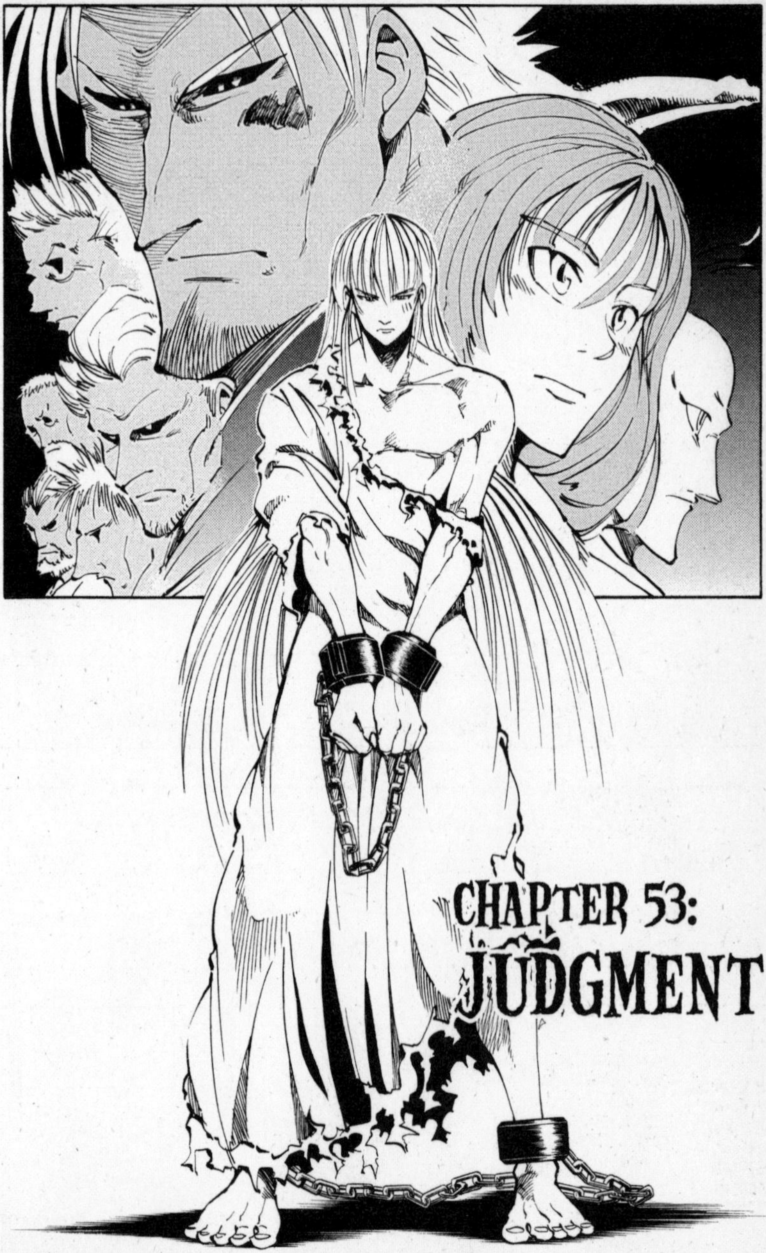
CHAPTER 53:
JUDGMENT

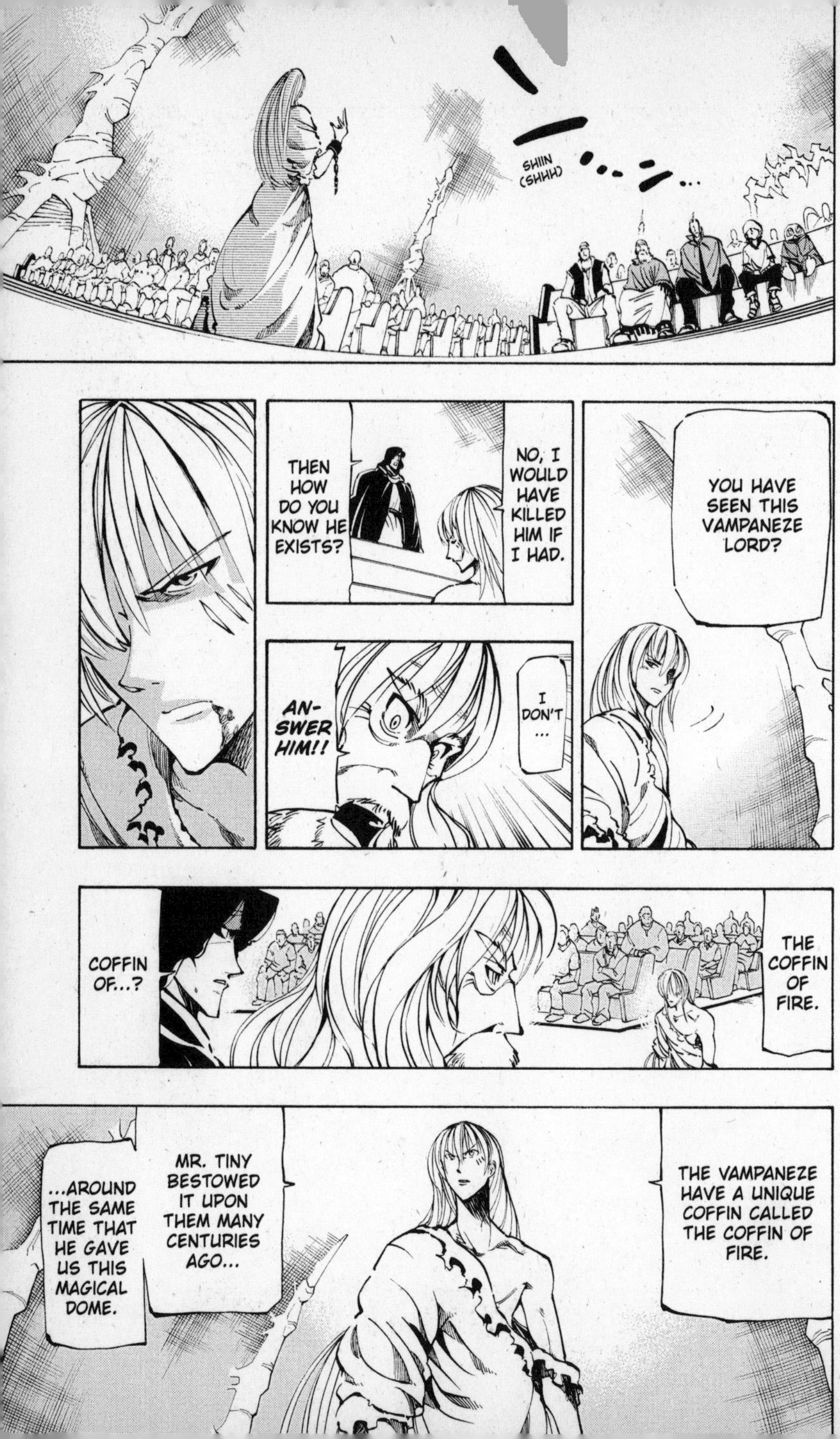
SHIIN (SHHH)
YOU HAVE SEEN THIS VAMPANEZE LORD?
NO, I WOULD HAVE KILLED HIM IF I HAD.
THEN HOW DO YOU KNOW HE EXISTS?
I DON'T ...
AN-SWER HIM!!
THE COFFIN OF FIRE.
COFFIN OF...?
THE VAMPANEZE HAVE A UNIQUE COFFIN CALLED THE COFFIN OF FIRE.
MR. TINY BESTOWED IT UPON THEM MANY CENTURIES AGO...
...AROUND THE SAME TIME THAT HE GAVE US THIS MAGICAL DOME.

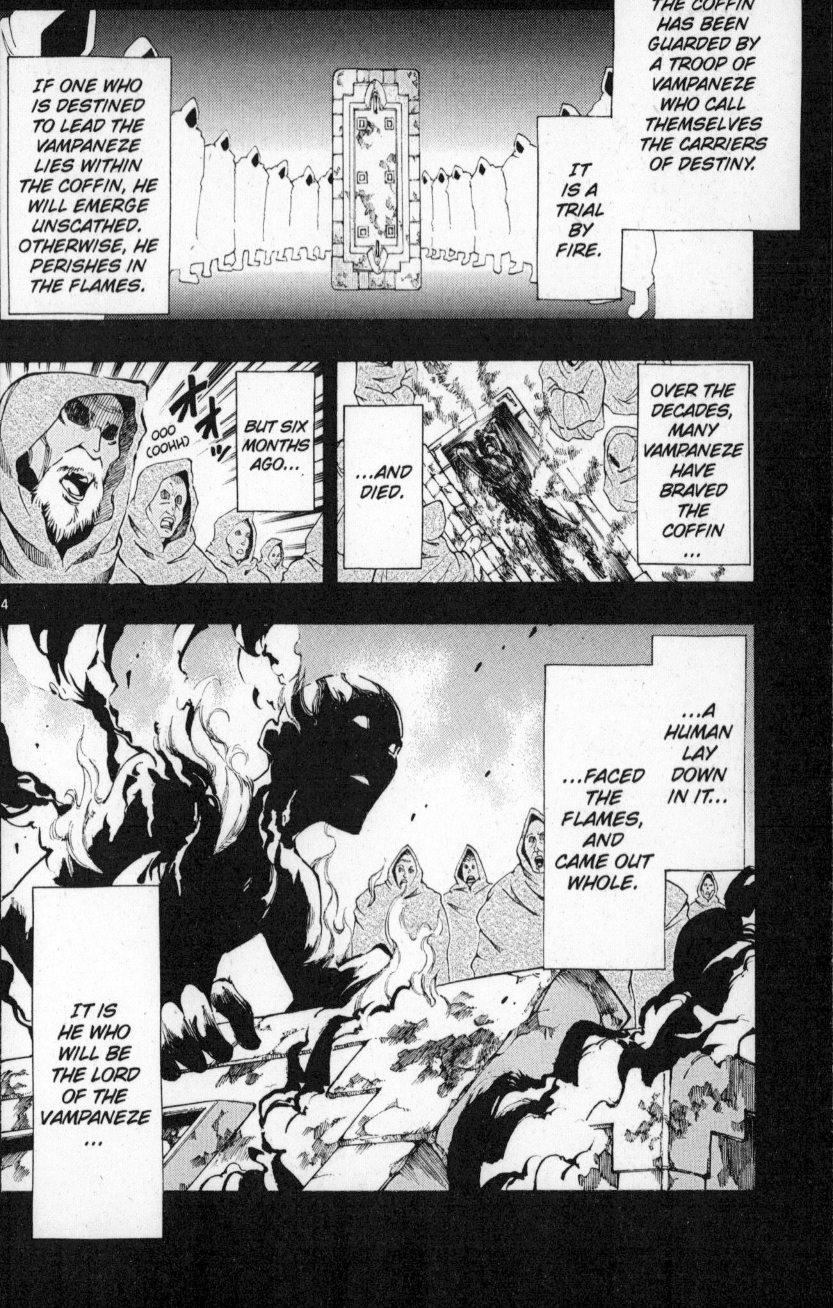
THE COFFIN HAS BEEN GUARDED BY A TROOP OF VAMPANEZE WHO CALL THEMSELVES THE CARRIERS OF DESTINY.
IT IS A TRIAL BY FIRE.
IF ONE WHO IS DESTINED TO LEAD THE VAMPANEZE LIES WITHIN THE COFFIN, HE WILL EMERGE UNSCATHED. OTHERWISE, HE PERISHES IN THE FLAMES.
OVER THE DECADES, MANY VAMPANEZE HAVE BRAVED THE COFFIN ...
...AND DIED.
BUT SIX MONTHS AGO...
オオッ
OOO (OOHH)
...A HUMAN LAY DOWN IN IT...
...FACED THE FLAMES, AND CAME OUT WHOLE.
IT IS HE WHO WILL BE THE LORD OF THE VAMPANEZE ...

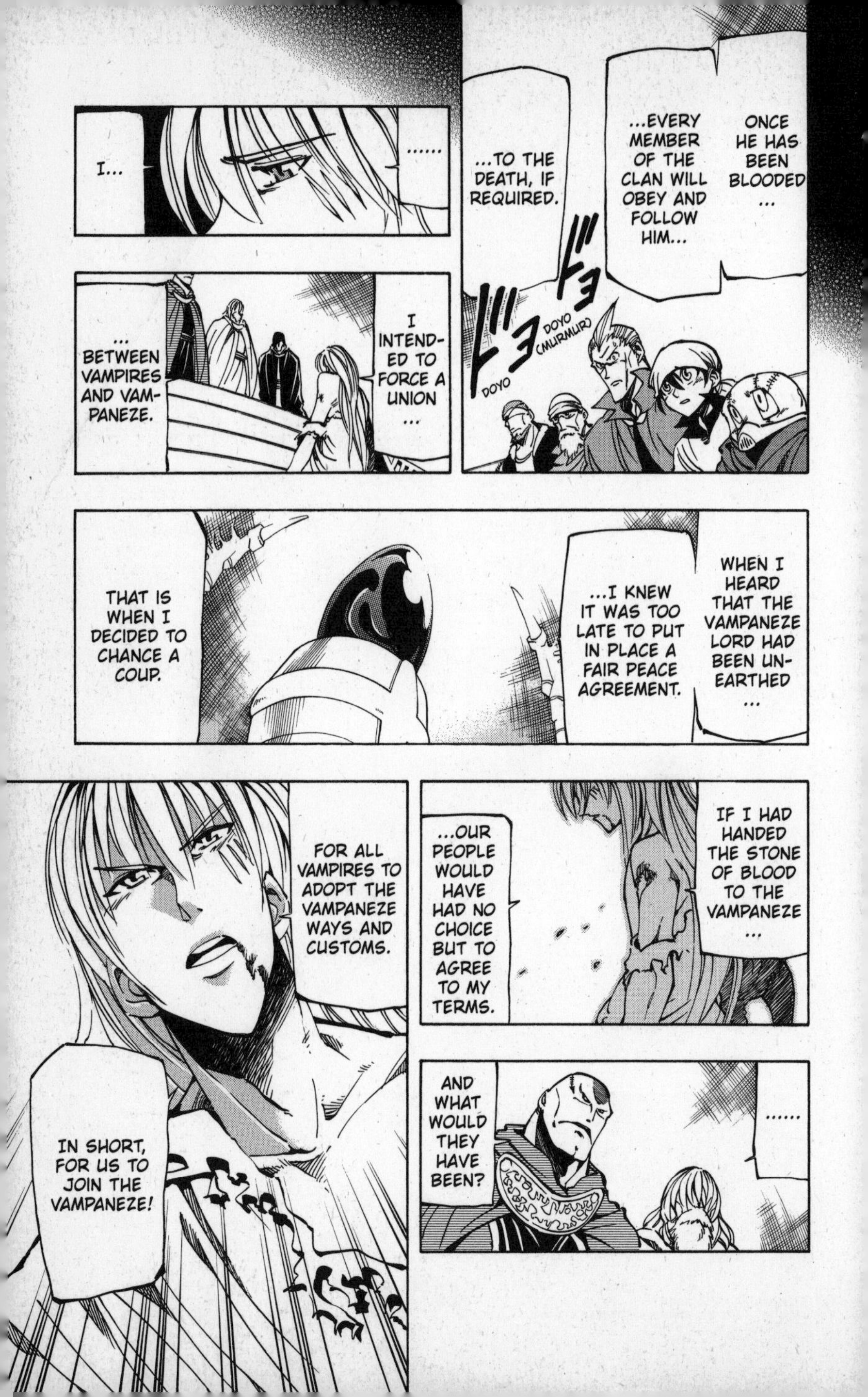
ONCE HE HAS BEEN BLOODED ...
...EVERY MEMBER OF THE CLAN WILL OBEY AND FOLLOW HIM...
...TO THE DEATH, IF REQUIRED.
ドヨ
ドヨ
DOYO (MURMUR)
DOYO
......
I...
I INTENDED TO FORCE A UNION ...
... BETWEEN VAMPIRES AND VAMPANEZE.
WHEN I HEARD THAT THE VAMPANEZE LORD HAD BEEN UNEARTHED ...
...I KNEW IT WAS TOO LATE TO PUT IN PLACE A FAIR PEACE AGREEMENT.
THAT IS WHEN I DECIDED TO CHANCE A COUP.
IF I HAD HANDED THE STONE OF BLOOD TO THE VAMPANEZE ...
...OUR PEOPLE WOULD HAVE HAD NO CHOICE BUT TO AGREE TO MY TERMS.
......
AND WHAT WOULD THEY HAVE BEEN?
FOR ALL VAMPIRES TO ADOPT THE VAMPANEZE WAYS AND CUSTOMS.
IN SHORT, FOR US TO JOIN THE VAMPANEZE!

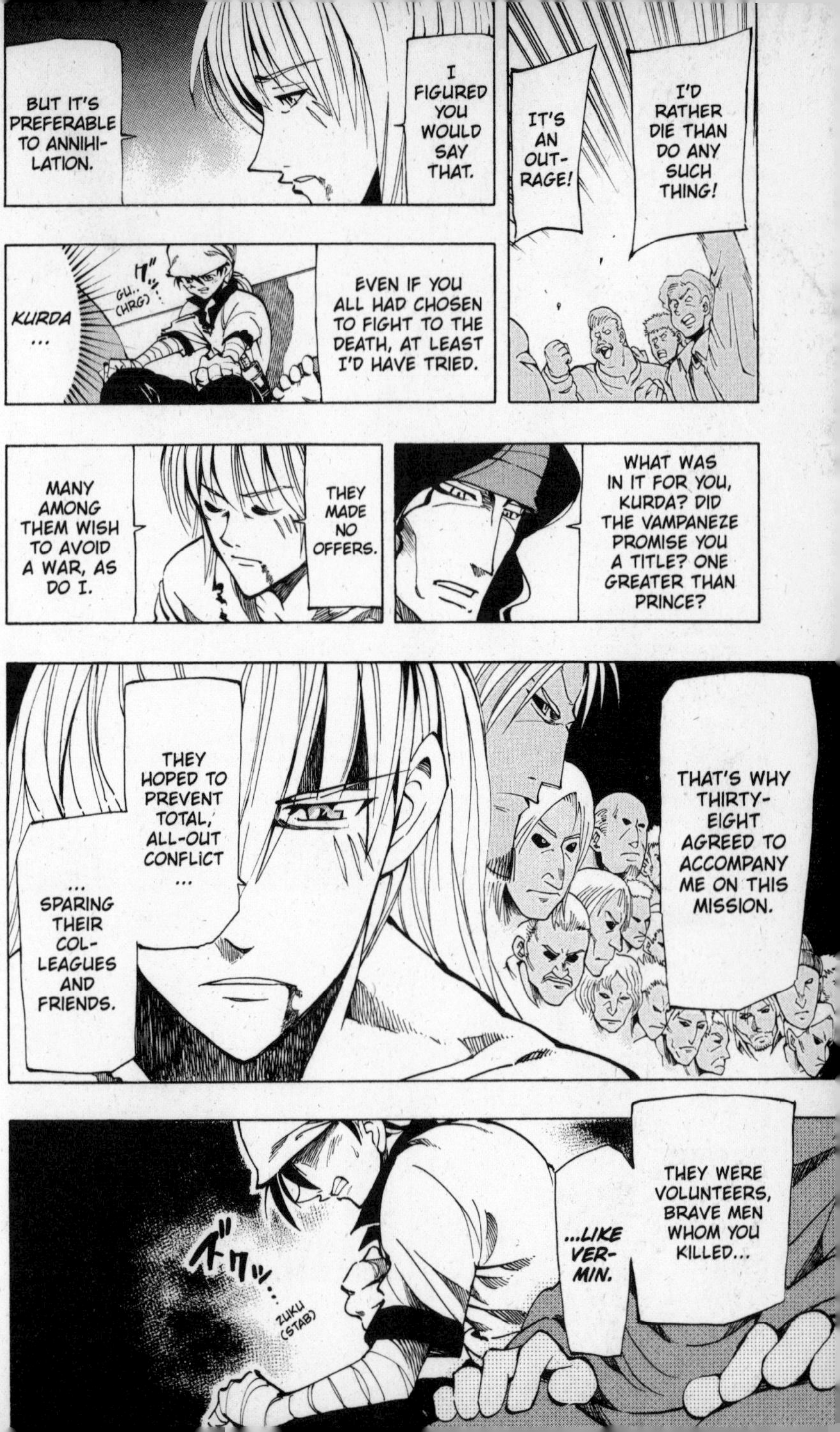
I'D RATHER DIE THAN DO ANY SUCH THING!
IT'S AN OUT-RAGE!
I FIGURED YOU WOULD SAY THAT.
BUT IT'S PREFERABLE TO ANNIHI-LATION.
EVEN IF YOU ALL HAD CHOSEN TO FIGHT TO THE DEATH, AT LEAST I'D HAVE TRIED.
GU.. (HRG)
KURDA ...
WHAT WAS IN IT FOR YOU, KURDA? DID THE VAMPANEZE PROMISE YOU A TITLE? ONE GREATER THAN PRINCE?
THEY MADE NO OFFERS.
MANY AMONG THEM WISH TO AVOID A WAR, AS DO I.
THAT'S WHY THIRTY-EIGHT AGREED TO ACCOMPANY ME ON THIS MISSION.
THEY HOPED TO PREVENT TOTAL, ALL-OUT CONFLICT ...
... SPARING THEIR COL-LEAGUES AND FRIENDS.
THEY WERE VOLUNTEERS, BRAVE MEN WHOM YOU KILLED...
...LIKE VER-MIN.
ZUKU (STAB)

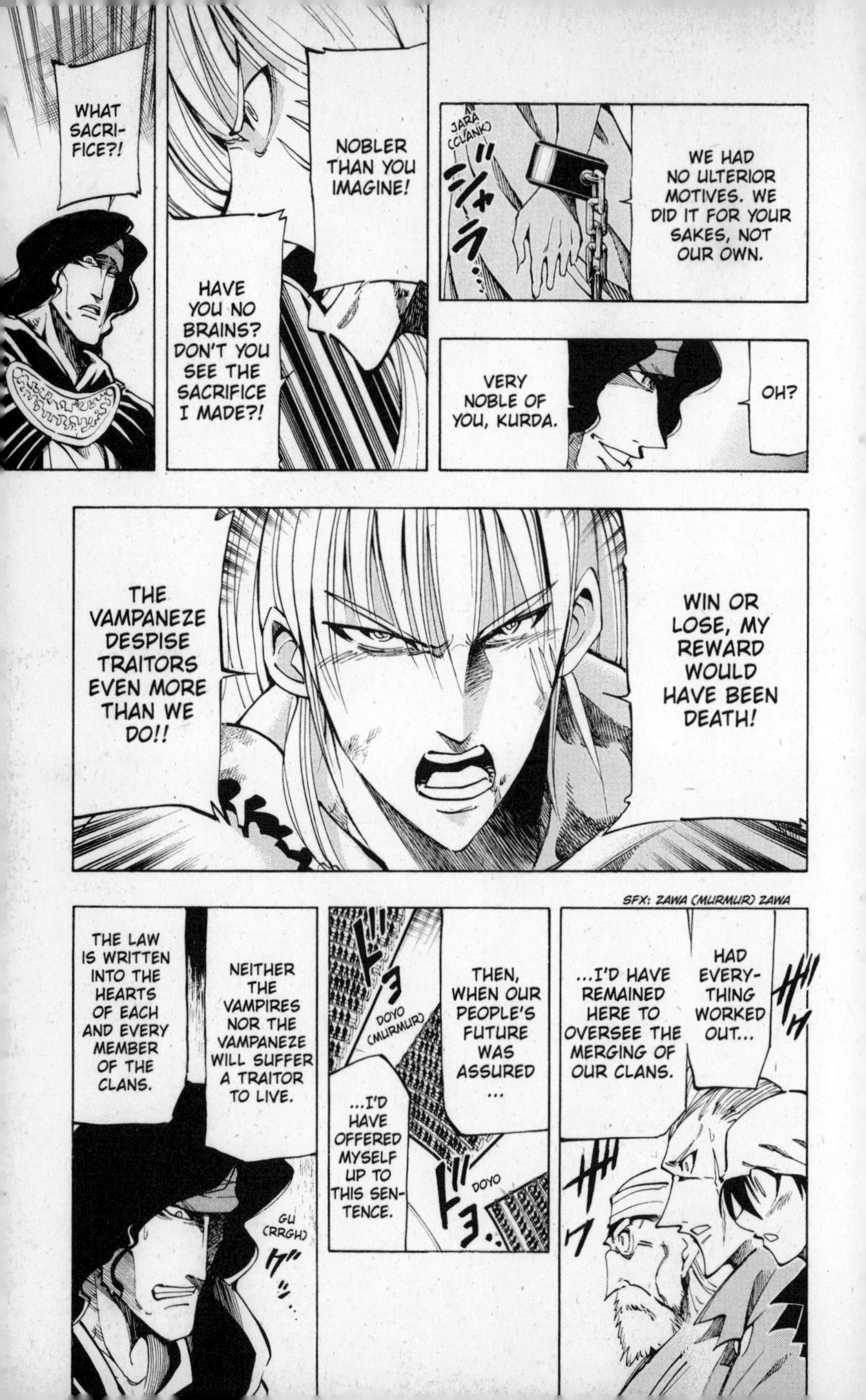
JARA (CLANK)
WE HAD NO ULTERIOR MOTIVES. WE DID IT FOR YOUR SAKES, NOT OUR OWN.
OH?
VERY NOBLE OF YOU, KURDA.
NOBLER THAN YOU IMAGINE!
HAVE YOU NO BRAINS? DON'T YOU SEE THE SACRIFICE I MADE?!
WHAT SACRIFICE?!
WIN OR LOSE, MY REWARD WOULD HAVE BEEN DEATH!
THE VAMPANEZE DESPISE TRAITORS EVEN MORE THAN WE DO!!
SFX: ZAWA (MURMUR) ZAWA
HAD EVERYTHING WORKED OUT...
...I'D HAVE REMAINED HERE TO OVERSEE THE MERGING OF OUR CLANS.
THEN, WHEN OUR PEOPLE'S FUTURE WAS ASSURED...
DOYO (MURMUR)
...I'D HAVE OFFERED MYSELF UP TO THIS SENTENCE.
DOYO
NEITHER THE VAMPIRES NOR THE VAMPANEZE WILL SUFFER A TRAITOR TO LIVE.
THE LAW IS WRITTEN INTO THE HEARTS OF EACH AND EVERY MEMBER OF THE CLANS.
GU (RRGH)

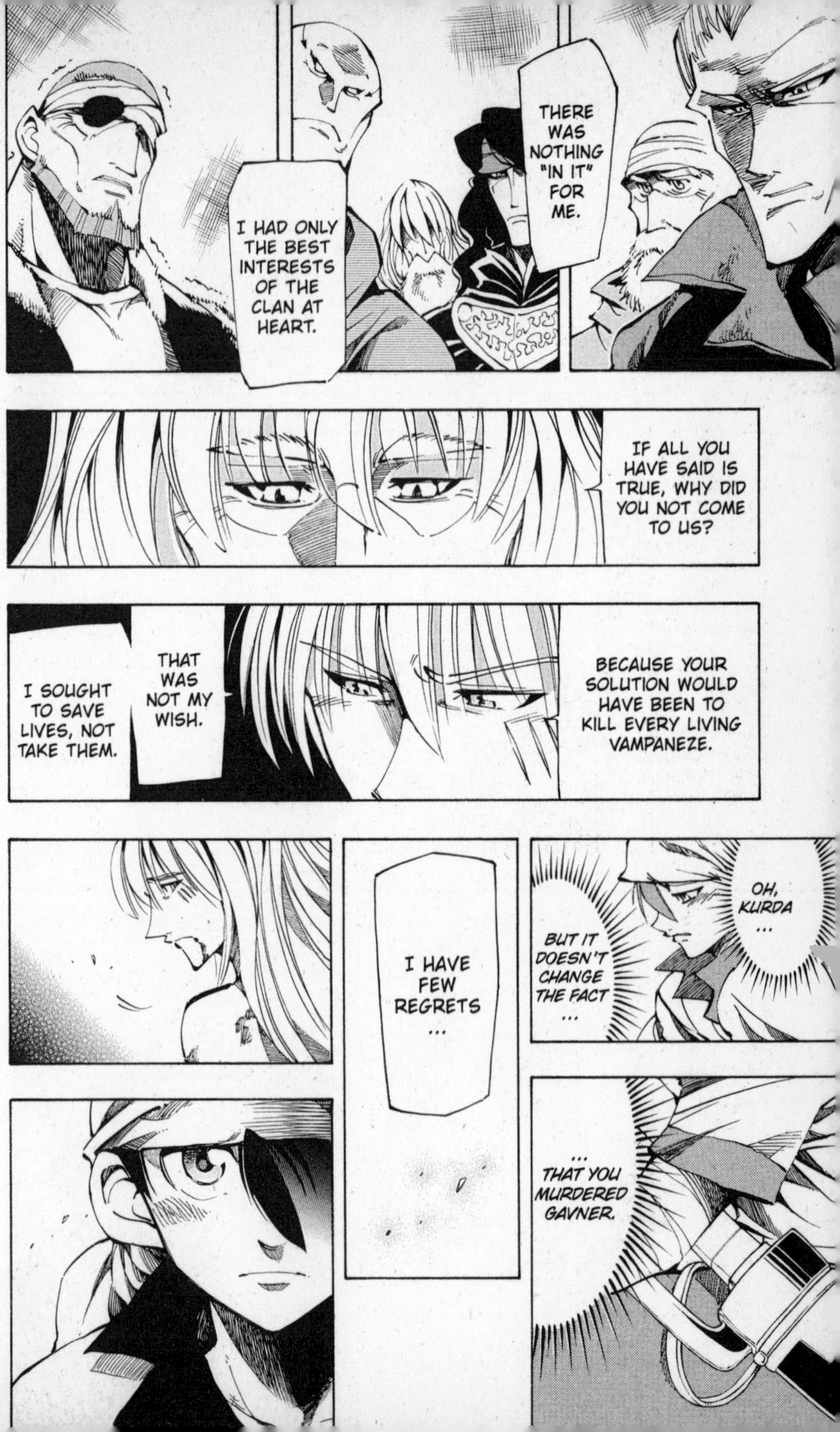
THERE WAS NOTHING "IN IT" FOR ME.
I HAD ONLY THE BEST INTERESTS OF THE CLAN AT HEART.
IF ALL YOU HAVE SAID IS TRUE, WHY DID YOU NOT COME TO US?
BECAUSE YOUR SOLUTION WOULD HAVE BEEN TO KILL EVERY LIVING VAMPANEZE.
THAT WAS NOT MY WISH.
I SOUGHT TO SAVE LIVES, NOT TAKE THEM.
OH, KURDA ...
BUT IT DOESN'T CHANGE THE FACT ...
... THAT YOU MURDERED GAVNER.
I HAVE FEW REGRETS ...

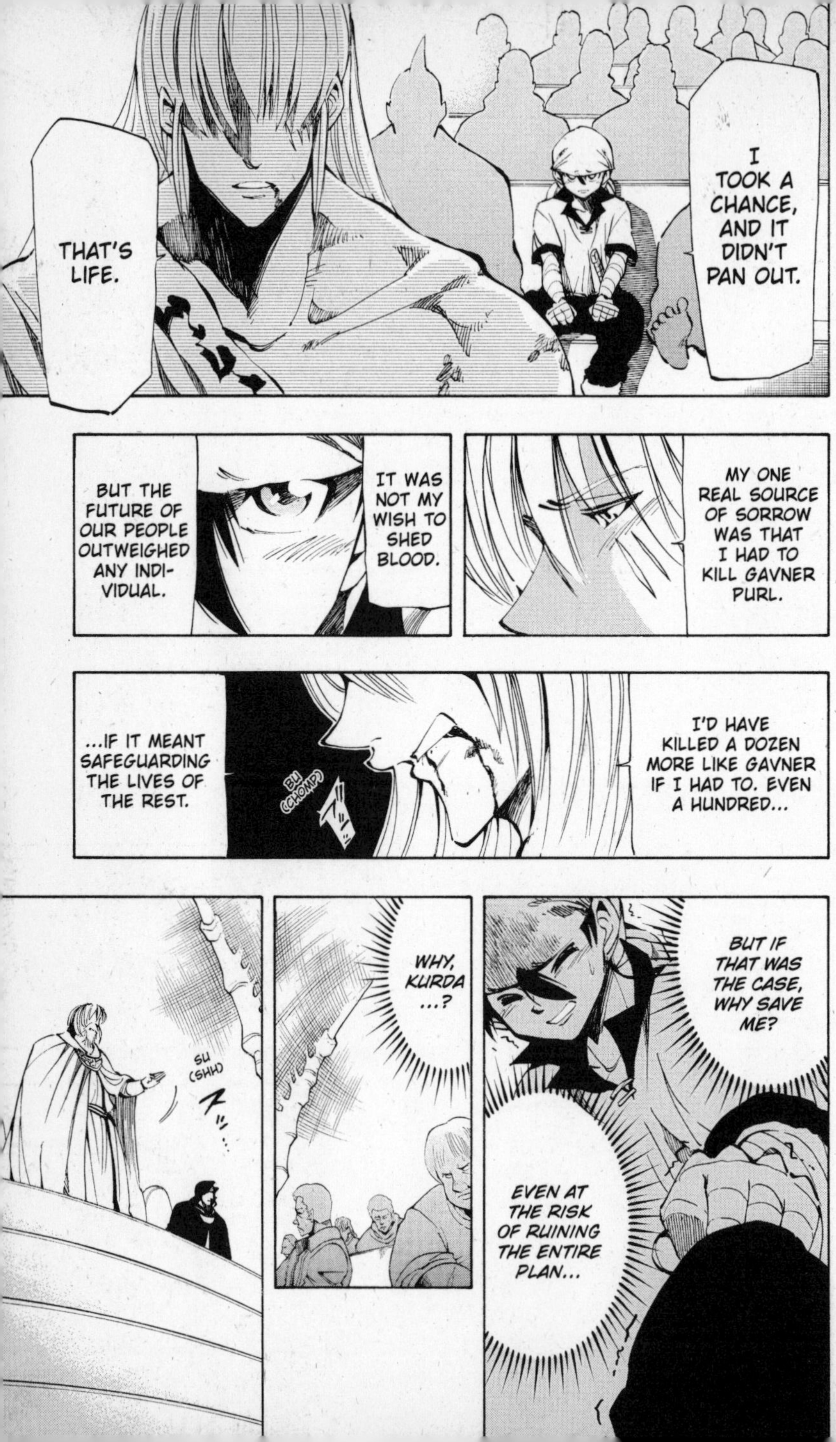
I TOOK A CHANCE, AND IT DIDN'T PAN OUT.
THAT'S LIFE.
MY ONE REAL SOURCE OF SORROW WAS THAT I HAD TO KILL GAVNER PURL.
IT WAS NOT MY WISH TO SHED BLOOD.
BUT THE FUTURE OF OUR PEOPLE OUTWEIGHED ANY INDIVIDUAL.
I'D HAVE KILLED A DOZEN MORE LIKE GAVNER IF I HAD TO. EVEN A HUNDRED...
BU (CHOMP)
...IF IT MEANT SAFEGUARDING THE LIVES OF THE REST.
BUT IF THAT WAS THE CASE, WHY SAVE ME?
EVEN AT THE RISK OF RUINING THE ENTIRE PLAN...
WHY, KURDA ...?
SU (SHH)

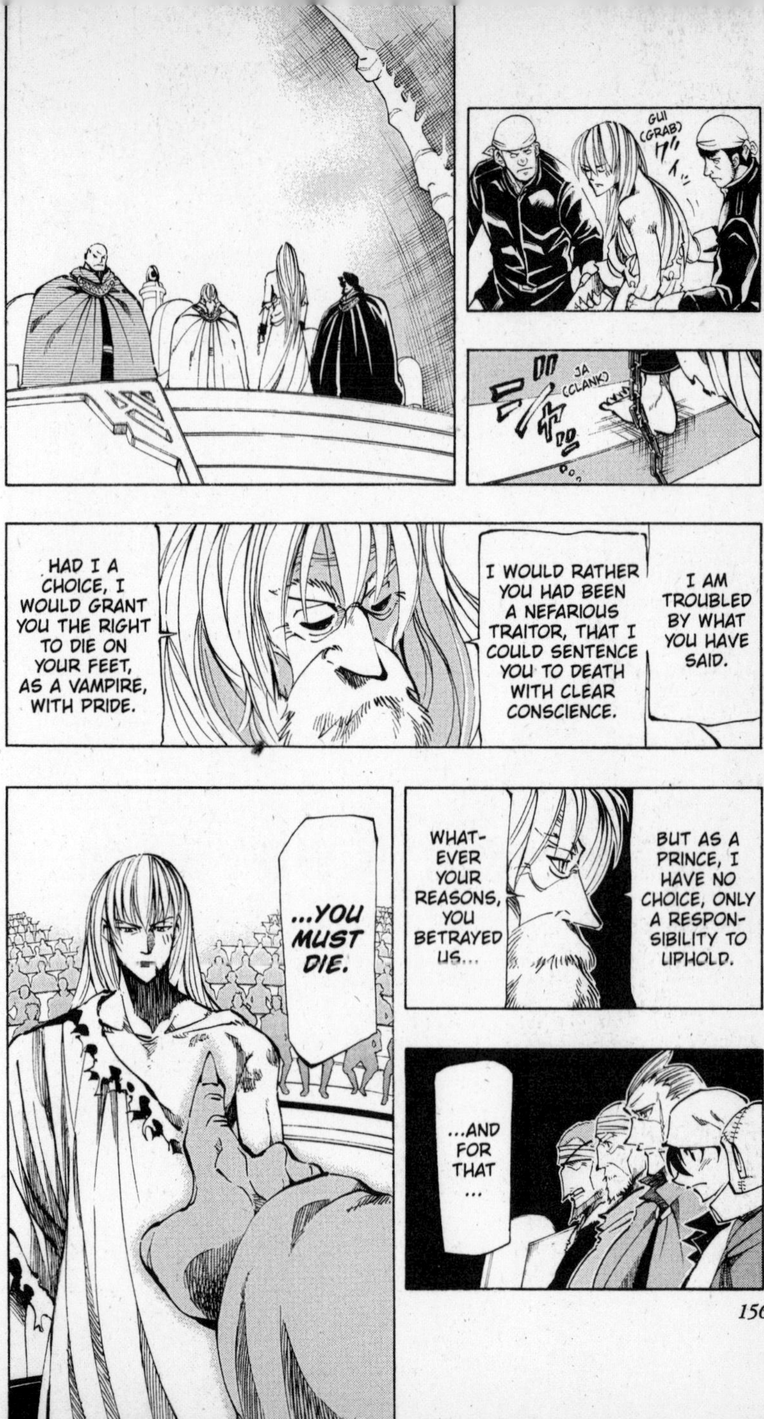
GUI (GRAB)
JA (CLANK)
I AM TROUBLED BY WHAT YOU HAVE SAID.
I WOULD RATHER YOU HAD BEEN A NEFARIOUS TRAITOR, THAT I COULD SENTENCE YOU TO DEATH WITH CLEAR CONSCIENCE.
HAD I A CHOICE, I WOULD GRANT YOU THE RIGHT TO DIE ON YOUR FEET, AS A VAMPIRE, WITH PRIDE.
BUT AS A PRINCE, I HAVE NO CHOICE, ONLY A RESPONSIBILITY TO UPHOLD.
WHATEVER YOUR REASONS, YOU BETRAYED US...
...AND FOR THAT ...
...YOU MUST DIE.

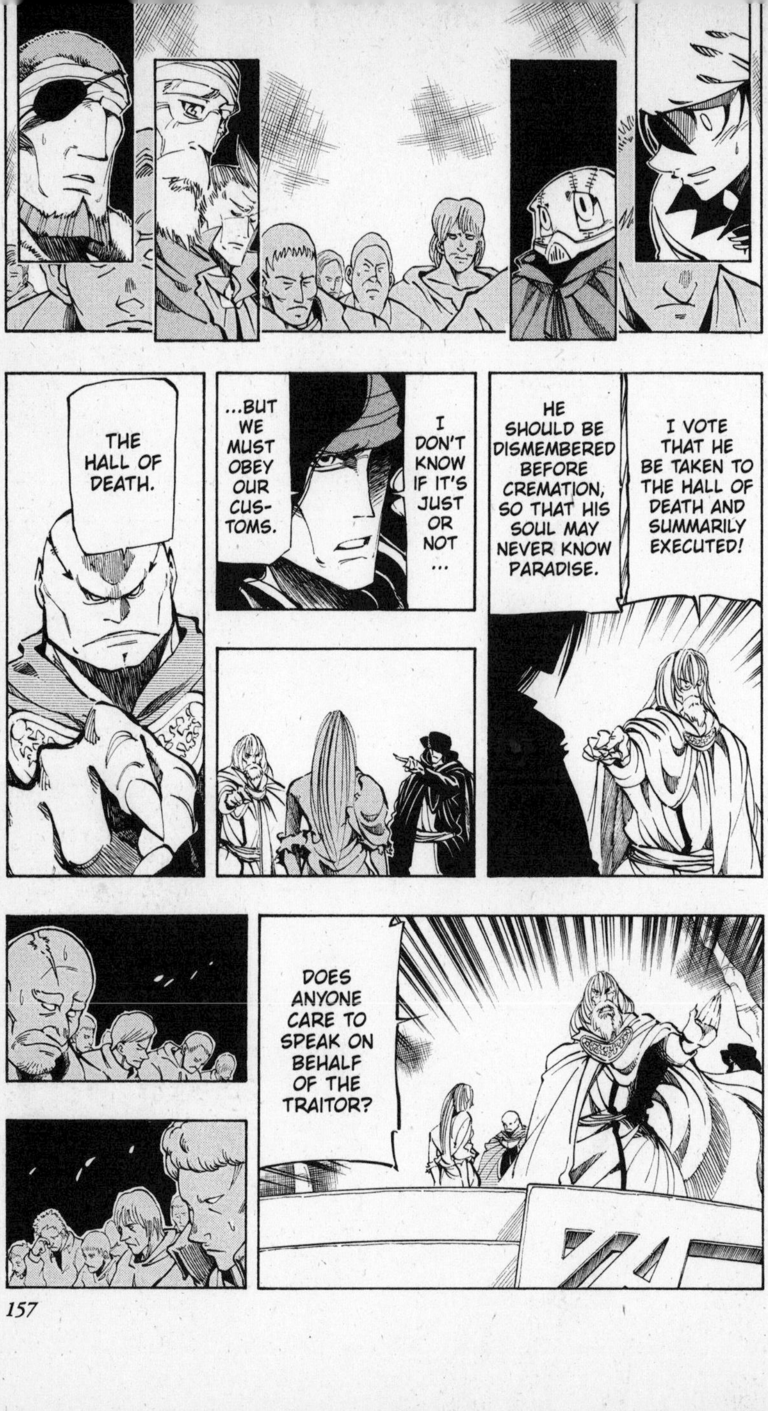
I VOTE THAT HE BE TAKEN TO THE HALL OF DEATH AND SUMMARILY EXECUTED!
HE SHOULD BE DISMEMBERED BEFORE CREMATION, SO THAT HIS SOUL MAY NEVER KNOW PARADISE.
I DON'T KNOW IF IT'S JUST OR NOT ...
...BUT WE MUST OBEY OUR CUS-TOMS.
THE HALL OF DEATH.
DOES ANYONE CARE TO SPEAK ON BEHALF OF THE TRAITOR?

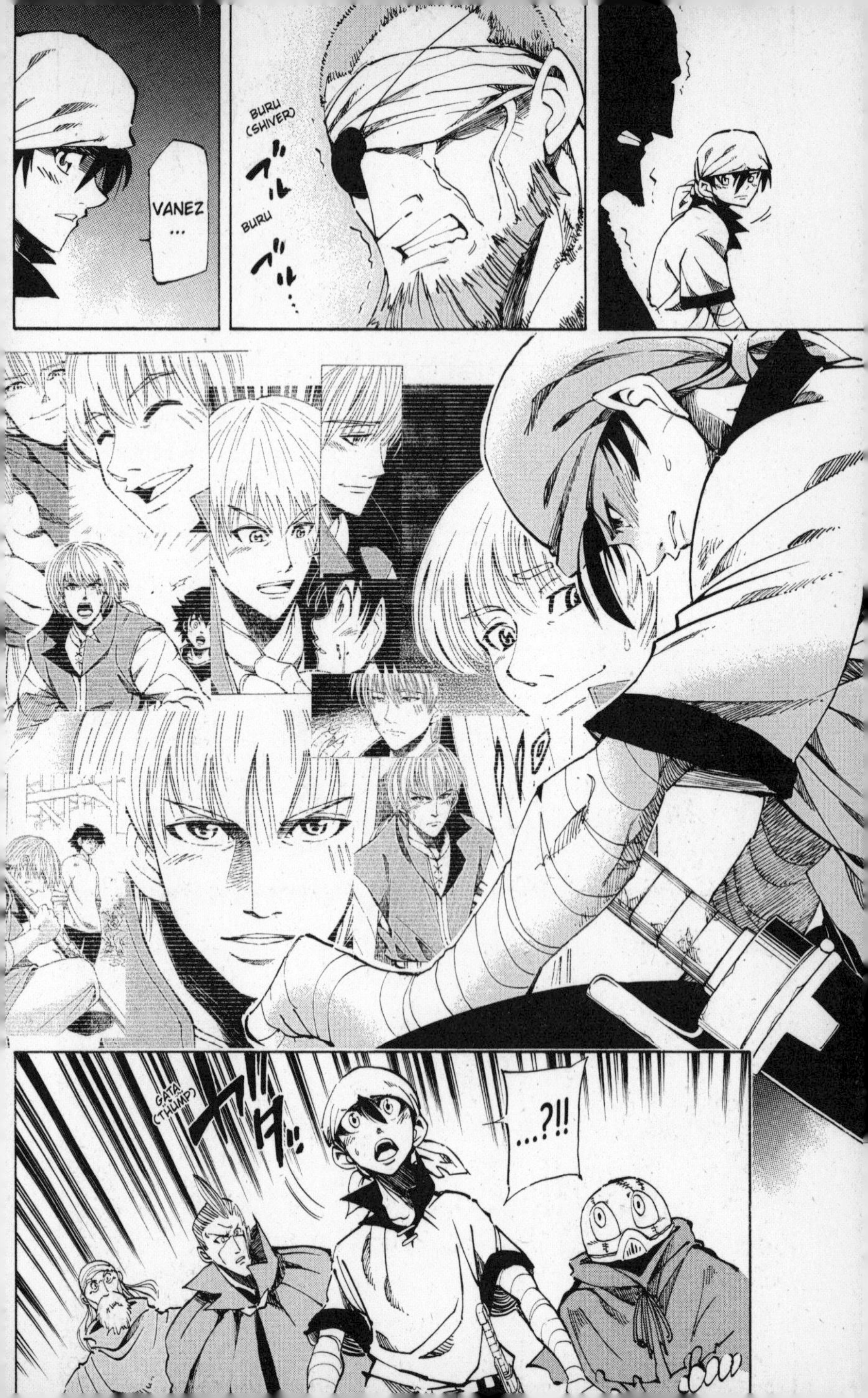
BURU (SHIVER)
ブル
BURU
ブル…
VANEZ ...
...?!!
GATA! (THUMP)
ガタッ

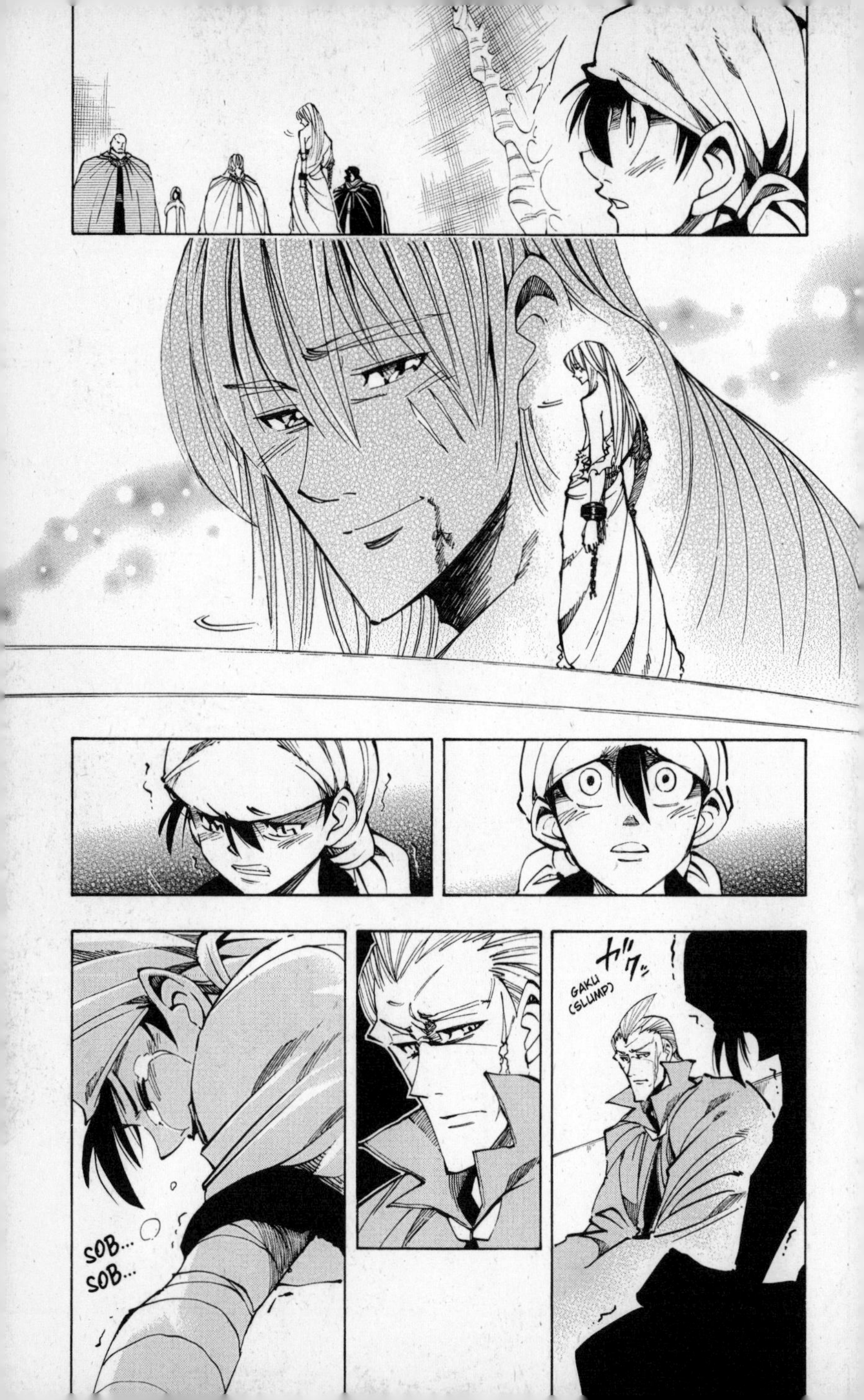
ガクッ
GAKU (SLUMP)
SOB... SOB...

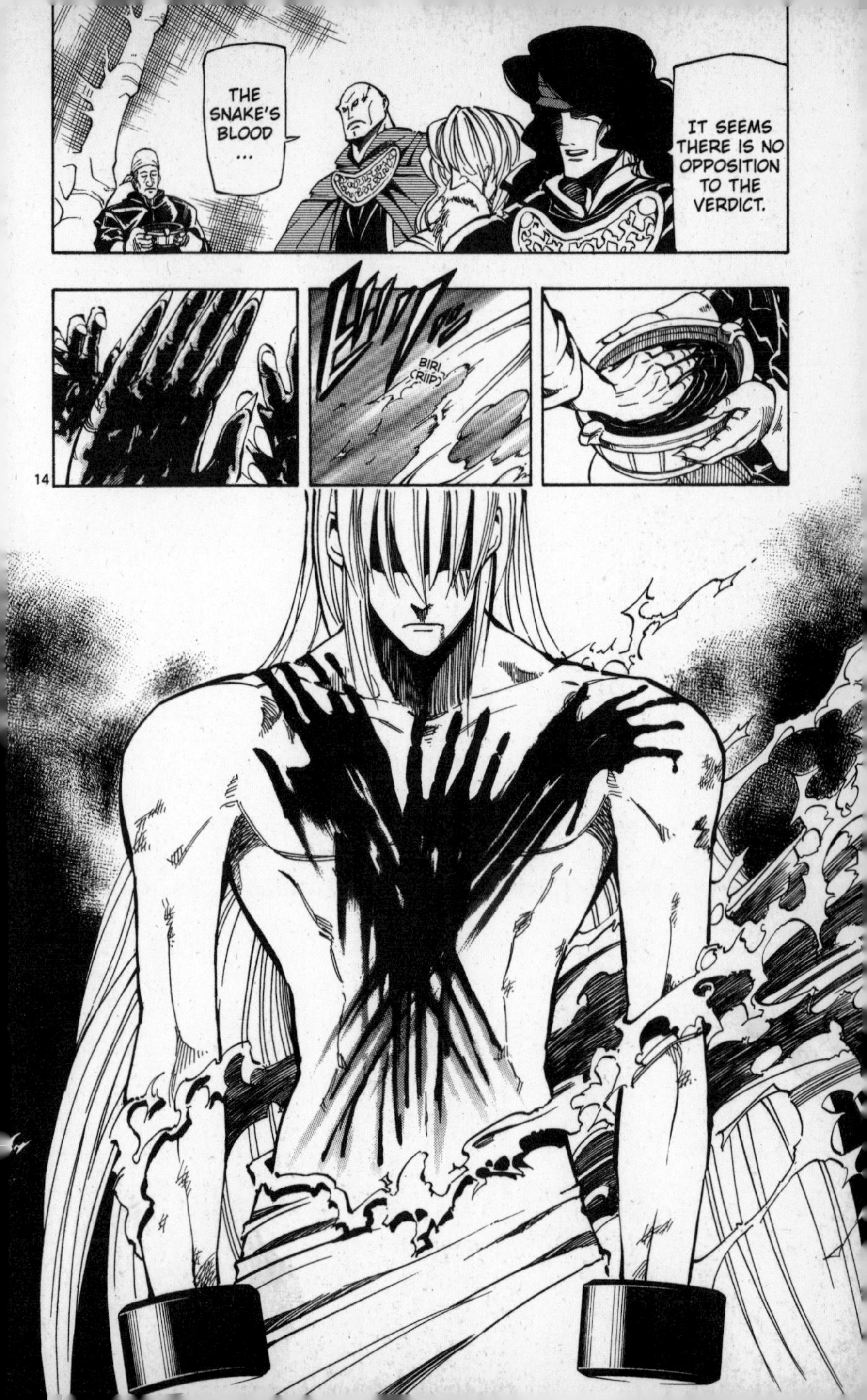
IT SEEMS THERE IS NO OPPOSITION TO THE VERDICT.
THE SNAKE'S BLOOD ...
BIRI (RIIP)

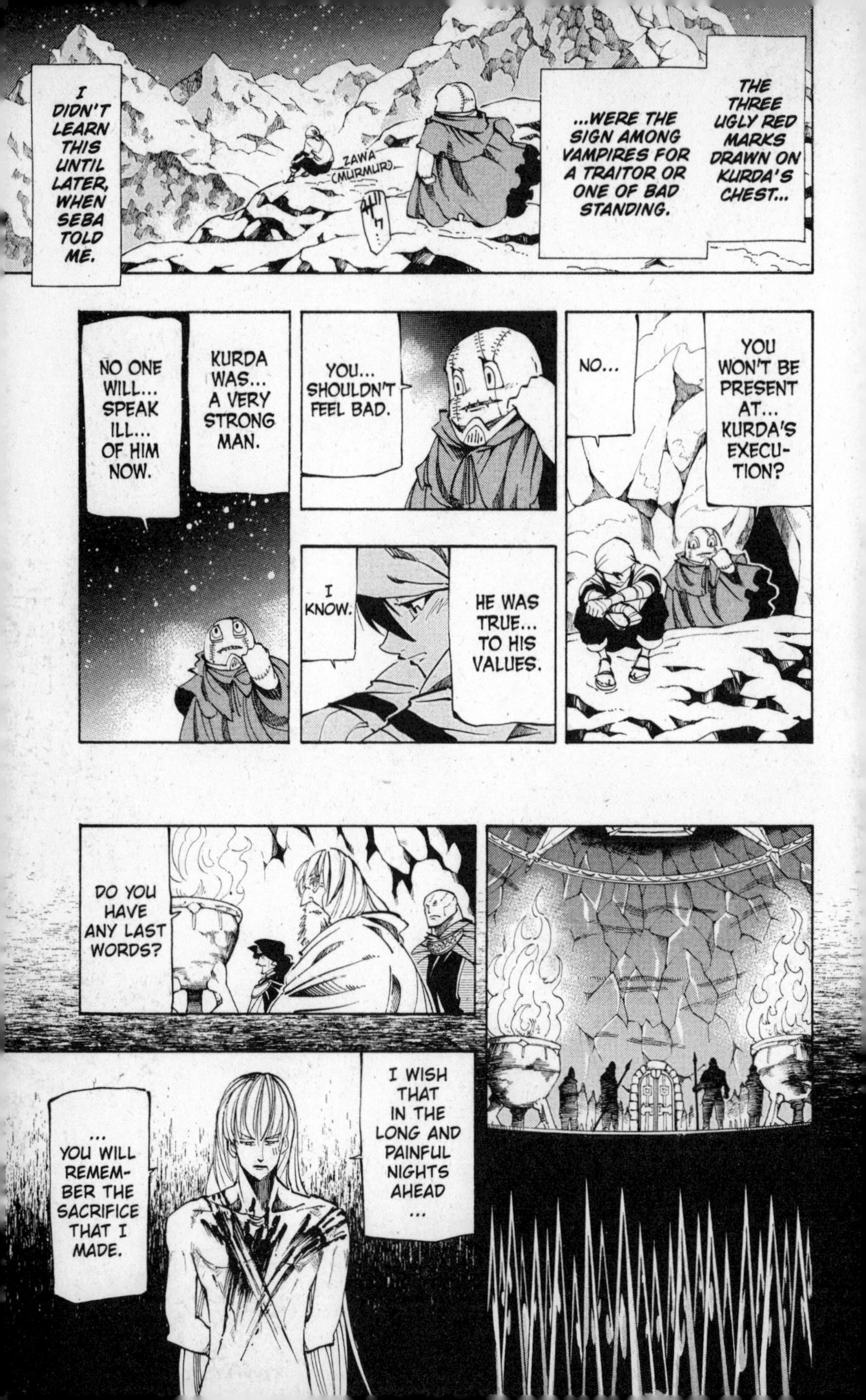
THE THREE UGLY RED MARKS DRAWN ON KURDA'S CHEST...
...WERE THE SIGN AMONG VAMPIRES FOR A TRAITOR OR ONE OF BAD STANDING.
ZAWA (MURMUR)
I DIDN'T LEARN THIS UNTIL LATER, WHEN SEBA TOLD ME.
YOU WON'T BE PRESENT AT... KURDA'S EXECUTION?
NO...
YOU... SHOULDN'T FEEL BAD.
HE WAS TRUE... TO HIS VALUES.
I KNOW.
KURDA WAS... A VERY STRONG MAN.
NO ONE WILL... SPEAK ILL... OF HIM NOW.
DO YOU HAVE ANY LAST WORDS?
I WISH THAT IN THE LONG AND PAINFUL NIGHTS AHEAD ...
... YOU WILL REMEMBER THE SACRIFICE THAT I MADE.

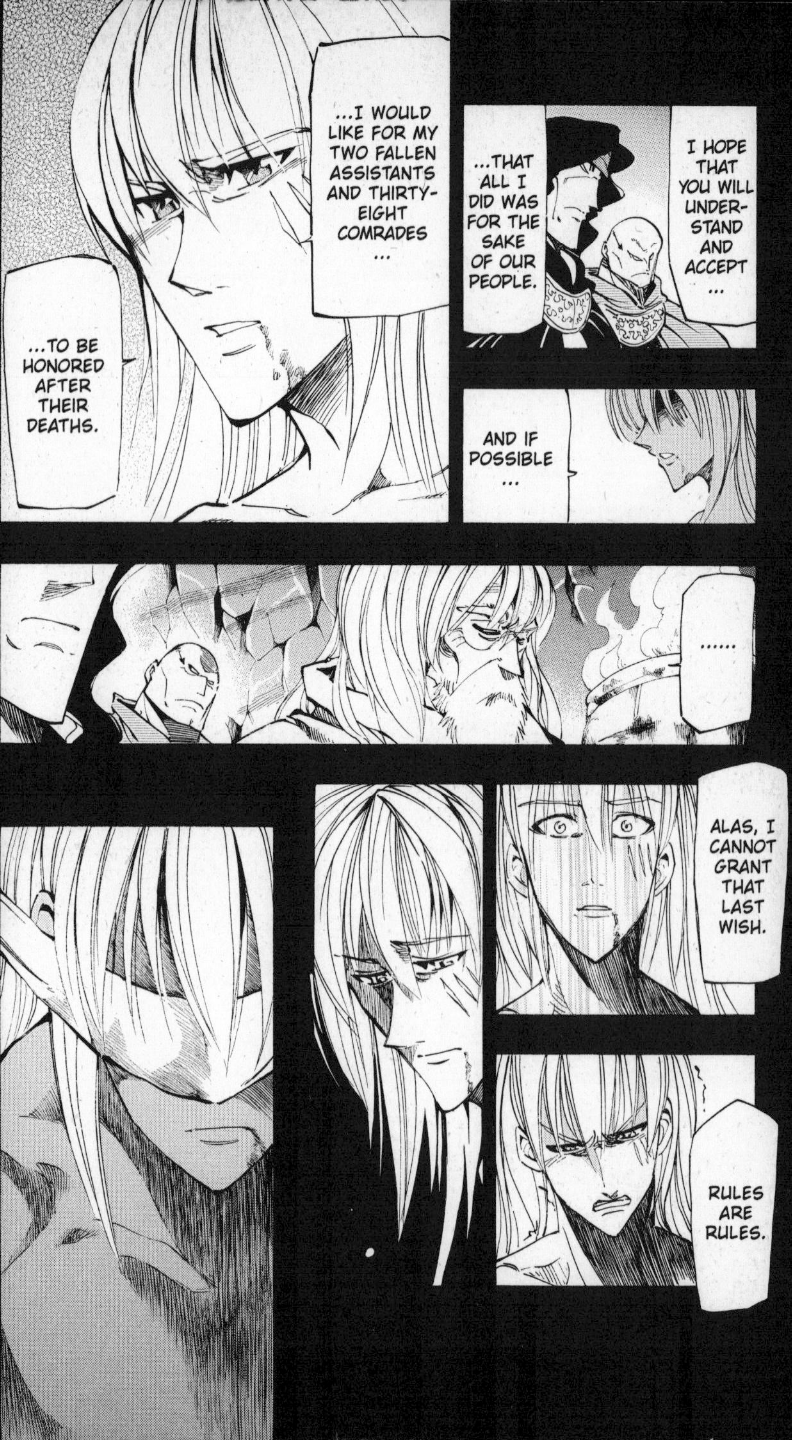
I HOPE THAT YOU WILL UNDER-STAND AND ACCEPT ...
...THAT ALL I DID WAS FOR THE SAKE OF OUR PEOPLE.
AND IF POSSIBLE ...
...I WOULD LIKE FOR MY TWO FALLEN ASSISTANTS AND THIRTY-EIGHT COMRADES ...
...TO BE HONORED AFTER THEIR DEATHS.
......
ALAS, I CANNOT GRANT THAT LAST WISH.
RULES ARE RULES.

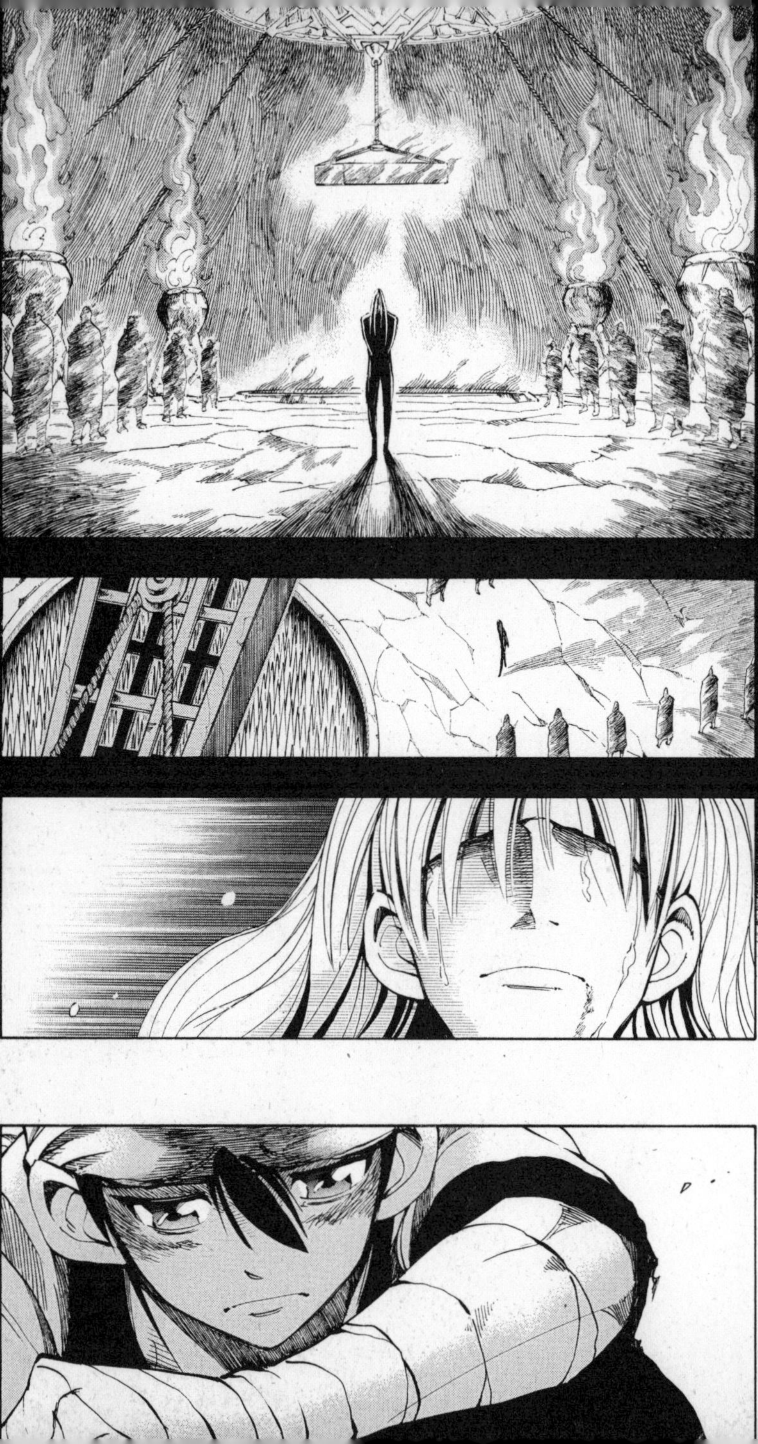

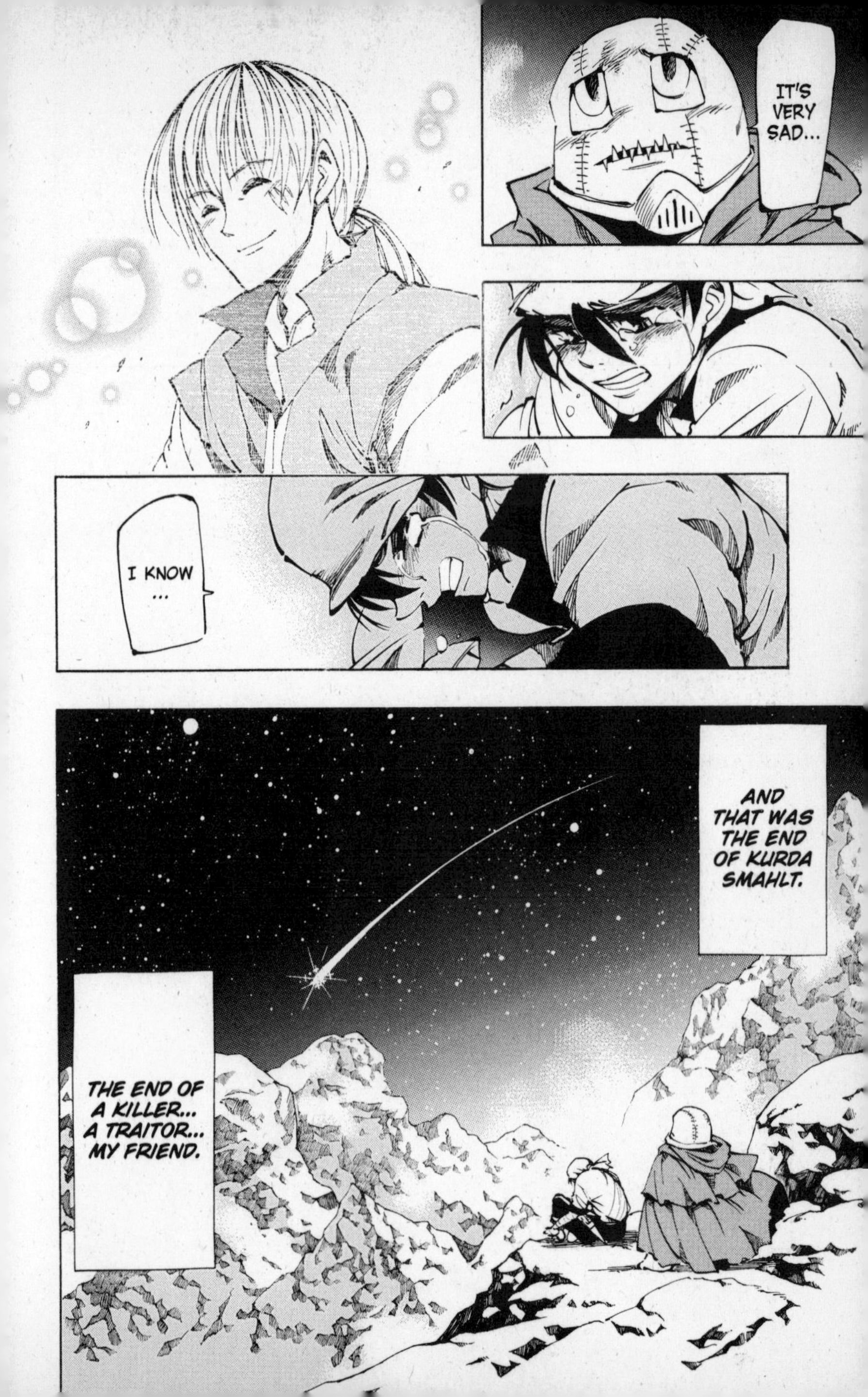
IT'S VERY SAD...
I KNOW ...
AND THAT WAS THE END OF KURDA SMAHLT.
THE END OF A KILLER... A TRAITOR... MY FRIEND.

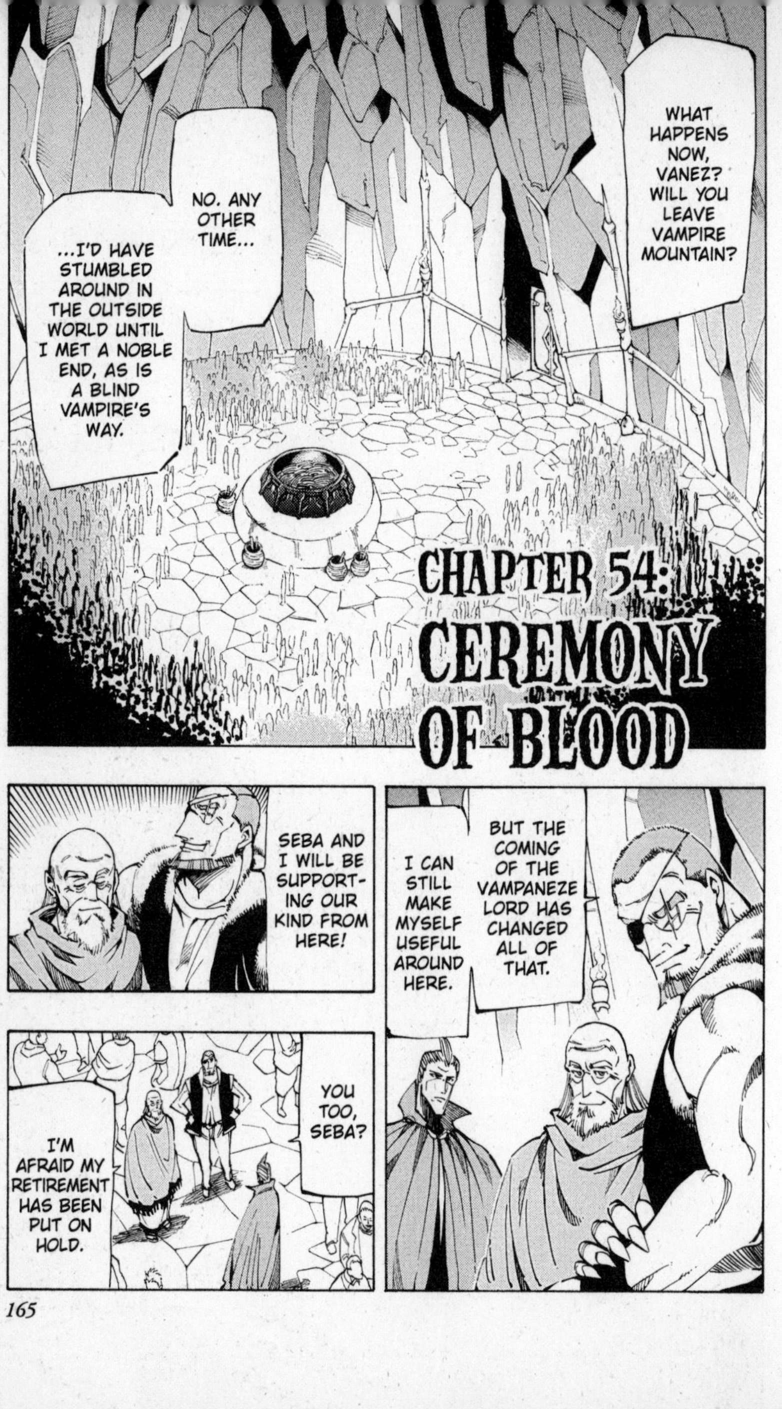
WHAT HAPPENS NOW, VANEZ? WILL YOU LEAVE VAMPIRE MOUNTAIN?
NO. ANY OTHER TIME...
...I'D HAVE STUMBLED AROUND IN THE OUTSIDE WORLD UNTIL I MET A NOBLE END, AS IS A BLIND VAMPIRE'S WAY.
CHAPTER 54: CEREMONY OF BLOOD
BUT THE COMING OF THE VAMPANEZE LORD HAS CHANGED ALL OF THAT.
I CAN STILL MAKE MYSELF USEFUL AROUND HERE.
SEBA AND I WILL BE SUPPORT-ING OUR KIND FROM HERE!
YOU TOO, SEBA?
I'M AFRAID MY RETIREMENT HAS BEEN PUT ON HOLD.

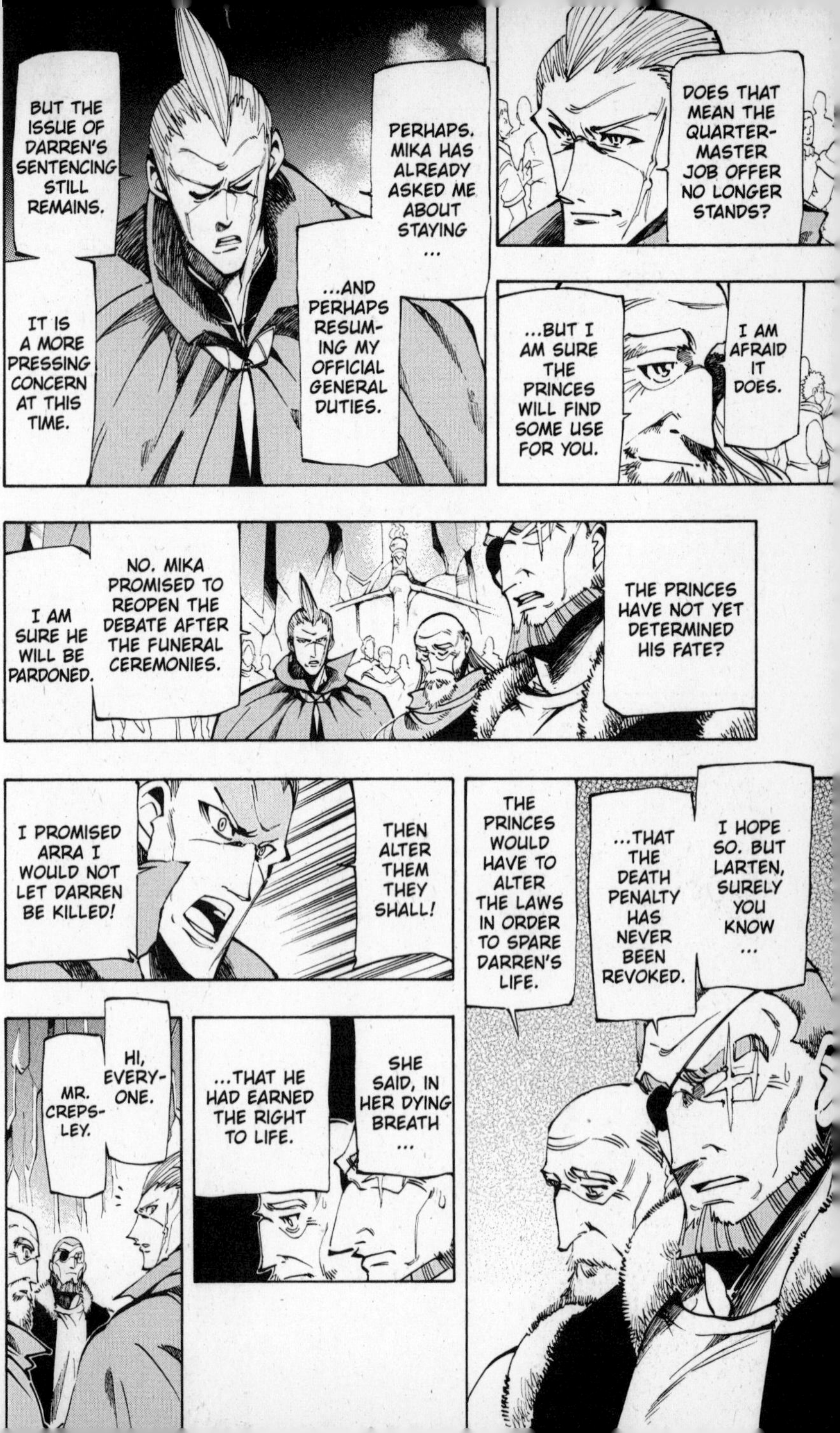
DOES THAT MEAN THE QUARTER-MASTER JOB OFFER NO LONGER STANDS?
I AM AFRAID IT DOES.
...BUT I AM SURE THE PRINCES WILL FIND SOME USE FOR YOU.
PERHAPS. MIKA HAS ALREADY ASKED ME ABOUT STAYING ...
...AND PERHAPS RESUMING MY OFFICIAL GENERAL DUTIES.
BUT THE ISSUE OF DARREN'S SENTENCING STILL REMAINS.
IT IS A MORE PRESSING CONCERN AT THIS TIME.
THE PRINCES HAVE NOT YET DETERMINED HIS FATE?
NO. MIKA PROMISED TO REOPEN THE DEBATE AFTER THE FUNERAL CEREMONIES.
I AM SURE HE WILL BE PARDONED.
I HOPE SO. BUT LARTEN, SURELY YOU KNOW ...
...THAT THE DEATH PENALTY HAS NEVER BEEN REVOKED.
THE PRINCES WOULD HAVE TO ALTER THE LAWS IN ORDER TO SPARE DARREN'S LIFE.
THEN ALTER THEM THEY SHALL!
I PROMISED ARRA I WOULD NOT LET DARREN BE KILLED!
SHE SAID, IN HER DYING BREATH ...
...THAT HE HAD EARNED THE RIGHT TO LIFE.
HI, EVERYONE.
MR. CREPSLEY.

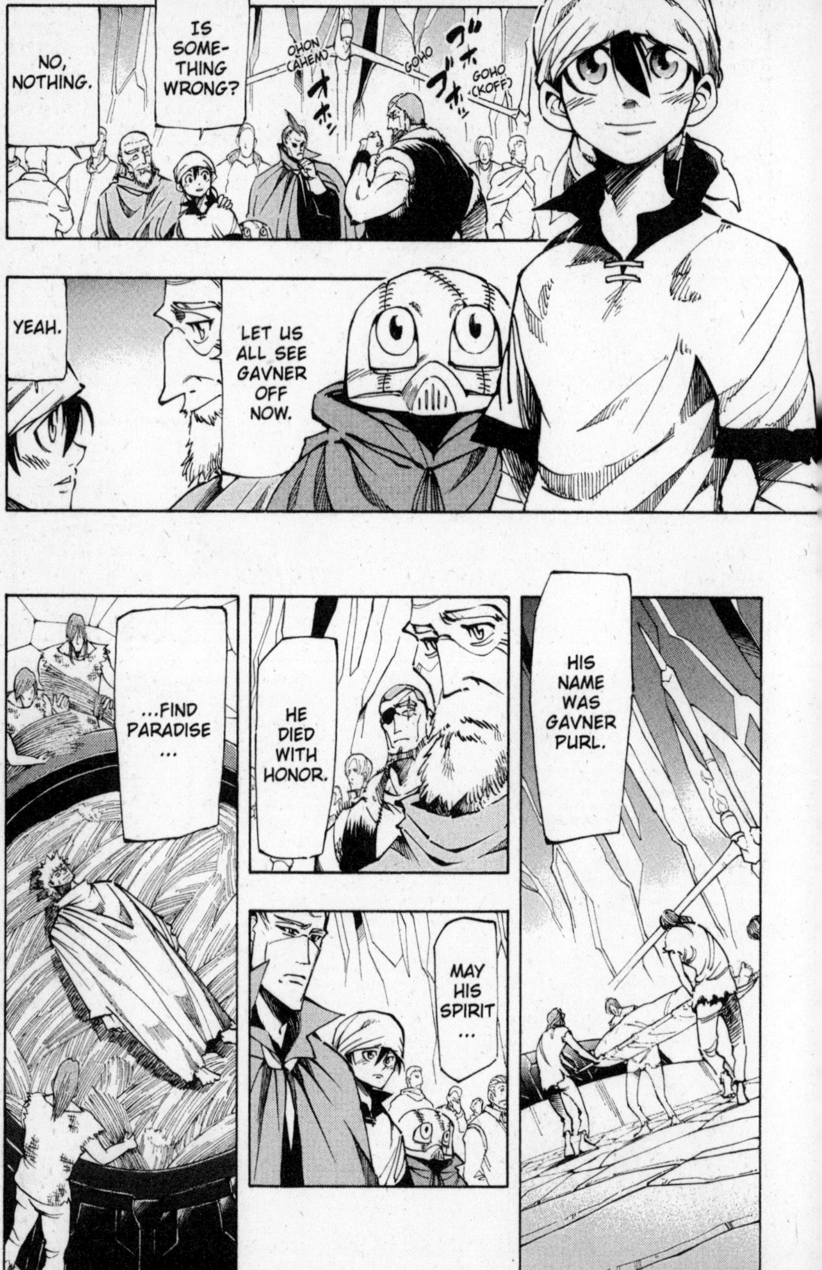
IS SOMETHING WRONG?
GOHO (KOFF)
GOHO
OHON (AHEM)
NO, NOTHING.
LET US ALL SEE GAVNER OFF NOW.
YEAH.
HIS NAME WAS GAVNER PURL.
HE DIED WITH HONOR.
MAY HIS SPIRIT ...
...FIND PARADISE ...

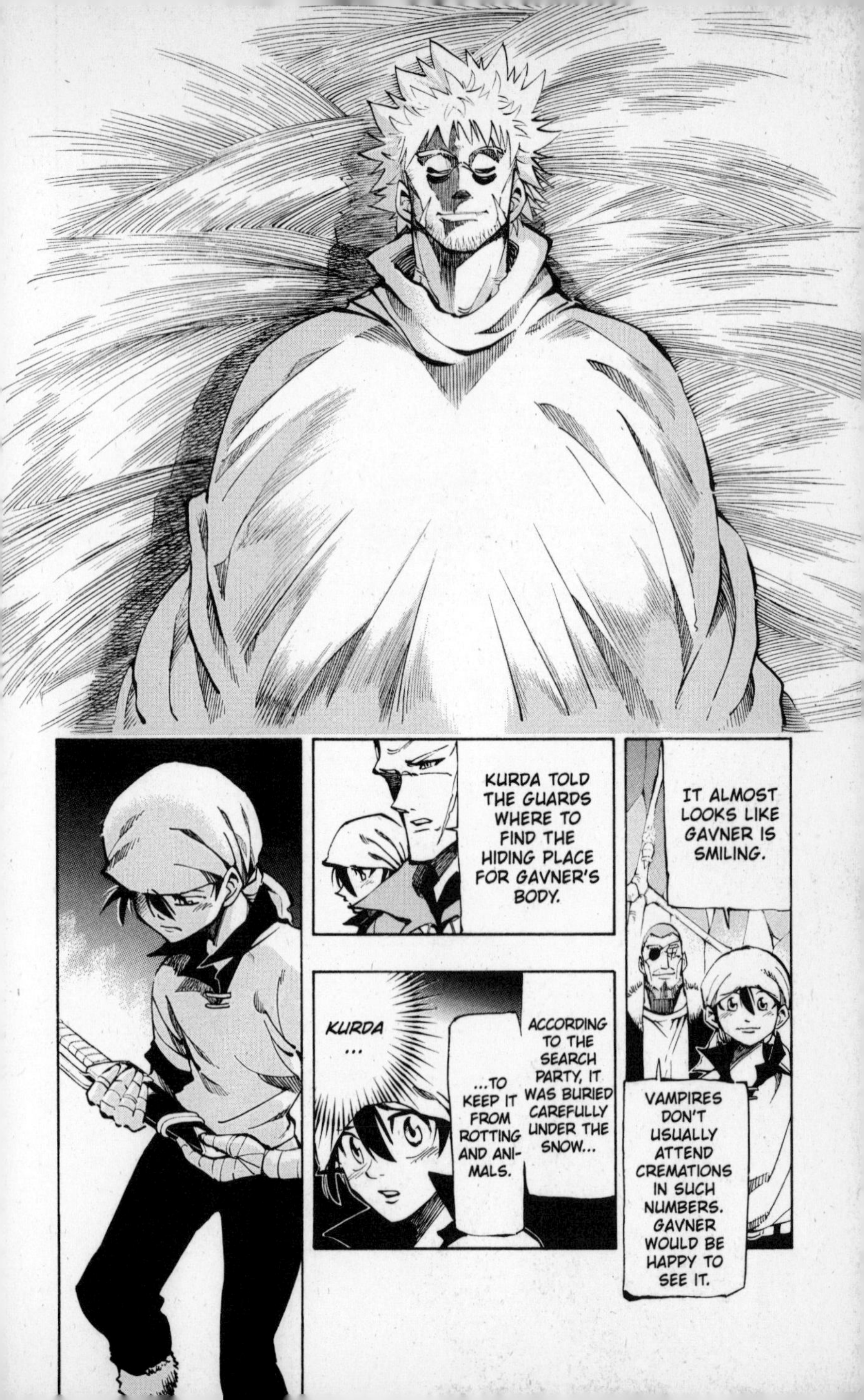
IT ALMOST LOOKS LIKE GAVNER IS SMILING.
VAMPIRES DON'T USUALLY ATTEND CREMATIONS IN SUCH NUMBERS. GAVNER WOULD BE HAPPY TO SEE IT.
KURDA TOLD THE GUARDS WHERE TO FIND THE HIDING PLACE FOR GAVNER'S BODY.
ACCORDING TO THE SEARCH PARTY, IT WAS BURIED CAREFULLY UNDER THE SNOW...
...TO KEEP IT FROM ROTTING AND ANI-MALS.
KURDA...

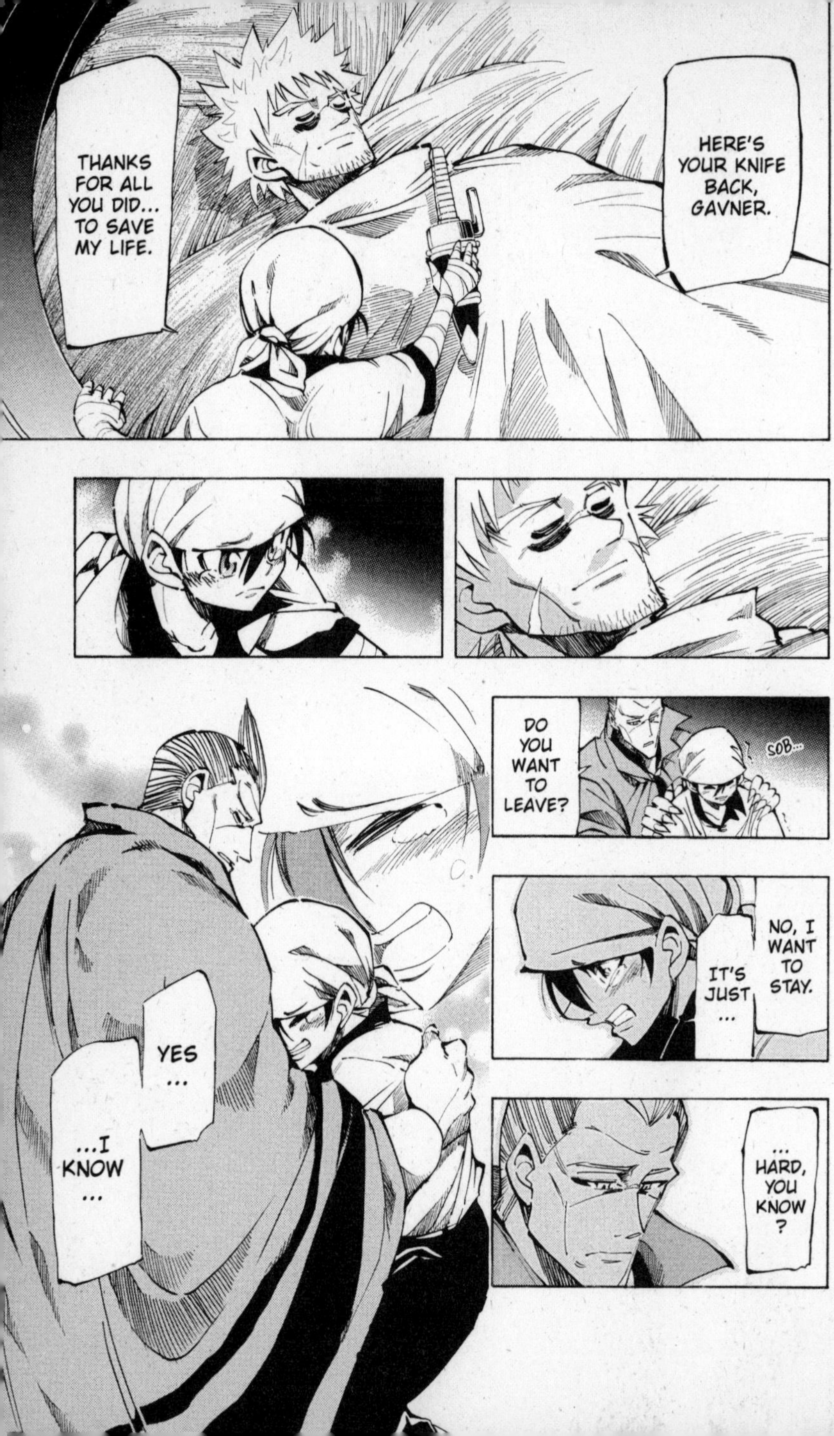
HERE'S YOUR KNIFE BACK, GAVNER.
THANKS FOR ALL YOU DID... TO SAVE MY LIFE.
DO YOU WANT TO LEAVE?
SOB...
NO, I WANT TO STAY.
IT'S JUST ...
... HARD, YOU KNOW ?
YES ...
...I KNOW ...

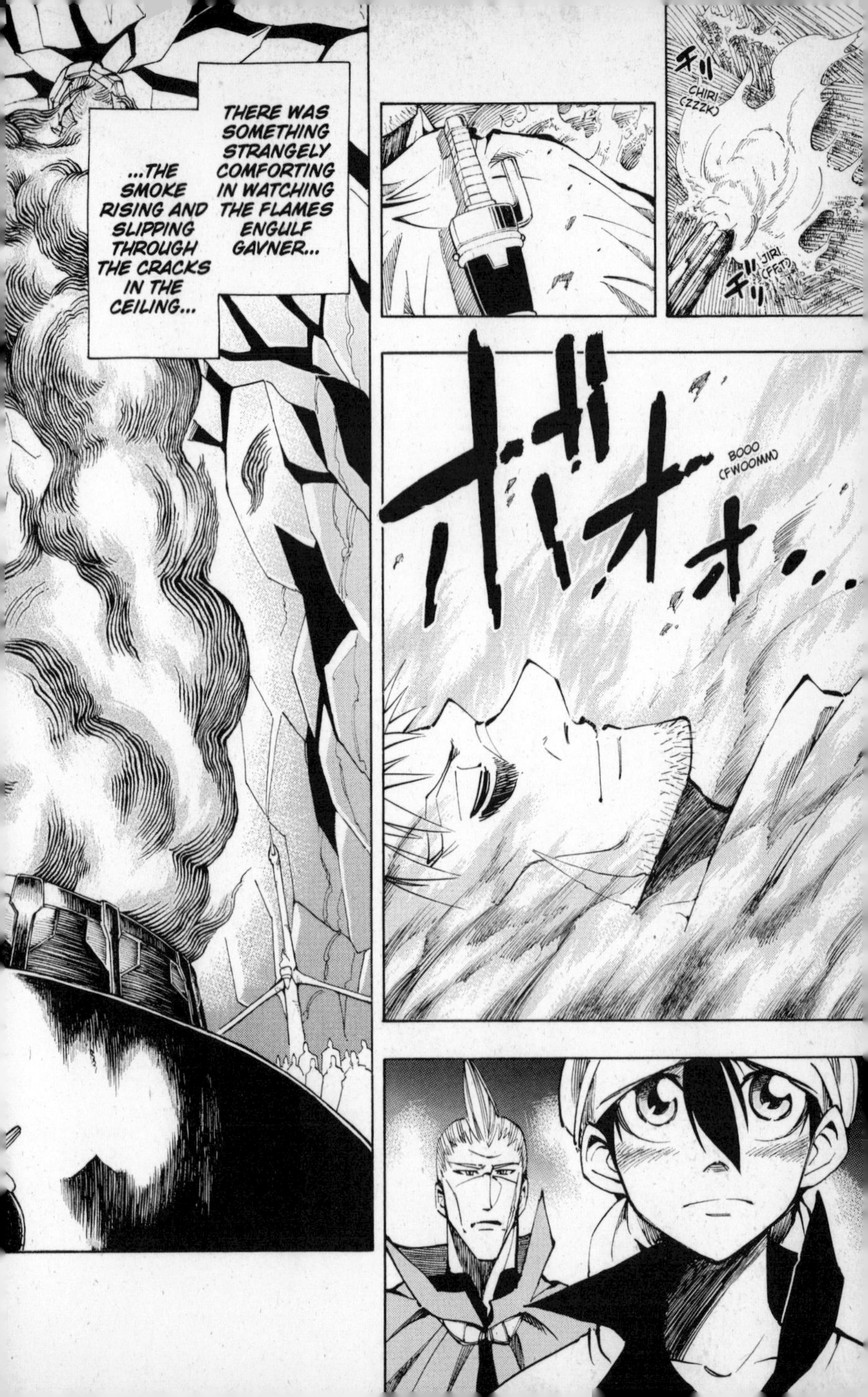
チリ
CHIRI (ZZZK)
ヂリ
JIRI
BOOO (FWOOMM)
THERE WAS SOMETHING STRANGELY COMFORTING IN WATCHING THE FLAMES ENGULF GAVNER...
...THE SMOKE RISING AND SLIPPING THROUGH THE CRACKS IN THE CEILING...

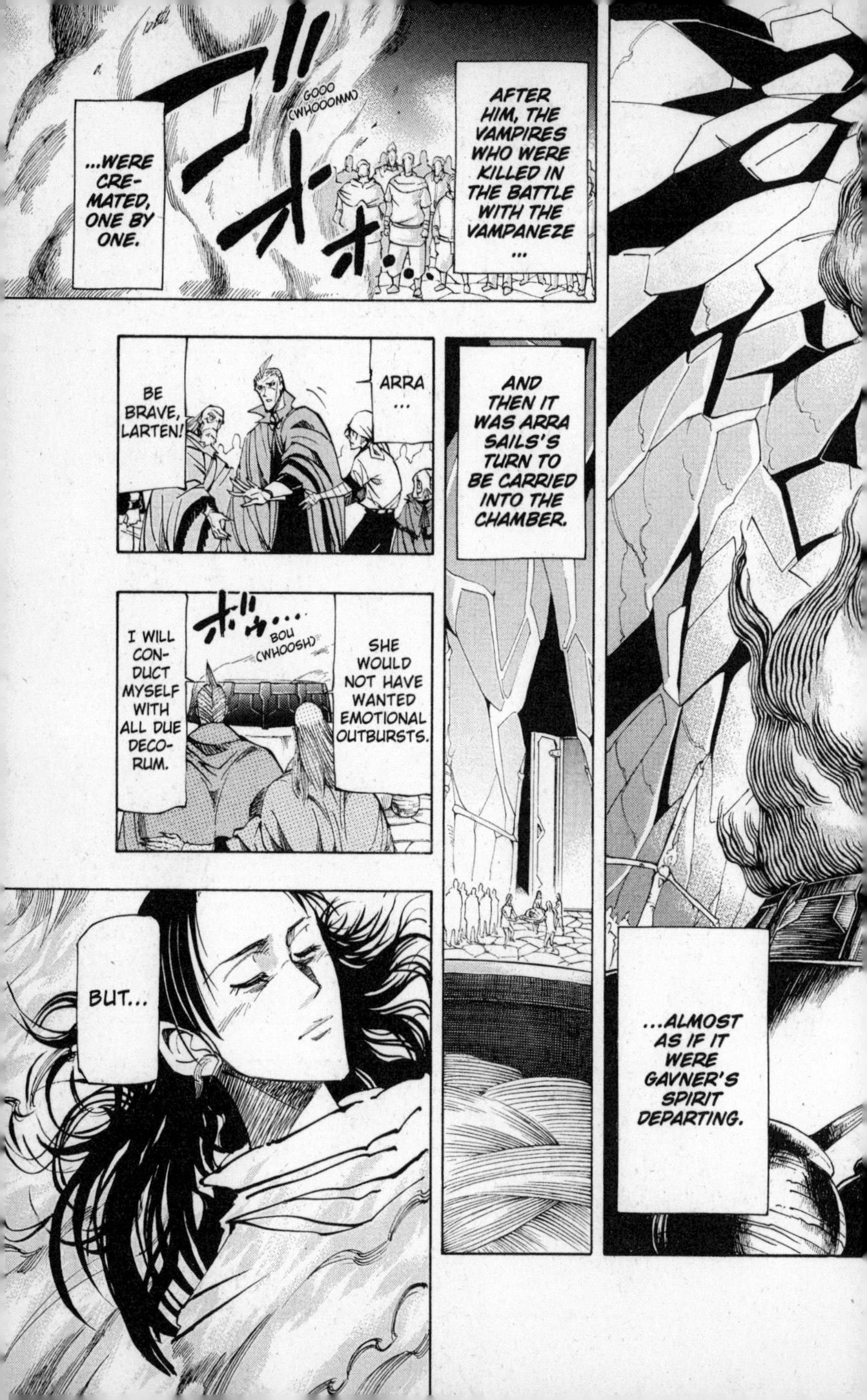
...ALMOST AS IF IT WERE GAVNER'S SPIRIT DEPARTING.
AFTER HIM, THE VAMPIRES WHO WERE KILLED IN THE BATTLE WITH THE VAMPANEZE ...
GOOO (WHOOOMM)
...WERE CREMATED, ONE BY ONE.
AND THEN IT WAS ARRA SAILS'S TURN TO BE CARRIED INTO THE CHAMBER.
ARRA ...
BE BRAVE, LARTEN!
SHE WOULD NOT HAVE WANTED EMOTIONAL OUTBURSTS.
BOU (WHOOSH)
I WILL CONDUCT MYSELF WITH ALL DUE DECORUM.
BUT...

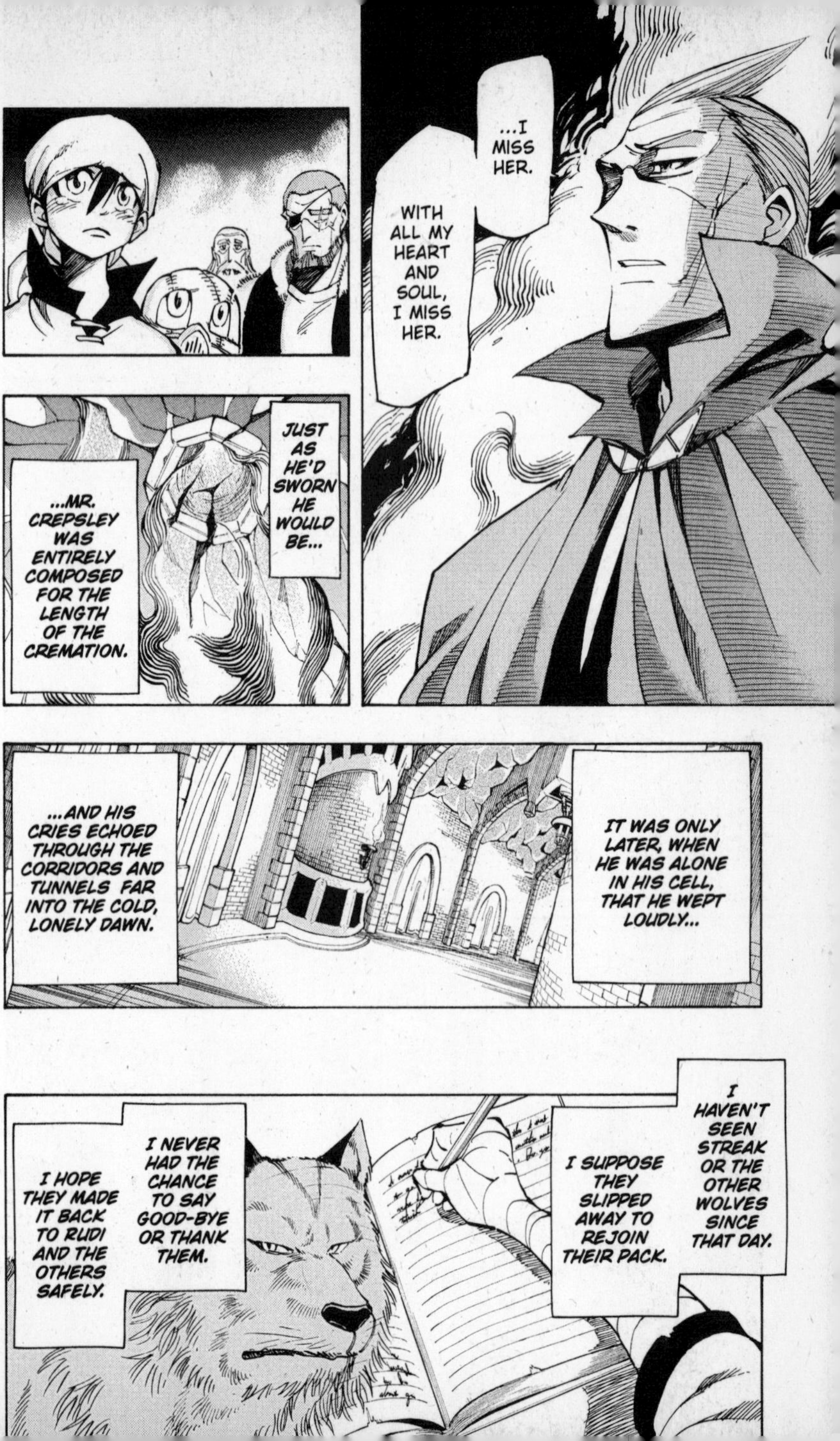
...I MISS HER.
WITH ALL MY HEART AND SOUL, I MISS HER.
JUST AS HE'D SWORN HE WOULD BE...
...MR. CREPSLEY WAS ENTIRELY COMPOSED FOR THE LENGTH OF THE CREMATION.
IT WAS ONLY LATER, WHEN HE WAS ALONE IN HIS CELL, THAT HE WEPT LOUDLY...
...AND HIS CRIES ECHOED THROUGH THE CORRIDORS AND TUNNELS FAR INTO THE COLD, LONELY DAWN.
I HAVEN'T SEEN STREAK OR THE OTHER WOLVES SINCE THAT DAY.
I SUPPOSE THEY SLIPPED AWAY TO REJOIN THEIR PACK.
I NEVER HAD THE CHANCE TO SAY GOOD-BYE OR THANK THEM.
I HOPE THEY MADE IT BACK TO RUDI AND THE OTHERS SAFELY.

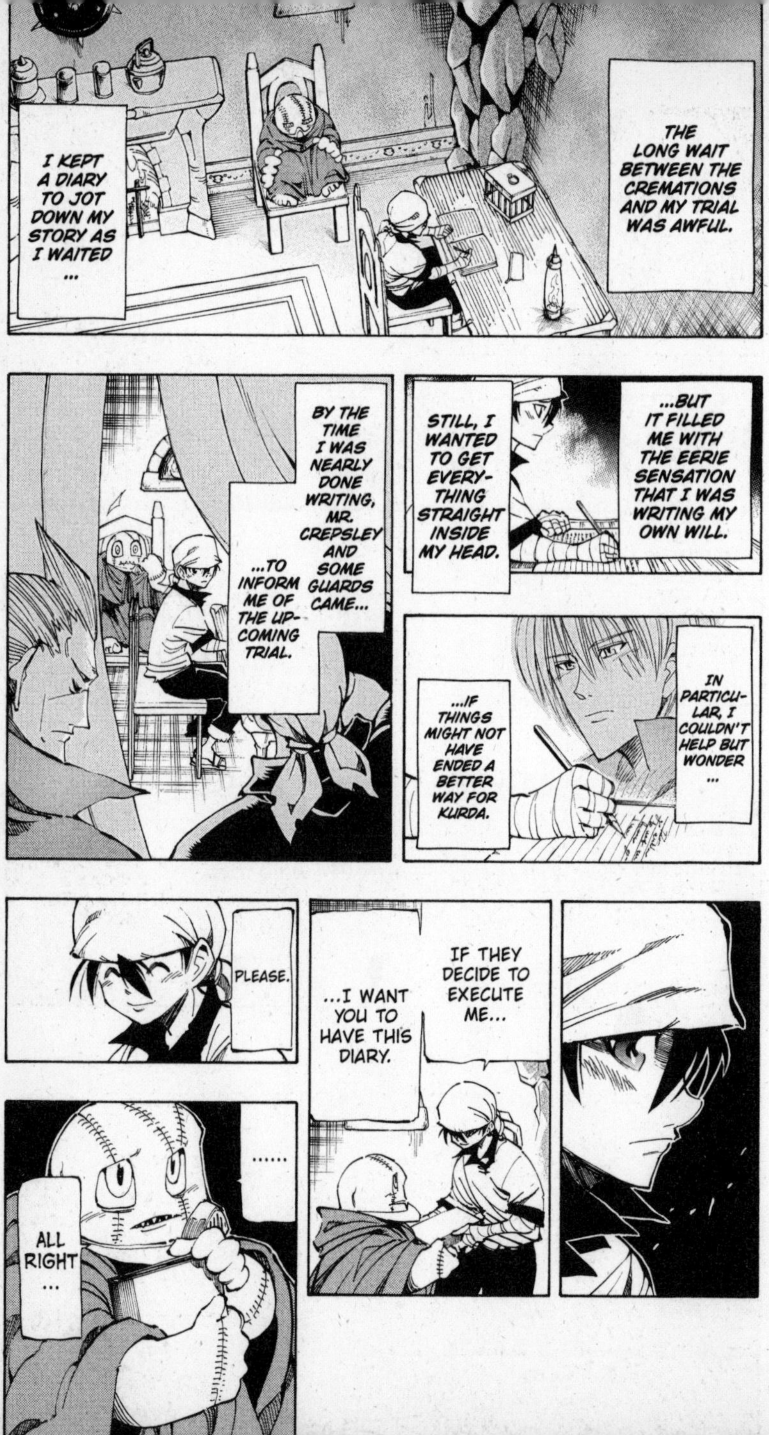
THE LONG WAIT BETWEEN THE CREMATIONS AND MY TRIAL WAS AWFUL.
I KEPT A DIARY TO JOT DOWN MY STORY AS I WAITED ...
...BUT IT FILLED ME WITH THE EERIE SENSATION THAT I WAS WRITING MY OWN WILL.
STILL, I WANTED TO GET EVERY-THING STRAIGHT INSIDE MY HEAD.
IN PARTICU-LAR, I COULDN'T HELP BUT WONDER ...
...IF THINGS MIGHT NOT HAVE ENDED A BETTER WAY FOR KURDA.
BY THE TIME I WAS NEARLY DONE WRITING, MR. CREPSLEY AND SOME GUARDS CAME...
...TO INFORM ME OF THE UP-COMING TRIAL.
IF THEY DECIDE TO EXECUTE ME...
...I WANT YOU TO HAVE THIS DIARY.
PLEASE.
......
ALL RIGHT ...

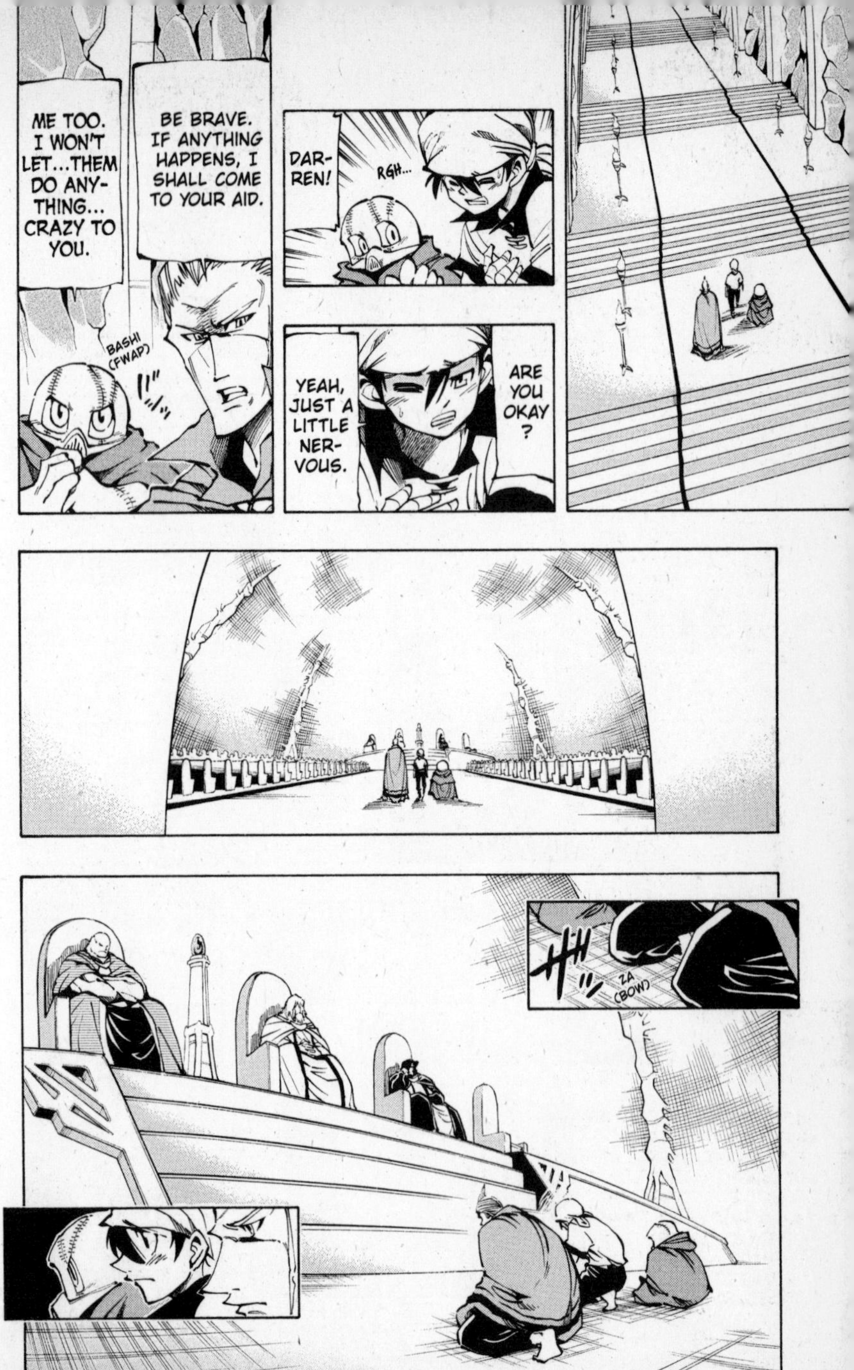
RGH...
DAR-REN!
ARE YOU OKAY?
YEAH, JUST A LITTLE NER-VOUS.
BE BRAVE. IF ANYTHING HAPPENS, I SHALL COME TO YOUR AID.
ME TOO. I WON'T LET...THEM DO ANY-THING... CRAZY TO YOU.
BASHI (FWAP)
ZA (BOW)

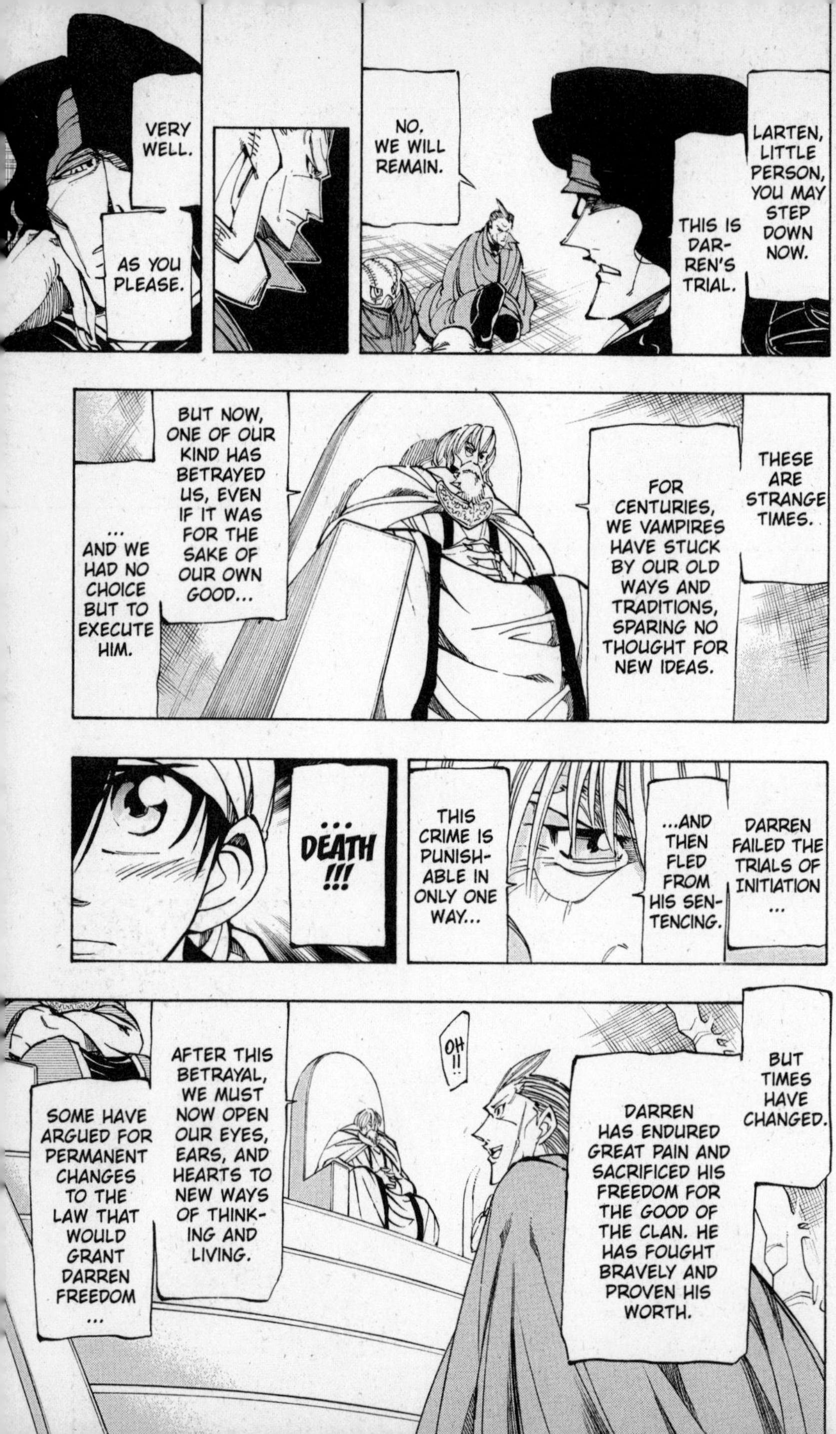
LARTEN, LITTLE PERSON, YOU MAY STEP DOWN NOW.
THIS IS DARREN'S TRIAL.
NO, WE WILL REMAIN.
VERY WELL.
AS YOU PLEASE.
THESE ARE STRANGE TIMES.
FOR CENTURIES, WE VAMPIRES HAVE STUCK BY OUR OLD WAYS AND TRADITIONS, SPARING NO THOUGHT FOR NEW IDEAS.
BUT NOW, ONE OF OUR KIND HAS BETRAYED US, EVEN IF IT WAS FOR THE SAKE OF OUR OWN GOOD...
... AND WE HAD NO CHOICE BUT TO EXECUTE HIM.
DARREN FAILED THE TRIALS OF INITIATION ...
...AND THEN FLED FROM HIS SENTENCING.
THIS CRIME IS PUNISHABLE IN ONLY ONE WAY...
... DEATH !!!
BUT TIMES HAVE CHANGED.
DARREN HAS ENDURED GREAT PAIN AND SACRIFICED HIS FREEDOM FOR THE GOOD OF THE CLAN. HE HAS FOUGHT BRAVELY AND PROVEN HIS WORTH.
OH !!
AFTER THIS BETRAYAL, WE MUST NOW OPEN OUR EYES, EARS, AND HEARTS TO NEW WAYS OF THINKING AND LIVING.
SOME HAVE ARGUED FOR PERMANENT CHANGES TO THE LAW THAT WOULD GRANT DARREN FREEDOM ...

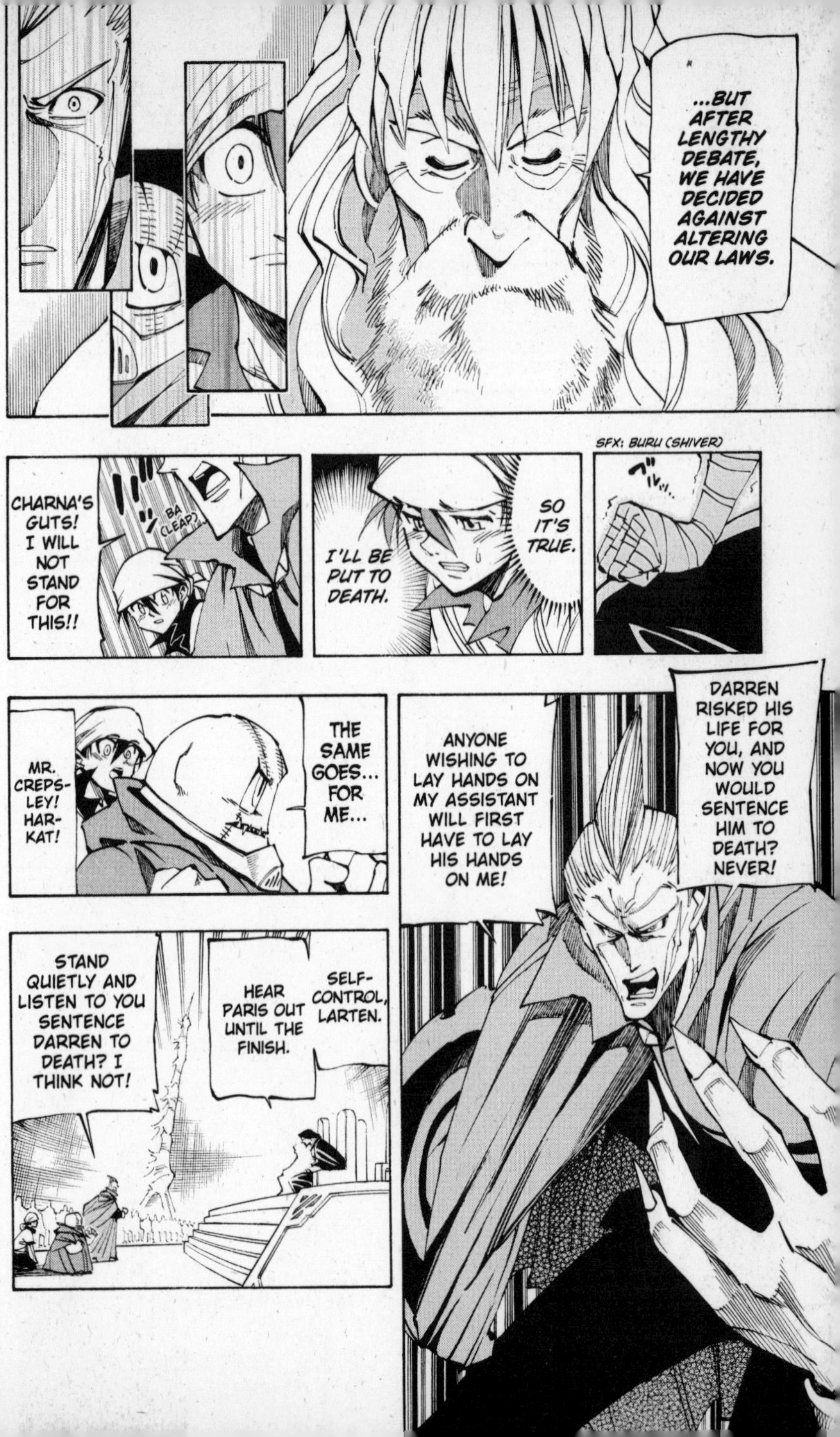
...BUT AFTER LENGTHY DEBATE, WE HAVE DECIDED AGAINST ALTERING OUR LAWS.
SFX: BURU (SHIVER)
SO IT'S TRUE.
I'LL BE PUT TO DEATH.
CHARNA'S GUTS! I WILL NOT STAND FOR THIS!!
BA (LEAP)
DARREN RISKED HIS LIFE FOR YOU, AND NOW YOU WOULD SENTENCE HIM TO DEATH? NEVER!
ANYONE WISHING TO LAY HANDS ON MY ASSISTANT WILL FIRST HAVE TO LAY HIS HANDS ON ME!
THE SAME GOES... FOR ME...
MR. CREPS-LEY! HAR-KAT!
SELF-CONTROL, LARTEN.
HEAR PARIS OUT UNTIL THE FINISH.
STAND QUIETLY AND LISTEN TO YOU SENTENCE DARREN TO DEATH? I THINK NOT!

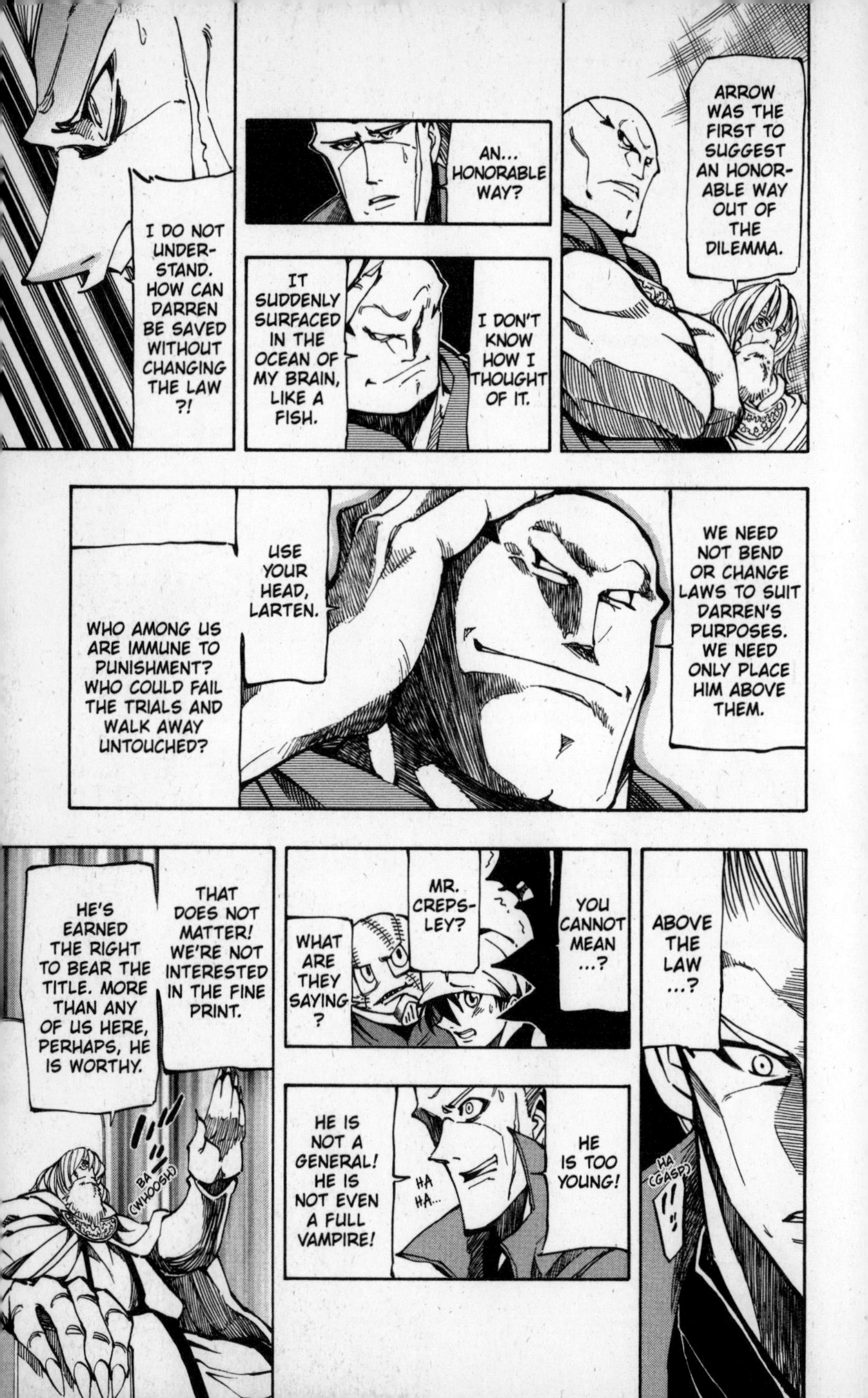
ARROW WAS THE FIRST TO SUGGEST AN HONORABLE WAY OUT OF THE DILEMMA.
AN... HONORABLE WAY?
I DON'T KNOW HOW I THOUGHT OF IT.
IT SUDDENLY SURFACED IN THE OCEAN OF MY BRAIN, LIKE A FISH.
I DO NOT UNDERSTAND. HOW CAN DARREN BE SAVED WITHOUT CHANGING THE LAW ?!
WE NEED NOT BEND OR CHANGE LAWS TO SUIT DARREN'S PURPOSES. WE NEED ONLY PLACE HIM ABOVE THEM.
USE YOUR HEAD, LARTEN.
WHO AMONG US ARE IMMUNE TO PUNISHMENT? WHO COULD FAIL THE TRIALS AND WALK AWAY UNTOUCHED?
ABOVE THE LAW ...?
HA (GASP)
!!
YOU CANNOT MEAN ...?
MR. CREPSLEY?
WHAT ARE THEY SAYING ?
HE IS TOO YOUNG!
HA HA...
HE IS NOT A GENERAL! HE IS NOT EVEN A FULL VAMPIRE!
THAT DOES NOT MATTER! WE'RE NOT INTERESTED IN THE FINE PRINT.
HE'S EARNED THE RIGHT TO BEAR THE TITLE. MORE THAN ANY OF US HERE, PERHAPS, HE IS WORTHY.
BA (WHOOSH)

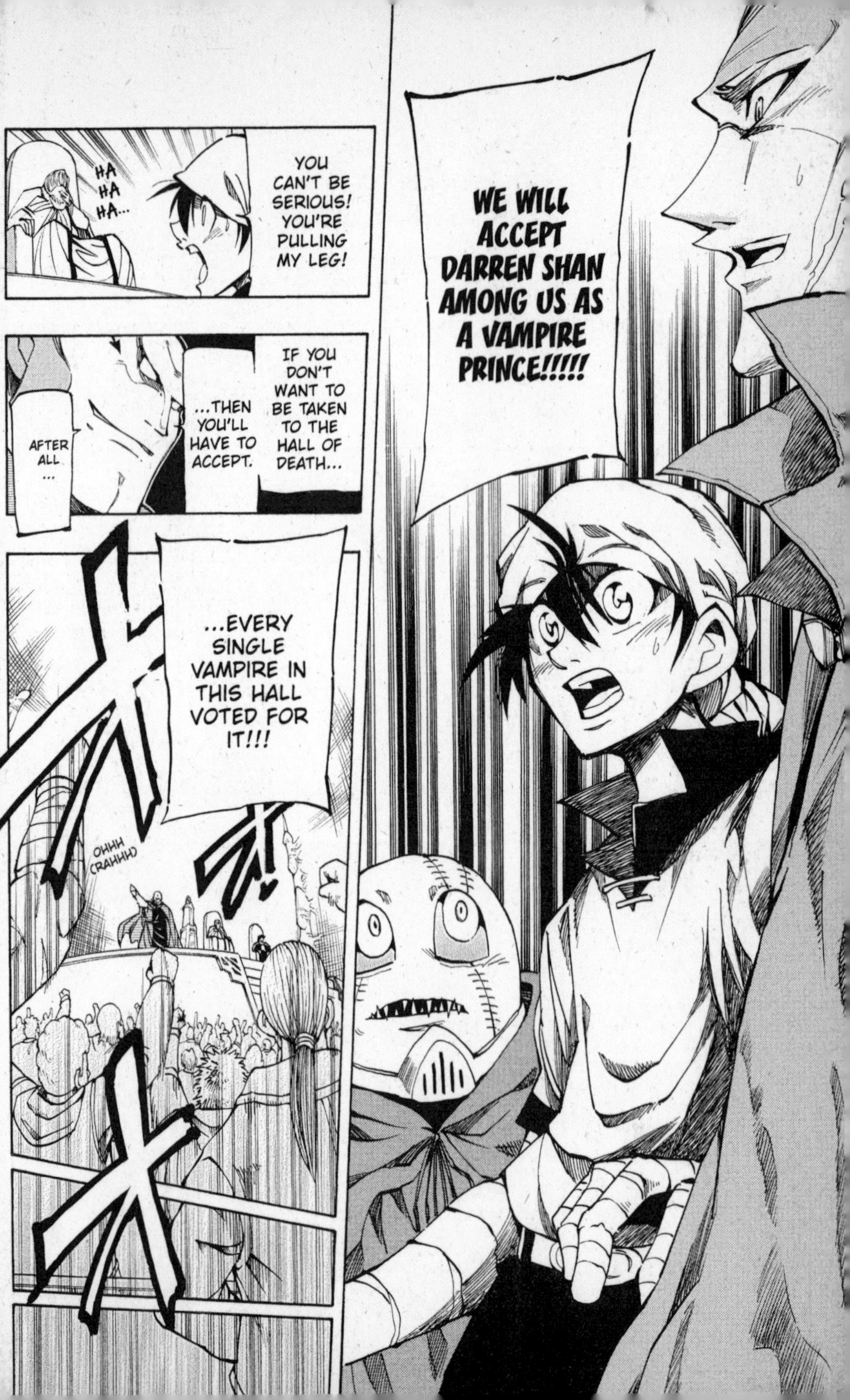
WE WILL ACCEPT DARREN SHAN AMONG US AS A VAMPIRE PRINCE!!!!!
YOU CAN'T BE SERIOUS! YOU'RE PULLING MY LEG!
HA HA HA...
IF YOU DON'T WANT TO BE TAKEN TO THE HALL OF DEATH...
...THEN YOU'LL HAVE TO ACCEPT.
AFTER ALL ...
...EVERY SINGLE VAMPIRE IN THIS HALL VOTED FOR IT!!!
OHHH (RAHHH)

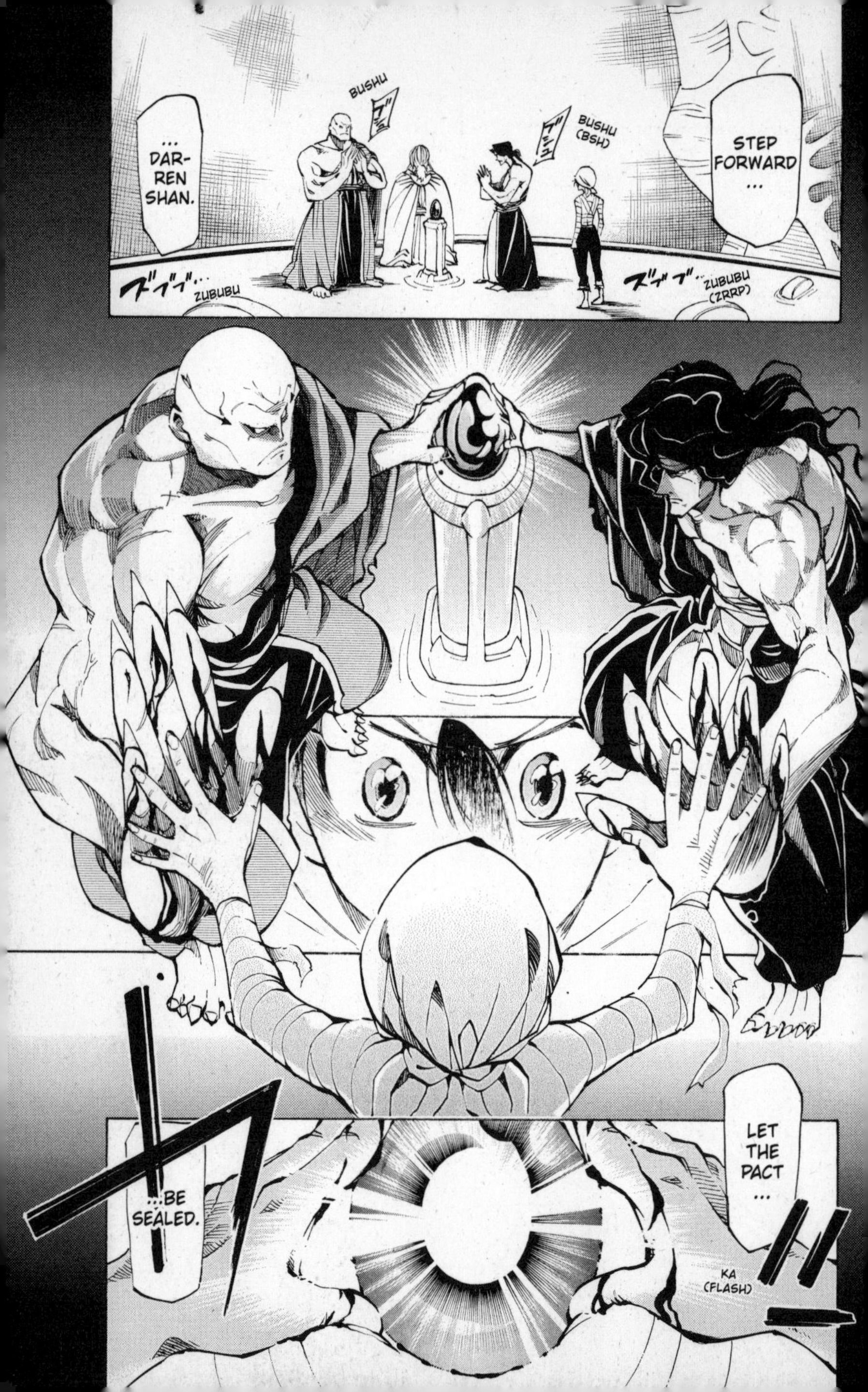

STEP FORWARD ...
BUSHU (BSH)
BUSHU
... DAR-REN SHAN.
ZUBUBU (ZRRP)
ZUBUBU
LET THE PACT ...
KA (FLASH)
...BE SEALED.

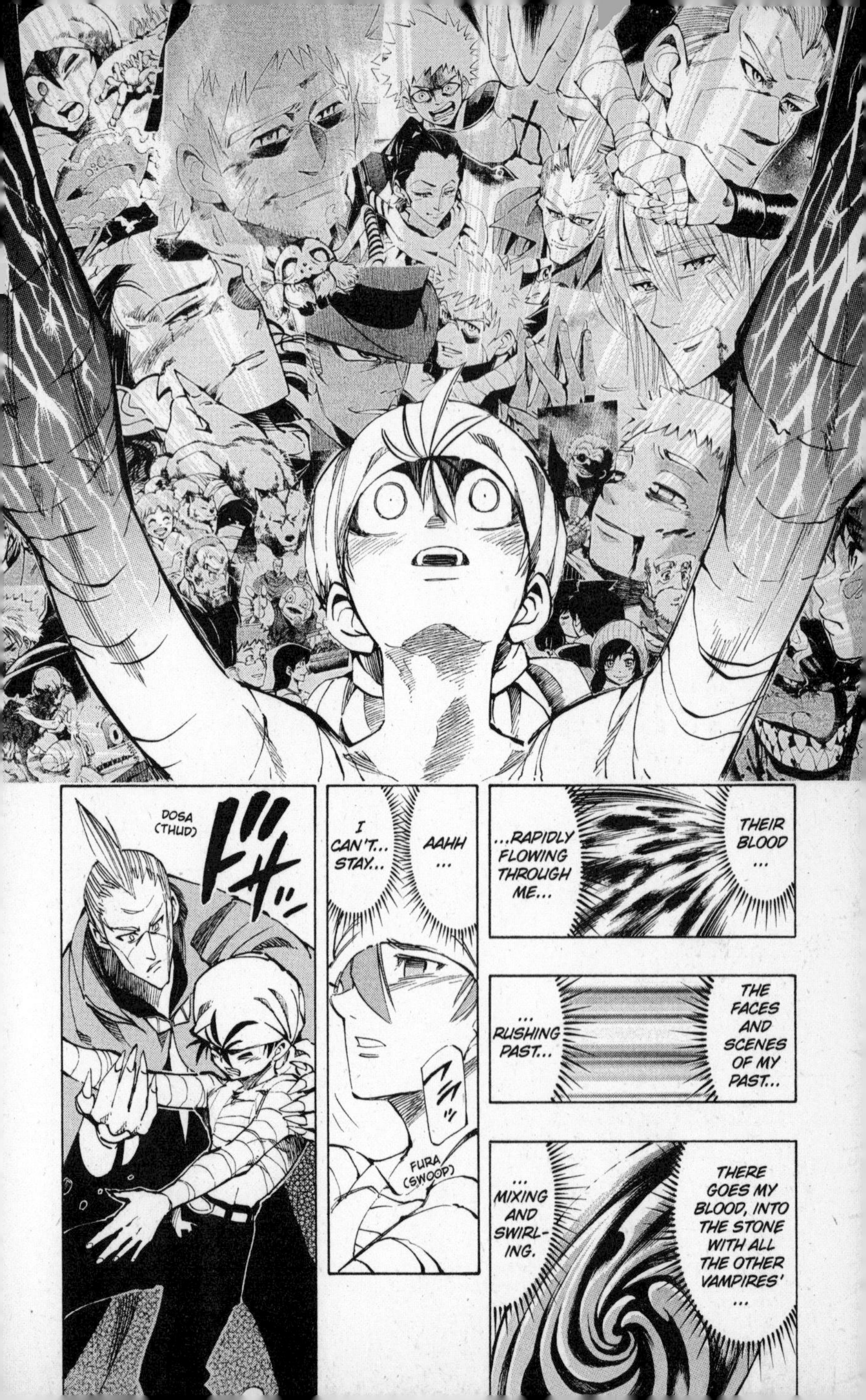
THEIR BLOOD ...
...RAPIDLY FLOWING THROUGH ME...
THE FACES AND SCENES OF MY PAST...
... RUSHING PAST...
THERE GOES MY BLOOD, INTO THE STONE WITH ALL THE OTHER VAMPIRES' ...
... MIXING AND SWIRL-ING.
AAHH ...
I CAN'T... STAY...
FURA (SWOOP)
DOSA (THUD)
ドサッ

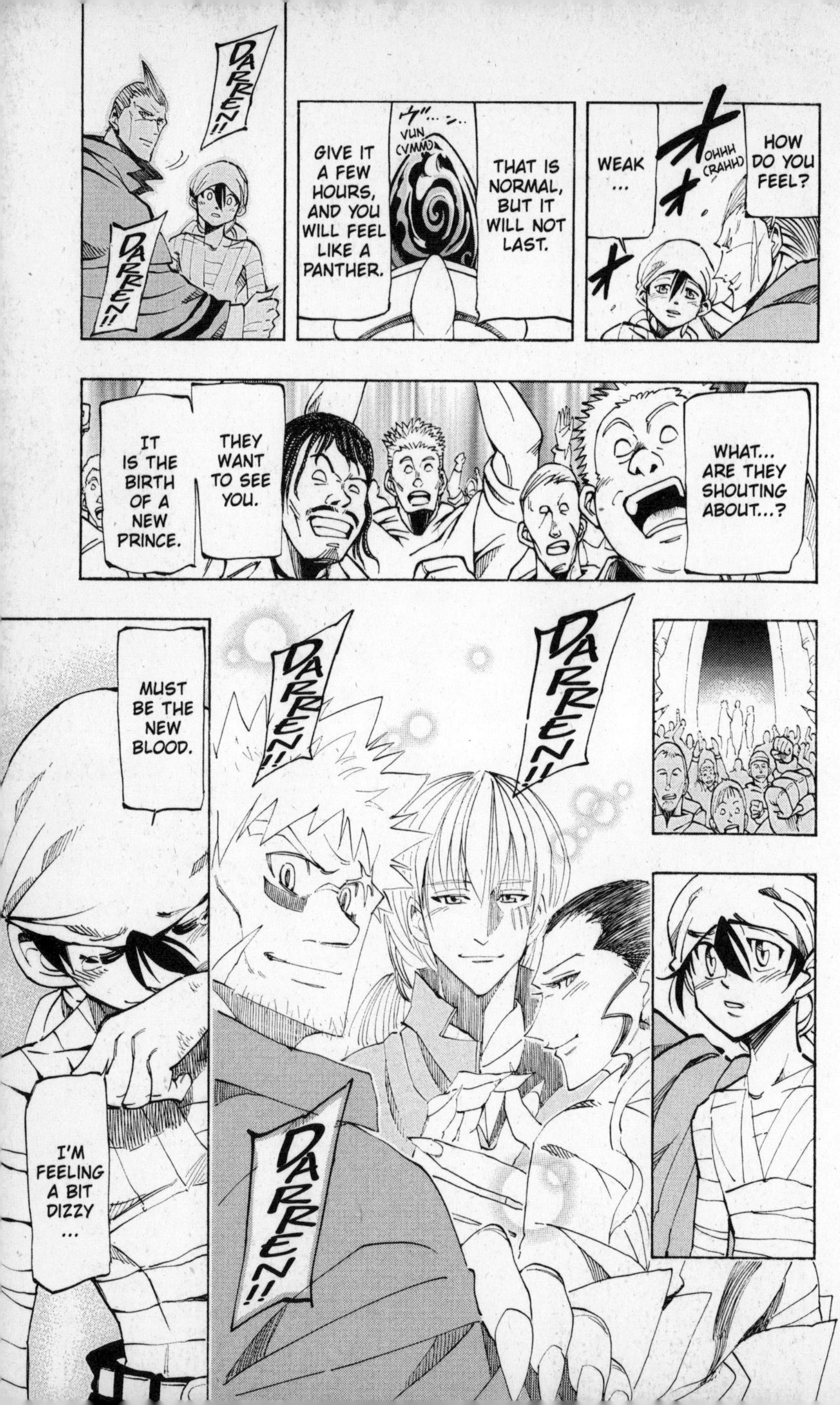
HOW DO YOU FEEL?
OHHH (RAHH)
WEAK ...
THAT IS NORMAL, BUT IT WILL NOT LAST.
ヴ"…ン
VUN (VMMM)
GIVE IT A FEW HOURS, AND YOU WILL FEEL LIKE A PANTHER.
DARREN!!
DARREN!!
WHAT... ARE THEY SHOUTING ABOUT...?
THEY WANT TO SEE YOU.
IT IS THE BIRTH OF A NEW PRINCE.
DARREN!!
DARREN!!
MUST BE THE NEW BLOOD.
DARREN!!
I'M FEELING A BIT DIZZY ...

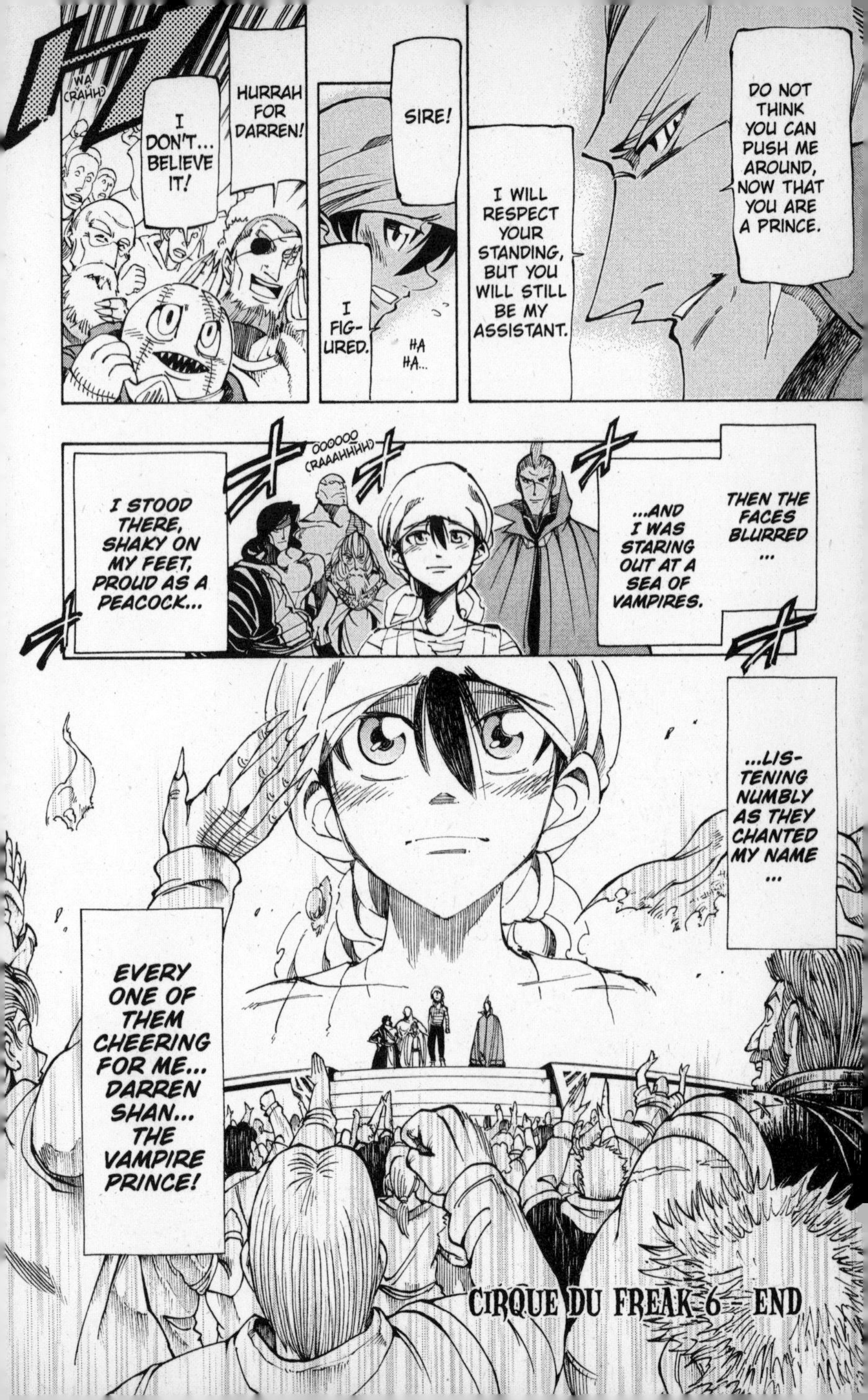
DO NOT THINK YOU CAN PUSH ME AROUND, NOW THAT YOU ARE A PRINCE.
I WILL RESPECT YOUR STANDING, BUT YOU WILL STILL BE MY ASSISTANT.
SIRE!
HA HA...
I FIGURED.
HURRAH FOR DARREN!
WA (RAHH)
I DON'T... BELIEVE IT!
I STOOD THERE, SHAKY ON MY FEET, PROUD AS A PEACOCK...
OOOOOO (RAAAHHHH)
THEN THE FACES BLURRED...
...AND I WAS STARING OUT AT A SEA OF VAMPIRES.
...LISTENING NUMBLY AS THEY CHANTED MY NAME...
EVERY ONE OF THEM CHEERING FOR ME... DARREN SHAN... THE VAMPIRE PRINCE!
CIRQUE DU FREAK 6 - END

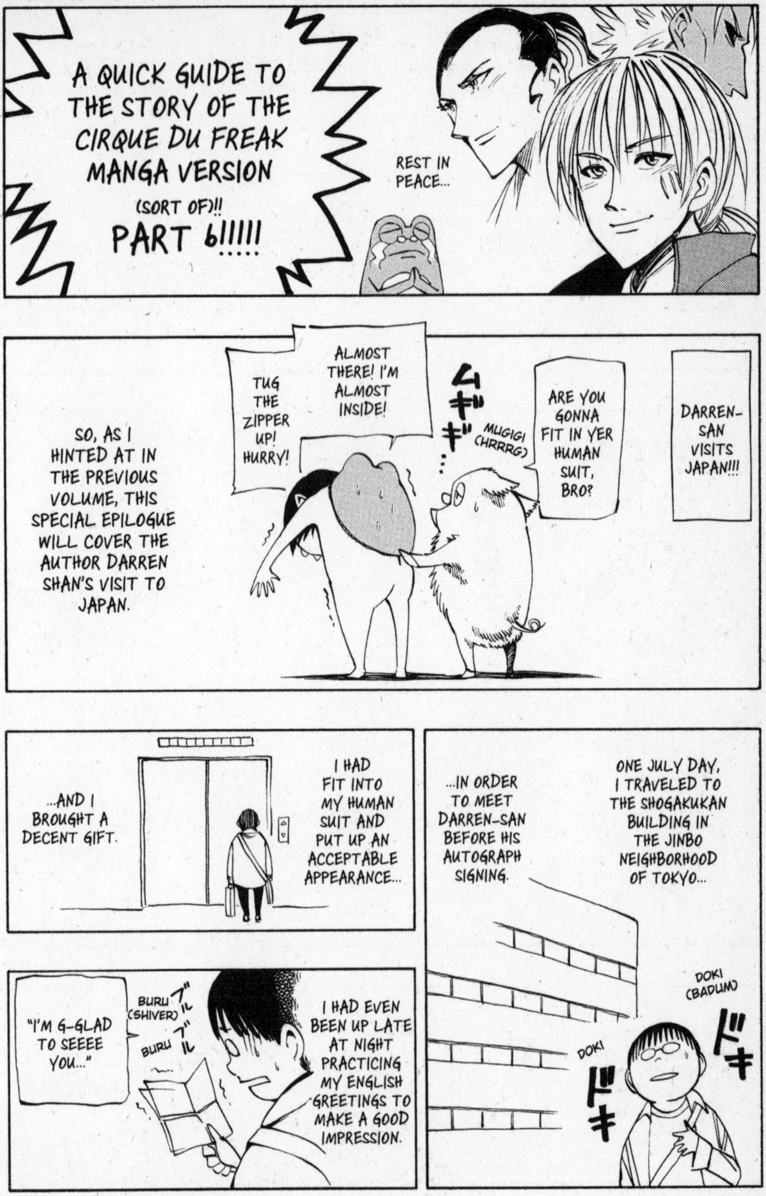

A QUICK GUIDE TO THE STORY OF THE CIRQUE DU FREAK MANGA VERSION
(SORT OF)!!
PART 6!!!!!
REST IN PEACE...
DARREN-SAN VISITS JAPAN!!!
ARE YOU GONNA FIT IN YER HUMAN SUIT, BRO?
ムギギ
MUGIGI (HRRRG)
ALMOST THERE! I'M ALMOST INSIDE!
TUG THE ZIPPER UP! HURRY!
SO, AS I HINTED AT IN THE PREVIOUS VOLUME, THIS SPECIAL EPILOGUE WILL COVER THE AUTHOR DARREN SHAN'S VISIT TO JAPAN.
ONE JULY DAY, I TRAVELED TO THE SHOGAKUKAN BUILDING IN THE JINBO NEIGHBORHOOD OF TOKYO...
...IN ORDER TO MEET DARREN-SAN BEFORE HIS AUTOGRAPH SIGNING.
ドキ
DOKI (BADUM)
ドキ
DOKI
I HAD FIT INTO MY HUMAN SUIT AND PUT UP AN ACCEPTABLE APPEARANCE...
...AND I BROUGHT A DECENT GIFT.
I HAD EVEN BEEN UP LATE AT NIGHT PRACTICING MY ENGLISH GREETINGS TO MAKE A GOOD IMPRESSION.
ブル
BURU (SHIVER)
ブル
BURU
"I'M G-GLAD TO SEEEE YOU..."

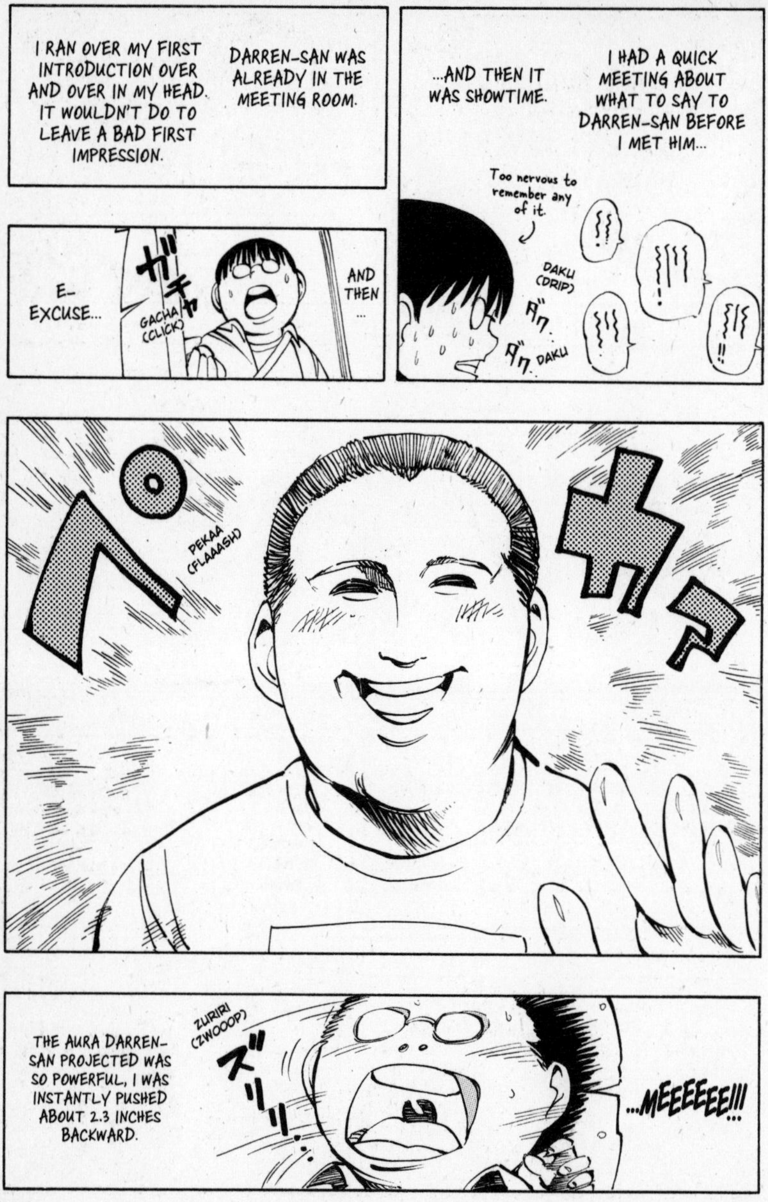
I HAD A QUICK MEETING ABOUT WHAT TO SAY TO DARREN-SAN BEFORE I MET HIM...
...AND THEN IT WAS SHOWTIME.
Too nervous to remember any of it.
DAKU (DRIP)
ダク
ダク DAKU
DARREN-SAN WAS ALREADY IN THE MEETING ROOM.
I RAN OVER MY FIRST INTRODUCTION OVER AND OVER IN MY HEAD. IT WOULDN'T DO TO LEAVE A BAD FIRST IMPRESSION.
AND THEN ...
ガチャ
GACHA (CLICK)
E- EXCUSE...
ペカァ
PEKAA (FLAAASH)
...MEEEEEE!!!...
ズリリ
ZURIRI (ZWOOOP)
THE AURA DARREN-SAN PROJECTED WAS SO POWERFUL, I WAS INSTANTLY PUSHED ABOUT 2.3 INCHES BACKWARD.

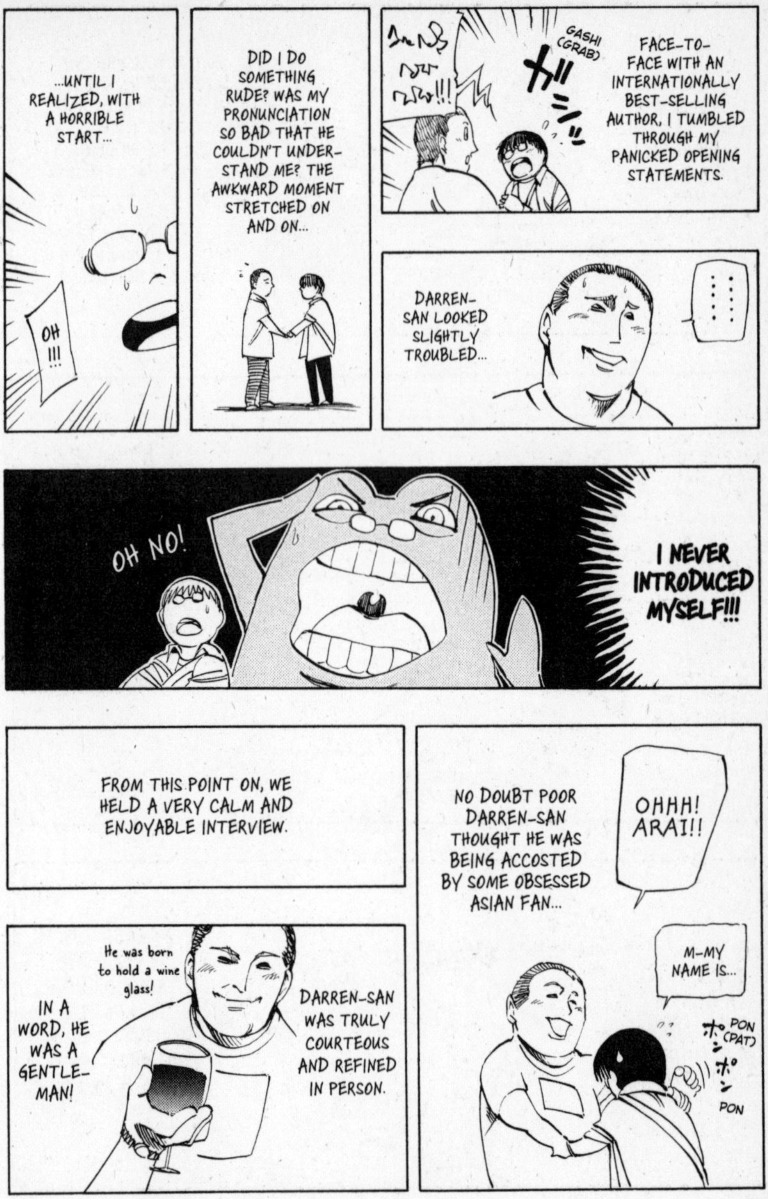
GASHI (GRAB)
FACE-TO-FACE WITH AN INTERNATIONALLY BEST-SELLING AUTHOR, I TUMBLED THROUGH MY PANICKED OPENING STATEMENTS.
DARREN-SAN LOOKED SLIGHTLY TROUBLED...
......
DID I DO SOMETHING RUDE? WAS MY PRONUNCIATION SO BAD THAT HE COULDN'T UNDERSTAND ME? THE AWKWARD MOMENT STRETCHED ON AND ON...
...UNTIL I REALIZED, WITH A HORRIBLE START...
OH!!!...
I NEVER INTRODUCED MYSELF!!!
OH NO!
OHHH! ARAI!!
NO DOUBT POOR DARREN-SAN THOUGHT HE WAS BEING ACCOSTED BY SOME OBSESSED ASIAN FAN...
M-MY NAME IS...
PON (PAT) PON
FROM THIS POINT ON, WE HELD A VERY CALM AND ENJOYABLE INTERVIEW.
DARREN-SAN WAS TRULY COURTEOUS AND REFINED IN PERSON.
He was born to hold a wine glass!
IN A WORD, HE WAS A GENTLEMAN!

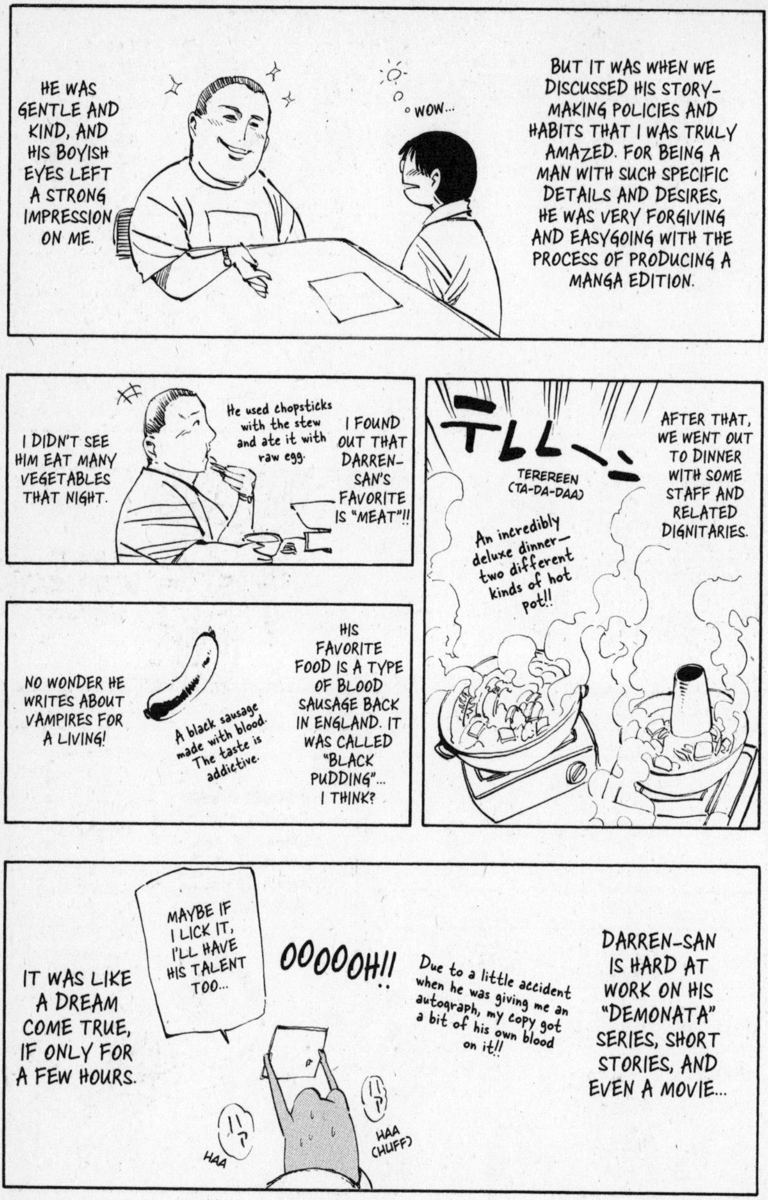
BUT IT WAS WHEN WE DISCUSSED HIS STORY-MAKING POLICIES AND HABITS THAT I WAS TRULY AMAZED. FOR BEING A MAN WITH SUCH SPECIFIC DETAILS AND DESIRES, HE WAS VERY FORGIVING AND EASYGOING WITH THE PROCESS OF PRODUCING A MANGA EDITION.
WOW...
HE WAS GENTLE AND KIND, AND HIS BOYISH EYES LEFT A STRONG IMPRESSION ON ME.
AFTER THAT, WE WENT OUT TO DINNER WITH SOME STAFF AND RELATED DIGNITARIES.
TEREREEN (TA-DA-DAA)
An incredibly deluxe dinner—two different kinds of hot pot!!
I FOUND OUT THAT DARREN-SAN'S FAVORITE IS "MEAT"!!
He used chopsticks with the stew and ate it with raw egg.
I DIDN'T SEE HIM EAT MANY VEGETABLES THAT NIGHT.
HIS FAVORITE FOOD IS A TYPE OF BLOOD SAUSAGE BACK IN ENGLAND. IT WAS CALLED "BLACK PUDDING"... I THINK?
A black sausage made with blood. The taste is addictive.
NO WONDER HE WRITES ABOUT VAMPIRES FOR A LIVING!
DARREN-SAN IS HARD AT WORK ON HIS "DEMONATA" SERIES, SHORT STORIES, AND EVEN A MOVIE...
Due to a little accident when he was giving me an autograph, my copy got a bit of his own blood on it!!
OOOOOH!!
MAYBE IF I LICK IT, I'LL HAVE HIS TALENT TOO...
HAA (CHUFF)
HAA
IT WAS LIKE A DREAM COME TRUE, IF ONLY FOR A FEW HOURS.

ゴオオ…
GOHHH (ZWOOOM)
DARREN-SAN HAD ANOTHER AUTOGRAPH SIGNING THE NEXT DAY.
SEE YOU AGAIN!
I'M SURE THAT SOME OF YOU READING THIS MANGA WERE PRESENT AT THE SIGNING TOO.
I WOULD LIKE TO THANK DARREN-SAN, THE FOLKS FROM THE EDITORIAL DEPARTMENT, OTHER DIGNITARIES, AND ALL OF THE READERS FOR MAKING THIS HAPPEN.
THANK YOU ALL SO MUCH!!!
NOT ONLY THAT, BUT THE TEXT OF OUR INTERVIEW WAS PRINTED ON DELUXE COLOR PAGES IN THE PAGES OF WEEKLY SHONEN SUNDAY TWO MONTHS LATER!
HOWEVER, ALL MY FRIENDS AND FAMILY WHO SAW THE PHOTO OF ME THAT RAN WITH THE INTERVIEW SAID, "YOU LOOK OLDER," OR, "YOU SHOULD EAT A BIT HEALTHIER, LAY OFF ALL THAT MEAT." NOT SURE HOW I FEEL ABOUT THAT.
......
PON (PAT)
PON
SO, AT THIS POINT, THE MANGA EDITION HAS COVERED PRECISELY HALF OF THE ORIGINAL STORY.
WHILE I FEEL ENORMOUS GRATITUDE AT WHAT I'VE ACCOMPLISHED SO FAR, I ALSO FEEL SAD THAT THERE'S ONLY HALF LEFT TO TELL.
WHAT HAPPENS NOW, MR. CREPSLEY?
HEH HEH HEH...
NOW THAT DARREN HAS SHOCKINGLY BEEN PROMOTED TO VAMPIRE PRINCE, WHAT MIGHT FATE HAVE IN STORE FOR HIM?
I'LL SEE YOU AGAIN IN VOLUME 7!!

The End

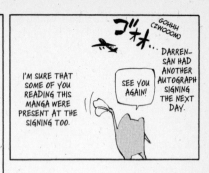

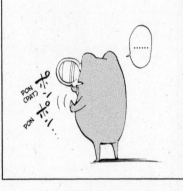

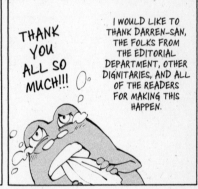

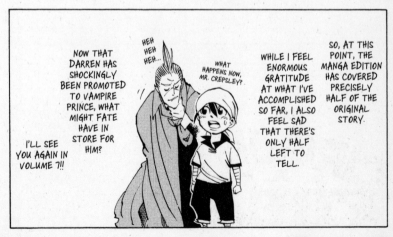

CIRQUE DU FREAK

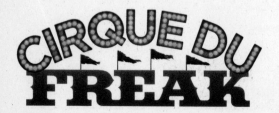

CIRQUE DU FREAK ⑥

DARREN SHAN
TAKAHIRO ARAI

Translation: Stephen Paul   •   Lettering: AndWorld Design
Art Direction: Hitoshi SHIRAYAMA
Original Cover Design: Shigeru ANZAI + Bay Bridge Studio

DARREN SHAN Vol. 6 © 2007 by Darren Shan, Takahiro ARAI. All rights reserved. Original Japanese edition published in Japan in 2007 by Shogakukan Inc., Tokyo. Artworks reproduction rights in U.S.A. and Canada arranged with Shogakukan Inc. through Tuttle-Mori Agency, Inc., Tokyo.

English translation © 2010 Darren Shan

Yen Press
Hachette Book Group
237 Park Avenue, New York, NY 10017

www.HachetteBookGroup.com
www.YenPress.com

Yen Press is an imprint of Hachette Book Group, Inc. The Yen Press name and logo are trademarks of Hachette Book Group, Inc.

First Yen Press Edition: July 2010

ISBN: 978-0-7595-3040-9

10 9 8 7 6 5 4 3 2 1

BVG

Printed in the United States of America